PLOTTING JUSTICE

PLOTTING JUSTICE
NARRATIVE ETHICS & LITERARY CULTURE AFTER 9/11
GEORGIANA BANITA

University of Nebraska Press | Lincoln and London

© 2012 by the Board of Regents of the University of Nebraska
Acknowledgments for previously published material appear on pages xiii–xiv, which constitute an extension of the copyright page. All rights reserved. Manufactured in the United States of America.

Library of Congress Cataloging-in-Publication Data
Banita, Georgiana.
Plotting justice : narrative ethics and literary culture after 9/11 / Georgiana Banita.
    p. cm.   Includes bibliographical references and index.
ISBN 978-0-8032-4038-4 (cloth : alk. paper)
1. American fiction—21st century—History and criticism.
2. September 11 Terrorist Attacks, 2001, in literature.
3. September 11 Terrorist Attacks, 2001—Influence. 4. Ethics in literature. 5. Psychoanalysis in literature. 6. Social change in literature. 7. Literature and morals. 8. Literature and society—United States. I. Title. II. Title: Narrative ethics and literary culture after 9/11.
PS374.S445B36 2012   813'.6093587393—dc23   2012014470

Set in Garamond Premier Pro by Kim Essman.
Designed by A. Shahan.

For Nicoleta Croitoru, with gratitude

If one has to do things for the good, in practice one is always faced with the question: for the good of whom? From that point on, things are no longer obvious. Doing things in the name of the good, and even more in the name of the good of the other, is something that is far from protecting us not only from guilt but also from all kinds of inner catastrophes.

JACQUES LACAN

The only true ethical stance is to assume fully the impossible task of symbolizing the Real, inclusive of its necessary failure.

SLAVOJ ŽIŽEK

Is it at all possible to read and interpret ambiguity *without reducing* it in the very process of interpretation? Are reading and ambiguity in any way *compatible*?

SHOSHANA FELMAN

CONTENTS

Acknowledgments xi

Introduction: New Ethics,
New Literatures, New Americas 1

1. Falling Man Fiction: DeLillo,
   Spiegelman, Schulman, and the
   Spectatorial Condition 59

2. Sex and Sense: McGrath, Tristram, and
   Psychoanalysis from Ground Zero to
   Abu Ghraib 109

3. Moral Crusades: Race, Risk, and
   Walt Whitman's Afterlives 165

4. The Internationalization of Conscience:
   Hemon, Barker, Balkanism 205

5. Reading for the Pattern: Narrative,
   Data Mining, and the Transnational
   Ethics of Surveillance 251

Conclusion: Postincendiary
Circumstances 289

Notes 301

Bibliography 321

Index 345

ACKNOWLEDGMENTS

This project first took shape in my mind in the fall of 2006. I had newly arrived in the United States, after six years in Germany, to study as a doctoral fellow at Yale University. On that fateful day in October, I was watching workers at Ground Zero as they laid the foundations for what was then called the Freedom Tower, the edifice meant to replace the Twin Towers that the terrorist attacks of September 11, 2001, had destroyed. The decision to embark on a book project about post-9/11 fiction seemed to me at the time as recklessly ambitious as the Freedom Tower itself. Only a handful of writers had responded to the attacks, and after a flurry of academic activity producing several books in 2003 (these were largely instant responses that had taken two years to be printed), little to nothing was going on in the field. Although I cannot entirely reconstruct the motives behind my decision (and the blurriness of the memory is significant in itself), my resolve was confirmed by 9/11 fictions that staged encounters resembling mine—resolutions and anxieties formed at Ground Zero—begging the question of what exactly I and other New York locals and pilgrims were responding to. And why did we feel impelled to take on life projects, as it were; what was the nature of this imperative, and what caused it? To what extent does the site elicit a personal reaction, and how do we, on an objective level, make sense of it as an ethical imperative? Part of my intention in this book has been to answer that question. In doing so I have attempted to put the ethical debates emerging from the attacks into conversation with transnational accounts of 9/11 as an event shaped and prefigured by global histories. In light of this international remapping of Ground Zero, the concept of post-9/11 ethics appeared even more stringent and unresolved, occluded by the imperious morality of the rapidly escalating War on Terror.

In the process of writing, I have incurred intellectual debts that are as transnational and wide-ranging as the book itself. I have been fortunate to receive financial support from several institutions. I am grateful to the Council for Gender Equality at the University of Constance for a generous fellowship in early 2006 and a three-month grant in 2009; the Baden-Württemberg Foundation for a two-year doctoral scholarship (LGFG) at the University of Constance, as well as for a ten-month doctoral fellowship at Yale University (2006–07); the German Research Foundation (DFG) for travel grants to attend conferences at the University of British Columbia and Syracuse University, as well as for a research grant to support my archival work at Columbia University in the fall of 2008. The staff of the Columbia Oral History Archives offered valuable suggestions in consulting the vast 9/11 archive hosted by the department.

This book reflects conversations with colleagues and friends in the research colloquia of my dissertation supervisor at the University of Constance, Prof. Dr. Reingard M. Nischik, who unstintingly supported this project from gestation to completion. None of this would have materialized without her nurturing generosity. I would also like to thank the students in my 9/11-themed seminars at the Universities of Constance and Paderborn, who were quick to engage in dialogue about the ethics and aesthetics of representing 9/11 and wrote fascinating essays as well as some remarkable poems about their own experience of the attacks. I have found their verve and emotional investment quite stimulating. I also benefited from a visiting teaching position at the University of Paderborn in 2009, and I am indebted to Christoph Ribbat for his friendship and professional guidance at an important (and precarious) time. And in ways that continue to teach me the value of intellectual generosity and sheer enjoyment of our profession, Jörn Glasenapp has been the best chair and supervisor I could wish for at the University of Bamberg.

I negotiated the publication process during my postdoctoral fellowship at the U.S. Studies Centre, University of Sydney (2010–11), where I got the opportunity to discuss both the book and the publishing world with Brendon O'Connor and Paul Giles. I will always remember this phase in my career as one in which I drew sustenance from Paul's unwavering support and encouragement. In the final stages of the project I learned from the comments of several anonymous reviewers on chapters published separately in journals. For permission to republish portions of this book, I gratefully acknowledge ZAA, LIT: Literature Interpretation Theory, Textual Practice, and Critique. The rigorous responses of the anonymous readers who reviewed the book manuscript were also invaluable. Like-minded audiences over the years at UBC, Syracuse, Amsterdam, FU Berlin, Konstanz, Bayreuth, Saarbrücken, and Frankfurt helped with challenging questions and excellent advice. I am indebted to my extraordinary editor, Merrin Lazyan, for her intelligence and meticulousness and the impeccable standards of her work. At the University of Nebraska Press, Kristen Elias Rowley has been an encouraging and accommodating guide, steering me through the publication process with confident, knowing, and always dependable hands. For her careful and perceptive reading of the manuscript, I thank my copyeditor, Judith Hoover. Much appreciation also goes to my project editor, Sara Springsteen, for her patience.

Rather quaintly, perhaps, I dedicate this first book to my high school English teacher Nicoleta Croitoru, who instilled in me a constant fear of inadequacy and a great hunger to excel. Though modulated by the intervening years, this imprint has remained an organic part of who I am. Finally, I am grateful to my family in Romania, and to Rudi, for being my closest, most generous interlocutor. Thank you.

Part of chapter 1 was previously published, in different form, as "9/11 Trauma and Visual Witnessing in Helen Schulman's *A Day at the Beach*," *Critique: Studies in Contemporary Fiction* 53.1 (2012): 1–15.

Part of chapter 2 was previously published, in different form, as "Scapegoating in 'Ground Zero': Patrick McGrath's Allegory of World-Historical Trauma," *Textual Practice* 26.2 (2012): 293–317.

Part of chapter 3 was previously published, in different form, as "Race,

Risk, and Fiction in the War on Terror: Laila Halaby, Gayle Brandeis, Michael Cunningham," *LIT: Literature Interpretation Theory* 21.4 (2010): 242–68.

Part of chapter 4 was previously published, in different form, as "'The Internationalization of Conscience': Representing Ethics in Pat Barker's *Double Vision*," *ZAA: A Quarterly of Language, Literature and Culture* 58.1 (2010): 55–70. Used with permission.

PLOTTING JUSTICE

widely than existing discussions, which tend to emphasize distinctions among literary genres in representing the posttraumatic experience (Versluys, *Out of the Blue*; Gray, *After the Fall*). It also avoids regarding the fictions at hand as a monolithic block that can be used to illustrate one specific critical approach. To that extent, a broad methodology informed by ethics seems especially suitable in teasing out both the textual and the political implications of this literature. Loose ends are left in, suggestive ambiguity being preferred to neat categorization of a literary field that is still burgeoning and unsettled. I wish to suggest that it is precisely because post-9/11 narratives puzzlingly problematize and redefine notions of alterity (through acts of witnessing, racial scapegoating, transnationalism, and surveillance) that they acquire ethical meaning beyond the jingoistic, moralizing discourses that prevailed in the immediate aftermath of the attacks. Rather than merely stating that literary ambiguity creates a resistant counterdiscourse to the overbearing reliance on certitude in the War on Terror, *Plotting Justice* scrutinizes how certainty and justice are brought into being through a set of narrative strategies operating across national borders and time scales.

So far 9/11 scholarship has focused on fiction that portrays the terrorist attacks overtly at the expense of more oblique intimations of a post-9/11 world, with its global risks and permutations (Keniston and Quinn; Versluys, *Out of the Blue*; Cilano; Gray, *After the Fall*). My readings of post-9/11 fiction attempt to elucidate the textual appearances and disappearances of the terrorist attacks as well as their narrative role in each case, a question that becomes gradually more penetrating as the analysis progresses and the texts qualify less and less explicitly as 9/11 literature. Notwithstanding their increasingly oblique association with the events in New York, Washington, and Pennsylvania—although their significance as post-9/11 fiction is never in doubt—these texts mutually illuminate each other across a wide thematic and geographical spectrum. Their points of contact count perhaps as the most rewarding confirmation of my claim that the exemplars I have chosen respond to a larger cultural provocation.

INTRODUCTION

Existing scholarship has also neglected to position post-9/11 literary culture within a broader historical context. The threshold that marked the end of the cold war, for instance, has been largely overlooked. Only two critical studies have addressed the interlude between the fall of the Berlin Wall and the collapse of the Twin Towers, and neither has decoded the adversarial ideologies of these two events in ethical terms. In his book *After the End of History: American Fiction in the 1990s*, Samuel S. Cohen conceptualizes the 1990s as "a time between wars, between times characterized by the fear of threat to America, and as a result, as a moment during which it became perhaps more possible for some to recognize and examine the binary orientation such fear encourages" (6). DeLillo, Pynchon, Morrison, and other major writers of the 1990s, Cohen proposes, succumbed to an impulse of retrospection (a deep immersion in national history), which is undoubtedly a fair assessment of such works as *Underworld*, *Mason & Dixon*, and *American Pastoral*. Yet although he briefly points out the moralist divisions that were mobilized in cold war discourse and are experiencing a resurgence after 9/11, Cohen doesn't explicitly bring into focus the *ethical* binarism galvanizing the historical imagination of the novels he chooses to examine.

Staking a similarly two-pronged vision of September 11 as a companion piece to 1989, Phillip E. Wegner makes effective if sparse use of an ethical apparatus in positing 9/11 as a "second death" repeating the earlier fall of the Berlin Wall in his eloquently titled study *Life between Two Deaths, 1989–2001: U.S. Culture in the Long Nineties*. September 11, Wegner argues, "enabled the United States . . . to assume a global mantle" (25) more expediently than the volatile aftermath of the cold war would have permitted. Both Cohen and Wegner clearly regard the 1990s through glasses thickly tinted with nostalgia and with an affinity for radical thinking stymied, from their perspective, by the patriotic euphoria of the War on Terror. I hope to show in this book that to imagine the 1990s as prelapsarian prelude to the post-9/11 era would be to make short shrift of the much deeper geohistorical forays undertaken by 9/11 literature (as far back as the Peninsular War of 1808–14, as laterally remote as Japan and Algeria).

INTRODUCTION

While September 11 and its aftermath may indeed serve to retrospectively historicize the late cold war era, what has happened in literature since the attacks testifies to a new set of anxieties about how to relate the present to the past, but also about how knowledge of the past (and its residual traces) inflects our understanding of the present, seen not as a break with history but as its organic outcome. This book shows that post-9/11 fiction highlights "the possibility of knowing history," in Cathy Caruth's words, as a "deeply ethical dilemma: the unremitting problem of how not to betray the past" (*Unclaimed Experience* 27). In doing so it reveals unforeseen connections between September 11 and other historical turning points of the past two centuries, drawing on their capacity—often portrayed as an ethical imperative—to cast contemporary fiction in a new cross-historical, transnational light. Isolating the so-called 9/11 decade (2001–11) as a neat historical and literary paradigm would detract from its cultural diversity, from its imperviousness to Western historicization (especially in Arab American fiction), and from its attempts to rewrite the tenets and responsibilities of narrative ethics, and in particular of the novel, as permanently charged and altered by the events of September 11.

The turn to ethics in literary studies has provoked a variety of both enthusiastic and restrained responses, although by now some trends in that direction have been absorbed into mainstream critical discourse, where they no longer incite skepticism. In order to make progress on the issue of literary ethics, this introduction recapitulates the main claims of ethical thought as it pertains to literature, pointing out the concepts that I presuppose or criticize throughout this book. Specifically I engage with Dorothy J. Hale's recent work on contemporary fiction and the "new ethics" (which does not, however, address the 9/11 moment) to argue that post-9/11 literature effectively illustrates the transition from theoretical discussions of post-9/11 ethics to an aesthetic debate around practical morality and narrative imperatives. Before turning to the ethical paradigm of this book, however, it is necessary to locate ethically invested narratives within the larger post-9/11 genre, thus offering a foretaste of my approach that will also facilitate the subsequent step of situating post-9/11 fiction within the broader, highly contested field of contemporary literature.

INTRODUCTION

Pathways to Ethics: The Moral Topology of Post-9/11 Fiction

I want to delineate several ethical leitmotifs in post-9/11 literature as a preliminary rejoinder to the question of why ethics is a productive theoretical framework and why the narratives I have selected for this study—ranging from Don DeLillo's *Falling Man* (perhaps the most predictable choice) to Lorraine Adams's *Harbor*, a likely modern classic in the making—are representative of the literature produced during the 9/11 decade. These adjacent themes testify that an ethical agenda has percolated most post-9/11 fiction to date—beyond the texts to which I speak in this study. The specific concerns that structure this book (ethical spectatorship, psychoanalysis, race, transnationalism, and surveillance) seek to encode the broad cultural reach of post-9/11 literature and its granularly sophisticated ethical questions.

Because the Ground Zero of my discussion is the moment of trauma and the long durée of its aftershocks, I will start with the first 9/11 novel I myself read, Jess Walter's *The Zero*, in which Brian Remy, a NYC policeman, experiences "gaps in his memory, or perhaps his life" (5) after the attacks. During his bouts of consciousness, Remy is ensnared in a federal counterterrorist investigation that polarizes the book between those who unquestioningly support the War on Terror and those who seek "another way, a political or economic route to morality and generosity" (75). Remy's dreamy condition, which prohibits emotional connections with others because he cannot remember them from one moment to the next, dramatizes a more generalized post-9/11 amnesia and disaffection, a state in which people "just drift past" each other and through their own dreams "like loosed worries" (103), nursing their grief in solitude. This amnesia, by further extrapolation, bespeaks a dissociative syndrome in contemporary consciousness about confusing "gaps" in memory and history, a generalized puzzlement about how we arrived at the present point and how to proceed. The novel ultimately boils down to the question of "how a man knows if he's done the right thing" (299)—"the right thing" being not an act in itself as much as an act of consciousness or recognition, all the more challenging in a climate of historical amnesia. "He generally knows when he's doing the *wrong* thing," Walter suggests, setting the tone here for the common practice in post-9/11 fiction—from Patrick McGrath and Aleksandar Hemon to Richard Flanagan—of deriving ethical norms from the representation of evil (rather than the good or the virtuous).

Sometimes the "wrong thing" is a goal in itself, as in J. G. Ballard's novel *Millennium People*, a speculative account of an insurgent London suburb, Chelsea Marina. Ballard applies the ethos of terrorism to British middle-class malaise, seen as erratically oscillating between "vicious boredom" and "meaningless acts of violence" (28). Turning their attention overnight from charity to apocalypse, these idle classes launch a bid to overthrow the reigning world order as well as their own liberal existence, which they perceive as impoverished and constraining. In this world, the essence of terror is revealed through its meaninglessness—of which the 9/11 attacks serve here as a prime example (139). On the surface Ballard's novel is devoid of any sense of morality. Yet the entire so-called revolution of the privileged classes is premised on the notion that their cultural sensibility has lulled them into a sense of "moral superiority denied to football fans or garden gnome enthusiasts" (154). The quest of Chelsea Marina residents, then, is toward the liberation afforded by *immorality* (in the form of transgression or bad taste), which is perceived as a basic human right. And somehow, despite its beating heart of immorality, something deeply ethical resides in the ambiguities of this book. Terrorism can by no means be regarded as a source of personal or political renewal, yet the meaningless violence extolled here as an "empty space we could stare into with real awe" (249) does conceal, in ways I explain in this book, a potential for productive disorientation, a new imaginary probing of what we thought we knew about terror and its effect on our lives. "A motiveless act stops the universe in its tracks," Ballard writes (255), and indeed post-9/11 fiction is replete with such acts of shock, horror, disgust, or even arousal meant to cast doubt on the naïve sentimentality and melodrama still coloring our memory of the terrorist attacks and their legacy.

This legacy often involves (or demands) a personal change toward greater empathy and accountability, and fictions that internalize this demand often invoke the visual archive of September 11 as a constant incentive to moral self-scrutiny. Lynne Sharon Schwartz's *The Writing on the Wall*, as its title suggests, seeks to provide the "writing on the wall" (a term for the informative cards attached to museum exhibits) that captions September 11 in the collective consciousness of the nation. A substantial part of the novel thus examines the moral nature of language as a supplement to the televised image. Yet Schwartz's greatest insight into the ethical underpinnings of literature after 9/11 is a catalyzing faith in the possibility of change for her protagonist, Renata, who symbolically collects newspaper clippings of radical makeovers in her "Transformed Lives or Everyone Wants to Be Changed folder" (10), and sees in the burning towers an image in need of an explanatory label or tagline that surpasses the swashbuckling rhetoric of the Bush administration. In search of this tagline, Renata changes her life—as do so many others in 9/11 literature. Her past is "reborn from the big bang" (220), and the language in which it speaks—carrying guilt, flaws, mistakes, and oversights—is profoundly moral. At the end of the novel, Renata (rather too swiftly) escapes her moral dilemma between forgetting the past and parsing it forever, between domestic happiness and a higher intellectual purity—a dilemma that Schwartz describes as producing "an impasse, a paralysis of the will" (293). To preserve this paralytic condition is one of post-9/11 fiction's central aims and a close correlative to the "new ethics" of the novel—a theoretical concept that will organize my examinations of post-9/11 fiction over the course of this book.

The more urgent the ethical questions raised by 9/11 literature, the more radicalized the responses become and the more provincial the novels' settings. Reynolds Price's *The Good Priest's Son*, set in rural North Carolina, projects a starkly moralizing voice through the sermon-like expositions of Tasker, a widowed African American Episcopal priest caught in a wrangle with his son, Mabry, for whom he has less-than-fatherly feelings. This book, like Hugh Nissenson's *The Days of Awe*, offers a religious reading of the terrorist attacks from the perspective of aging, judgmental characters hypocritically advocating restraint in judgment. American crimes over the ages—such as the country's willingness to flaunt its Christian faith while allowing "mankind to starve and tear each other to shreds like always" (Price 45)—is less a matter of punishable and therefore partly redeemable crime than of absolute, indelible sin. And because sin is ingrained in the fabric of the nation, Tasker contends, after 9/11 "*nothing* will happen—nothing new" (46), not even, or especially, if we dare to interpret the devastation as "partial payment on the nation's counts" (141): for the sins of slavery, and for a sum of international transgressions. Indeed back in New York, we are told, "the world was proceeding on its terrified or indifferent way," few people seeming "so much as mildly unnerved" (227). But despite such sweeping assertions about the state of the nation, the mental space of Price's novel is confined to Mabry's isolated consciousness, as he puzzles over a work possibly attributable to another solitary man, van Gogh. Here as in many of the post-9/11 fictions I address in this book, art mediates the direct experience of the terrorist attacks and facilitates their ethical-historical contextualization. Above all, however, by reworking 9/11 as a flashlight shone on personal drama, *The Good Priest's Son* can be seen to dramatize the inwardness of pain, its *confinement*—despite the gigantic proportions of national tragedy—to the home, the close relationships between fathers and sons, the old and the young, the ailing and the fit, authenticity and surrogacy.

Confinement—to a mind, a house, a nation, a moment in time—also haunts Ward Just's *Forgetfulness*, a novel that looks at the aftermath of the 9/11 attacks from a perspective both domestic and international, personal and political. Just provides the most profoundly European treatment of America's aggressive response to 9/11, from the wars in the Middle East and the tensions with European allies about Bush's invasion of Iraq to conflicts of a subtler psychological nature between Americans who support retaliation for 9/11 (they are lambasted in the novel as "so quick to act . . . so slow to repent" [187]) and those who prefer a more contemplative view of world affairs. Ward's protagonist, an American living a secluded life in the French countryside, is one of the contemplative types: sympathetic to the American plight yet uninterested in its motivations, even mildly disgusted by the excessive anger of his compatriots, "anger of the sort that swept all before it and became a cause in itself" (132). When his French wife is killed by terrorist mercenaries (out of expediency rather than maliciousness), the War on Terror practically enters his living room and lingers there, among his portraits (Thomas is an artist), presenting him with an ethical dilemma: Is he now as American as the country he has so adamantly renounced? What fate should befall the perpetrators? And more important, is he entitled to a personal vendetta? When the opportunity for revenge arises as he is facing his wife's killer, all he can do is sketch his portrait—that is, engage in an act of ethical spectatorship—although the two are seated in an interrogation room and torture is an equally viable option. This kind of ethical spectatorship in response to terror (spectatorship often mediated by art) recurs in countless post-9/11 fictions, many of which I discuss in this book.

Yet far from ennobling, Thomas's refusal to shed blood haunts him after he returns to America, and he files it away, along with other false starts and misperceptions, as a so-called Lebenslüge, a convenient narrative ("the lie that makes life bearable" [103]) that allows him to move on, a sealant in the cracks of his identity, a systemic illusion without which he would succumb to the unbearable quest to learn the truth, do the right thing, wage a war that is just and rewarding. In between espressos, calvados, and French oysters, he settles on a "truth" whose main virtue is its ability to breed contentment: that mistakes were made (although to dissect them would be a waste of time); that terrorism may strike randomly no matter how sheltered we foolishly assume we are (and isn't that a good reason to stop pretending that we can ever have it under control?); that forgetfulness is the best weapon in our struggle for survival and the antidote to corrosive ideology, seen as "a belief in the righteousness of your cause and the squalor of all other causes" (189); that forgetfulness is, in fact, the ultimate ethical act.

One of the most puzzling and haunting of post-9/11 novels, *Forgetfulness* starts out as a book about how to become insulated from the past, using art as one means of detaching from worldly engagement and as an excuse for locking oneself away in a French cottage. To ward off any objection that Thomas's sequestered vision might be warped by incuriosity or self-interest, Just portrays him as a politically savvy former intelligence operator, who used to ply his trade by drawing portraits of his subjects, thus unobtrusively prying into their lives. (Surveillance, as we shall see, is a recurrent trope in post-9/11 literature.) By the last chapter, when night falls over Thomas and his troubles (a blend of guilt, remorse, and the desire for indifference), merely obscuring rather than resolving them, the notion that literature—even poignant, evocative fiction such as this—might be ethically enlightening seems itself a Lebenslüge, reassuring and delectable. In a world that is "dark by nature," much like the places where Thomas chooses to reside, life boils down to a "watch of the night" (the novel's last words), which is a spectatorially interesting if rather fatalist vision of the things to which, even in the aftermath of wild injustice, we are reasonably entitled: weighing the measure of chaos that always threatens to interrupt our routine, expecting nothing (or everything) to happen, waiting it out, playing another record, opening another bottle, listening to the creaks of the old French house.

The premise of Just's spatial displacement of the War on Terror is his protagonist's freedom to leave America as soon as the country's politics contravene his personal moral standards. Civil liberties, personal self-determination, and moral choice are also the central concerns of Jonathan Franzen's *Freedom*. According to the Republican voices of this novel, after 9/11 the onus is on the president "to exploit this unique historical moment to resolve an intractable geopolitical deadlock and radically expand the sphere of freedom" (266–67). "We have to learn to be comfortable with stretching some facts" (267) is the slogan of the day, both in Washington and in daily life. In this age of political and personal dissimulation, Franzen anatomizes the body of freedom, or rather the corpse that remains after 9/11 and Iraq, questioning what may have led to its demise—long-term ailments as well as fresher blows. From Walter Berglund (the novel's prime "moralistic irritant" [349], adored by his wife for his "goodness" [515]) to the companies that exploit the war in Iraq for quick financial gain, Franzen references a whole gamut of moral transgressions in a society that has ceased to question its readiness "for the *push*" (412): into war, financial speculation, or sexual infidelity. Although it predictably returns, in Tolstoyan fashion, to the marriage as a safe, alternative-free principle, *Freedom* is steeped in grave ethical reflection entertainingly paired with sarcasm about the positionality of moral judgment, about the petty motives and calculations behind the apparent judiciousness and rationality of ethical decisions. Importantly the narrative's many implausible turns sustains Franzen's vision of contingency as a determinant of ethical life—a contingency that ultimately translates into an unassailable belief in human resourcefulness under conditions that lie beyond human control. This is a theme that informs, in the guise of risk ethics, a number of post-9/11 fictions I address in this book.

While Franzen longs for a "simpler world in which a good life could be had at nobody else's expense" (438), Paul Auster, whose fiction since 9/11 bears the imprint of the attacks with evident (if somewhat fleeting) consistency, has abandoned all hope for a good life, and in *Sunset Park* he elucidates ethical optimism as being predicated on the notion of futurity. *Sunset Park* is firmly anchored in the post-9/11 perpetual present—that is, in the understanding that it would be futile to pin one's hopes on the future when irreversible damage can be wreaked at a moment's notice. In this novel sudden catastrophe in private life (a car accident, a moment of rage) is coextensive with national downfall—in this case, the global financial crisis of 2008 as a late aftershock of 9/11, a crisis that confirms what some may already have suspected in 2001: that the future is unwarranted and unsafe. On the verge of personal collapse, Auster's central character, Miles Heller, "thinks about the missing buildings, the collapsed and burning buildings that no longer exist" (the Twin Towers, but also the abandoned house from which he and other financial outcasts were violently evicted), "and he wonders if it is worth hoping for a future when there is no future" (after financial speculations in "futures" have failed so miserably), "and from now on, he tells himself, he will stop hoping for anything and live only for now, this moment, this passing moment, the now that is here and then not here, the now that is gone forever" (307–08). This is the novel's final sentence, and perhaps an admission of the impossibility of closure in post-9/11 literature, which is permeated by the sense of an ominous past that chance, coincidence, or fate might cause to fall shut, like a long-set, forgotten trap, at any moment.

This cursory overview cannot, of course, do justice to the complexity of these novels, yet I hope it reveals the abiding concern of various post-9/11 fictions with the moral landscape of an era still in the shadow of "no

INTRODUCTION

towers." It also exposes the broad scope and shifting basis for narrative ethics as the attempt to encapsulate and safeguard a sense of empathetic identity constantly torn between individual insecurity and the interpersonal imperative of engaging with Otherness. By attending to literary rhetoric and form, we espy a process of ethical narration that unravels types of knowledge, identification, and sentiment in ways that reaffirm traditional ethical mandates as newly pertinent in the light of September 11 and its continuing aftermath. As for the narratives I discuss in the following chapters—a mixture of canonical and underrated works by DeLillo, Art Spiegelman, Helen Schulman, Patrick McGrath, Michael Cunningham, and others—I have selected them for their explanatory, predictive, and normative value. They illustrate the broad palette of post-9/11 literary discourse, from its most soothing to its most rancorous tones. Some of these texts foreshadowed, at the time of publication, political events they couldn't realistically have foreseen. And they have set the tone for what literature *ought* to be after 9/11. At times forswearing their ethical burden, sometimes openly embracing it, these texts puzzle the reader into a painful awareness of moral crisis and sanction the operative task of narrative in defining a post-9/11 ethical agenda. This impulse might stem from the suspicion that post-9/11 literature can only be a short-lived phenomenon and another "post-" will soon interfere to derail it. But even as new catastrophes demand literary attention, 9/11 is likely always to partake of their significance. Most new fiction about the Iraq War and the global financial crisis—the two key milestones of the post-9/11 era—acknowledges the terrorist attacks as the political Ground Zero of the twenty-first century. A critical vision of contemporary literature that doesn't pay tribute to that event is, by now, virtually unthinkable.

Stopwatch History: Post-9/11 Fiction and Contemporary Culture
Historicizing contemporary literature is a paradoxical task whose stringency has only recently become apparent. In her essay "On the Period Formerly Known as Contemporary," Amy Hungerford defends the right of contemporary scholars to acknowledge literature since 1945 as a legitimate component of the American literary canon, thus relinquishing the

disputed institutional restrictions that have stymied research on this era, or at least relegated that research to a status largely subordinate to more "serious" work on periods that lend themselves to easier historicization. Although Hungerford's essay does not refer to the terrorist attacks or their aftermath, her assessment provides a useful starting point in historicizing post-9/11 literature on a number of fronts.

While "post-45" refers less to the aftermath of a discrete event than to the long throes of a waning conflict—the march of cultural forces abandoning a battlefield—Hungerford tellingly begins her analysis of the contemporary moment with a reference to the "genuine historical transformation" marked (more or less directly, more or less causally) by the events "on or about 9 November 1989" (410). Clearly, then, even though the gist of her approach is generally indifferent to scrupulous dating, Hungerford does concede some significance to the punctual historical moment. She also allows for the Bosnian War as a determining aftershock of the 1989 revolutions, referring to it as "the most dramatic example of resurgent sectarian strife in Eastern Europe after the fall of the Soviet Union" and positing a stark contrast between the domestic and the international in terms of how the United States experienced this tectonic shift: "On the American literary scene, pluralism defined the moment; in the international scene, sectarianism" (410). In the aftermath of 9/11 we are witnessing yet another reversal: while the diminishment of American power abroad has led to a new pluralism in international relations that sees the United States as one among several nuclei of power, new domestic tensions have emerged that the benign multiculturalism of the 1990s had almost entirely appeased. Racial friction spurred by counterterrorist discrimination and surveillance, along with the fear of home-grown terror, has resulted in a discourse of suspicion that sees ethnic minorities again at the forefront of cultural wars—wars that gained in intensity and became deterritorialized with the Bush administration's invasions of Afghanistan in 2001 and Iraq in 2003.

Attending to literature after 9/11 allows us to see how this rise of sectarianism modifies the history of the contemporary as delineated by Hungerford and as it is ingrained in the works of established writers who have come to embody the contemporary imagination. The effects of 9/11 are palpable in the changing shapes of their careers: DeLillo's *Falling Man*, addressing the WTC attack head-on, may have seemed a fluke (and an unsuccessful one at that) before the publication of *Point Omega*, by which time it appears that the deepest influence of the attacks on DeLillo's work lies in the understated, elliptical quality of his recent prose. I read this narrative inertia from an ethical viewpoint as an injunction to slowness in judgment, with absolute-zero narrative momentum meant to counteract the speed of historical change. In this sense the 9/11 moment only "accelerates," as it were, the decelerating plunge in which DeLillo's fiction already found itself before the attacks. A similar reinforcement occurs with Art Spiegelman, whose work since 9/11 is inseparable from his Holocaust comics. In other cases the attacks triggered radical reorientation. September 11 proved so devastatingly futuristic that it prompted William Gibson to write his first novel set in the present. The 2009 National Book Award winner, *Let the Great World Spin*,[1] also marks a shift, though less in Colum McCann's work to date than in literary representations of New York and its cultural memory. By using the tightrope walk of Philippe Petit between the Twin Towers in 1974 as the suspended axis around which the multivocal world of his novel may be seen to rotate, McCann illustrates the kinds of oblique fictional references to 9/11 that would render virtually boundless any study of exactly how far the reverberations of the attacks have reached.

Another way of registering where post-9/11 literature is located on the larger map of the contemporary is to assess the scholarship on these texts. Relatively little has been done in the field since the early flurry of activity in 2003 (J. Greenberg; Hauerwas and Lentricchia) and 2004 (when *Studies in the Novel* published a special issue on literature and terrorism).[2] Since then two monographs and two edited collections have been published exclusively on 9/11 literature, and I must add that many of the texts I analyze in this book probably wouldn't have made the cut as 9/11 fiction in those critical works, which I see as hamstrung by three problems: an almost exclusive interest in the most "iconic," mainstream responses to the September 11 attacks; an extreme focus on explicit, generally descriptive fictions about the attacks at the expense of more oblique works addressing the post-9/11 era; and a disabling lack of commitment to theory, as if the attacks themselves, with their immense historical and political heft, were sufficient to ground an analysis of literature. While in my own work I honor the value of close reading, I find that this scholarship too often stops short of asking the tough theoretical questions about narrative form, the cultural work of fiction about 9/11, and the contribution of this genre to a cultural-historicist study of literature. What this criticism has accomplished, however, is a study of how media narratives inflect post-9/11 literary discourse, although even here few have ventured beyond Slavoj Žižek and Jean Baudrillard or asked, as I attempt to do in the final chapter of this book, how the imaginative structures of the digital in a post-9/11 surveillance culture, with its attendant problem of archiving, are changing aspects of narrative and stylistic form. By discussing, for instance, the work of Lorraine Adams, who has already published two intriguing post-9/11 novels (*Harbor*; *The Room and the Chair*), I hope to draw early attention to the kind of narratively ingenious and politically nuanced writing the next decades are likely to produce. In this book I use an ethical framework to describe precisely this complex symbiosis of politics and narrative. Implicitly, then, through critical discoveries and new theoretical framings, I aim to identify a stronger, more varied 9/11 literary canon than has been acknowledged so far.

To some extent the problems I see in 9/11 scholarship also reflect an understandable uncertainty about which 9/11 works will stand the test of time and which are merely ephemeral. Yet topicality itself can be productively contextualized. In fact the datedness of some 9/11 fictions (such as Claire Tristram's *After*, a novel whose reception was hijacked by the Abu Ghraib scandal; see chapter 2) helps historicize the post-9/11 era in ways that should alleviate any discomfort at focusing so much energy on the literary production of a single decade. Yet where Hungerford proposes to abandon the hieroglyphics nominated to head the post–World War II period (Post•45, the missing hyphen nicely anticipating her verdict of that era as "long modernism," a decimal, as it were, of modernism itself), "9/11" strikes me as well worth keeping. Its chronological specificity aptly characterizes a decade whose events have precipitated at stopwatch speed: September 11, 2001; October 7, 2001 (launch of Operation Enduring Freedom); March 20, 2003 (launch of Operation Iraqi Freedom); April 28, 2004 (Abu Ghraib news report); November 8, 2004 (launch of Operation Phantom Fury in the Second Battle of Fallujah); July 7, 2005 (London bombings); May 2, 2011 (killing of Osama bin Laden). Yet at the same time, despite its temporal specificity, 9/11 remains, as Donald Pease has noted, "inherently nonsynchronous" and discordant with the "mode of historical eventuation the Bush administration has inaugurated in its name" (651). In other words, the attacks articulate a history of which they are no part by brutally terminating a buoyant post–cold war era in which they had seemed unimaginable, and inaugurating an age that quickly overstepped (with a litany of fresh conflicts) the seemingly insuperable caesura of September 2001. This is a paradox that several fictions have explored, both by contextualizing the attacks historically and through their narrative decisions about where in the text the towers should fall, how catastrophic the collapse should be, and whether or how the story (or history) should proceed.

"For this generation, the 1960s are history, not memory," Hungerford writes, and concludes that distance from the past is "an advantage when it comes to the business of historicizing" ("On the Period" 416). Certainly 9/11 is memory rather than history for all of us writing today. More than any of the other seismic shifts in the history and geography of modern times, 9/11 marks a transformation of which we are still in the midst, not only because it is most recent but also because its effects and enduring consequences have been occluded by moralistic knee-jerk reactions, political demagoguery, and institutional disdain of the topical as an aesthetic (and ethical) category. Post-9/11 fiction has gone a long way toward contextualizing the 9/11 event both as a historical phenomenon and as a stage in literary history. This fiction is different from other kinds of contemporary literature, not for any additional moral messages it might deliver about post-9/11 life, but for the profoundly ethical anxiety it communicates. In questioning established opposites and newer dichotomies launched by the Bush administration (between East and West, right and wrong, us and them), it postulates the unforgiving complexity of contemporary culture while acting out dramatically the shifting allegiances mobilized by the War on Terror and America's military ventures abroad. Fiction after 9/11 also asks how we as individuals and communities have superficially accepted (though not fully internalized) the formulaic morality of political discourse. It shows how the ensuing sense of disorientation has allowed smaller things—everyday kindnesses and cruelties—to become suddenly clear. And it stakes out the role of literature as a realm in which responsibilities and compassions begin and grow.

Literary Ethics between Causality and Immanence

Even when they do not openly declare their ethical approach, the works I have selected nevertheless contain what Geoffrey Harpham calls "a factor of 'imperativity'" (*Getting It Right* 5). Consequently my approach requires some rehearsal of narrative ethics to foreground its tradition before 9/11 and its manifestations since then. To begin with the foundational premise of literary ethics, "narrative ethics" is a coinage that denotes a reciprocal correlation—narrative discourse evinces an ethical status, while ethical discourse hinges on narrative structures—and is therefore particularly pertinent to fiction, whose reception (in the act of reading) may itself be construed as an ethical act. In Adam Zachary Newton's understanding, ethics "signifies recursive, contingent, and interactive dramas of encounter and recognition, the sort which prose fiction both crystallizes and recirculates in acts of interpretive engagement" (12). Quite a large number of post-9/11 fictions align with this description of narrative ethics in obvious ways. The texts I have chosen to discuss, along with others that address the "clash of civilizations" and the political vilification of the Islamic Other, not only illustrate ethical behavior or its opposite but also assume the fundamental contribution of literature itself to the realm of ethics and morality, particularly in the aftermath and continuing challenge of terror.[3]

The prevalent view among literary ethicists is that ethical approaches to literature fall into two categories, each associated with one seminal theorist. The work of Martha Nussbaum epitomizes the practice of reading in order to tease out values and norms that are applicable outside of the literary text. Questioning too-rigid boundaries between philosophy and literature (a stance inspired by her work on classical antiquity, where such boundaries did not exist), Nussbaum contends that "moral attention and moral vision finds in novels its most appropriate articulation" (*Love's Knowledge* 148). According to Nussbaum, the "patterns of possibility—of choice and circumstance" (171) that literature delineates are not only descriptive of human lives and problems, but may also be taken normatively as a prescription for living. By contrast, the practice of attending to the ethical in the text itself, rather than establishing a rapport between text and exterior world, finds its passionate advocate in J. Hillis Miller, who insists, against Nussbaum, on a textually immanent ethic. Historical and personal context, Miller suggests, interpose an opaque screen between the reader and the text. For Miller, reading is a transformative act that defers to the heterogeneity of a text and its potential for dislocation and surprise rather than to the historical predispositions (derived from extratextual evidence) we might bring to bear on literature. While for Miller the literary text is free of determinate ethical content, the act of reading, which "cannot be accounted for by the social and historical forces that impinge on it" (8), nevertheless becomes ethical by virtue of its individual, particular power. And while this power is not predetermined by its extratextual environment, it actively inflects this environment. "There must be an influx of performative power," Miller writes, "from the linguistic transactions involved in the act of reading into the realms of knowledge, politics, and history" (5).

My analysis of narrative ethics after 9/11 contains ingredients from both Nussbaum and Miller, historicist criticism and deconstruction. Fiction after 9/11, a genre that is already historically predetermined, dramatizes both the interaction of character and circumstance (corresponding to Nussbaum's normative understanding of ethics) and the textually immanent ethics of fiction. It engages the reader in a journey of ethical self-discovery through idiosyncratic literary forms not straightforwardly reducible to social practices and ways of thinking. Extrapolating from this binary to a psychoanalytic vision of ethics, I also show that post-9/11 fiction presupposes both a preontological ethical relationship to the Other in the Levinasian tradition and a nonpersonal ethical relationship to the unconscious revealed by language, in the terms put forward by Jacques Lacan. To the extent that it has been recruited for the imaginative production of alterity in the post-9/11 era, literature thus also exposes a conceptual impasse between tendencies in ethical thought that have become combatively self-defensive and mutually exclusive. The structural ambiguity of these narratives highlights the conciliatory synthesis underlying their ethical engagement: their moral vision is normative even as their understanding of (inter)subjectivity is not; they evidence formal imperatives that are seldom substantiated. And when they draw on cultural and historical contexts (such as the Balkan civil war and the Holocaust), they tend to homogenize historically and geographically discrete moral visions, rather than differentiate them.

Literature after September 11 is especially attuned to the triangular entwinement of ethics, politics, and literature and to Nussbaum's conviction that a theoretical understanding of ethics would only be diminished if divorced from its manifestations in literary form. Justifying the enterprise of her book *Love's Knowledge* against acerbic criticism from the legal theorist Richard Posner, Nussbaum advances the claim "that moral philosophy needs certain carefully selected works of narrative literature in order to pursue its own tasks in a complete way" ("Exactly and Responsibly" 346). "I do believe," she writes, "that ethical and political issues are non-optional, in the sense that every human being ought to reflect about them in some manner. I also hold that the ethical and political criticism of literature is potentially helpful to most human beings in this reflective activity" (347). This is not to say that Nussbaum attempts to use fiction to prescribe concrete norms or a moral hierarchy of human endeavor; her stance is an egalitarian tolerance of the particularity of moral choices. In advocating the role of the imagination in promoting compassion, Nussbaum argues "that certain specific literary works develop those imaginative abilities in a valuable way and are therefore helpful to citizens" (350)—where "helpful" implies not merely the ability of fiction to develop and assess ethically instructive scenarios, but also its capacity to foster "helpfulness": empathy, support, humane and humanitarian insight. I rely heavily on Nussbaum's work and use one of her essays (in chapter 4) that goes a long way toward illuminating how sudden disruptive events such as 9/11 may act as a catalyst to release waves of empathy that it is our responsibility to channel toward morally defensible goals.

Above all I borrow from Nussbaum's flexibility about the use of ethical criticism, which, though not always a good guide (and sometimes even misleading), *can* be an exceptional heuristic in some cases. Clearly the post-9/11 fiction I address here does not culminate in the unequivocal, Dickensian moral imperative "It is up to you to make society better." But if the authors do not demand to be read ethically, their characters certainly do, and in a very specific sense, with attention to values that have been thrown into disarray by the terrorist attacks and are now in need of some rearrangement. When these books repudiate empathy (as some of them do), it is only to suggest that compassion itself is no solution and may therefore be discarded, which releases these narratives into a void where they must devise their own alternative salvations. Within this void we are alerted to different perspectives of the world and of America's role in it, in ways that help us overcome what Nussbaum calls the "common human tendency to think of one's own habits and ways as best for all persons and all times" (*Cultivating Humanity* 156).

Overwhelmed by the gravity of the events recounted, readers and critics may look to embrace their shared human response, yet it is precisely such homogenization that many post-9/11 fictions set out to eradicate. And here is where the work of J. Hillis Miller proves useful in reading literature ethically yet capturing its transformative potential, primarily in its textual features. In his seminal study, *The Ethics of Reading*, Miller argues that "there is a necessary ethical moment in [the] act of reading as such, a moment neither cognitive, nor political, nor social, nor interpersonal, but properly and independently ethical" (1). He de-emphasizes the complex linkages of ethical values with political and social interests, and by doing so unmoors the process of reading from the reader's self-interest, politics, and even cognition, projecting it onto a zone of pure isolation from everything that to Nussbaum had constituted a reader's sphere of responsibility. Although Miller does acknowledge that, in addition to the immediate ethical response to the text, there must be a later political reaction, an immense chasm opens up between the two. The post-9/11 fictions I discuss attempt to bridge this gap and reconnect the two levels of response without glossing over the difficulties of moving from textual to extratextual realms.

The Otherness Provocation: New Ethical Theory, New Literatures

It is from Dorothy J. Hale's recent work on "new ethical theory" that I have learned most in developing my own vision of narrative ethics in post-9/11 fiction. "The return to ethics," Hale writes, "is not just the attempt to recuperate the agency of the individual reader or author for positive political action but also an attempt to theorize for our contemporary moment the positive social value of literature and literary study" ("Fiction as Restriction" 188). In another essay she reiterates her claim that "the return to moral reflection in contemporary literary theory is in fact a double return: the renewed pursuit of ethics has been accompanied by a new celebration of literature" ("Aesthetics" 896). In defining post-9/11 literature as a potent ethical force, I rely on her insights while suggesting that *contemporary* literature in particular echoes the theoretical work that concerns Hale. My book thus gives precedence, in a way that Hale does not, to the idea of *new* fiction as a site of "new ethical" transaction and contestation.

Reading Hale's work next to that of Spivak, Butler, and Nussbaum (with whom Hale most frequently engages) has helped me devise a framework of interpretation that will guide my theoretical investment in post-9/11 fiction throughout this book. What I want to do is extrapolate from the "new ethical" paradigm mapped by Hale to a discussion of how post-9/11 literature resonates with this paradigm, unfolding as a parallel discourse to its main concerns. The most obvious correlation between the ethical theory and the fictions that interest me here lies in what may be called the Otherness provocation. Hale writes, "For the new ethicists, the novel demands of each reader a decision about her own relation to the imaginative experience offered by novels: Will I submit to the alterity that the novel allows? An affirmative answer launches the novel reader into a transactional relation with another agent, an agent defined by its Otherness from the reader" ("Fiction as Restriction" 189). The post-9/11 novel builds on Otherness as a fundamental structural principle. I say *structural* to point out that the post-9/11 novel's interest in Otherness exceeds the thematic. As I will show, formal narrative choices contribute as much as the notions of foreignness and distance to the post-9/11 novel's concern with alterity.

Despite the complexity of Otherness as narrative strategy—a complexity that emerges from every text analysis included in this book—the idea that literature after 9/11 manifests unparalleled interest in the Other is unlikely to elicit tremendous surprise. Yet unexpected reversals do occur. *The Lazarus Project*, a novel by the Bosnian American writer Aleksandar Hemon, effectively turns Otherness on its head, insisting instead on the recognition of Sameness in ways that echo Hale's pronouncement that "ethical knowledge is the experience of irresistible encounter with what one does not try to know, what one cannot but know" ("Aesthetics" 903). In many cases the distant Other (a threatening nation or person nearly in possession of devastating power) mirrors more proximate lethal figures: the estranged wife, the irresistible lover, the deranged prostitute. Both categories share the potential to wreak moral havoc in ways that allow the international and the domestic to effortlessly collude.

The investment in Otherness both in theory and in literature becomes troubling, however, as soon as we begin to think about the larger social and political implications of reading such fiction and of deriving practical wisdom from our reading experience in a world fraught with transcultural tensions—a world in which many of the traditional concerns of ethical theory before 9/11 (empathy, identification, translation) have acquired a tense immediacy.[4] Hale's gloss on how new ethical theory understands the social and political embeddedness of reading provides some guidance on this issue:

> The social good of diversity and cultural difference can be accomplished, these new ethical theories of literature argue, as much through the felt-efficacy of reading—reading as a personal and inti-

mate activity—as through legal judgments or state policy. The novel reader's experience of free submission, her response to the "hailing" performed by the novel, becomes, for these theorists, a necessary condition for the social achievement of diversity, a training in the honouring of Otherness, which is the defining ethical property of the novel—and is also what makes literary study, and novel reading in particular, a crucial pre-condition for positive social change. ("Fiction as Restriction" 189)

Partly because Hale never locates "new ethical" theory in a concrete historical moment or uses any recent fiction to illustrate her claims and those of the critics she discusses, this statement doesn't appear to fully apprehend the implications of "state policy" and "positive social change" in current discourse. In ways that help specify and complicate Hale's position, post-9/11 literature, I would suggest, constantly oscillates between dissent from and complicity with sociopolitical norms and, through its ethical interpellation, provokes readers to assess how they relate to these norms.

What the post-9/11 novel also illustrates is the incomplete transition from what Hale terms "the old ethical account of novel reading" (190)—revolving around insight and epiphanic emotion—to poststructuralist ethical theory. Although Hale's account doesn't fully illuminate this, the traditional and the contemporary still mingle and coexist in the work she refers to as new. "The name given by poststructuralists to their valorization of readerly experience is anything but 'love'" ("Aesthetics" 902), Hale remarks, with reference to Nussbaum's work in *Love's Knowledge*. Yet it seems to me that the "humanist values of readerly emotion" (190) as they were defined by George Eliot, Charles Dickens, or Lionel Trilling (as sympathy, feeling, or love) still have some purchase for "new ethical" theory and, in ways that strike me as equally important, for new literature. For Hale, what distinguishes the "new ethical" theory is "the self-consciously unverifiable status of the alterity that the ethical subject seeks to produce—an unverifiability that retains the post-structuralist's scepticism about knowledge as a tool of hegemony while bestowing upon epistemological uncertainty a positive ethical content" ("Fiction as Restriction" 190). Nussbaum, however, to whom Hale's account establishes a rather fraught relation, has emphatically continued to stress the emotional component of ethical provocation and response. Post-9/11 fiction, as my analysis of Pat Barker's novel *Double Vision* will reveal, invites interpretation along lines best delineated by Nussbaum, yet at the same time is at pains to challenge the preponderance of sympathy and feeling in post-9/11 public discourse, resenting the instrumentalization of emotion in promoting public and foreign policy agendas of questionable value and efficacy (especially the War on Terror and the wars in Afghanistan and Iraq).

Even more, isn't the "love" associated by Trilling and Nussbaum with the novel's ethical accomplishment nothing other than a traditionally packaged form of what Hale defines as the "new ethical" sense of the novel, "a means of self-binding, that would limit the self and, through this limitation, produce the Other" ("Fiction as Restriction" 190)? To oppose this self-restriction to love is to misunderstand emotion by equating it with a kind of prepossessing benevolence that completely evacuates its subtler exercise of self-restraint. Hale agrees with Lynne Huffer that narrative should leave us with something more than emotion, something "we can never fully grasp, articulate or understand" about the Other (21), yet this may not be as far from love as both Hale and Huffer suppose. Trilling perhaps exaggerated in stating that emotional relationships with a novel's characters lead to a critique of policies that see in social Others "the object of pity, then of our wisdom, ultimately of our coercion" (26). Love for the Arab American characters of post-9/11 fiction (especially in Updike, Brandeis, and Halaby) results only on a superficial and ineffectual level in criticism of the current War on Terror. Rather these fictions mount a successful critique of foreign policy in general and readerly response to the unfamiliar in particular, and they do so by representing situations that fail to achieve their potential for sympathy: dispassionate visual witnessing of the terrorist attacks (DeLillo, Spiegelman, Schulman), the fraught psychological and physical encounter with the Other (McGrath, Tristram), abusive risk assessment in the War on Terror (Halaby, Brandeis, Cunningham), the nationalist core of "evil" as an acute form of self-interest (Hemon, Barker), or the dehumanizing effects of surveillance across national borders (Kirn, Raban, Gibson, Flanagan, Adams), situations that evince a greater capacity for indifference—or even cruelty—than for empathetic response.

Nor is contemporary literature entirely unaware of theoretical debates around alterity, of "the untheorized understanding of the form of the novel as inherently politicized" (Hale, "Aesthetics" 899), and often engages these debates in narrative form through the texts' authorial choices, as well as in their degree of focalization. With self-flagellating abandon, some of the fictions I discuss in this book elevate the production of self-awareness and guilt to a severe ethical commitment, both thematically and formally. As Hale rightly notes, drawing on J. Hillis Miller's discussion of the reader's accountability in the process of reading, "The reader's response to the call of the text makes her as judge judgeable, accountable. The very uncomfortableness of this position is proof of the ethical efficacy of ethical self-binding. The production of alterity is what hurts" ("Fiction as Restriction" 193). The stakes of "hurt" are, of course, different and more concrete in the aftermath of an event as painful as the terrorist attacks—painful both in abstract and more localizable terms. Post-9/11 fiction makes visible not only the reader's agency in the production of narrative alterity, but also the failure of individual agency in safeguarding this alterity in more broadly political terms. For me, this realization has resulted in a new set of interpretive questions, grouped around a central concern: How does the agency involved in the production of textual alterity alert the reader to the political construction of alterity in the post-9/11 era, and to her own (acquiescent or resistant) involvement in this process?

Certainly the ethical unknowability posited by Butler and Hale poses different problems in political life than it does in fiction. Where the novel holds back in self-suppression to open up spaces of alterity, policy makes suppositions, takes risks, and judges without assuming accountability. While "the reader feels he or she comes to know more each time his or her current knowledge is confounded" (Hale, "Aesthetics" 903), political failures to "know" (assess a situation in advantageous ways) may have catastrophic outcomes that are not remedied through mere repetition. An acritical study of literature (as prescribed by Butler, Spivak, and others) is possible while amoral policy is not, because policy lacks a similar potential for endless renewal and experimentation. This is a paradox that post-9/11 fiction eloquently exposes, staging its contradictions in ways that advance the reader's ethical and political education. By positioning the reader in relation to this paradox, it blocks the kind of imperialist identification that Trilling and Spivak lament (Spivak, *Death of a Discipline* 250) without, however, producing the "suspension of judgment" that Butler locates at the heart of literary ethics ("Values of Difficulty" 208). The post-9/11 novel is manifestly different from the Jamesian novel, which implies an ethical position without stating it overtly, thus demanding the reader's judgment—a demand as pressing as it is unfulfillable. By contrast, the aim of the post-9/11 novel is not to cease judging the Other but to show how we are judging even when we think we are not, how we have judged wrongly and how to make amends for it, how simply ceasing to judge is not the solution to a political crisis where judgment continues on, no matter how loftily we might condemn it in the realm of literary study. It is not enough for this literature to leave the reader, as James does, "exasperated, cursing, staring" (Butler, "Values of Difficulty" 208); it also asks for a more productive frustration that doesn't eradicate the value of judgment, inviting the reader to actively evaluate some of the more flagrant misuses of justice in the period following the 9/11 attacks.

The model that underpins Hale's and Butler's understanding of narrative ethics revolves around the self as much as around the Other: "Incomprehension of the other yields knowledge of the self," Hale writes, opening "the possibility that we might change for the better" ("Aesthetics" 901). The fictions I look at ask exactly how—and whether at all—this transition may be achieved. Some of them completely defamiliarize for the reader ideas of sympathy, love, and identification, partly to show how they have been thrown into contingency by the terrorist attacks, partly to expose their manipulative aspects in the service of both narrative and policy. The identification of some characters with the man falling from the North Tower, as captured in Richard Drew's famous photograph, is only the beginning of a laborious struggle toward a reconsideration of what witnessing such horrors implies for the viewer, pointing the reader toward a process of change triggered by the clash-ridden encroachment of politics into intimate life. Sympathy with distant victims of conflict does not necessarily foster the capacity for similar emotions in our private lives, Pat Barker's *Double Vision* suggests, while Claire Tristram's representation of casual sex gone wrong echoes torture practices in ways that follow Liliana Cavani's long-overgrown trail into the thicket of sexuality and political violence, famously dramatized through the erotic relationship between a concentration camp survivor and her former tormentor in the controversial 1974 film, *The Night Porter*.

To be sure, the post-9/11 novel isn't unique in extrapolating from text to context or to allow an appreciation of how political power operates. Martha Nussbaum and Richard Rorty in particular have long held that by expanding our moral imagination, all forms of literature promote tolerance, respect for other viewpoints, and recognition of one's own contingent perspective in ways that enhance the practice of liberal democracy. Though overly deterministic, these formulations certainly help undermine the vehemence of individual, solipsistic truth claims. There is an element of that in most post-9/11 fiction, which often stages a clash of subjectivities pitting Christians against Muslims, Americans against foreigners, Western literary traditions against Eastern aesthetics. The guilt with which the texts confront us is the guilt of "incuriosity" (Stow 413) about what lies beyond the immediate perimeter of our self-loving tolerance, the guilt that makes itself felt when we finish a novel "rubbing our heads, worrying about whether we are all right, wondering whether we like ourselves" (Rorty xiii). This guilt is even more troubling than the ambiguous ending of Henry James's novel *Washington Square*, which leaves Butler feeling betrayed as a reader, betrayed in the same way an addict feels betrayed by a drug when realizing it is only a placebo. The frustration caused by the post-9/11 novel is closer to Rorty's than to Butler's. Not only are we denied access to meaning, but a rather distasteful understanding of ourselves, of our willful solidarity in ignorance, becomes palpable.

Much has been made of reading not only as politicized, but as a political act in itself. "We are hard at work trying to fulfill the impossible task of reading from the moment we are born until the moment we die," J. Hillis Miller writes in *The Ethics of Reading* (59), suggesting that the imperative to grasp and decode language inevitably "enters into the social, institutional, political realms" (4). Especially through the representation of data mining as an inherently political reading process that establishes moral boundaries and oppositions, in post-9/11 fiction it is often the act of reading itself that guides our understanding of literature at the current historical juncture. Without seeming to conveniently sidestep the receptive fallacy imputed to both Rorty and Nussbaum (i.e., the fallacy of speaking from a reader's perspective while engaging the text rather than the audience itself), over the following chapters discussions of narrative and of reading go hand in hand without starkly separating the realm of reader reception from the issue of how these texts are politically instructive on their own terms. I do not do this to complicate the connections between literature and life that have informed ethical debate as much as to allow for the possibility that the post-9/11 novel enters this discussion with a much broader knowledge of its poststructuralist audience than the classical objects of ethical inquiry (James, Eliot, Dickens) can be said to do, and as such already attempt to map out their reader relation on a textual level.

That these fictions open up ambiguities and irresolvable ethical questions is part of my point about the challenge they pose to policies that eschew such ambiguity, policies that act in the spirit of a contrived certainty eloquently lampooned by Spivak: "If Paul Wolfowitz had had serious training in literary reading and/or the imagining of the enemy as human, his position on Iraq would not be so inflexible" ("Ethics and Politics" 23). Of course, the line of equivalence between literature and politics is not as clear-cut as Spivak's quip might suggest, and in this book I seek to decode the relations between political and narrative choices in ways that do not obfuscate the ethical value of ambiguity, which I identified earlier as a dominant characteristic of the post-9/11 novel. Beyond the statements made by characters and narrators, and beyond narrative strategies that I discuss specifically in the contemporary context (an ethical reading of counterterrorist surveillance and data mining is one step I take in this direction), I want to allow these fictions the freedom of not signifying. Far from constituting the ultimate purpose of literary ethics, new or otherwise, their refusal to signify should be considered in the broader context of a culture whose propensity for oversignification and reckless judgment we should take very seriously in our capacity as both readers and citizens. And while each of the novels discussed in this book must be approached on its own terms, looming large behind their negotiations of ethics and morality for our age is the concept of just war. We cannot begin to understand these fictions' obsessive return to questions of revenge, retaliation, preemption, and scapegoating without exploring the moral underpinnings of the War on Terror, both at home and abroad.

Justice and Security

I want to start from Fredric Jameson's observation that "it is ethics itself which is the ideological vehicle and the legitimation of concrete structures of power and domination" (*The Political Unconscious* 114) to elaborate on the political contexts undergirding the moral discourse of the War on Terror—discourses that inform many of the fictions addressed in the following chapters. Ethical rhetoric after 9/11 has steered a middle path between mainstream moralism (espoused especially in American political discourse and the Bush Doctrine) on the one hand and subtle finessing of existing ethical positions on the other. America's immediate reaction to the attacks was to affirm a single moral paradigm (encapsulated in the conflict of good versus evil or "us" and "them," a grotesque reprise and radicalization of Samuel Huntington's "clash of civilizations") rather than grapple with the messiness of conflicting choices that call for repeated judgment and compromise. At the opposite pole, a plethora of critics have rushed to align ethics with "human affectivity and passions as the motor of subjectivity" (Braidotti 13) against an essentialist moralism. In his book *Moral Philosophy after 9/11*, Joseph Margolis rightly locates moral contention and concession at the heart of the contemporary era: "The sources of moral conviction drawn from the life of different societies cannot be shown to converge toward any uniquely valid moral vision" (viii). I want to argue that fiction inspired by the 9/11 attacks displays a similarly polarized engagement with ethics, rejecting the War on Terror's exclusionary norms while dramatizing the constraints under which the ethical questions of our time are being raised. In its ramified scenarios post-9/11 fiction demonstrates that "an objective moral vision focuses more on a defensible *modus vivendi* than on any isolated act or proposition" (101), moving beyond ideological and theoretical doctrines to engage with practical commitments whose miniature dynamics literature is particularly apt to investigate.

The events that form the backdrop of post-9/11 fiction (the war in Afghanistan, Homeland Security policies, the passage of the Patriot Act, the invasion of Iraq,[5] and the Abu Ghraib scandal) certainly open up a Pandora's box of moral questions that gel around the encounter with the Other. A "foundational question of US-ness," Cynthia Weber writes in her study of post-9/11 political morality, *Imagining America at War*, is "what does it mean to be a moral America(n)?" (2). While Weber's argument that post-9/11 debates on American identity at home and abroad were primarily moral seems powerful and trenchant, her position illustrates precisely the kind of binarism that sees a moral response to the attacks as tilted toward either humanitarianism or vengeance (5). Here, as in other accounts of how the events of September 11 challenge us in ethical terms, morality is understood as a morality tale in which good and evil play discrete parts and engage in a struggle, or in which moral choices are made whose content is incontestable. But what exactly *is* morality, and how does it come about? On what grounds can we differentiate, as Weber does, between moral certainty, which may be simplified or misguided, and a purer, underdetermined idea of "morality itself" (155)? Weber condemns Michael Moore's 2004 documentary *Fahrenheit 9/11* as expressing Moore's "own morally certain opposition to the moral certainty of the Bush administration" (129). Yet a persuasive critique of the Bush administration's moral fundamentalism requires a finer-tooled revision of the relationship between justice and security since 9/11, a revision that fiction might be well equipped to undertake.

Specifically the literature I analyze displays a critical awareness of how the War on Terror has deployed the vocabulary of moral panic around citizens deemed to be suspicious and around nations that form so-called axes of evil. On a concrete narrative level, fictions that discuss surveillance practices (chapter 5) respond to the cybernetically driven forms of moral control that James Der Derian has termed "virtuous war." Yet it would be simplistic to state that works by Laila Halaby, Michael Cunningham, Gayle Brandeis, and Lorraine Adams are merely critical of the proliferation of moral discourses that justify violence against individuals and sovereign nations. More interestingly, these novels reenact the ways judgments used to justify the War on Terror are formulated and enforced, and they perform these judgments by narrative means. To some extent these texts are also complicit in the strategies of moral racialization associated with the War on Terror, as I argue in chapter 3. Throughout, post-9/11 fictions cannily construe plots and characters that illustrate for the reader the mechanics of justice, particularly the potential of the War on Terror to cause miscarriages of justice by vilifying the innocent. The most ethically complex narratives I have chosen revolve around such tragic figures, whose racial and cultural diversity exposes the mutability of this war's moral guidelines, as well as the importance of pursuing its narratives to their final implications: deportation, torture, or death.

When they refrain from imposing a rigid ethical framework on their narratives, these writers implicitly question the inflexible terms in which the War on Terror has been couched—terms that appear to tap into the tradition of just war. A stalwart proponent of just war theory, the political philosopher Michael Walzer endorsed the Afghanistan invasion as "just," as a morally acceptable alternative to what he terms "the 'dial 911' response to 9/11" (xiv), namely the misguided notion that calling on international law enforcement will suffice to reorganize a newly disjointed transnational map of alliance and enmity. Even though the just war argument may appear established and coherent (which it is in its original outline, with all its caveats in position), it may not in fact be the primary justification behind the War on Terror. In responding to Jean Bethke Elshtain's understanding of the War on Terror as a political ethic of responsibility (264), Anthony Burke expresses his concern about "the naivety of [Elshtain's] belief that the just war framework is the one actually being applied by

INTRODUCTION

the Bush administration" (144). This is a valid point, and indeed many have criticized the Bush Doctrine on a number of ethical grounds. Yet the fictions I analyze go far beyond the tenets of an American doctrine, as they range across several nations engaged in the global War on Terror (the United States, the United Kingdom, and Australia) and nations positioned at the receiving end of Bush-style moral opprobrium: Jordan, Palestine, an increasingly powerful Russia, Algeria, and Iran. The wars described here have progressed beyond the initial stages of deliberation: in Afghanistan and Iraq, the rules are no longer *jus ad bellum* (a set of criteria consulted and debated *before* engaging in war) but *jus in bello* (laws regarding conduct *during* war). Once we find ourselves embroiled in the War on Terror with no end in sight, these fictions ask, how do we extricate our understanding of ethics and justice from the strategic moralism that started this war? For better or worse, we have inherited, as has the Obama administration (often lambasted for its moral indecisiveness), the War on Terror started in 2001. Writers who seek to explore uneasy questions about how this war permeates our lives have been thrust into a situation that has less to do with just war than with the ethical realities of *already* living with an indeterminate, perpetual battle waged in the name of peace. How exactly has this paradox infiltrated and corrupted our daily lives?

Patrick McGrath and Claire Tristram suggest that we have become inured to the practice of inflicting pain, that we are likely to single out scapegoats for the uncertainty we feel and to be cruel with less remorse and a greater sense of moral justification; that the images of Abu Ghraib have negatively inflected our views of interracial sexuality and tainted, through abuse and oversimplification, the ways we see the Other as an object of care and desire. In Tristram's novel *After* a woman who sets out to sleep with the Muslim enemy to enable a sense of shared humanity mysteriously proceeds to tie him up and beat him with coat hangers in a dingy hotel room. For a woman in McGrath's *Ghost Town*—this one trained in the allocation of sympathy (a psychoanalyst)—September 11 muddles the distinction between the morality of political retaliation and the ethics of everyday life: terror is transplanted from the Homeland Security state into her client's bedroom, while the ultimate evil is not bin Laden but her client's Chinese lover. Both McGrath and Tristram use highly unreliable narrators to probe the narratives of exculpation we tell ourselves and others. Laila Halaby, Gayle Brandeis, and Michael Cunningham enact in their post-9/11 fictions the end of civilian immunity heralded by inflammatory arguments in favor of authorizing civilian targets in the War on Terror. Most infamously, the international security scholar Barry Buzan dismisses "the idea that in war, peoples and their governments should be treated separately" as nothing but "a Western fetish, a way of asserting the West's claim to be civilized" (85). In post-9/11 fiction concerned with the War on Terror, innocent individuals appear as national and moral ciphers, imbibing much of the hostility and righteousness mobilized by this war.

The post-9/11 politics of justice, Debra Bergoffen has argued, is rooted in a concept of innocence derived from the ethical figure of the innocent victims brutally murdered in New York, Washington, and Pennsylvania: "the innocence of the victims has spilled over into the nation" (74), Bergoffen writes, imbuing national politics with a self-righteous notion of collective blamelessness and vindictive entitlement of which violence against the Other is the inevitable paroxysm. To transcend or preempt the violence of post-9/11 intersubjectivity, not only is the self required to recognize the Other's destabilizing effects; the self must also, Bergoffen insists, acknowledge that it is "experienced by the Other as a threat" (75), not as a result of any concrete hostile actions but as an existential suspicion from which no one can be exempted. "Renouncing the claim to innocence," Bergoffen concludes, "is essential to the project of the ethical, for in claiming the mantle of innocence, I position myself as absolutely wronged" (75). Post-9/11 fiction divests the self of its innocence by recasting it as violent, condemnable, and abject through narratives that effectively block the path of self-exoneration and raise suspicions about the self's rhetorical reliability and coherence. Contrary to America's self-image as an innocent and resilient world power, fictions by Claire Tristram and Patrick McGrath in particular distill from the violence of the pathological encounters they describe an ethics of contingency and desire that reinscribes the post-9/11 American self within the sphere of inconclusive intersubjectivity. Seduced by "an imaginary investment in its invincibility," Bergoffen remarks, the United States devised a symbolic construct that left no room for "critical self-reflection, for the experience of uncertainty," tying itself instead to a myth of global invincibility (78). Post-9/11 fiction effectively critiques this mythical frame by inverting the collective humiliation experienced by Americans on September 11. What drives self-reflection and the admission of ethical uncertainty in these texts are experiments in self-abasement and brutal denials of American innocence by characters who become ruthless perpetrators—of sexual abuse, torture, and narrative gaslighting.

In a state of emergency that suffers few legal restraints, these novels find an ethical responsibility in revealing how moral obligations are spurned and left unfulfilled despite the prominence of morality in political discourse. In ways that cut against the absolute certainty of moral dogma underpinning post-9/11 ideology, post-9/11 literature is most effective when its ethics is not the overt theme and when it focuses on the experience of physical suffering to cut through the abstractions of ethical theory and to show how theoretical impartiality (as encapsulated in the "just war" concept) obscures the material contingencies of the ethical relation. In exposing this self-consuming form of ethics, many post-9/11 fictions resort to technologies of visuality, and in so doing articulate what I call "ethical spectatorship," a concept to which I devote the first chapter and that runs through the entire book, surfacing in discussions of racial profiling, photography, and surveillance.

Ethical Spectatorship

Although the dynamics of applying ethics to one field of study or another is far from unusual, most often such constructions rest precariously on an ambiguous genitive (J. Hillis Miller's "ethics of reading" or Booth's "ethics of fiction"). By intentional contrast, my approach does not take this form ("ethics of spectatorship"), but rather implies simply spectatorship *as* ethics, and also, more important, ethics *as* spectatorship. The term *ethical spectatorship* thus yokes together both the ethical significance of vision and the visual undercurrent of ethics itself. I want to use this compound concept as an umbrella term for a series of engagements with the obsessive interest of post-9/11 fiction in the terrorist attacks as a visual event. My claim is that the explicit or implicit presence of visual discourse in the novels discussed here bespeaks a distinctly contemporary investment in the appellative power of the visual. While both ethics and visuality independently have come to saturate the discourse of contemporary literary and cultural theory, together they have made little impact, although their nearly simultaneous popularity (both have experienced a surge since the 1990s) may suggest a degree of interconnectedness.

In the *Timaeus* Plato explains that vision, despite the potential for illusion it conceals, may be seen as a path to ethics. Vision is necessary, he writes, so that "we should see the revolutions of intelligence in the heavens and use their untroubled course to guide the troubled revolutions in our own understanding" (65). It is through vision, Plato argues, that we can adjust our measurements to the "right" standards, yet such vision need not—in fact possibly *should* not—be derived from visual artifacts such as works of art, of which Plato was notoriously suspicious. If we take ethics in the sense proposed by Emmanuel Levinas and his followers as based on a relation or encounter between self and Other, it is in the work of the phenomenologist Maurice Merleau-Ponty that the ethics of vision is most precisely articulated. Given that the physicality of the "look" must leave its imprint on the object of vision, to Merleau-Ponty the seer is continuous with the seen, and to look at the Other is essentially to look at oneself. "Since vision is a palpation with the look," he writes, "it must also be inscribed in the order of being that it discloses to us; he who looks must not himself be foreign to the world that he looks at" (134).

A very similar pronouncement comes from Kaja Silverman, who proposes in the introduction to *The Threshold of the Visible World* that "to look is to embed an image within a constantly shifting matrix of unconscious memories" (3). The encounter between the outside image and the inner realm of private memory seems to occur on the plane of interior subjectivity, yet, somewhat counterintuitively, it also draws out the self. As Silverman writes, "When a new perception is brought into the vicinity of those memories which matter most to us at an unconscious level, it too is 'lighted up' or irradiated, regardless of its status within normative representation" (4). The interior memory can thus be said to shade into the exterior perception, or at least come into fleeting "contact" with it. It is thus not only the outer image that falls in step with the visual repository that absorbs it; the gesture is reciprocal, occasioning an illumination and a renewal of the unconscious self. Reciprocity is what makes this visual investment profoundly ethical.

Yet looking is often prestructured, its forms determined by technologies that simultaneously make looking possible in the first place and restrict its possibilities.[6] In the historical moment that I discuss here, what has most radically influenced regimes of representation is the technology of video, especially as live feed and amateur footage, with its attendant social practices and domains of knowledge. Video borrows from the aesthetics of the photographic image and profits from its digitalization. For an ethics of vision that reflects the democratization and provisionality of the visual in contemporary culture, video aesthetics is the arena that hosts the ethical relation between the visualizing self and the visualized Other. Being much more disembodied than previous visual formats (easily transferable, embeddable, and minimizable on screens so small that they fit in the palm of one's hand), video is the medium of the portable gaze, a semicorporeal optical device that redefines traditional notions of spectatorship, witnessing, and presence. Although photography remains significant in interpreting the aftermath of the terrorist attacks (especially with regard to the fiction discussed in chapter 1), including the ways it serves to chronicle and juxtapose disparate historical events (a point on which I elaborate in chapter 4), it is video that constitutes the signature visual medium we will associate with 9/11 and its violently photogenic, video-streamable aftermath for years to come.

Various references to this medium recur in 9/11 fiction: the image of train passengers filming with their cell phone cameras a performance artist who poses as one of the World Trade Center jumpers; entire families in thrall to the repetitive footage of the collapsing towers and the dust cloud billowing through the deep canyons of downtown Manhattan; the impromptu documentary footage of the attacks by the Naudet brothers encouraging a war correspondent to write a book about representations of war; a surveillance video that turns an innocent Australian woman into a public scapegoat onto whom an array of crimes and transgressions are projected; mysterious footage disseminated via the Internet and through video-sharing platforms, which, as I have argued elsewhere, have proliferated partly as a response to the visual traumas of the September 11 attacks and of other conflicts they have engendered.[7] It may be argued, with Eduardo Mendieta, that contemporary technologies undermine the traditional, face-to-face proximity associated with ethical relations because the ethical is predicated on distance, spatial and temporal (113). Mendieta rightly notes that ethics consists precisely in the active attempt to "reach across space and aid and respond to the other" (116), and this gap is less evident or enticingly prohibited in a hypervisible, shrinking world. However, it seems to me that new visual technologies also encourage an interesting sense of impersonal accountability toward images of pain and suffering not despite the deterritorialized anonymity of the medium but as a result of it. As I aim to show in this book through a number of textual readings against the grain of traditional ethics, intimate interpersonal relations and impersonal visual traffic are not mutually exclusive but constitutive of a new social geography favorable to ethical investment.

Considering the ubiquity of screens and the largely unfiltered visuality they permit, the question of how visibility underpins ethical address gains added urgency. To a limited degree the visual nature of ethical relations has already found its way into ethical criticism, yet this has occurred mostly by accident. Nussbaum, for instance, defends Henry James's view of art as moral exemplary "because human beings do great damage to themselves and others through obtuseness and refusal of *vision*" ("Exactly and Responsibly" 343–44, my emphasis). While the visual presence of the Other is often recognized as the foundation of ethics, especially through the frequent and largely unreflected invocation of Levinas, rarely is ethical discourse sensitive to the subtle negotiations implied in this act of mutual engagement. Before any Other can be *seen*, the self must *look* with some degree of interest. No longer, then, is "the decentered center of ethics . . . its concern for 'the other,'" as Harpham would have it; nor is ethics merely "the arena in which the claims of otherness ... are articulated and negotiated" (394). Ethics is something at once very simple and altogether more complicated: it is the locus of communication that binds the self and the Other without emanating explicitly from either one, emerging instead from the act of recognition, intersubjectively, in "a process of witnessing that connects us through the tissues of language and gestures" (Oliver 223), a process that clearly implies visuality.

In an explicit, albeit inchoate study of ethics and contemporary spectatorship, Rey Chow does away with Levinas altogether by relegating his influence to a footnote, although Chow's own approach stands squarely in the tradition of Levinas's attachment of ethics to Otherness. "Because engagement with otherness almost always involves some kind of imagistic objectification (of the other)," Chow astutely remarks, "it is difficult, if not impossible, to segregate considerations of otherness from visual relations (even if such relations are only implied, passed over, or suppressed)" ("Toward an Ethics of Postvisuality" 676). Unfortunately this insight has not prevented ethical theory from mobilizing a profound distrust of the visual image and of representational practices, particularly in the encounter with cultural alterity, which always seems in need of rescuing from falsifying or abusive representations. At no time was the iconophobia of ethical discourse articulated with more conviction than in the days following September 11, as cultural critics condemned both the instrumentalization of the visual by the terrorists on the one hand, and the media's endless repetition of the same images on the other. Moreover at that emotionally charged historical juncture, visuality was often employed as a weapon of racial profiling and discrimination rather than as a means of intercultural mediation. When images were indeed meant to provoke compassion (as in the publication of victims' portraits by the *New York Times*), they tended to facilitate the process of mourning as primarily introspective rather than ethically extroverted.

Other attempts to overthrow the apartheid of ethics and vision bypass the linkage altogether as either too obvious or misguided. "What I wish to caution against," Mieke Bal notes in a particularly ruthless commentary on Levinas, "is the conflation of the *slogan* of the face-to-face with an ethics of vision, as long as it remains as vague as it tends to be, easily slipping into a pseudo-anthropological reasoning that is, indeed, unhistorical" (151). Such groping for an ethics of vision—which Bal does not distinguish from an ethics of visuality (see Chow, "Toward an Ethics of Postvisuality")—confirms my initial supposition that not only does ethical criticism do relatively little with visuality, but visual studies do precious little with ethics as well.[8] Bal's "commitment to look" sounds radical and innovative mainly because the straw man premise against which she argues—"the pseudo-ethics . . . of the discourse of the face" (159)—is vague and easily denounceable in the first place. Rather than act as an interdiction to violence, as Levinas would have it, in Bal's estimation the face evokes an empty compassion without identification. It reduces the gaze to passive recognition of alterity instead of imbuing it, as she aims to do, with the responsibility of not merely seeing, but looking—not *at* the face (to which Bal attributes the permeability of skin) but through and beyond it.

While the theories put forward by Chow and Bal prepare my own intervention, it is the work of Levinas—ignored or dismissed by both Chow and Bal—to which I am most indebted. The French philosopher and ethicist not only has unambiguous opinions concerning the visual dimension of ethics, but he plainly fetishizes vision as a source of knowledge and as the primordial medium inside which the ethical encounter takes place. In *Totality and Infinity* Levinas writes, "Ethics is an optics. But it is a 'vision' without image, bereft of the synoptic and totalizing objectifying virtues of vision" (23). The implications of this statement cannot be properly gauged outside Levinas's long-standing interest in the face of the Other. "The first word of the face," he explains, "is 'Thou shalt not kill.' It is an order. There is a commandment in the appearance of the face, as if a master spoke to me. However, at the same time, the face of the Other is destitute; it is the poor for whom I can do all and to whom I owe all" (*Ethics and Infinity* 89). This rhetoric of the face grounds Levinas's optical ethics as a self-committing system of looking and spectatorship rather than mere visual detection of Otherness.

INTRODUCTION

Levinas's concept of an optical ethics also lends new valences to his paradoxical definition of the face as an image that signifies the impossibility of its own representation: "The way in which the other presents himself, exceeding *the idea of the other in me*, we here name face. This *mode* does not consist in figuring as a theme under my gaze, in spreading itself forth as a set of qualities forming an image. The face of the Other at each moment destroys and overflows the plastic image it leaves me" (*Totality and Infinity* 50–51). "Optics," then, is one way of describing this appearance of Otherness—which is not an appearance at all in that it remains exterior to itself as well as to its temporary visual traces and to the attributes that might attempt to fix it.[9] The optical demand of the face is related to what Levinas calls the relation without relation ("le rapport sans rapport"), referring to the subject that aspires to an Other that exceeds its relational capacity. Insofar as the subject feels inadequate to make good on the ethical demand of Otherness, vision fails to cohere into an absolute image yet constantly strives to achieve this fullness. Such obsessive ambition constitutes what Levinas describes as trauma, understood here as a persecuting responsibility toward Otherness. "This trauma," he insists, "this affectivity ... takes shape as a subjection to the neighbor. It is thought thinking more than it thinks, desire, the reference to the neighbor, the responsibility for another" (*Basic Philosophical Writings* 142). Trauma implies a complex mix of passivity and agency, presupposing an unfulfillable responsibility toward Otherness fueled by the impossibility of a concrete response, as well as by an infinite supplement of affection seeking to latch onto a fervently desired subject. "In short," Simon Critchley quips, "the Levinasian ethical subject is a traumatic neurotic" (*Infinitely Demanding* 61), and such neurosis is evidently at work in many of the post-9/11 fictions I discuss in this book. My approach thus perceives Levinasian ethics as enmeshed with the broader conceptual framework of trauma theory. Rather than being easily subsumed to either one of these monolithic interpretive imaginaries, post-9/11 fiction both sustains their premises and registers their volatilities. By narrativizing ethical mandates, these texts ultimately annotate and reshape the trajectories of current critical thought.

INTRODUCTION

To predict where the dialogue between post-9/11 ethics and visuality will lead it is safe to say that the former exerts more pressure precisely at the most intensely visual moments of the text. The visual can thus be conceived as the Other of narrative, and insofar as the Other is, according to Derek Attridge, not merely recognized but actively created, visuality becomes something else through its absorption into narrative, which is in turn re-created through the influence of visuality.[10] Yet this reciprocal inflection contains the same insurmountable aporia that characterizes all discourses of Otherness, because "insofar as I apprehend the already existing other, it is not other: I recognize the familiar contours of a human being, which is to say I accommodate him or her to my existing schemata" (Attridge 24). Indeed once it enters the narrative, the visual inhabits other hybrid forms, such as ekphrastic discourse, descriptive performance, or racist psychotherapy. The visual and the verbal merge in post-9/11 fiction to produce narratives that not only question literary judgment and moral values, but also are distinctly ethical through their aesthetic heterogeneity.

We know from reading both Attridge and Critchley that ethics makes impossible demands, that in fact no demand has any ethical validity unless it is never fully realizable. Or, as Levinas himself remarks, "one is never quits with regard to the Other.... At no time can one say: I have done all my duty" (*Ethics and Infinity* 105). The only post-9/11 novel so far that distinctly attempts to calculate the precise responsibility of the text to the image, Jonathan Safran Foer's *Extremely Loud and Incredibly Close*, is also the one that most notably fails in its ethical mission. Whereas Foer includes a series of documentary images depicting a man falling from the North Tower in a reverse sequence that propels him upward, the 9/11 texts on which I have chosen to linger retain the visual as a dangerous supplement.[11] Instead of making an obvious textual appearance, the images invoked in these fictions materialize the paradox of simultaneous presence and absence, as well as the ethical imperative it formulates.

Certainly the mere proliferation of visual references in 9/11 fiction shows that visuality can indeed be signified in some manner through narrative language, even though its singularity will never be rendered in full. There are instances when looking at (through ekphrastic discourse) rather than seeing (i.e., reproducing) the visual traces of the attacks more successfully epitomizes vision by denying it concrete representation. The reader is thus prohibited from interpreting the violent images in terms of their visible qualities, and the Others that populate such fictions—the figure of a man falling from the North Tower, a Chinese woman who epitomizes alien evil, or a woman raped and murdered in a bombed-out building in Sarajevo—likewise display a noncoincidence with their visual portrayals that indicates the incompleteness and nonrepresentability of the traumatic image as a coherent whole. Such visuals occupy the place of narrative's impossible, expressing something the text needs to convey but cannot articulate in its own terms. This inarticulateness brings to mind one of the most incomplete and nonrepresentable images of the 9/11 victim, an image that is both fetishized and carefully avoided both in literature and in public discourse: the image of the dead body, which is simultaneously potent, empty, and deterritorialized. The image of the falling man is particularly haunting because it elicits and implies another image that we never see but also cannot completely ignore: the victim's body just after he has hit the ground.

This tension between facing the Other (and, implicitly, the horror of death) and looking away circumscribes the discursive locus for my analysis over the following chapters. Could this intersection help redefine the intense appeal of the visual in contemporary culture, especially since September 11, 2001, and even take us toward a different—and more binding—kind of ethics altogether? To put it differently, are moral imperatives closely dependent on visual injunctions and interdictions, and if so, how does post-9/11 narrative stage or suppress this relation? With these questions in mind, my analysis offers a response and addition to that strain of ethical criticism that singles out literature for debates around the authenticity of testimony and the responsibility of representing atrocity as a step toward punishment, reparation, or prevention. I argue that far from ignoring the increasingly visual pressures on ethical discourse, post-9/11 fiction is precisely the ground on which many of the battles between an ethics of representation and one of active responsibility are being waged.

INTRODUCTION

Transnational Ethics

The assumption driving this book is that crucial junctures in the development of literature after 9/11 have been shaped by the challenges of ethical thought. The roller coaster of momentous history triggered on that day appears to have "outstripped the capacity of traditional forms of reflection on the ethical life" (Sullivan and Schmidt, Introduction 2), challenging us to live justly in a world replete with ethical ambiguities, the world itself the most ambiguous of all. By revealing the difficulty of moral choice, according to Nussbaum the novel encourages "a posture of agency that is porous and susceptible of influence" (*Love's Knowledge* 180) and constructs an understanding of life as "richer, fuller of enjoyment, fuller too of whatever is worth calling knowledge of the *world*" (181, my emphasis). I want to take this phrase literally and ask to what extent an ethical reading of the post-9/11 novel facilitates knowledge of the "planet"—to use the term favored by Wai Chee Dimock ("Literature for the Planet") and Gayatri Spivak (*Death of a Discipline*)—knowledge that is geographically flexible and in transit, that further complicates and questions our ability to judge a deterritorialized Otherness, while inviting a critique of the ways such judgment has been made. The transnational perspective I adopt adheres to an ethics of global responsibility toward the Other as individual or as nation, but it also reveals interpellations derailed by shifting coordinates. It is, in the words of Jeffrey Paul Melnick, as "our cultural Esperanto: our language of grief and anger, of loss and steadfastness" (7), that September 11 has galvanized a transnational ethics of care, anxiety, and exclusion. A symbol of endless, perpetually remote, and essentially unfulfillable ethical appeal, the global strikes me as not only an ideal environment in which to carry out an ethical debate, but possibly as the only one that truly does justice to the challenge of ethical thought today. A transnational approach to post-9/11 ethics redirects ethical obligations "above, below and beyond the state" (Burke 165), a state that has forsaken responsibility for the Other in favor of an uncritical moralism of emergency aimed to safeguard a fetishized national self.

A complex argument about the long durée and transnational repercussions of September 11 has been made by Martin Halliwell and Catherine Morley, who see in the terrorist attacks less a "moment of historical rupture" than a "tipping point in which 9/11 intensified certain emergent patterns through a process of reterritorialization" (5). Over the course of this book, I advocate a similarly intertwined global and historical perspective on September 11 to bring into focus and interrogate the ethical binarisms mobilized in its aftermath. Writers such as Aleksandar Hemon and Pat Barker effortlessly contextualize September 11 in time and space by linking the terrorist attacks with the Bosnian War. To draw such historical analogies, as Amy Kaplan has noted, "would be to trouble the very binary oppositions and exceptionalist narratives . . . between before and after, between being 'with us' or 'with the terrorists,' between the 'American way of life' and the 'axis of evil'" (84). It is precisely this opposition between the Virgin Land and the postcatastrophic Ground Zero, Donald Pease writes, that supplies Americans with a "moral rationale: their native land was inviolate because the American people were innocent" (640). Especially when September 11 is linked with the suffering inflicted by the United States on civilian populations, to locate the United States within world history amounts to an indictment of American foreign policy of the kind that has met with public opprobrium ever since Susan Sontag was castigated in the days following 9/11 for her suggestion that the attacks may have been a direct consequence of American alliances and actions. Although Frank Lentricchia reiterates Sontag's point in his editor's note to *Dissent from the Homeland* (Hauerwas and Lentricchia), global historical events that may have prefaced or prefigured the terrorist attacks were quickly forgotten in post-9/11 cultural discourse, while a vociferous counterdiscourse emerged around how 9/11 ushered in, seemingly out of the blue, a new transnational era.

The idea that September 11 opened a "window on the world" entered post-9/11 vocabulary very early on. "Will Americans decide to fortify further their 'sphere,' or will they risk stepping out of it?" Slavoj Žižek asks in "Welcome to the Desert of the Real!" (135). Succumbing to a similar kind of presentism, or what Amy Kaplan referred to as the historically exceptionalist antinarrative of September 11,[12] Jean Baudrillard projects on the attacks the same kind of insularity that he bemoans in the American nation: "We have not yet had any symbolic event of such magnitude that it is not only broadcast all over the world, but holds globalization itself in check—not one" ("L'Esprit du Terrorisme" 149). In typically chiastic, inwardly spiraling fashion, Baudrillard sees in the clash of civilizations nothing less than "globalization grappling with itself"—a "world" war whose stake is the world as a whole, leading him to the perplexing conclusion that "it is the very world itself that resists globalization" (152). Baudrillard handles the ethical implications of this struggle in equally hermetic terms: "Terrorism is immoral. The World Trade Center event, this symbolic defiance, is immoral and responds to a globalization that is itself, also immoral" (153). It is left to other writers and critics to elucidate the meaning of this immorality, beyond the self-evident assumption that murder is wrong and globalization is not a level playing field but a more or less surreptitiously preserved hierarchy that acts of terror such as September 11 attempt to usurp, at least temporarily.

"In our cultural moment," Hale writes, "the novel and its aesthetics of alterity define the literary for most readers" ("Aesthetics" 902). What also defines the literary since 9/11 is an understanding of the novel as profoundly deterritorialized in ways that pose new challenges for ethical criticism. Jill Bennett attempts to answer these challenges by questioning the term *national trauma* and its exclusionary effects. "When trauma is coextensive with nation," she asks, "where do the limits of empathy lie? Is the construction of 'national trauma' an impediment to recognizing traumatic experience beyond the boundaries of the nation and national identity?" (133). Bennett sees in the War on Terror the kind of "transnational identification" that operates through the rejection of subjects classed separately from the so-called true victims of the attacks. Post-9/11 fiction confirms Bennett's assessment, although in analyzing this fiction along several stages of development (from a focus on national interest, toward dissent and discord within the multicultural nation, and finally to a global gauze of vigilant fear), I try to bring some nuance to Bennett's division between a national and a transnational trauma, as I see the two as distinct but also closely intertwined.

INTRODUCTION

This is not to unquestioningly embrace those responses to September 11 that derive from the attacks "a sense that there once were clear differences between home and away . . . but that those distinctions have been lost" (Rothberg, "There Is No Poetry in This" 151), or a sense that "there is no difference" and that "over there is over here," as Suheir Hammad puts it in her poem "first writing since" (139, 142). There are differences indeed, many of them based on spurious moral guidelines, and in reading post-9/11 fiction ethically we become entangled in these constructions and learn to be suspicious of them. Each chapter thus dwells on a particular "part of no-part," which is how Jacques Rancière describes the subversive elements negated by the articulation of ideological totality, elements that strive toward recognition:[13] the shocking images of 9/11 victims and the textual disruptions they cause; racialized subjects inspiring both fear and an uncanny attraction; territories distant in space and memory that emerge into visibility as linked or resonant with the attacks of 9/11; the systemic surveillance media we use to capture and apprehend the Other.

As I advance through my analysis, the texts I address increasingly appear as symptoms of a transnational cultural terrain. This is why I am interested in the connectivity implied by what Emily Apter calls "oneworldedness" ("held in place by the paranoid premise that 'everything is connected'" ["On Oneworldedness" 366]) less as a descriptor for the world or any part of it than as a function of literary discourse. The first question I thus raise is how post-9/11 fictions cue their narrative and stylistic structures to broader patterns of globalism as well as on a temporal stratum emphasizing historical predictors; and how narrative in particular as a discursive mode responds to a culture obsessing about how to "connect the dots," implementing in fiction what Apter refers to as "the psychotic dimension of planetarity" (370). The first to engender uncertainties about the status of the post-9/11 era as defining the American nation and its status in the world are those fictions that focus on immigration and racialized discourses in the War on Terror. These narratives disturb a sense of national identity in the domestic sphere without directly engaging global networks of exchange, exposing the post-9/11 experience of deterritorialization as bound up with traditional discourses around migration, citizenship, and national identity, all rendered more fractious in the aftermath of the attacks. The invocation of race in these fictions becomes a comforting notion in assuming that the new danger is in fact an old, familiar problem rather than the new risk landscapes of global securitization, an idea that is much harder to conceptualize and narrate.

Fictions that more explicitly situate the 9/11 attacks in space and time are organized around a fluid conception of place, whose instabilities define not only literary tendencies in contemporary literature but also the current political moment. The terrorist attacks against the United States, these narratives suggest, should be seen as a continuation (whether directly causal or circumstantial) of earlier conflicts in the second half of the twentieth century, particularly in the Balkans, as well as posing questions around the political and textual constitution of cruelty in liberal society—debates that took off after the Holocaust and have continued unabated since then. In Paul Giles's words, "The powerful impact of 9/11 might thus best be understood in terms of how it appeared not as an entirely unexpected event, a bolt from the blue, but how, on the contrary, it resonated as a symbolic culmination of the various kinds of deterritorializing forces" (18), which Giles associates with the transition to the Reagan era and, in particular, with the end of the cold war. Although Giles does not mention the Balkan War of the 1990s, post-9/11 fiction has shown that it effectively marks off the post–cold war era and the redistribution of power that came with the diminishment of American influence abroad, while instantiating another transnational vector of great potency: the proliferation of sympathy, hand in hand with military intervention and nation building in conflict zones. Literature's concern with the geographically dislocated pasts of the 9/11 turn is also of a piece with a broader interest in transnational circuits of knowledge and information that have only recently been assimilated into fiction. Global surveillance, for instance, serves as the underlying grid for the narratives discussed in chapter 5, for their vacillations between the panoptic nation (through measures in the service of Homeland Security) and a much more inscrutable global supervision system, ranging from corporate surveillance to web 2.0 networking platforms, from street-level CCTV to the wiretapping of terrorist sleeper cells.

The point here, quite simply, is that the reason why post-9/11 literature has not achieved a sense of territorial grounding has less to do with the still developing nature of this literature than with the lack of enclosure that the post-9/11 era allows, in literary production as in the political realm. In his overview of recent American literature, *The American Novel Now: Reading Contemporary American Fiction since 1980*, in a chapter aptly titled "Relations Stopping Nowhere," Patrick O'Donnell identifies the contemporary era as one in which "the mobility of identity and globalization would seem to throw a monkey wrench into notions of limitation and sovereignty" (199), notions that "are conceivable only as transitional states" (200). Or, as Paul Giles notes, "9/11 has become for the United States the most visible and haunting symbol of the new permeability of the country's borders, its new vulnerability to outside elements" (17). In mapping the attachments to home and the vulnerability of the homeland after 9/11, Giles detects "ethical affinities ... grounded not in direct relations to territory or patrimony but in more circuitous ways" (180). However, even though Giles is certainly right to point out that the perimeters of the post-9/11 state "can never again be entirely self-regulating" (180)—the implication being that the Other exerts as much pressure on the perimeter of the state as do the coalescing forces of nationhood—the national self continues to be aggressively regulated and regimented by the rhetoric of the War on Terror, racial politics, and neoconservative agendas in ways that post-9/11 fiction effectively interrogates. To adopt the benign vision of a postnational humanism would be to obscure the tensions roiling underneath the glossy mantle of global electronic media, tensions that are most apparent in countercanonical literature that has so far been silenced by critical neglect and that rebels against (rather than embracing) the paradoxes of the post-9/11 age.

Just as some American fictions since 9/11 "provoke not a sustained meditation on the status of the other, but on the self, the American self, and the processes of writing and fictional plotting" (Morley 247), so too does criticism of literature since 9/11 apply itself to the task of "othering" rather conventional and conventionally "national" fictions, searching for eloquent Other figures that invariably turn out to be terrorists. Catherine Morley analyzes "the narrative's relegation of Hammad to its periphery" (252) in DeLillo's *Falling Man* as "a formal embodiment of the ostracism of minority groups in current-day America," overlooking the ways so much fiction by Arab Americans that clearly foregrounds the various ostracisms of the War on Terror has been dismissed by readers and critics alike. Why dwell on Updike's naïve Muslim protagonist in *Terrorist* to study Islamic fundamentalism when so many other fictions do an ample job of scrutinizing not only fundamentalism itself but also the moral panics that we have constructed around it? Inexplicably Kristiaan Versluys concludes his study *Out of the Blue: September 11 and the Novel*—which discusses narratives by DeLillo, Spiegelman, Foer, Beigbeder, and Updike—by classing as "a matter of mere conjecture whether the new 9/11 fiction will remain the preserve of male white writers or whether it will be marked by more gender and ethnic diversity or acquire a more outspoken international dimension" (183). Gender, ethnicity, and transnationalism should, I think, be granted more than mere walk-on parts in discussions of post-9/11 literature, since so many of the texts responding to that event clearly do not occupy the white male realm.[14] Nor is it entirely productive to divide the genre into the mainstream American and the "international," or posit, as Versluys does, the ethical importance of describing terrorism from within (i.e., from the terrorist's point of view), when much more interesting novels have been written about the nonterrorists caught up in the oversensitive web of the War on Terror.

"Does the interpellation of the Other," Versluys asks, "the exercise of imaginative identification and the practice of viewing a situation in its full complexity also entail the obligation to encompass the viewpoint of the terrorist?" (*Out of the Blue* 151). Not necessarily, I would suggest, at least not before we have fully dissociated our "interpellation" from the kinds of interrogations going on elsewhere and vigorously questioned the images we have been led to associate with suspected or alleged terrorists. The perils of equating representations of the Other with narratives from

INTRODUCTION

the Mohammed Atta point of view have been articulated by Jacques Derrida,[15] who points out that "certain parties have an interest in presenting their adversaries not only as terrorists—which they in fact are to a certain extent—but *only* as terrorists" (Borradori 110), and who condemns the logic of such easy (m)alignments. Versluys rightfully seeks to "escape binary thinking" that pits terrorist hatred against counterterrorist retaliation (156), yet in doing so he neglects the multiple shadings in between. These shadings invite assiduous critical work in line with Dorothy Hale's "new ethics" and the global remappings of American literature charted by Dimock and Giles, in tandem with a willingness to consider, once we have assumed the subtle and oblique effects of September 11 on literature, those fictions that address us diffidently or evasively on the subject of terrorism and, more generally, as readers.

The Chapters

Unlike Hale, I separate "new ethics" from the Jamesian literary canon and apply it to contemporary fiction as an incomplete, process-oriented inquiry, what I call ethical anxiety or disorientation. To illustrate this anxiety I want to challenge the rather ossified canon of post-9/11 literature itself and look beyond the familiar names to draw attention to the canonical alterity of texts themselves, particularly texts that step much further back in time and space to renarrate 9/11 from a seemingly marginal perspective. This isn't simply a matter of including lesser known or eccentric writings, but of showing that the tone and style of post-9/11 fiction are changing, while increasing the kind of ethical openness and ambiguity organizing this book. I have grouped the novels under discussion according to the ways their narrative form and plot structure invites an ethical reading. Each chapter thus elaborates on a specific trope: narrating images in chapter 1; cruelty, violence, and psychoanalytic discourse, as well as narrative unreliability in chapter 2; the narrativization of risk in chapter 3; deterritorialized emplotment in chapter 4; and data mining as a reading strategy in chapter 5. The overall vision and progression of the book rests on this important continuity.

INTRODUCTION

The narratives that interest me in chapter 1, "Falling Man Fiction: DeLillo, Spiegelman, Schulman, and the Spectatorial Condition," engage with complex visual regimes of representing and responding to the attacks on the domestic front. My first example here is Don DeLillo's novel *Falling Man*, which adduces several visual media (photography, painting, and performance art) to suggest that ethical responses to 9/11 entail increased attention to the visibility of the world and to the demand it formulates for the training of responsibility. DeLillo's narrative operates through affective channels that attempt to bridge the rift between the post-9/11 image overload on the one hand and the salutary effects of increased visual attention in the aftermath of the attacks on the other hand—attention not to the overwrought visuality of media spectacle but to the visible, if low-key eventfulness of everyday life. The second section of this chapter analyzes Art Spiegelman's account of his 9/11 experience in his book *In the Shadow of No Towers*, which addresses the issue of secondariness in the transmission and representation of trauma. To Spiegelman, the terrorist attacks are mediated both through his inherited memories of the Shoah and by the televised images that he struggles to separate from his own impressions of the attacks. The two historical events remain, however, closely entwined, and Spiegelman resorts to a technique of substituting one for the other, which I call ethical surrogacy. By repeatedly invoking images of the attacks (especially the figure of a WTC jumper), and by constructing a bridge back to his previous novel *Maus* through the visual motifs of smoking and suicide, Spiegelman asks whether visual fetishism facilitates the process of mourning or further deepens the impact of trauma. The last section of this chapter examines Helen Schulman's novel *A Day at the Beach* to show how narrative can function as a palliative to the visual brutality of the terrorist attacks, especially as depicted on television. The protagonists' reaction to the brutality of terrorism is to turn over a new leaf and reshape their personal relationships, thus testifying to Zygmunt Bauman's pronouncement that "the only space where the moral act can be performed is the social space of 'being with'" (185). It is through her visual memory of September 11 that the novel's main protagonist achieves a new moral identity manifested in revived personal commitment and in her newly regained interest in the small successes and pleasures of everyday life. This chapter leans on the works of theorists such as Raymond Williams, John Ellis, Susan Sontag, Barbie Zelizer, Paul Frosh, and Eric Satner to address the links between ethical discourse, narrative theory, and contemporary media witnessing.

Chapter 2, "Sex and Sense: McGrath, Tristram, and Psychoanalysis from Ground Zero to Abu Ghraib," reads post-9/11 fiction through a critical lens that joins ethical and psychoanalytic theory. Through a close reading of Patrick McGrath's *Ghost Town: Tales of Manhattan Then and Now* (especially the section "Ground Zero"), I argue that McGrath responds to the post-9/11 conversation by articulating traumatic transference in ethical, psychoanalytic, and narratological terms. By staging the dissolution of the barrier between an analyst's personal and professional lives, McGrath points to the transference of world-historical trauma into the minor-scale trauma of interpersonal relationships. In ways that characterize a broader subgenre of post-9/11 fiction, he also stages a scapegoating plot (which I interpret with René Girard) that singles out a racialized Other as symbolically responsible for the evil of September 11. The second section of this chapter turns to Claire Tristram's controversial novel *After*, which similarly describes a post-9/11 revenge plot. Although conceived and published before the release of the Abu Ghraib torture images, the novel features an uncannily analogous scenario of racial and sexual humiliation. This section draws on Judith Shklar's work on moral psychology and liberalism as a theoretical grid in revealing how *After* resonates with the broader climate of political cruelty in post-9/11 America. Along with discussions of transference informed by the work of Peter Brooks and of sexuality in psychoanalytic criticism building on Shoshana Felman, I lean on Leo Bersani and Jacques Lacan to elucidate the "ethics of psychoanalysis," a concept to which the fictions analyzed in this chapter make a valuable contribution.

Chapter 3, "Moral Crusades: Race, Risk, and Walt Whitman's Afterlives," examines the ways racial perceptions manifest themselves across a range of post-9/11 fictions that not only openly address racial fear, but can also lead to a more nuanced understanding of literature's response to the erosion of human rights and civil liberties in the War on Terror. I argue in this chapter that literature after 9/11 has sought to alleviate the pressure of racial discrimination by replacing a moral discourse based on race with a more ambiguous ethical approach that emphasizes risk. Importantly this concept of risk tacitly includes (without foregrounding) subtle forms of racial profiling. By examining Ken Kalfus's *A Disorder Peculiar to the Country*, Chitra Divakaruni's *Queen of Dreams*, Laila Halaby's *Once in a Promised Land*, Mohsin Hamid's *The Reluctant Fundamentalist*, Gayle Brandeis's *Self Storage*, and Michael Cunningham's *Specimen Days*, I aim to show how these novels oscillate between a morally simplistic understanding of post-9/11 racial fear and a complex ethics of risk. I begin this chapter by examining moral discourses in the War on Terror, suggesting ways that racialized Others in novels by Kalfus, Divakaruni, Halaby, and Hamid at once condemn and internalize strategies of racial profiling, becoming increasingly isolated and insecure in a society that both objectifies and marginalizes them as a part of no-part. In the second section I consider the ethics of risk in the discourse of counterterrorism more generally, as well as in its narrative implementation. Drawing on a selective vision of Walt Whitman's cultural legacy, Brandeis and Cunningham clearly (if perhaps unwittingly) politicize the overlaps and divergences between risk and morality, showing how perceptions of safety and danger both in fiction and in contemporary culture often repress their reliance on a moralization of race. My readings of these novels also point the way toward some of the implications that racial profiling and an ethics of risk might have for a consideration of narrative and literary form.

The purpose of chapter 4, "The Internationalization of Conscience: Hemon, Barker, Balkanism," is to study the connections proposed in some post-9/11 fiction between the September 11 attacks and other conflicts of the twentieth century, in particular the war in Bosnia and Herzegovina (1992–95). Specifically the first section of this chapter explores the difficulty and ethical importance of inscribing the 9/11 attacks within deep time and transnational imagination. Aleksandar Hemon's novel *The Lazarus Project* proposes a contextualization of post-9/11 paranoia against a vast historical canvas, ranging from the Kishinev pogrom of 1903 through

INTRODUCTION

the anti-anarchist paranoia of early twentieth-century Chicago to the siege of Sarajevo in 1992. Hemon connects these disparate historical moments through the recurrent image of evil through the ages. Consequently my reading of this novel correlates ideas of transnationalism and exile with the ethical thought (especially on the good/evil dichotomy and its political functions) of Alain Badiou. Turning to Pat Barker's novel *Double Vision*, the second section of this chapter examines the ways the internationalization of empathy shored up by media representations of global war dovetails with the failure of the individual to internalize sympathy in its intimate underpinnings. I aim to establish a set of parallels between the internationalization of conscience enacted in *Double Vision* (spanning the layered traumas of the Bosnian conflict, the attacks of September 11, and the subsequent U.S. invasion of Afghanistan) and the narrative crystallization of emotional truth on the micro level of interpersonal and romantic relationships. My discussion of the novel's ethics is indebted to Martha Nussbaum's insights on the cataleptic experience as knowledge occasioned by suffering, on which she elaborates in her work *Love's Knowledge*.[16] Ethics, like love, is revealed (i.e., represented or made visible) by a cataleptic impression that has a key role in constituting it. Just as for Nussbaum a cataleptic feeling of love cannot be had in the abstract, so too does the suffering of war take palpable shape for this novel's protagonist only when it enters his personal life, wreaking havoc and reordering his experience in the same way that the attacks of September 11 organize the temporal and geographical sequence of the novel's multiple conflict zones.

Throughout my analysis I seek not to lose sight of the extent to which ethics is subject to cultural-historical constraints. Chapter 4 as a whole, in uncovering the Balkan prehistory of 9/11, shows precisely how ethical imperatives are shaped by the historical conditions from which they emerge and those in which they are received. On the other hand, ideas of evil can be remarkably atavistic, and several post-9/11 fictions develop transhistorical and international concepts of evil that belie a too rigid understanding of ethics as either culturally specific or a product of historical circumstance. Rather than settle for a historicist interpretation, the chapters highlight these consistent ethical formations that effectively undermine the exceptionalist view of 9/11 as an event unique in time and space.

The final chapter, on the transnational ethics of surveillance, looks into several post-9/11 fictions—Walter Kirn's *The Unbinding*, William Gibson's *Pattern Recognition*, Jonathan Raban's *Surveillance*, Lorraine Adams's *Harbor*, and Richard Flanagan's *The Unknown Terrorist*—that are premised on strategies of political watchfulness. To investigate how these writers simultaneously describe and subvert watchful politics after 9/11, I develop a threefold argument. First, I suggest that surveillance has influenced character construction and development in the post-9/11 novel, interfering with familiar notions of omniscience, focalization, and readerly experience. Second, the novels under discussion reflect the centrality of spectatorship (seen here as pervasive, invasive, and abusive) to the definition of the modern subject, gesturing at the same time toward the problems and opportunities that this panoptic turn in narrative poses for the ethics of literature. Third, increased visibility is also an essential element of global commoditization and consumption, so another question raised sharply in these texts is how surveillance measures implemented internationally with the aim of preempting transnational terrorism impinge on contemporary discourses of globalization. September 11 and its aftermath are embedded in a transnational society of the spectacle, understood to be the environment in which terrorism is produced, experienced, and ultimately also combated. Current narratives of hypersecuritization thus run parallel to a deterritorialization of surveillance as it embraces the ambiguities of both domestic and international intelligence in a context that no longer distinguishes between state governance and the global sphere.

Circling back to the critical evaluation of ethical theory offered in this introduction, I conclude by arguing that ethical engagement with post-9/11 literature can effect a repositioning of the political that may effectively combat the moralizing displays of current public discourse. My two main interlocutors here are Chris Adrian, a writer whose post-9/11 short stories I briefly appraise to sum up the insights of this book, and John Guillory, whose contentions about the ineffectual entwinement of politics, literature, and ethics I enlist as a shorthand for wider debates on ethical codes and their application, debates that post-9/11 narrative has forcefully revived. Drawing on the foregoing chapters, I argue in this conclusion that an ethical reading of post-9/11 fiction has the potential to dispel some of the entrenched lack of faith in the productive entanglement of ethical and political categories.

A careful reader will note that although I begin by differentiating my stance from posttraumatic approaches to 9/11 literature, some of my textual readings overtly employ the apparatus of trauma theory and psychoanalysis. My focus here is on fetishism and transference, two concepts that are deeply lodged in trauma discourse. Although posttraumatic approaches have been useful in addressing early works on the terrorist attacks, it seems to me that fiction has gradually moved away from introspective accounts of how Americans are "working through" the effects of 9/11, toward a vivid interest in the human impact of the War on Terror on diasporic communities and in the larger implications of the wars in Afghanistan and Iraq. To reflect the complexities of this dynamic, I have structured the entire book around the development in 9/11 fiction away from narratives of mourning and toward a complex elucidation of psychoanalytic issues and social dynamics. This by no means entails a dismissal of trauma as a concept or heuristic, nor does it imply that I am trying to replace it with something else entirely. Rather, in focusing as I do in this book on the Other (the foreign, the remote, the unknowable) instead of the self, I suggest that it might be more productive to explore the shift in literature from a posttraumatic consciousness (driven by memory and self-reflection) to one of responsibility and engagement.

Importantly post-9/11 fiction has absorbed the discourse of transnationalism and deterritorialized Otherness in ways that propose an ethics located, with Rey Chow, "after idealism." Though subjugated by the new security policies of the War on Terror, the Other is not an idealized entity, victimized and as such ethically untouchable. Nor does globalization feature in these fictions as a smooth operation, melting borders and mixing peoples with no clumpy matter left behind, but as a messy affair fraught with power abuses and imbalances. The structure of this book is meant to reflect such ethical ambiguities and paradoxes while providing a

INTRODUCTION

lengthy answer to Amy Kaplan's question "What is the opposite of homeland? Foreign lands? Exile? Diaspora? Terrorism?" (86). Like charity, the responsibilities engendered by September 11 should begin at home, as this book does, rotating along ever-widening circles from Ground Zero to Middle Eastern desert wars, retracing and respooling over some twenty novels the circuitous routes that have brought us, one decade and two wars later, to where we are today.

1. FALLING MAN FICTION

DeLillo, Spiegelman, Schulman, and the Spectatorial Condition

David Friend's visual record of post-9/11 New York, documenting and analyzing the stories behind the powerful images of that day, opens with the troubling sentence "The eyes were everywhere" (xv). This remark—initially meant to suggest the sheer number of cameras and recording devices aimed at the towers, as well as the stunned reactions of witnesses to the attacks—aptly describes literary representations of the 9/11 events. The attacks have gelled into stock images that recur obsessively in post-9/11 literature, pointing to a deep-seated traumatic reaction on both a visual and a textual level. Many literary depictions of September 11 can in fact be regarded through the filter of a single photograph, which, however, did not circulate widely in the immediate aftermath of the attacks. On September 12, 2001, the *New York Times* published Richard Drew's picture of one man tumbling out of the North Tower straight down the side of the building ("A Person Falls Headfirst from the North Tower of the New York World Trade Center, Sept. 11, 2001"). The man is falling upside down in what looks like an uncannily peaceful—even graceful—position. The picture's composition is perfectly symmetrical, the man's body running parallel to the vertical girders of the World Trade Center in a harmonious gradation of blacks and grays.

In highlighting the aesthetic qualities of the scene he witnessed, Drew runs headlong into a minefield of ethical problems, most eloquently formulated by Roland Barthes in his essay "Shock-Photos." Such images, Barthes writes, fail to convey horror "because, as we look at them, we are in each case dispossessed of our judgment: someone has shuddered for us, judged for us; the photographer has left us nothing—except a simple right of intellectual acquiescence" (71). Drew, one could argue, not only arouses a prurient interest in the plight of 9/11 victims, but seems exceedingly invested in the compositional aspects of his picture as he tries to find beauty in the twisted forms of its anguished subject. The inherent danger is that this aestheticization of tragedy may ultimately anaesthetize the feelings of those who are witnessing it. Moreover by diverting attention from the sobering subject of the WTC jumpers and turning it toward the medium of photography itself, Drew may also be said to compromise his picture's status as a historical document of the tragedy, thereby replacing evidence with spectacle. The image induces self-centeredness in the viewers, who get caught up in noticing how they react to its beauty, a beauty that becomes reflective and melancholy rather than immediate and distressing. Yet the picture is partly redeemed by the ways it questions the function of vision and visual representation in shaping a personal and collective response to 9/11. Importantly Drew's image encapsulates some of the most visibly destructive and dehumanizing effects of the terrorist attacks. Two weeks after 9/11 Anthony Lane observed in the *New Yorker* that "the most important, if distressing images to emerge from those hours are not of the raging Towers, or of the vacuum where they once stood; it is the shots of people falling from the ledges" (79).[1] Whereas most images of the explosions and collapses display the spectacular vaporization of glass and steel structures, the falling man gives this destruction a material embodiment, evoking a tangible sympathy in viewers toward the events they witnessed from afar.

The still photograph also suspends the body's descent in time as if to prevent the tragedy from taking its indomitable course and allow viewers to entertain the irrational hope that death might not occur. In a culture of overwhelming media potency, Susan Sontag defended precisely this capacity of the photograph to break through a parade of atrocious images by capturing the intervention of death: "To catch a death actually happening and embalm it for all time is something only cameras can do, and pictures taken by photographers out in the field of the moment of (or just before) death are among the most celebrated and often reproduced of war photographs" (*Regarding the Pain of Others* 59). Barbie Zelizer refers to this arrested position as the "about-to-die moment," which she analyzes in light of the "subjunctive"—open-ended or speculative—dimensions of an image ("The Voice of the Visual" 175).[2] Part of this speculation rests on the uplifting hope that the photographer or viewer may interfere with the flow of events. As Susan Lurie remarks, while "contemplating this image, one wishes that the camera's ability to freeze the moment might have made a magical intervention in the fall itself" (44). This mood of contingency fuels the impression that death may not be impending after all and distinguishes the image of the falling man from representations of dead bodies, which have almost entirely been stricken from the visual record of that day.[3]

In ways that greatly expand upon the ethical provocation contained in Drew's image, fiction that explicitly depicts the terrorist attacks has integrated the photograph into its very fabric, both thematically and as a structural device. I argue in this chapter that Don DeLillo, Helen Schulman, and Art Spiegelman facilitate an ethical response to the iconic photograph by creating a path of engagement between text and image that guides close readership toward a form of ethical spectatorship. Their works bring both the unreflected act of looking and the overdetermined practice of artistic visualization into close proximity with the ethics of narrative. Taken together, my readings of *Falling Man*, *In the Shadow of No Towers*, and *A Day at the Beach* draw the outline of a wide-ranging argument about the ethics of visual representation: from the intrinsic ethical challenge of 9/11 photography and the ways ekphrastic discourse around these images feeds into the morality of post-9/11 storytelling, to the reluctant or predatory forms of identification inspired by images such as Drew's, and finally to the catalyzing effect of visual witnessing and its contribution to the transformative, "makeover" rhetoric endemic to post-9/11 narratives of change and rebirth.[4]

Narrative as Still Life: Visual Attention in Don DeLillo's *Falling Man*

Falling Man imagines how ethical tenets divorced from traditional concepts of empathy and compassion persist in literary forms, and how they do so by drawing on visual experience. While DeLillo's previous works often acknowledge and unpack the visual underpinnings of memory and narrative, it is only in *Falling Man* that visuality relates ethically to characters and to the situations in which they interact, even though these characters are not particularly compelling as objects of pity and compassion, or as typical bastions of moral strength.⁵ They all display bizarre, questionable motives, they are not consistently characterized, and it is often difficult to distinguish between the narrator's voice and the characters themselves. The novel seems, in fact, extremely dispassionate and impersonal despite its emotional theme and DeLillo's efforts to dwell on harrowing visual details. And even though here, "as in Henry James's fiction, the way one responds to art is an index of moral character" (Kauffman 360), we learn very little about how DeLillo's characters distill visual experience into ethical insight and moral behavior. Nor do Jamesian ethics, as I suggested earlier, seem pertinent to the ethical dynamic evidenced by the post-9/11 novel. Instead I want to argue that *Falling Man* proposes an ethical response to the 9/11 attacks by highlighting the redemptive value of incisive (albeit passive) attention to the visual world, a form of attention that impinges deeply upon the novel's narrative structure. DeLillo isn't alone in exploring the ethical potential of impassiveness and indifference in response to the shock of 9/11: Claire Tristram's novel *After*, which informs my argument in chapter 2, displays a very similar fascination with restrained, distant subjectivity—although in DeLillo the distance is less intersubjective than ontological, capturing the relationship between the self and the world rather than juxtaposing alienated selves.

John McClure has noted that DeLillo "insistently interrogates secular conceptions of the real, both by focusing the reader's attention on events that remain mysterious or even 'miraculous,' and by making all sorts of room for religious or spiritual discourses and styles of seeing" (143). It is these "styles of seeing" that enable my own approach to the novel and the departure I make from existing scholarship on the narrative embeddedness of Drew's photograph, particularly with regard to Jonathan Safran Foer's novel *Extremely Loud and Incredibly Close*, which I see as a direct antithesis to DeLillo's unsympathetic vision. While, as Laura Frost has claimed, Foer's novel "attempts to memorialize the people who jumped from the WTC" but also "steers away from the very problems that these people present" ("Still Life" 185), DeLillo frontally confronts the more disturbing aspects of the falling man's fate. In doing so, he rejects the tendency of post-9/11 fiction to offer an "unerring emphasis on redemption, courage, noble sacrifice, dignified human connection and, above all, heroism" (200). Whereas Frost concludes that "literary treatments of 9/11's falling bodies constantly circle around . . . failures of knowledge" (187), partly derived from a dearth of visual evidence, I want to examine how an exceedingly rich and explicit visual record of 9/11 creates spheres of knowledge that inure viewers to the compassion such images would normally summon up.

Extremely Loud and Incredibly Close concludes with a flip-book narrative that defies the gravity of the falling man's death plunge, replacing the unstoppable fall with an angelic flight away from the towers and the reader's field of vision. DeLillo, at the end of his novel, returns to its opening scene, which takes place during the attacks and in their immediate aftermath. The novel's protagonist limps out of the burning tower and finds himself in a haze of dust and debris. Rather than magically recasting the fall as a reassuring ascent with overt religious undertones, DeLillo opts to replace the falling man with a shirt descending in slow motion, prolonging the illusion of life (and criticizing our longing for this illusion) while simultaneously implying that the falling man had been dead all along: "Then he saw a shirt come down out of the sky. He walked and saw it fall, arms waving like nothing in this life" (246). DeLillo's and Foer's stances could not be more dissimilar, yet to castigate *Falling Man* as a heartless and alienating rendering of horror corresponding to "nothing in this life" and to extol Foer's as the only compassionate vision would be missing the point that the two writers diverge appreciably in their understanding of compassion and the moral responsibilities of fiction.

DeLillo's consistent attempt to resist rather than advance affective responses to the 9/11 events, while recognizing the sway of emotion and feeling in public discourse, sets *Falling Man* apart from most treatments of the terrorist attacks. His stance, though unconventional, also chimes with recent criticism of the so-called therapeutic turn that identifies emotion rather than reason as the logic of public life.⁶ DeLillo points to media narratives of trauma and survival as well as to stock images of domestic affect as the key locus of this development toward a culture of sentiment, further fueled by the intensity of large-scale media events. To counterbalance their emotional overload, he proposes an anesthetization of emotion in everyday life—not as the "proper" response to the 9/11 attacks but as the only means of tracing their deeper repercussions without risking involvement in affect-driven nationalist euphoria. In what follows I chart the novel's engagement with painting, photography, and performance art as a conceptual undercurrent to DeLillo's concern with the ethical and narrative possibilities of visual attention more generally, and with the specific role of visuality in memorializing September 11.

"Ways of Seeing": Imagining Spectatorship

Falling Man shows that "literary language does not remain unaffected by the language of visuality that has encroached on the public throughout the twentieth century," as Marco Abel presciently suggests in relation to DeLillo's essay "In the Ruins of the Future," published in late 2001 (1239). In the ruins of representational language, DeLillo turns to imaging processes in ways that intensify the concept of narrative as intertwined with visual experience and establish vision as the basic function of cognition itself. In keeping with this close link between subjectivity and visual apprehension, *Falling Man* fastidiously describes the characters' individual perception of what they see, whether as direct witnesses or through intermediary visual artifacts. The image of the WTC jumper is central among these. DeLillo begins by invoking Drew's photograph indirectly to describe the peculiar Otherness of the human being in flight, suggested here through a subtle metonymy. As the novel's protagonist and secondary "falling man" of the title, Keith Neudecker, exits the North Tower shortly after the impact of the first plane (and the separation from his wife, Lianne), it is, as I noted earlier, not a man but a shirt that he watches gliding down the side of the building. This substitution allows DeLillo to delineate a surreally decelerated movement: "There was something else then, outside all this, not belonging to this, aloft. He watched it coming down. A shirt came down out of the high smoke, a shirt lifted and drifting in the scant light and then falling again, down toward the river" (4). The slowness of the shirt's descent offers a more palatable alternative to the fall of a living person, whose life would have been terminated within a matter of seconds. The trajectory of the fall is further modified and prolonged by the shirt's progression "down toward the river"—toward a definitive end but also, implicitly, into a continued presence within the reader's imagination.

This slowness is essential to the novel's dispassionate tone and heightened visual sensitivity. In the long term the attacks instill in Keith a sense of increased alertness to what occurs within the perimeter of his vision, as if his sight had been sharpened by the aggressive visibility of the attacks. The fire and ash, instead of impairing his sight, only lower the threshold of his perception. In contrast, life before 9/11 suddenly strikes him as a form of blindness, where not noticing used to be a quality and a condition of living. Returning to his apartment in the aftermath of the attacks, Keith "sees" for the first time the overwhelming emptiness of his life: "Everything else was the same as it had been when he walked out the door for work that Tuesday morning. Not that he'd noticed. He'd lived here for a year and a half, since the separation, finding a place close to the office, centering his life, content with the narrowest of purviews, that of not noticing" (26). Not only does Keith now perceive his surroundings with unprecedented clarity, but he also takes the time to "look"—and the insalubrious nooks and crannies of his existence are exposed by this searching gaze: "Some light entered between splashes of window grit. He saw the place differently now. Here he was, seen clear, with nothing that mattered to him in these two and a half rooms, dim and still, in a faint odor of nonoccupancy" (26). The vacuity surrounding him allows Keith to take stock of his life and place himself at its center, where he traces the contours of his physical and mental possessions. This self-scrutiny facilitates an ethical self-cleansing that shines an unsparing light on personal prejudices and foibles of questionable morality.

Keith thus contents himself with watching smaller, more trivial events as an antidote to large-scale horror. He begins to notice "all the small strokes of a day or a minute, how he licked his thumb and used it to lift a bread crumb off the plate and put it idly in his mouth," feeling "strange to himself" due to his regained ability to watch his surroundings at leisure (65). Being close to his family and more attuned to the slower rhythms of days and minutes, he experiences the familiar as alienating, the close as distant and dispassionate. Time stretches and balloons into a miraculously suspended dimension, as the narrative becomes increasingly dense with detail. Repetitions of imagery, a clutter of mundane details, the inertness of characters who shuffle along at soporific speeds, the constant injunction to look and watch rather than simply see (which forces the reader to linger on the text instead of moving along ahead of the characters who are left gazing at things)—all of these elements impose an emphatic slowness and a sense of doomed stasis on the narrative pace. The reader follows the story in fits and starts, drifting in and out of focus, much like Keith, who "finds himself drifting into spells of reflection, thinking not in clear units, hard and linked, but only absorbing what comes, drawing things out of time and memory and into some dim space that bears his collected experience" (66). Watching insignificant happenings and the refreshing ambiguity of their significance ultimately prepares Keith for the ethically charged effort of redefining his position in the world he currently inhabits. Sight, then, becomes the opposite of movement as well as the facilitator of a certain human groundedness that Keith seeks and eventually finds by relinquishing all conscious effort to achieve it. On a secondary level the novel adopts a similarly fraught passivity in looking at art from a postapocalyptic standpoint.

Pittura Metafisica and the Twin Towers

After witnessing the demise of what had seemed untouchable and intractable—the Twin Towers and with them the exceptionalist mentality of an entire nation—DeLillo's characters long for a vision of the eternal, of what cannot be destroyed or removed, and whose existence is not in doubt or immediate danger. In such times of insecurity Lianne's mother, Nina, retreats to a museum, where she isolates herself in aesthetic contemplation. Hers is an escapist experience of not merely seeing, but prolonged, intense looking, less with the purpose of decoding the images that surround her than with the dogged faith that they will remain mute, solid, and dependable. Nina expects the paintings to offer an alternative to the visual brutality of televised terror by opening up a space where the self can be unpacked and unfolded in safety: "She looked at three or four pictures in an hour and a half of looking. She looked at what was unfailing. She liked the big rooms, the old masters, what was unfailing in its grip on the eye and mind, on memory and identity" (11). After the brutal images of the attacks, Nina yearns for a sheltered moment of pause and the reassurance that images may be reliable and enduring rather than aggressive agents of terror and alienation. While Keith seeks ethical ambiguity, she longs for the strength of moral certainty, for a visually familiar alternative to violently invasive evil. Yet despite her need for consolation in certainty, it is again ambiguity that seduces and provides solace.

Significantly, then, the only paintings that the novel names explicitly and describes at some length are works by the Italian painter (of the metaphysical school) Giorgio Morandi, the creator of compositionally minimalist and formally pure still lifes. At significant points in the narrative, these paintings puzzle the characters, themselves collected like an unmatching assemblage of things quietly occupying their set positions: "The two dark objects, the white bottle, the huddled boxes. Lianne turned away from the painting and saw the room itself as a still life, briefly" (111). Lianne and her mother's art collector lover, Martin, project the Twin Towers onto Morandi's innocuous still life assemblages. Yet to Nina, comparing the "two dark objects" with the Twin Towers would be missing the deeper objecthood of Morandi's forms, far superior to the limited and indeed short-lived solidity of the towers. "Architecture, yes, maybe," she remarks, "but coming out of another time entirely, another century. Office towers, no. These shapes are not translatable to modern towers, twin towers. It's work that rejects that kind of extension or projection. It takes you downward, down and in. That's what I see here, half buried, something deeper than things or shapes of things" (111). Compared to the distinctly perishable nature of human life, the bottles and boxes appear eternal, their forms assembled harmoniously to reveal their fragile yet imperishable natures: "Being human, being mortal," is what they invoke to Nina; "I think these pictures are what I'll look at when I've stopped looking at everything else. I'll look at bottles and jars. I'll sit here looking" (111), she confesses. The paintings encapsulate for her a deep ethical essence that is divulged when the "modern towers" of morality and faith have crumbled.

The immobile frames of Morandi's still lifes clearly resonate with the frozen quality of the falling man photograph, and it is certainly no coincidence that DeLillo focuses on still life painting in a novel that questions the effectiveness of still images in capturing the 9/11 attacks. The narrative itself displays static features in its spare, compact sentences that resemble dabs of paint. Its carefully composed images are devoid of context or feeling, breaking into lyric utterance and the occasional aphorism. The literary critic James Wood in fact begins his review of the novel by noting, "Don DeLillo's new book is not a 9/11 novel but a 9/11 short story, or perhaps a 9/11 poem. It is not a synthesis or an argument or even, really, a sustained narrative, but an arrangement of symbolically productive elements" (47). DeLillo deploys these elements in a spirit of absolute economy and precision like objects on a canvas, all the while smearing and obscuring their meaning.

In ways that concretize the ethically ambiguous crisis at the core of the novel, the book remains trapped in a curiously static formation that employs pressurized formal patterns, clusters of symbolism, and depthless, impressionistically sketched characters. Morandi himself is a congruous addition to the novel's cast of characters. His paintings were often condemned as antihuman, a diagnosis further exacerbated by the myth of Morandi as an isolated artist figure, a shy man who valued his privacy. Yet above all DeLillo employs Morandi's works as timeless symbols—calm reflections on objects originating in what the painter called "il mondo visibile" (Abramowicz 58). Paradoxically these serene and peaceful works were painted during one of Europe's bloodiest conflicts in an attempt to evade the grim reality of World War I, which nevertheless manages to seep into the texture, color scheme, and obsessively structured composition of the paintings. Morandi's works are deeply ambivalent in this sense and offer DeLillo a fertile ground for positioning his own narrative minimalism as an ethical response to historical trauma. As Janet Abramowicz remarks, "It wasn't only that Morandi chose to paint objects that were used ambiguously, but also that he used them in intriguing and ironic ways. Morandi's bottles and containers are not to be seen or understood as bottles and containers, but as objects that have been given new meanings that transcend their primary or explicit functional use" (59–60). In Lianne's eyes, "the irregular edges of vases and jars" encapsulate "a mystery she could not name . . . some reconnoiter inward, human and obscure" (*Falling Man* 12), indexing the rough exposure and vulnerability of the demolished buildings while providing a transgressive insight into their continuing presence on the edge of public consciousness.

Two tower-like objects, "dark and somber, with smoky marks and smudges" (*Falling Man* 49), fill one of Morandi's paintings just as the Twin Towers dominated New York's skyline: with a suffusive naturalness, or as DeLillo writes in *Mao II*, like "two black latex slabs that consumed the available space" (165). Although the dark objects are "too obscure to name" (*Falling Man* 49), Martin and Lianne recognize the shapes of the towers in a visual analogy that situates them on a plane of shared feeling: "They looked together," DeLillo writes, recruiting visuality as the vehicle of togetherness and ethical alliance, in reference both to the two observers and to the intrinsic cohesiveness of the objects, whose obscurity channels a sense of belonging to the same space, of soundlessly inhabiting it with utter naturalness and gravity. The novel's straightforward language similarly accumulates into a series of solid, powerful images producing a subdued narrative voice that, like Morandi's painting, transports its audience "downward, down and in." Visual restraint and silence are key to Morandi's provocation, just as narrative and emotional austerity is to DeLillo's.

When Lianne attends an exhibition of Morandi's paintings at a Chelsea gallery, she is searching for a moment of visual respite after the invasions of television footage, so she can focus her gaze on immobile objects, which create an impression of continuity both among themselves and among the paintings, but also among the events and spaces of her own life. Alone with the paintings she can communicate with them and with herself: "She noted the nature and shape of each object, the placement of objects, the tall dark oblongs, the white bottle. She could not stop looking. There was something hidden in the painting. Nina's living room was there, memory and motion" (210). Despite the limited view offered by the paintings—close-ups of trivial things extricated from their mundane environments—simply looking at them helps Lianne to disentangle the threads of her life and recover an ethical sense of self by projecting her own being onto the objects themselves, instantiating the materiality of visual ethics to the point where the images become part of her living body (and she part of their *natura morta*): "She was passing beyond pleasure into some kind of assimilation. She was trying to absorb what she saw, take it home, wrap it around her, sleep in it. There was so much to see. Turn it into living tissue, who you are" (210). Watching the planes collide with the towers had elicited a similar visceral reaction from her. Yet while the footage caused a wound, the paintings help to cauterize it and reinstate a sense of coherence through the tidy arrangement of things in space and the ethically charged deceleration of experience.

Witnessing Performance Art

Ritualistic forms of voyeurism have a sedating effect on DeLillo's narrative even when the images described, unlike Morandi's paintings, are meant to shock rather than soothe or anesthetize. Lulled by the effects of Morandi's muted appellation, DeLillo's protagonists respond with the same torpor even to the unsettling exhibitionism of an artist impersonating Drew's falling man. The collective witnessing encounter that ensues adds further proof of spectatorship's ethical function in creating communities of memory and experience. DeLillo's use of the falling man theme in this key subplot performatively extends and complicates the premise of Drew's photograph while explicitly acknowledging its initial influence. The visual implication of the performance plot is that the textual dynamics of that image cannot be circumscribed to a single, isolated artifact, but are compounded by multiple and repeated forms of spectatorship. What had seemed impossible to represent is thus subsumed within a paratactic regime that illustrates the contradictions and conflicts among different forms of representation—photographic, filmic, and performative.

Critics of 9/11 visual culture have asserted the superiority of photography as a medium in which to process and contemplate traumatic experiences. Marianne Hirsch proposes that "still photography, not film, is the visual genre that best captures the trauma and loss associated with September 2001—the sense of monumental, irrevocable change that we, as a culture, feel we have experienced. This is related to the photograph's temporality. Photography interrupts time. It is inherently elegiac" ("I Took Pictures" 72). Even more elegiac is the performance in DeLillo's novel of Drew's photograph, a performance that becomes a compelling vehicle of affect and collective engagement as it involves a zone of "interperformance" (Fisher) or what Sontag would call "co-spectatorship" (*Regarding the Pain of Others* 60) and the conceptual artist Bracha Ettinger describes as "wit(h)nessing" (qtd. in Pollock 235). According to Zelizer, "the frozen images of the still photographic visual record are a helpful way of mobilizing a collective's post-traumatic response. They help dislodge people from the initial shock of trauma and coax them into a post-traumatic space, offering a vehicle by which they can see and continue to see until the shock and trauma associated with disbelieving can be worked through" ("Photography" 49). The performance artist's mimetic reenactment of the photographic pose makes explicit what Zelizer's remark does not, namely the ways in which posttraumatic *collectivities* of engaged spectatorship emerge around an image.[7]

In watching the performance act, the spectators see beyond their own trauma, but also beyond the falling man himself, to an ethically potent acknowledgment of the presence of other viewers and their reactions. In contrast to the immediacy of photography, performance art thus opens a space of connection and facilitates an encounter with the traumatic event that allows it to be worked through by means of collective mourning. While Sontag rightly notes that witnessing images of horror can serve as a call to action, the awareness of other viewers may generate a context even more favorable to ethical involvement as well as concretize the responsibilities that accrue from regarding other people's pain. Whereas the falling man himself, "who'd stood above her, detailed and looming" (*Falling Man* 224), continues to elude her, Lianne "could believe she knew" the other people with whom she watched him perform.[8] While Marita Sturken has stated that feelings of community after 9/11 depend on "finding the good ... that has come from pain" (382), DeLillo shows that communities are forged by exposure to pain itself or its reenactment, experienced collectively. The closest correlative to DeLillo's vision is what Deborah Nelson has called an "ethics without empathy" (88)—not a substitute for traditional ethical engagement with the Other but an equally viable alternative to it. "The ethical models of relation ascendant since the tragedies of the midcentury," Nelson writes, "have tried to bring the self face-to-face with the Other. . . . We might imagine a contratradition of ethical relation, one that seeks not to come face-to-face with the Other but to come face-to-face with reality in the presence of others" (88). Through the Falling Man's active inducement of memory at various locations, the presence of the spectators becomes a copresence of each to the other. What had seemed insufferable when experienced alone or with close friends and family thus becomes bearable in a wider scene of conjoint commitment and recollection.

The impersonator raises another ethical issue that is central to falling man fiction as a whole, namely the ambiguity surrounding the man's decision to jump. To Lianne, the performance artist "brought it back, of course, those stark moments in the burning towers when people *fell* or were forced to jump" (*Falling Man* 33, my emphasis).[9] The agency involved in replicating the plunge clearly excludes the possibility of an accidental fall. Not merely falling and certainly not forced to jump, the artist *chooses* to fall while his viewers consciously watch him, both for the horror of what they, not seeing the safety harness, believe might happen to him, and for the relief and consolation afforded in seeing that he, unlike the true victims, is ultimately saved. The performer thus creates the comforting illusion that the collective gaze directed at him seems to have stopped death in its tracks. One might indeed argue that this repetition of the fall as simulation, which renders the prospect of actual death more elusive, does not differ greatly from Foer's flip-book fantasy. Yet unlike Foer, DeLillo does not "move beyond photographic time into narrative time" (Frost, "Still Life" 196). Instead he distends the duration of the fall inwardly—much the same way that he puts the brakes on narrative pace—to suggest not temporal progression but the temporal investment of spectatorship itself. The temporality of the falling image does not refer merely to the time sequence it contains, but also (and more interestingly) to the more subjective time needed to absorb the image and formulate a cognitive and emotional response to it.

By demanding the spectators of his performances to remember and record the image that his fall conjures up, the Falling Man thus effectively wrests the power of visual replication away from the media and places it in the hands of his viewers, showing how vision may induce an ethical sense of responsibility and community that cannot be derived merely from a passive reception of ready-made and easily manipulable TV images. In other words, Lianne comes to enfold, however temporarily, the image of the Other as part of herself: "There were no photographs of that fall. She was the photograph, the photosensitive surface. That nameless body coming down, this was hers to record and absorb" (*Falling Man* 223). The fall becomes a personal event, one that relates more to the circumstances of the spectators' own lives than to the motivations of the jumpers (both the original and his copy), motivations that after all remain impenetrable to outside observers. An unframed ethical perception—free from the moralistically consoling frame of photography and television—becomes possible, which results in a disorientation of the characters as though they too, like the Falling Man, were dangling from some viaduct, kept alive by a precarious balance. In line with Dorothy Hale's "new ethics" and its productive ethical puzzlement, this disorientation is not to be confused with ethical nihilism. What DeLillo attempts to reconcile is, on the one hand, visual literacy in assigning meaning to the disaster and, on the other hand, the moral problematic of guilt or shame accompanying sight and the vicissitudes of empathy.

The novel also implicitly wrestles with the challenging problem of whether fiction can reclaim its role as arbiter of meaning and ethical responsibility. It poignantly explores this issue by considering several artistic forms—photography, painting, and performance art—in ways that barely disguise the question that is foremost on DeLillo's mind: What about fiction in an age where "world news is the novel people want to read" (*Conversations* 101)? How does fiction relate to the increasing array and proliferation of media, and to what extent does this relation raise an ethical challenge? In his review of the novel, Tom Junod, the journalist who first investigated the identity of Richard Drew's falling man, expresses his disappointment with the book, which, he laments, fails to do justice to the victims and to their ineffable suffering. "I have a pretty good idea who the Falling Man was," Junod protests, "and he was neither a performance artist nor a totem of severed human connections. . . . And so what I asked of DeLillo's *Falling Man* was not that it be inventive, but that it be commensurate—commensurate to all the falling men, and the falling women, and their agony. And it's not. It's a portrait of grief, to be sure, but it puts grief in the air as a cultural atmospheric without giving us anything to mourn" ("The Man Who Invented 9/11" 38). Junod makes a valuable point, one that DeLillo clearly addresses in his novel. His treatment of the falling man through photography and performance art dissects the function of images as affective stimuli that goad viewers to feel more, which ultimately backfires into rote affective pathways and the exploitation of sentiment. In admitting that fiction, like visual images, shouldn't give us "anything to mourn" (i.e., prescribe suffering as the mandatory reader response) and cannot ever be commensurate with anyone's true suffering, DeLillo takes the alternative (and far more interesting) route of looking into exactly how literature "stops for death," that is, pauses over its own representational impossibility, and how we as readers react to loss that is not readily assigned as an object of mourning. Mediated sympathy of the kind Junod expects is, to DeLillo, highly suspect and counterproductive. Instead of seeking formulaic relief, DeLillo sinks the reader into a "cultural atmospheric" that leaves us exasperated (as Butler suggested literature should) and that cuts against received notions of how we regard the pain of others, revealing, instead, how we learn to closely watch and internalize it on our own terms.

Suicide, Smoking, and Ethical Surrogacy in Art Spiegelman's *In the Shadow of No Towers*

The pitfalls of sympathetic identification also traverse Art Spiegelman's autobiographical account of the terrorist attacks in a more explicitly visual text than DeLillo's *Falling Man*, a text concerned with the broader narrative mechanisms of mediation in the transmission of trauma. The tension between his parents' traumatic experiences during the Holocaust and his own as a direct witness to the 9/11 attacks looms large in Spiegelman's *In the Shadow of No Towers*, a comic book that calls attention to the psychic repository of what Marianne Hirsch has called "postmemory" in the context of secondary traumatic survival.[10] Living through the 9/11 events is the second traumatic incident of Spiegelman's life, experienced partly by direct exposure and partly by ingesting media images after the event. Because Spiegelman can relate to the first traumatic incident, the Holocaust, only on a secondary level inflected by his parents' experience and survival, at its core *In the Shadow of No Towers* is a meditation on the dynamic of transmission and secondariness in the representation of trauma. Spiegelman invokes and critiques visual mediation in particular by reconstructing his own memories of 9/11 at a remove from the media accounts that have distorted them.[11] "I wanted to sort out the fragments of what I'd experienced from the media images that threatened to engulf what I actually saw," he writes in the two-page essay that prefaces the book. At the same time, he seeks to disentangle his own reactions to the chaos in Manhattan from his father Vladek's harrowing reports of the concentration camp, as well as from the suicide of his mother, Anja, in 1968. More often than not, however, disparate realms of transgenerational experience are superimposed and bleed into each other to create a tight grid that entraps Spiegelman inside his own memories and the paralyzing anxieties of the historical moment.

As I read *In the Shadow of No Towers*, my attention was systematically arrested by two details that help recast Spiegelman's 9/11 report in light of his previous graphic narrative, *Maus*. These details are suicide and smoking, two very different tropes that elicit prejudice and disparagement, forming a key site around which Spiegelman evinces particular concern about the overlapping terrain of the Holocaust and September 11. In what follows I want to consider the ethical centrality of self-harm to both *Maus* and *In the Shadow of No Towers* as a theme that ripples out into broader issues of silence, representation, and historical commemoration.[12] Spiegelman's treatment of the "falling man" trope and its implications for an ethics of representing suicide turns on what I call ethical surrogacy—the practice of using one event or image to substitute for another in order to enact the ethical tension at work in their juxtaposition. The images analogized here are suicide on the one hand and smoking as posttraumatic, self-destructive addiction on the other. Connections between smoke and physical destruction, as well as the idea of smoke as a symbol for what is left behind after forgetfulness and indifference have set in following the shock of trauma, are worth considering here—especially if we remember the billowing clouds of dust filling the cavernous Manhattan landscape after 9/11. Underlying these connections is an understanding of trauma as a fetishistic mechanism that relies on substitution and displacement. In part this mechanism supports what the French sociologist Luc Boltanski has called tele-suffering, or "souffrance à distance," where distance is not only a gap that must be bridged for a politics of pity to come into being, but also an energizing, necessary space in which self and Other are negotiated and exchanged, so that empathy and compassion can arise. According to Geoffrey Hartman, a central question raised by distant witnessing is "whether we can learn from the suffering of others without overidentifying" (78). The power of the image to relay affect and invoke ethical responsiveness in the viewer could indeed result in a predatory appropriation of trauma that, Hartman claims, "may have consequences as grave as to identify with the aggressor" (78–79). I am interested in why this appropriation takes place and how it enfolds Spiegelman's Holocaust-determined predispositions as well as his status as a witness—direct or by proxy—to traumatic events, brushing up against and trying to make sense of historical tragedy.

Ethics and Visual Fetishism

What haunts Spiegelman in this book is the lattice-like image of the North Tower shortly before its collapse, an image that escaped the eye of the media and creates a forbidding screen, accentuating the incomprehensibility of the collapses. Like DeLillo and, as we shall see, Helen Schulman, Spiegelman registers the 9/11 events through images imprinted with sensation: "What I actually saw," he insists, was "burned into the inside of my eyelids" (2). Much of the book's appeal in fact relies on its promise of visual authenticity, which Spiegelman uses to separate historiographic image technologies (photography, television footage) from literary fictionality (his own memory of the prelapsarian tower). *In the Shadow of No Towers* differs in this sense from *Maus*, which subsumed both literalness and fictionality under a broader responsibility to history. As Joshua Brown writes, "*Maus* is not a fictional comic strip, nor is it an illustrated novel: however unusual the form, it is an important historical work that offers historians, and oral historians in particular, a unique approach to narrative construction and interpretation" (91). If *Maus* proved revealing to oral historians, *In the Shadow of No Towers* provides historians of visual culture with substantive ammunition for their debates around the historiographic function of images and, implicitly, of the spectatorial condition.

I want to argue that Spiegelman's efforts to separate public history from personal memory are entangled with the idea of visual access to Otherness in ways that carry a distinct potential for ethical interpretation. While ethics and visuality haven't been paired in studies of *In the Shadow of No Towers*, Hillary Chute has cursorily proposed an ethical reading of *Maus*, distinguishing Spiegelman's approach—"moving forward from a moral center"—from an authoritative morality tale. The story's lack of closure and the projection of the Holocaust experience into the present suggest to Chute "the ethical value of narrative" as well as "the work of memory as a public process" ("The Shadow" 215). Chute does not elaborate, however, on how the ethics of narrative converge with an ethics of the image, and what the concept of ethics in its various interpretations brings into this discussion. In her analysis of seriality in *In the Shadow of No Towers*, she invokes the use of old comic strips as a means of imposing an "ethical shape to trauma," asserting that the author is "open to ethically remembering the past" ("Temporality and Seriality" 240), but she does not attempt to elucidate the meanings underlying her idea of ethics here as in her reading of *Maus*, or how ethics relates to trauma. A crucial connection between the two books in fact resides in their singular engagement with the ethics of memory and trauma.

To clarify this connection, I propose that *In the Shadow of No Towers* revolves around three distinct if interdependent patterns of self-injury: the suicide of Spiegelman's mother, the death of an unknown man jumping out of the burning WTC on September 11, and Spiegelman's own tendencies toward self-harm (inflicted by excessive smoking after the attacks). To link these suicidal plots, Spiegelman represents each through the prism of the others, raising questions about the ethics of substitution and mediation in testimonial speech. Some of these questions are carry-overs from the earlier *Maus* and follow logically from what Katalin Orbán refers to as that book's "somewhat sacrilegious suspicion of its own testimonial project—its own impulse to self-consolidate and purify by exclusion and erasure" (*Ethical Diversions* 38). The "real" images that *In the Shadow* invokes, as well as those that duplicate existing 9/11 footage, slip away from their original function as material, archival traces and instead *simulate* the process of historical reference. The absence of a referential network stimulates both Spiegelman and his readers to create their own through a substitutive gesture that turns on the concept of fetishism and its narrativization.

The Freudian definition of fetishism situates this phenomenon on the boundary between neurosis and psychosis. The fetishist, Freud asserts, denies the unwelcome fact of a woman's lack of a penis, which he perceives as a castrated condition. In order to compensate for this absence, a series of mental processes is put in play that substitutes a sign for the object thought to be missing. This compensatory gesture covers over and disavows the traumatic sight of absence, thus creating the comforting illusion that everything is in place. Yet the substitution, as Laura Mulvey points out, is never complete, nor does it fully conceal the workings of the unconscious. "For Freud," she writes, "the fetish . . . represents a memorial, marking the point of lack (for which it both masks and substitutes) and ensuring that the fetish structure . . . includes, through its very presence, a residual knowledge of its origin. It is in this sense that the fetish fails to lose touch with its original traumatic real and continues to refer back to the moment in time to which it bears witness, to its own historical dimension" (11). One cannot help detecting an uncomfortable parallel to the arguably phallic Twin Towers and the empty space where they once stood, a space that 9/11 fiction often attempts to cover by locating the origin of trauma in a different place (from Dresden and Hiroshima in Jonathan Safran Foer to Vietnam in Paul West's novel *The Immensity of the Here and Now*). Eric Satner usefully applies this circumventing strategy to narrative forms of commemorating the Holocaust that, he argues, spring from the opposite desire to gloss over its reality. Satner's concept of "narrative fetishism" circumscribes

> the construction and deployment of a narrative consciously or unconsciously designed to expunge the traces of the trauma or loss that called that narrative into being in the first place. The use of narrative as fetish may be contrasted with that rather different mode of symbolic behavior that Freud called *Trauerarbeit* or the "work of mourning." . . . Narrative fetishism, by contrast, is the way an inability or refusal to mourn emplots traumatic events; it is a strategy of undoing, in fantasy, the need for mourning by simulating a condition of intactness, typically by situating the site and origin of loss elsewhere. Narrative fetishism releases one from the burden of having to reconstitute one's self-identity under "posttraumatic" conditions; in narrative fetishism, the "post" is indefinitely postponed. (144)

Fetishistic about Spiegelman's book is its dexterous replacement of objects and rituals derived from an earlier trauma—the author's vicarious experience of the Holocaust through his parents' testimony—with objects and images specific to a later traumatic event experienced up close. Such surrogacy, however, remains haunted by the fragility of the mental mechanism that sustains it. What is missing (and, implicitly, what Spiegelman wants to substitute for) is a lack that he disguises through over-inscription: of past memories over present events and of symbolic images over evidential traces of history-in-the-making—from the suicide of his mother to the death of a WTC jumper to his own ritualized smoking habit.

Regarding Self-Harm

Virtually no interpretation of *Maus* has neglected to discuss the conspicuous absence of Anja Spiegelman's testimony. This approach only perpetuates what I consider to be a critical misconception. No doubt Artie's mother absents herself by committing suicide and erasing her own version of the Holocaust experience, implicitly subverting the survivalist element in the narrative that she and Vladek pass on to their son. Yet she continues to haunt the story precisely through her absence from it, and her specter still plays a supporting role in Spiegelman's 9/11 testimony.

Although *In the Shadows of No Towers* never mentions Anja Spiegelman directly, both her suicide and the 9/11 attacks are nodal moments in Art's life, which force open the floodgates of his creative expression. Spiegelman stresses the catalyzing effects of September 11 in his introduction to *In the Shadow of No Towers*: "The unstated epiphany that underlies all the pages is only implied: I made a vow that morning to return to making comix full-time." His mother's death played a similar role by channeling his energies toward the *Maus* project. Spiegelman's first comic strip of true aesthetic validity, "Prisoner on the Hell Planet: A Case Study"—featured in the collected edition of *Maus*—appeared five years after Anja's suicide and was clearly prompted by this traumatic event. "So the larger or perhaps divine purpose of Anja's suicide," Stephen E. Tabachnick contends in his religious analysis of *Maus*, "albeit certainly not her own motivation for it, was to provide the shock that forced Art into drawing seriously" (11). Equally significant to Spiegelman's creative outburst after Anja's death is the loss of her journals, which his father destroyed in a moment of aggressive grief: "No. You'll not find it. Because I *remind* to myself what happened.... These notebooks, and other really nice things of mother, ... one time I had a very bad day ... and all of these things I destroyed" (*Maus* 158). For a glimpse of her character, readers must rely on the testimonial narratives of the two men. Given my focus on how Anja's suicide is fetishistically reconstituted by *In the Shadow of No Towers*, it is particularly relevant that Anja's motives are far from conclusive.

Considering her independence and resilience—both as a survivor of the concentration camps and as the bereaved mother of a lost son, Richieu—Anja seemed unlikely to succumb to the psychological degeneration or momentary imbalance that are common causes of suicide. On the other hand, the mere fact that Anja survived the concentration camps is not sufficient indication of her ability to persevere through whatever subliminal, chronic damage that ordeal may have inflicted. "The survival of trauma," Cathy Caruth notes, "is not the fortunate passage beyond a violent event, a passage that is accidentally interrupted by reminders of it, but rather the endless inherent necessity of repetition, which ultimately may lead to destruction" (*Unclaimed Experience* 63). This repetitive, retraumatizing pattern may, in the long run, alter and damage the chemical structure of the brain, thus explaining, according to Caruth, "the high suicide rate of survivors ... who commit suicide only after they have found themselves completely in safety" (63). Itself in line with Freud's understanding of fetishism as traumatic displacement, Anja's death can thus be read as a sign of her inability to escape her past, echoing other survivor suicides who, to quote Elie Wiesel, "died at Auschwitz forty years later" (qtd. in Stark 102), their inconclusive survival forcefully reinstating the danger they only temporarily escaped.

Vladek's destruction of Anja's diaries is a secondary erasure that reinforces the suicidal loss of Anja's integrity as a survivor. Her wartime diaries did not, in fact, survive the war but were rewritten from memory much later; these are the Polish notebooks that Spiegelman remembers were lying around the house during his childhood: "What you saw she wrote after: her whole story from the start," Vladek explains (*Maus* 84). Thus the notebooks are themselves a secondary record of testimony and, as such, a fetishistic substitute for the originals that will never reach their assigned reader, Artie, epitomizing through their absence the enduring specter of what cannot be retrieved and recuperated.[13] The incineration of the diaries thus simulates the deadly conflagration that both Anja and Vladek narrowly escaped, as well as Anja's own suicide, in an ethically complex substitutive strategy by which destruction follows upon destruction, vanishing upon vanishing.[14]

Through the mystery that surrounds her death, coupled with Art's guilt for not having been sufficiently affectionate toward her, Anja becomes the object of a powerful fetishistic obsession revived by the carnage of September 11. The scenes he witnesses on that day leave an indelible imprint, yet Spiegelman claims to be even more intensely "haunted now by the images he didn't witness . . . images of people tumbling to the streets below . . . especially one man (according to a neighbor) who executed a graceful Olympic dive as his last living act" (*In the Shadow* 6).[15] Spiegelman pictures himself as one of the WTC jumpers through a series of five self-portraits in various stages of tumbling as he glides along the edges of a skeletal, glowing tower. Yet his dive is, of course, more figurative than deadly, as he "keeps falling through the holes in his head, though he no longer knows which holes were made by Arab terrorists way back in 2001, and which ones were *always* there" (6). The mental shaft through which the multiple Spiegelman figures are rattling downward, I would suggest, is shaped by the loss of his mother and the void left by her unwritten legacy. Neither Anja's personal account of the Holocaust nor the jumpers' individual stories can be recovered. To counteract this loss, Spiegelman produces his own, secondary testimonial that blends the visual and the discursive, of which the repeated falling man motif is the most compelling ethical synthesis, revolving as it does around both personal metaphor and political allegory.

Interpreting the Fall

James Young and Erin McGlothlin have thoroughly dissected *Maus*'s temporalities, detecting no less than three narrative strands.[16] In addition to Vladek's experience of the Holocaust and his account of that experience to Artie, on a third level the text reflects on the problems of shaping Vladek's harrowing story into a visual narrative. Some sections of *In the Shadow of No Towers* also ponder the problems of the text's production and reception, particularly in light of the book's suppression on the American market. Yet compared to the triadic narrative mode of *Maus*, *In the Shadow* contains little metafictional layering. Although not situated on a single temporal plane—the story extends from September 2001 up until August 31, 2003—its interlacing micronarratives do not occupy starkly different diegetic levels. The relation between these planes is one of mediation and transfer rather than contrast. Specifically Spiegelman presents his own testimony as metaphorical impresario to the more immediate experiences of closer witnesses or victims, such as the man falling from the North Tower. Since these victims cannot communicate their stories directly, Spiegelman's relationship to their testimony is different from Artie's role as coproducer of Vladek's account and more reminiscent of how Artie's compensatory speculations fill the void of Anja's silence, seeking to elucidate her behavior.

Ever since September 12, 2001, when Drew's photograph of the falling man was published, debate has been rampant over whether the jumpers were committing suicide or being forced to jump by the raging fires (or, in yet another scenario, simply being pushed out of the building by the force of the explosions inside). Rather than proposing a theory to clarify the accident-suicide conundrum, Spiegelman links the image of the 9/11 jumpers with that of other people "landing in the streets of Manhattan" as a result of the "economic dislocation" (*In the Shadow* plate 6) that followed upon the attacks. Invoking a man "who executed a graceful Olympic dive as his last living act" (plate 6), Spiegelman depicts himself as a falling figure in increasingly disheveled tumbling poses, which reflect not the aesthetic sublimity and elegance of Drew's image but, in a more realistic perspective, the less harmonious or dignified stages of the real jumper's descent, "legs splayed, arms spread, jacket flapping" (Friend 136). Far from conveying poise and nobility, Spiegelman's self-portrait as falling man suggests a loss of humanity and impending horror, instating visually the fetishistic aesthetic of posttraumatic narrative, both through the visual stutter of the repeated drawing and in the emollient reencoding of the fall as (merely) economic decline.

The liberties Spiegelman takes with the image of people "landing in the streets of Manhattan" have exposed him to a slew of moral accusations. *New York Observer*'s Adam Bengley accuses Spiegelman of narcissism, claiming that "he has no access to the desperate terror of the people actually in the towers, and no words or images to communicate the aching grief of that day" (2). Kristiaan Verslyus similarly remarks on the apparently gratuitous and ethically questionable transfer of identity: "To fall through holes in one's head is not the same as being forced to jump from 110 stories high by a raging fire. To be exploded on the pavement in front of the towers is not the same as 'landing in the street' as a homeless person" ("Art Spiegelman's *In the Shadow*" 996). Yet the five identical replicas of a blue-tinged Spiegelman superimposed over the image of the tower extend beyond a mimetic view of the fall by projecting selfhood onto an image of profound Otherness: the death of another person under circumstances that remain unknowable. By imagining himself in the place of the anonymous figure, Spiegelman does not "personalize" the photograph, as Mitchum Huehls suggests (43). Instead he takes possession of an image that had been devoid of identity and open to sympathetic identification by the viewer in ways that reenact the emotional investment inherent in ethical spectatorship. Spiegelman's gesture of ventriloquism, then, is a first step toward performing ethical identification and responsiveness to the suffering of others.

Beyond this performative retooling of Drew's photograph, Spiegelman incorporates the falling man trope in other pages and panels of the book. The eighth broadsheet page features a collection of old comic book characters falling through space after being kicked into the air by a turbaned, bearded goat vaguely suggestive of Osama bin Laden. The same suspended cartoon characters adorn the front cover of the book, cutting across the nearly imperceptible, blackened image of the towers, while the back cover continues the theme in black-on-black, featuring the same characters in various postures of tumbling. While the exact placement of the colored slot against the colorless background may seem incidental or decorative, it is worth noting that it was from about this height that many of the WTC jumpers plunged. The evocation of comic characters raining down in a colorful group as a counterpoint to the more somber image of the WTC jumpers echoes *Maus*'s gesture of situating a real, harrowing story in what Michael Rothberg called "a highly mediated, unreal, 'comic' space" (*Traumatic Realism* 206).

Further, several pages in Spiegelman's 9/11 diary adopt one of the falling man's most conspicuous features: the upside-down position of his body, which Spiegelman casts as a metaphor for the absurdity of the post-9/11 universe into which he awakens with a mixture of horror and bewilderment. Confusion about the right and wrong course of action in response to the attacks, a recurrent theme in post-9/11 literature, obfuscates distinctions between up and down, reason and absurdity in Spiegelman's eyes. Even the image of the melting North Tower serves as a substitute for the falling man. Both conform to the paradigm of Drew's photograph, which captured the "moment before death" in its full intensity and traumatic effect: "The pivotal image of my 9/11 morning—one that didn't get photographed or videotaped into public memory but still remains burned onto the inside of my eyelids several years later—was the image of the looming North Tower's glowing bones just before it vaporized. I repeatedly tried to paint this with humiliating results" (*In the Shadow* 4). Like the image of the falling man, Spiegelman's vision of the collapsing North Tower remains unique while inviting infinite repetitions and approximations, all of which fail to congeal into anything but a temporary stand-in for the unrepresentable, another fetishistic substitute for the primal scene of terror.

As I suggested earlier, Spiegelman's desire to inhabit the visible body, if not the consciousness, of the WTC jumpers is a throwback to Art's feelings of guilt after his mother's suicide. Although on September 11 Spiegelman failed to witness the WTC jumpers firsthand, the implied dignity of their act generates a moral imperative for visual representation that echoes Art's impulse to imagine and describe his mother's suicide. Art (over)compensates for his inability to intervene in Anja's suicide by drawing her lifeless body floating naked in a bathtub, with black liquid seeping onto the bathroom floor and up to Vladek's feet in the doorway. With the falling man, through an act of ethical surrogacy, Spiegelman portrays himself as the victim rather than retreating into a mock-witness position. By opening up the "holes in his head" (with connotations of a burial), he allows the image to enter his psyche at the risk of tearing open deeper wounds—or curing them. In looking at the falling man, Spiegelman implies, we become the falling man; in our attempts to represent terror we must learn to accommodate, even internalize its fragmentation and destruction. Following the theme of memory by substitution that is developed and sustained in both books, Spiegelman thus proposes visual ventriloquism as a way of remediating trauma by extricating it from media representation and by placing it on a personal path of transference (a term whose psychoanalytic nuances I parse in the next chapter) along which suicide and genocide are conjoined, making it possible to bear witness to one in lieu of the other.

Spiegelman also approaches the suicidal gesture from another direction altogether: as an iconic symbol for more pervasive images of social decay. *In the Shadow* ruthlessly condemns the unreflected patriotism that American citizens and mainstream media embraced after September 11 and up to the invasion of Iraq. Such spurious and misguided enthusiasm seemed discordant with voters' lack of allegiance to the two ruling political parties, regarded here as inefficient, outdated, bogged down by pettiness and self-interest, and generally ill-equipped to face the challenges of the post-9/11 world: "Rampaging Republican elephants . . . dimwitted Democratic donkeys . . . no wonder real Americans don't bother to vote! The two party animals are both 19th century dinosaurs, interested only in their own survival, not ours! We need a third party that actually represents us . . . a new and revolutionary Ostrich Party! Join your fellow Americans before it's too late. . . . Rise up & stick your heads in the ground!" (5). Illustrating this call for inaction is a large group of people who bury their heads in the sand and sport bull's-eyes on their rears. The only reasonable reaction to the political downturn in post-9/11 America, Spiegelman implies, is to relinquish the democratic right to political self-determination through voting and opt instead for apathetic self-destruction. Such estrangement and betrayal of trust between a government and its people inevitably gnaws at the fabric of social life, loosening the networks that hold individuals together and sending them into free fall. Several panels as well as the book cover show this suspended state. The excoriation of smokers is one symptom of this social decline, substituting for the broader exclusionary tactics initiated by the Bush administration, ranging from the Patriot Act to smaller, though no less preposterous domestic invasions. Yet smoking as a visual trope far exceeds Spiegelman's concern with misguided counterterrorism policies. Throughout *In the Shadow of No Towers* smoking dramatizes the ethically productive clash between suffering from a distance and the physical reenactment of trauma through rituals of self-harm.

Smoke: The Trauma of Exclusion

Spiegelman's testimony distinguishes among three categories of witnessing in a hierarchical triptych: "not seeing," exposure to live images, and primary witnessing through sensorial presence in the events. It is within this last category that smoke plays a decisive role by transforming a surreal spectacle into a space of real malodorous disintegration. The third page of the book is framed by two thin bars: on the left-hand side, the North Tower glows red and gold seconds before its implosion. To the right, the title of the book is reprinted in bold letters over the image of a gigantic cigarette, complete with glowing tip and puff of smoke. As a counterpoint to the iridescent tower on the left, the cigarette conveys the material congealment of trauma around toxic hapticity rather than imagery, aligning the book's ethical vision with the imaginary of smoke as transhistorical physical trace of death and evil.

Although the color scheme used for the cigarette matches that of the burning tower, the visual pairing does not invite readers to imagine the towers as two enormous cigarettes miraculously burning away for 102 minutes. Rather the cigarette functions as a lightning rod for a multiplicity of tobacco-related images in this book that have escaped critical attention despite their unambiguous allusions to *Maus* and to Spiegelman himself as an inveterate chain smoker. One of the most emblematic images in Holocaust iconography, the smoking crematorium chimney occurs repeatedly in *Maus* as a trace of lost human lives. Auschwitz smoke controversially merges with the smoke of Artie's cigarette in two adjacent panels.[17] While *Maus* includes several episodes in which smoking—in the guise of Vladek's mild rebukes and suggestions that Artie put out his cigarette—interferes as a non sequitur at delicate points in the narrative, derailing stories that may have taken a distasteful turn, *In the Shadow of No Towers* accords smoking a more insidious role. Here Spiegelman's habit evolves from a socially reviled vice to an emblem of political risk taking, from a conversational distraction to a vehicle in the transmission of trauma.

Smoking iconography in this book warrants discussion both as a thematic trope and as a structural device supporting the deeper phylogeny of Spiegelman's posttraumatic condition. Spiegelman draws himself as a smoker a total of sixty times, and several panels explicitly discuss his smoking habit, usually in derogatory terms. As he and his wife, Françoise, rush to find their daughter, Nadja, in the immediate aftermath of the attacks—at that time she was a freshman at Stuyvesant High School, at the foot of the Twin Towers—Spiegelman admits that "his 2-pack-a-day habit wasn't great training for this sort of thing" (3), and Françoise has to drag him by his collar through an overpass merely four blocks south of the towers. In a series of panels that depict him in his mouse attire, in a nod to the allegorical connotations of victimhood associated with animal physiognomy in *Maus*,[18] Spiegelman even extracts a cigarette from a pack that bears the imprint Cremo Lights—the same brand that Art smokes in *Maus*, where two fuming smokestacks adorn the packaging in a flippant reference to the Auschwitz crematoria. "With each pull on his cigarette," Michael Levine suggests, "Art inhales the incinerated bodies of Auschwitz. Every drag confounds what is internal and external, the past and the present, the inflamed airways of the living and the airborne remains of the dead" (333).

Levine's cogent reading of smoking as a malleable visual trope that mediates between present and past reinforces my claim that smoking iconography ties Spiegelman's books together by means of a somatic parallelism, linking two similar—if not equivalent—catastrophic conflagrations. The same urge impels Art/Artie to light one cigarette after another and Spiegelman to approximate the ambient smoke and psychological pollution in the aftermath of 9/11 through images of toxicity, both exterior and interior. Seemingly indifferent to the damage he is inflicting on himself, or perhaps celebrating his habit as a retributive act of free will and controlled, even pleasurable repossession of the once murderous fires, Spiegelman ruminates on the ineffable smell of death both in the camps and in Lower Manhattan: "I remember my father trying to describe what the smoke in Auschwitz smelled like.... The closest he got was telling me it was... 'indescribable.'... That's exactly what the air in Lower Manhattan smelled like after September 11!... Asbestos, PCBs, lead, dioxins, and body parts.... Lower Manhattan's air is a witch's brew that makes Love Canal seem like a health spa" (3).[19] More than a symbol for the tragic loss of life, 9/11 smoke enforces the transition from distant visual experience to firsthand suffering.[20] Yet unlike the smoke we associate with the Holocaust—an undefined mist filling spaces like steam or with the uncanny fluidity of gas (the aftermath of death rather than its cause)—9/11 smoke actively contributed to the death of people trapped on the upper floors above the zones of impact. More important, it may also have played a part in pushing WTC jumpers toward their fatal decision.

While this morbid connotation comes through forcefully in the book, so do the more pleasurable aspects of addiction. On the face of it, smoking is a fairly common habit aimed at obtaining pleasure.[21] In tune with this hedonistic vision, *In the Shadow of No Towers* features silent smoking panels that suggest an inhalation break and the quiet relish of puffing out smoke, illustrating the viscous temporality of what Spiegelman calls his "slow-motion diary" (2)—much the same way that DeLillo's contemplative, hypervigilant silences punctuate a newly regained intimacy with the visible world.[22] Images of Spiegelman with a cigarette dangling from the corner of his mouth often project a sense of visual silence—the disorientation of an individual (and of a nation) who cannot regain his bearings. But they also imply a sense of thoughtless compulsion, a reeling on the fault line between trauma and reckless action. A common component of posttraumatic stress disorder is indeed the compulsion to relive the traumatizing experience ad nauseam in dreams and in waking life.[23] Spiegelman's smoking habit provides an objective correlative for this repetition compulsion through its reliance on the principles of sameness and incremental accumulation.[24] Specifically smoking allows Spiegelman to open a parenthesis within trauma and slow down the narrative pace by offering the visual detail of the cigarette as a counterweight to the dizzying speed of events. The more peaceful moments in which he inhabits several successive panels by himself, alone with his indecent habit, enable a certain intimacy with the reader, a private conversation despite the unfolding horror. Located somewhere between activity and idleness, Spiegelman's permanently lit cigarettes also generate a sense of accomplishment in an era of misdeeds and painful inactivity—his own (as he struggles to meet his deadlines) and that of a nation benumbed and bewildered by unexpected tragedy. Smoking, then, indicates Spiegelman's longing for individual time beyond the solidified mappings of social time and outside the precipitated lurches of political time, which seems to be running ahead of itself in an effort to preempt attacks lurking in the future.

Spiegelman reacts to the government's post-9/11 paranoia by smoking "more than ever"; he coughs and directs his bloodshot eyes at the reader, doubting he will stay alive long enough for cigarettes to kill him. All the while he mocks the absurd displacements that occurred after the attacks, displacements that allowed serious issues to recede into the background or be placed on an indefinite "back burner" while the country was encouraged to focus on comparatively insignificant issues, such as the law against smoking in bars. The speech bubble in the panel that discusses the smoking ban emerges from Spiegelman's arm, his head having been replaced by his hand holding an outsized cigarette. In a morally repressive atmosphere in which the U.S. government imposes a smoking ban so as to help Americans live long enough to be blown to smithereens by al Qaeda, Spiegelman's dedicated smoking can be read as a form of willful self-destruction in the service of absolute freedom, not unlike the anonymous man's decision to jump from the towers. Rather than a mere tic or aesthetic maneuver with a merely decorative function, smoking endows Spiegelman with a defiant, self-sufficient aura pitted against politically opportunistic constraints.

Smoking is also proposed as symbol of a post-9/11 American culture outside the economy of health and strength, epitomizing the pernicious post-9/11 policies that were as likely to spread anxiety as to check it—just as smoking itself may induce both relaxation and malaise, as much illness as relief. Spiegelman exposes the antismoking campaign as a mean-spirited and discriminating crusade that goes beyond a critique of the habit to denigrate smokers themselves, providing a heuristic for the discriminatory practices against racially vilified groups in the aftermath of the attacks.[25] He alludes to these practices twice: by noting that he "grew a beard while Afghans were shaving off theirs" and by giving a politically incorrect reply to an NBC reporter's query on "the greatest thing about America." Aware of the duplicity that encroached upon American public life—one that draws a spurious line of demarcation between tolerable and damnable anti-Americanism—Spiegelman defines American greatness as the unwavering defense of the American way of life at the expense of intercultural tolerance and free speech ("that as long as you're not an Arab you're allowed to think America's not always so great" [10]). The images of Spiegelman relentlessly lighting up accentuate the volatility of those practices of inclusion and exclusion that were implemented after 9/11 in the process of achieving a highly regimented society defined by what was permitted and what was outlawed.

By depicting the smoke of his own cigarettes as a stand-in for the toxic clouds of 9/11, and the victimization of smokers in the aftermath of the attacks as a substitute for other discriminating practices, Spiegelman thus offers an example of what he calls "mass displacement" (9). The ethical responsibility of witnessing, he suggests, cannot be expressed without partial recourse to strategies of self-numbing, self-deception, and even self-harm. While most of the images I have cited here can be subsumed under an aesthetic of performative self-destruction, they also support a commitment to memory through transfer, projection, and substitution.

Witnessing already entails a certain degree of self-display and self-conscious ventriloquism to the extent that the basis of sympathy is an appropriation of the victim's position, a repossession of trauma. Yet Spiegelman's paradigm compellingly involves an even clearer duplication derived from his moral makeup as a second-generation Holocaust survivor whose original (if vicarious) trauma is reactivated and reembedded by the 9/11 events. In a review of the book, Elisabeth Anker expresses her concern that "Spiegelman's art becomes inadvertently complicit with the powers he aims to disrobe. By politicizing the individual experience of fear through broad-stroked and melodramatic images of terror, might Spiegelman's comics function to reinforce these fears and strengthen their contagious reproduction?" ("The Only Thing" 14). Spiegelman in fact demonstrates that not unlike trauma itself, the potency of fear hinges on its contagious reproduction and transference. The value of *In the Shadow of No Towers*, particularly in its echoes of *Maus*, lies precisely in its convincing argument that terror, fear, and trauma can be elucidated only by focusing on their interlinked mechanisms of ethical substitution, mechanisms that permeate the implicitly intermedial emplotment strategies of many other 9/11 fictions, from Helen Schulman's *A Day at the Beach*—which shares with Spiegelman's account an abiding interest in media representation—to intersubjective (rather than memory-driven) psychosexual plots of trauma transference.

Trauma and Visual Witnessing in Helen Schulman's *A Day at the Beach*

The soporific conjugal life rattled by an epiphanic event is a fairly common literary trope. Several novels that prominently feature the 9/11 attacks (including Jay McInerney's *The Good Life*, Hugh Nissenson's *The Days of Awe*, and Ken Kalfus's *A Disorder Peculiar to the Country*) depict crumbling marriages as their protagonists attempt to escape the fallout by fleeing toward the haven of their relationships, only to realize that marriage cannot protect them. Yet Schulman's *A Day at the Beach* marks a departure from the image of the disintegrating Twin Towers as shorthand for the dissolution of domestic intimacy. Set on a single day in the life of

Gerhardt and Suzannah Falktopf, *A Day at the Beach* communicates the tensions and traumas generated by September 11 as a violent threat to domestic security. Unlike McInerney's *The Good Life*, Schulman's novel does not conclude on a ringing note of affirmation by salvaging the marriage of its protagonists or downplaying the effects of trauma. Instead Schulman takes seriously the moral ambiguities of the 9/11 marriage as a microcosm of urban America in search of a "good life" in its ethical sense—not a life of luxury and privilege, as in McInerney's novel, but a life that recognizes (and here the visual ingredient is essential) an ideal or image of goodness.

Schulman's approach may be read as a synthesis between DeLillo's interest in emotional disorientation and estrangement within the post-9/11 family and Spiegelman's critique of media narrativization in shaping responses to the attacks—although Schulman's text adheres more closely to the precepts of classic narrative emplotment than either *Falling Man* or *In the Shadow of No Towers*. Caught up in the daily routines of early morning, the German choreographer Gerhard Falktopf and his wife, the former prima ballerina Suzannah (a Polish Jew from the Bronx), who have been married for thirteen years, witness the aftermath of the plane attacks from their Tribeca loft within view of the WTC. Suzannah is shocked and moved by the sight of a man plunging to his death from one of the towers. To deflect the fear provoked by this harrowing encounter with terror, Gerhard resolves to take his wife and their four-year-old son, Nikolai, to a house in East Hampton, picking up a terrified French woman and her baby along the way (strangers who quickly join and disturb the family dynamics). Once in safety, both Gerhard and Suzannah are briefly reunited with friends, acquaintances, and finally each other as they are able to achieve a shared acceptance—after years of denial—of their son's autism and regain a sense of intimacy through violent, precipitous change, which in a less propitious scenario may have harmed their marriage irreparably.

I approach Schulman's novel through the lens of this change triggered by the sight of a WTC jumper both as a televised event and as a scene of immediate witnessing. The tension between these two forms of visual experience helps articulate ethical imperatives that Schulman anchors firmly in daily life. Through a straightforward narrative that prods its protagonists through puzzlement, horror, and uncertainty toward a sense of transformation "for life, as it were" (to recall the Jamesian phrase), Schulman adapts the ethical dynamic of the novel as formulated by Spivak, Hale, and Butler to the visual mediascapes of the post-9/11 world. To prove this point I want to draw attention to an issue that has not yet attracted much critical interest in 9/11 literary scholarship, namely the ubiquity of television in fictional accounts of the events, and the even more intriguing function of television and the rituals of TV viewing as a subtle axis around which the currents of family life and relationships quietly revolve. Because of their very obviousness, the connections between television—which, unlike most other media, is received overwhelmingly in the home—and domestic life are often overlooked. "Television made the act of witness into an intimate and domestic act," writes John Ellis, and although he made this statement before 9/11, the attacks constitute a prime example of his diagnosis (*Seeing Things* 32). Many post-9/11 novels other than the ones included in this chapter (such as Ian McEwan's *Saturday* and Lynne Sharon Schwartz's *The Writing on the Wall*) rely on television as an intermediary between the smoldering debris at Ground Zero and the equally smoldering passions within the family.

My contention in what follows is that vicarious trauma through the medium of television on the one hand and unmediated witnessing on the other can be juxtaposed in ethically illuminating ways. I should emphasize, however, that I am by no means equating the posttraumatic phenomena that result from these distinct forms of witnessing. It is true that critics who have discussed the effects and symptoms of vicarious image-induced trauma (among them Susan Sontag and Joshua Hirsch) have observed belated responses and evidence of "working through" that are hardly distinguishable from classic trauma symptoms. Yet as E. Ann Kaplan astutely remarks, the bar for such symptoms may have been set far too high. "Would it be useful," she asks, "to open the term to refer to related but lesser discomfort—and a discomfort of shorter duration? And in any case, what may be the socially useful effects of either symptoms or discomfort?" (91). Considering the expansion of media witnessing over the past few decades and bearing in mind the explicit example of September 11, we may find that the discomfort of millions of viewers is as relevant, from an ethical viewpoint, as the more disturbing symptoms of the few who were physically caught up in the events.

Paul Frosh and Amit Pinchevski argue that the "repeatable singularity of 9/11" interpellates television viewers as witnesses "in ways that those physically present at the horror of ground zero are not and cannot be" (9, 8). Frosh in particular calls attention to the "mass morality" of media witnessing as "a primary mode of generalized moral response to otherness" that may appear at odds with "traditional emphases on the personal nature of both testimony and care" (66). While it seems to foster indifference and complacency about how we relate to others, media witnessing as a "moral force," Frosh suggests, locates the other "within the framework of those whom we recognize as equally human" (68). In *A Day at the Beach* Suzannah's response to the unidentified yet intimately familiar WTC jumper instantiates the kind of empathetic noncommitment that Frosh interprets as "morally enabling" (69). The fictions I discuss in chapter 2 illustrate a form of impersonal intimacy with the Other that comes very close to Frosh's vision of TV as an equalizing moral force. Yet in Schulman's novel a spiritual intimacy evolves that urges Suzannah as a witness to the jumper's suffering to also become a witness to her own. Her bond with this faceless man creates an imperative for change that surpasses the ethical civility with which Frosh describes the inflationary, nondescript empathies of media witnessing. This transformative thrust is, as we shall see, partly a consequence of the novel form (in its more conventionally teleological incarnation), whose narrative impetus demands a resolution usually achieved through connectedness with the Other, however fleeting or elusive this contact may be.

From Medium to Ethical Practice

In an insightful essay on the shared ironic modes of television and postmodern fiction, David Foster Wallace distinguishes between television and classic voyeurism. The latter, he observes, entails "watching people who don't know you're there as those people go about the mundane but erotically charged little businesses of private life." By contrast, television "is performance, spectacle, which by definition requires watchers. We're not voyeurs here at all. We're just viewers" (23). On September 11 voyeurism and viewership converged to produce a complex form of ethical spectatorship that was both distanced and involved. On the one hand, the terrorists applied enormous ingenuity in hurling images at the viewing public, so what we saw was proffered rather than stolen. On the other hand, watching the WTC employees plunge to their deaths counts as visual theft, since the victims had not prepared a watchable self and presumably did not intend for their act to create visual impressions. Schulman conflates voyeurism and the megagaze of television by positioning Suzannah in the orbit of two visual media: the TV set and the window through which she sees the WTC.[26]

The haptic nature of the image seen through the apartment window emerges most clearly in Gerhard's impression of the towers, especially in his queasy anxiety about the inhabitants scurrying within, whom he compares to "chiggers beneath the skin, . . . chiggers you couldn't see" (*A Day at the Beach* 51). By contrast, television is rooted in optical perception and construed—even though it clearly also contains its own concrete medium of transmission—as the opposite of material life, as the axis around which social networks evolve and interact. In his seminal essay "From Medium to Social Practice," Raymond Williams attempts to release the study of media forms from an emphasis on their material support and direct it toward an understanding of the medium as a form of social organization, as "work on a material for a specific purpose within certain necessary social conditions" (160).[27] This gesture of de-reification is particularly germane to an analysis of 9/11 as a televised event and especially useful in gauging Schulman's interest in the microrelations that are established *around* the medium of television. Williams locates the medium in the middle ground between materials and the uses to which they can be put, proposing the phrase "material social practice" (165) to sketch this intermediary function. Schulman's vision likewise oscillates between the ambient and the material functions of television. In the gap created between their direct witnessing of the attacks and the narrativization of events, television comes to occupy an important intermediary space for the Falktopfs, functioning as a kind of transitional object that mediates between the environments in which terror is produced (as weapon) and endured (as wound).

The novel unfolds over a single day, chronicled from dawn to dawn, which precludes it from including the wars in Afghanistan and Iraq as well as the media narratives put forward to make sense of the terror and its aftermath. The narrative is thus confined to a narrow slice of life whose limited perspective doesn't encompass the longer durée required to digest traumatic experience. A reduced temporal scale also allows Schulman to focus on the very first stage of the process by which televisual material is converted into narrative, a process that television theory conceptualizes as coterminous with posttraumatic signification over time. "The events cannot be poignant," John Ellis writes, "because they are radically incomplete: they exist in almost the same moment as we do when we see them. They demand explanation, they incite curiosity, revulsion and the usually frustrated or passing desire for action. We need, in other words, to work them through" (*Seeing Things* 80). The term *working through* originates in psychoanalysis, of course, where it denotes the assimilation of a sudden disclosure into already existing opinions, whereby everything else is reordered and the revelation itself is continually worried over.[28] For Ellis, "television finds itself in a similar position. It works over new material for its audiences as a necessary consequence of its position of witness. Television attempts definitions, tries out explanations, creates narratives, talks over, makes intelligible, tries to marginalize, harnesses speculation, tries to make fit, and, very occasionally, anathemizes" (79). Most of these strategies can be observed in the chaotic TV coverage that the Falktopfs watch in their Hamptons house. Significantly the "working through" of television is punctuated with conspicuous repetitions, as the same images of the crumbling towers are shown over and over again, much the same way that the falling man's plunge is replayed in Suzannah's mind in an infinite loop.

This repetitive dynamic, enlisted here primarily as a narrative device, draws on existing 9/11 footage. Replicating the structure of trauma itself, multiple television updates broadcast on that day were organized around discrete, sequential segments of minimum duration, which repeated the basic problematic of the plane impacts rather than aspiring to elucidate it. Instead of closure and totalizing vision, television coverage of the attacks offered a continuous reconfiguration of the events in an open-ended, perpetual rehearsal that kept returning to a temporal ground zero: the moment of impact. Indeed information was so scanty for at least two hours after the planes crashed that slow-motion footage of the second plane hitting the South Tower was repeated every few minutes. As James W. Carey observes, "Without a framework of coverage that could be supplied only by the state this was a national emergency after all—the television networks and stations lost control, repeating endlessly, as time-filler, the scenes of the plane striking tower two, the collapse of both buildings and the carnage and chaos on the ground" (74). Yet far from being mere time-filler, as Carey suggests, in Schulman's novel these images help recalibrate the viewers' sensibilities and attenuate their shock through the reassuring effect of repetition: "It was almost as if the network were presenting fresh and breaking news each instance—it took a while for the most recent members of this waxing and waning audience to realize that they were gawking at the same repeating news coverage, and that the unimaginable was now familiar" (*A Day at the Beach* 125–26).

Television also mimics the structure of trauma in the way images of devastation in Manhattan intrude into the narrative flow of the novel without being given meaning. The initial shock of unmediated witnessing is thereby at once alleviated and amplified as the emotional pitch of traumatic feeling rises with every repetition of the familiar yet increasingly alienating images of the crippled towers. In troubling ways that other post-9/11 narratives of vitiated (sexual) domesticity exacerbate (see chapter 2), the resulting paradox reveals the uncanny underside of domesticity in a gesture that equates extreme familiarity with alienation. Gerhard invokes "Jasper Johns and his flags, Jasper Johns and his alphabet" to make sense of the "looping reruns, the inveterate and persistent imagery" that "continue to carry the weight of the familiar but also transmogrify into something unreserved and different, as if conceptually the image itself had just been born" (129).[29] While standard news television prefers flickering pastiche to the richness of a single image, on September 11 the simplicity of the static footage showing the WTC towers burning and emitting smoke was not counterbalanced by rapid cutting. The image was held on screen long after its information value was exhausted, with variation provided by the talking heads rather than by adding further visual material. In contrast to DeLillo, then, Schulman expresses posttraumatic inertia not through the fixity of narrative but through the media's equally transfixed stare at the towers' dramatic collapse. Not unlike a Jasper Johns painting of a common flag or his series of almost identical representations of everyday objects, the image of the smoking towers conveys both soothing familiarity—Gerhard compares it to "the yule log at Christmas time . . . burning merrily for hours on Channel whatever" (61)—and a sense of uncanny lifelessness reminiscent of Morandi's hypnotic dark boxes, rendered even more disturbing by the sudden flashes of bodies falling off the upper floors, their features impossible to discern on the miniature screen.

Television indeed reduces the attacks to the minimal image it can transmit and reproduce: "The horror of the bomb and that gaping hole was less difficult to process on a small screen than it was in life, where it was so much larger and more visceral" (53–54). And since the TV image is stripped down and lacking in detail, the events appear sketchy, distant, and inoffensive. To Suzannah, it functions as a "relay, a kind of scanning apparatus that offers to present the world beyond the familiar and the familial, but to present them in a familiar and familial guise" (Ellis, *Visible Fictions* 163). In her apartment, at one remove from the endangered buildings, she glances over them from a position of relative security: "It was only if you looked outside Suzannah's window that the air was filling with smoke and people plummeted from the gaping hole. . . . On the screen the world was silent. . . . Here in Suzannah's home, sirens screamed" (*A Day at the Beach* 58, 59). Her spatial proximity to the towers undermines the sense of security conveyed by the diminutive TV image. This double exposure shapes Suzannah's traumatic response as she attempts to make sense of both avenues of experience at the same time. As we shall see, the dialectic oscillation between vicarious spectatorship and direct witnessing complicates the traditional dynamic of how trauma interferes with and reshuffles the continuity of experience and narrative form.

Traumatic Blockage and Identity Change

In his analysis of how accelerated communication has impacted on the way we perceive the world beyond our immediate experience, John Ellis writes, "No-one would claim that to witness an event in all its audio-visual fullness is the same as being present at it. There is too much missing, both in sensory evidence (no smell, no tactile sense) and, more importantly, in social involvement." Consequently "the feeling of witness that comes with the audio-visual media is one of separation and powerlessness: the events unfold, like it or not.... So for the viewer, powerlessness and safety come hand in hand, provoking a sense of guilt or disinterest" (*Seeing Things* 11). Yet Suzannah Falktopf displays neither guilt nor disinterest. Since her experience of the attacks involves a double exposure to both televised image and direct witnessing, albeit from a safe distance, her reaction is correspondingly multifaceted. For one thing, she plays the two channels of experience against each other and seeks to dispel the recurrent flashbacks of the WTC jumper by focusing instead on the more manageable images on television: "When she closed her eyes now, on the insides of her lids she saw that man diving, headfirst, tie flying, in a glowing red outline like some awful neon sculpture, a scorched negative, blinking and cheap. So Suzannah kept them open, her eyes, open and wide and focused on the TV" (*A Day at the Beach* 56). Because experiencing events at a distance may be conducive to overlooking and underacting, we might expect that Suzannah's dangerous proximity to the attacks would, on the contrary, provoke a concrete, visceral response. This is not immediately the case.

Rather than helping her derive from her experience an injunction to action—thereby obeying the falling man's voice urging her to "change her life"—the image of the jumper only sinks Suzannah even further into self-conscious introspection and marital gloom. According to Judith Herman, such apathy is a classic symptom of trauma victims, whose "perceptions may be numbed or distorted, with partial anesthesia or the loss of particular sensations. . . . These perceptual changes combine with a feeling of indifference, emotional detachment, and profound passivity in which the person relinquishes all initiative and struggle" (43). Suzannah does imagine concrete measures that she can take to respond to the falling man's appeal: "She should donate blood. As soon as she went home, Suzannah would volunteer at a local hospital. She would go to nursing school. Get her M.D. Ideas, they flew in and out through her mind like so many swooping birds. In her head, she heard a voice. Instructing her. *You must change your life*" (*A Day at the Beach* 119). But none of these intentions materializes. And yet although she fails to react by implementing concrete changes, she feels profoundly transformed, as if the attacks had invalidated the fundamental beliefs that gave her life meaning, resulting in an acute emotional paralysis and the obstruction of grief.

That Suzannah should experience both stagnation and change is in keeping with a larger paradox that investigations of trauma and its aftermath have not fully elucidated. While acknowledging the blockage caused by the incomprehensibility of trauma, Irene Kacandes makes the following, quite opposite claim: "Contact with uninvited disaster, the working through, and the acceptance of the presence of the impossible in one's life will *change one*. . . . Exposure to certain kinds of events may transform one's view of the world, and, consequently, one simply cannot be in the world in the same way as prior to exposure" (171). To support this theory Kacandes discusses Holocaust survivors forced by their experiences and memories to adopt a traumatized worldview, which creates an unbridgeable gap between the individual survivors and most other people with whom they attempt to interact. Both Holocaust survivors and witnesses to massacre (like Suzannah) experience subtle psychological changes that may or may not result in an attempt to actively redesign their lives in order to better cope with these transformations. In a classic catch-22 situation, Suzannah cannot "change her life" in a sustainable manner unless she acknowledges the change already effected by the initial shock of her vision. It is to the possibility of this initial change that I now turn my attention.

Suzannah's susceptibility to the sight of the falling man is sharpened by the condition in which the image finds her before lodging itself into her brain. The young wife displays symptoms of domestic disaffection, especially in dealing with her disabled child, her emotional antennae already abristle long before disaster strikes. Her posttraumatic self manifests itself in familiar symptoms: shock at first, followed by a roller coaster of numbness, pain, denial, and paralyzing bouts of fear. Once the initial tremor has subsided, it becomes clear that Suzannah's 9/11 trauma has wrought some collateral damage. Her relationship with Gerhard becomes fraught with tension, his usual uxoriousness being replaced by impatience and wonder at his wife's frequent mood swings. Kacandes coins the term "concomitant loss" to refer to such secondary manifestations of trauma, which habitually play out in the traumatized person's reaction to others, involving especially a loss of trust (175–76). Indeed throughout the day Suzannah becomes suspicious of everyone around her as well as increasingly and indiscriminately hostile, displaying feelings contrary to what Gerhard describes as "her paralyzing sense of compassion. Her empathy" (*A Day at the Beach* 75). It appears that witnessing the tragic fate of a stranger has cast a pall over Suzannah's own family life, exposing anxieties that had been concealed beneath the humdrum rituals and routines of domesticity. In her discussion of posttraumatic detachment in the aftermath of 9/11, Annabelle Sreberny makes the valuable point that the attacks shocked the viewers from a position of relative safety into one of victimization. As a result, lack of affect and compassion fatigue—symptoms of an era of "listless ennui" (Tester 28) in regarding the televised pain of others—swung in the opposite direction, giving rise to what Sreberny calls "over-identification" (223). Underpinning the change that Suzannah undergoes is a wave of extreme empathy congruent with Sreberny's remarks.

Paradoxically the image that precipitates this change is itself entirely free from development. As in the case of the towers burning away like giant Yule logs, it is the fixity of the jumper's image that ensures its transformative effect. Nor can Suzannah couch the man's descent into a full narrative despite her attempts to imagine a prehistory for the fall to deflect her attention away from its inexorable outcome. The details she adds reconstruct trivial aspects of the jumper's outfit, the peculiarities of his free fall, and the unexceptional domesticity of his life before September

11. Again the rituals of the everyday serve to solidify a dissolving identity by anchoring it in the safe and the familiar: "She thought of *him*, the man in free fall framed outside her window, she thought of *him*, just hours before standing in front of his bathroom mirror, maybe in his briefs, maybe with a towel around his waist, tying his tie ... the tie that he hadn't taken off, the tie that flew behind him like a loosed tether when he dived" (72). Throughout the book the jumper thus remains the protagonist of what Herman terms traumatic "prenarrative," an inchoate plot that "does not develop or progress over time" (174), inhibiting Suzannah's own creative reactions. Indeed despite the narrative ruffles she keeps adding to the image she witnessed, the initial event is not revised but merely reiterated within a closed, entropic system that Suzannah cannot escape. Her emotional blockage is certainly not helped by her failure to communicate with her husband about what they have both experienced, and particularly about the image of the falling man jutting incessantly into her consciousness.

Eventually, out of a sense of responsibility toward the death she witnessed, Suzannah applies more agency and intentionality to the mundane proceedings of her life by forcing it into a coherent narrative and giving it a new direction in response to the falling man—"a messenger, a rescuer, a winged angel sent to save her" (146–47). In ways that disclose the ethical subtext of posttraumatic experience (and Schulman's attempt to recast trauma as a fundamentally ethical event), Suzannah struggles to render productive the tension between Other and self, between passivity and agency in coping with her vision of the falling man. The final section of the book attempts to resolve this tension through familiar narrative tropes. Suzannah and Gerhard are joined in a "duet" that Gerhard plans to include in his ballet piece, *A Day at the Beach*. This sudden refocusing of attention on an object of art seems surprising, especially in light of Gerhard's earlier dismissal of a valuable painting he left behind in the Manhattan apartment, and of his intimation to Suzannah that "art doesn't matter" at this moment of historical urgency (210). Far more than an artistic product, however, the duet is also a miniature version of the Falktopfs' relationship—a marriage within a marriage that reflects the bifurcation of Suzannah's erotic identity in the aftermath of the attacks: on the one hand her attention is captured by the image of a dying man who becomes something of a spiritual lover; on the other hand her husband takes control of the situation and of the marriage, misjudging Suzannah's weakness and taking her resilience for granted, too easily and too early on. In fact throughout their flight from the city toward the vast landscape of suburbia (another classic duality and a much-loved, easily destabilized fictional trope), the Falktopfs manifest an unhealthy obsession with issues of misrecognition, ranging from the pathological (Suzannah suspects the French woman's blue-eyed baby to be her husband's) through the mnemonic (she battles with conflicting memories of a childhood acquaintance, now a full-grown seducer) and finally to her confusion about the identity of the falling man.

Suzannah comes to regard her mysterious relationship to him as her most intimate connection. She feels "inexplicably close" to him, "closer than anyone she actually knew really" (173). What Suzannah experiences at this moment is far from the civil indifference that Frosh associates with media witnessing as a form of indiscriminate sympathy toward any suffering subject, *despite* its unknowability. Her passionate rapport is energized precisely by the jumper's anonymity, so starkly opposed to familiar others. Rather than establishing a channel of communication with her estranged husband, for a long time she lingers on memories of the falling man and lavishes affection on her autistic son (as inaccessible as the WTC jumper), who can hardly provide the wall against which the echoes of her own crisis can productively resound. The anonymous WTC employee thus becomes entangled with the lives of others even as he opts to renounce his own. Suzannah's final decision to make herself accountable to others is not completely dissimilar. Her reunion with Gerhard in a setting that stages the novel's title heralds a luminous phase in their relationship and marks Suzannah's "self-binding" (in Dorothy Hale's words), her desire to dim self-consciousness and grief, to resolutely dismiss any act of self-coercion as prescribed by the jumper, and desist from it. Ultimately it is her conscious decision not to attempt any violent change that allows Suzannah to regain her composure and establish the limits of the self.

The ethical significance of the narrative rests precisely in the infinite, unanswerable appeal for change emanating from the act of witness. Change in this sense may be understood either as a *transformation* of the original, precatastrophic self or as the effort of the psyche to *return* to its initial completeness. Yet due to the insidious irreversibility of trauma, one can no longer speak simply of a change in the original self; nor can one speak of posttraumatic healing as a change, since its primary function would be to erase the effects of traumatization and to prompt the return to a pretraumatic consistency, which essentially constitutes *un*changing the self. More likely, as Robert Lifton explains, the traumatized self is not "a totally new self, it's what one brought into the trauma as affected significantly and painfully, confusedly, but in a very primal way, by that trauma" ("An Interview" 137). Importantly this traumatic duet of present and past selves takes place in the aftermath of Suzannah's visual encounter with the falling man, who serves as an appendage to her own identity, a partly malignant, unexcisable growth of her psyche.

At first the intruder does not pose any threat to the integrated self. His image is sheltered temporarily in what Abraham and Torok term an "intrapsychic tomb" or crypt that preserves the alien element until the psyche rebels against it and attempts to force it out:[30] "*He swan-dived out of the blazing building and into her head. He was in her head and she was no longer alone. They were falling together forever down the black hole inside her head*" (*A Day at the Beach* 182–83). The obsessively recurring image of the WTC jumper triggers psychosomatic changes as well, manifested primarily in Suzannah's loss of appetite, growing hostility, and callous abuse of her son. Describing the night of September 11, Schulman dwells on the peculiar appearance of the sky, whose sudden permeability reflects not only the gaping hole left behind by the impact of the planes but also Suzannah's physical vulnerability to an otherwise benign exterior (familial or natural) that now consists solely in potential triggers for syncope and collapse. "The stars," Schulman writes, "looked like tears in the sky, little rents in the fabric of the firmament, as if the protective skin that surrounded life on Earth and kept it from infinite nothingness were wearing away" (180). After a moment of extreme crisis in which Suzannah breaks down and starts howling, Gerhard slaps her with unexpected force (again it is a physical shock that shifts her consciousness), the couple is reunited, and Suzannah finally seems to have conquered her demons.

The description of the sky over Ground Zero the morning after the attack suggests, however, that this is a pyrrhic victory; notice especially the paradoxical assessment of what has "changed" in the course of the night, and implicitly since 9/11: "[Gerhard] . . . turned on the television. Nothing had changed overnight. Nothing but everything. On the TV screen, above the dark circle of the city there was a hole in the skyline, a hole filled with pink, smoky light, glowing like a comet had hit the Earth. It was a shot of the remains of the towers at daybreak" (208). As this ambivalent image indicates, Schulman does not clarify whether Suzannah's fractured self has come to terms with its duality. The duet that Gerhard wants to include in his composition might signify regained connubial harmony or, on the contrary, an understanding that the self will never be fully healed and an acceptance of its implicit, irresolvable division. Suzannah's pathological appropriation of the falling man's imaginary self is thus obscured by an illusory togetherness that allows the couple to temporarily restore both their individual identities and the identity they share as a couple.

Underneath this marital truce, Suzannah maintains a relationship to the falling man that fuses a sense of intimacy with the ethically serene acceptance of his death as the ultimate Other. Rather than reconcile herself to this loss, she continues to confer with him while remaining aware that her communication is mere ventriloquism. By entering into an imaginary "duet" with the falling man, Suzannah thus concedes that her responsibility to him will never end or be fulfilled. This, after all, is the change that she has attempted to implement all along, a change that does not emerge from her active intervention in her own life but through her admission of her own vulnerability to the death she witnessed, a vulnerability that approximates, in a minor key, that of the falling man at the moment of his death and the plea for protection contained in his image. Suzannah's belated response to the dilemma of changing her life in response to 9/11 is, then, an ambivalent one. While the concrete changes she undertakes are neither striking nor permanent, she becomes more attuned to slight alterations and nuances in the world around her in ways that link her with DeLillo's Keith Neudecker, who undergoes a similar transformation toward receptivity and self-restraint. Just as Suzannah's transformation entails not the recovery of a complete, harmonious self but the acknowledgment of Otherness and of her own responsibility to it—whether the Other be a dying stranger, her own husband, or her autistic child—so too does Gerhard perceive the impact of September 11 as an increase in his capacity to recognize the worth of his own life and of life in general, rather than as effecting a substantive modification of character: "Surrounded by his family and friends in this big, gracious house, flush with the awesome gratitude and relief of survival, was Gerhard in some strange sense actually more content? Clearly he was more appreciative" (163). And clearly while the traumatic narratives of the "disaster novel" might lead us to expect dramatic reversals, the more muted (and all the more effective) emplotment of trauma in this book encodes mourning as a subliminal, visual conversation engaging both the material solidity and ephemeral presence of what we see.

Extrapolating on the ethical framework of Schulman's novel, this increased perceptivity and appreciativeness can also be applied to the realm of politics. In this sense, though Schulman skirts political statements, *A Day at the Beach* may be read as a critique of opportunistic voices that hastened to proclaim the advent of "change" after 9/11. "This is a moment to seize," Tony Blair famously exclaimed. "The kaleidoscope has been shaken. The pieces are in flux. Soon they will settle again. Before they do, let us reorder this world around us."[31] To counter the avalanche of collateral profiteering, David Simpson argues, we must take our time in recognizing and assimilating whatever change resulted from the 9/11 events, or learn to live with its inassimilability: "The breakneck speed with which the tragic events of 9/11 have been cashed in for the pursuit of long-meditated military adventurisms and global realignments (intended or not) must make us wonder whether taking the time for sustained reflection is still worth doing" (11). DeLillo, Spiegelman, and Schulman dramatize the necessity for sustained reflection by training the rituals of self-scrutiny through halting narratives of trauma and survival. Yet the responsibilities these novels address remain symbolic—as does the falling man—a cipher for a deeper, unarticulated political task. In this sense they illustrate the disjunction between fiction and politics in the first wave of post-9/11 fiction, which gives virtually no expression to the politics of terrorism or the War on Terror. Writing about Jay McInerney's *The Good Life*, Joyce Carol Oates bemoans the "implausible sort of political vacuum in which the airplanes crashing into the World Trade Center towers seem to have simply appeared out of the sky as a grotesque sort of accident labeled vaguely as 'terrorism,'" and wonders why "no one speculates on the reasons for September 11, no one speculates on the (political, ethnic, national, religious) identities of the terrorists, no one speculates on the United States government's response to September 11, or, indeed, indicates that there has been and will be a response" ("Dimming the Lights"). Only hinting at the long-term political ramifications of the attacks, DeLillo, Schulman, and Spiegelman set resistant mourning against the opportunistic demagoguery that plays on fear, paranoia, and retaliation. Their novels end with only partial diagnoses—morally enabling through their impartiality—and an intimation of the responsibility for "change," partly constative, partly performative, always a matter of dueting subjectivities, and ultimately open-ended.

2. SEX AND SENSE

McGrath, Tristram, and Psychoanalysis from Ground Zero to Abu Ghraib

In his influential essay "Open Doors, Closed Minds: American Prose Writing at a Time of Crisis," Richard Gray underscores the failure of post-9/11 literature to formally articulate the crisis of imagination precipitated by the terrorist attacks. Gray encapsulates his position in asserting that 9/11 narratives such as Jay McInerney's *The Good Life*, Ken Kalfus's *A Disorder Peculiar to the Country*, and Don DeLillo's *Falling Man* "simply assimilate the unfamiliar into familiar structures. The crisis is, in every sense of the word, domesticated" (134). Rachel Greenwald Smith continues this argument when she states that 9/11 novels "articulate the attacks as world-changing while remaining formally familiar" in ways that reflect the post-9/11 historical conditions in the United States, particularly the misuse of the attacks for "political and economic goals that were more ideologically continuous than disruptive" (155). In other words, Greenwald Smith justifies the reluctance of post-9/11 fiction to engage in formal experimentation or posttraumatic renewal by invoking "the expansion of existing political policies" (159) in the years following the attacks. My discussion of the falling man trope, which post-9/11 writing has metabolized into a conventionally emplotted and answerable (if ultimately unfillable) ethical challenge, partly confirms Gray's and Greenwald Smith's diagnosis. Yet Spiegelman's and Schulman's gloss on the mechanics of substitution, transference, and self-restraint suggests that the task of responding to September 11 may also result in an oblique (and all the more interesting) evacuation of the familiar. It is precisely by drawing on clichéd narrative tropes that post-9/11 fiction manages to disrupt, with the violence of surprise, the benign domesticity of the terrorist plot as a painful yet ultimately surmountable personal and national crisis.

The challenge of representing the attacks does not relate to formal strategies alone, which are merely an envelope for rhetorical tropes that may insidiously prey on the conventional, planting the seeds of a productive and aesthetically experimental ethical disorientation. Gray and Greenwald Smith do not entertain the possibility that even though in many fictions since 2001 the traumatic events of 9/11 "are measured purely and simply in terms of their impact on the emotional entanglements of their protagonists" (R. Gray 134), the transference of the public into the personal (with all the clinical and aesthetic connotations such transference contains) may constitute precisely the kind of defamiliarizing, formally innovative strategy they had been seeking. And even though Greenwald Smith compellingly locates the transformative aspects of 9/11 fiction in disorienting corporeal sensations and affective provocations, she remains oddly uninterested in the psychosexual, which strikes me as a core site for the emergence of uneasy bodily and emotional shifts.

In what follows I consider Patrick McGrath's novella "Ground Zero" and Claire Tristram's novel *After* to show that far from merely oscillating "between large rhetorical gestures acknowledging trauma and retreat into domestic detail . . . reducing a turning point in national and international history to little more than a stage in a sentimental education" (R. Gray 134), fiction that bears witness to the 9/11 events can indeed enrich our understanding of trauma and its mediation. Rather than allowing "a kind of imaginative paralysis" (135), in McGrath and Tristram the ethical encounter with the Other becomes bound up—with the precision and elusiveness of allegory—with narrativization itself, particularly with that most obsessively introspective of narratives, psychoanalysis, as well as with the discomfiting vectors of sexual desire both within and outside the analytic relationship, in the bedroom, and on the geopolitical world stage.

McGrath reworks the strategies of allegory to address unmediated trauma, and in doing so he neither simplifies that trauma nor abolishes what critics such as Cathy Caruth have proposed as its determining feature, "the impossibility of . . . direct access" (*Trauma* 4). In fact allegory strikes me as a particularly apt category in the discussion of trauma due to the unreadability built into the concept, which denotes, in Paul de Man's formulation, the very impossibility of reading. De Man's phrasing can be taken to describe as much the workings of allegory as those of trauma: "The meaning constituted by the allegorical sign can then consist only in the *repetition* ... of a previous sign with which it can never coincide, since it is of the essence of the previous sign to be pure anteriority" (207). Allegory is, of course, also a common emplotment strategy in mining the consequences of historical events and a frequent configuration in post-9/11 literary culture. As Elizabeth Anker has observed, "If a distinctive feature coheres the burgeoning genre of the 9/11 novel, it is a reliance on self-conscious political allegory to grapple with the perception of historical rupture and decay induced by 9/11" ("Allegories of Falling" 463). Yet while Anker enlists post-9/11 fictions to argue that contemporary allegory "stifles indeterminacy, and suppresses what might otherwise be insurrectionary dissensus" (469), my reading of allegorical fictions emphasizes the ethical potential of their ambivalent, subversive, and ultimately unresolved crises.

Scapegoating in "Ground Zero": Patrick McGrath's Allegory of World-Historical Trauma

Patrick McGrath's novella "Ground Zero" is the third in his short story cycle *Ghost Town: Tales of Manhattan Then and Now*, which explores through an unreliable narrator the fraught relationship between a New York therapist and her client in the days and months following the September 11 attacks. Commissioned for Bloomsbury's The Writer and the City series, McGrath's collection assembles several layers in Manhattan's history, from the War of Independence, through nineteenth-century class and ethnic warfare, and finally to Ground Zero. Each of the three stories contextualizes the others, formally and thematically,[1] while examining various forms of trauma—a theme rehearsed in most of McGrath's other works (comprising one short story collection and seven novels so far). The author's own family background—his father served as chief superintendent of an institution for the criminally insane—seems to have contributed significantly to the formulation of this overarching theme: "My father would have liked me to become a doctor, but what growing up in Broadmoor gave me, that glimpse of the limits to which men and women can be driven by psychotic illness, has stimulated instead the writing of fiction" ("A Childhood" 62).

As the manner in which McGrath frames this causality suggests, his work originates in a perceived affinity between psychotic illness and psychotherapy on the one hand and narrative discourse on the other. On the face of it, this is a self-evident contention, not least because it comes from a writer who has devoted a substantial part of his work to an exploration of literature through the prism of psychoanalysis, whose impact on McGrath's formative years would have made it inseparable from his writing; or one could go even further and accuse McGrath of merely taking fiction as a pretext for surreptitiously practicing psychotherapy on his characters. As I aim to establish, however, in investigating emotional structures disturbed by the events of 9/11 and further complicated by psychotherapy, McGrath recasts them as emblems of a world-historical trauma transferred to personal lives.

More specifically he teases out the complex analogies between the traumatic impact of the attacks and the fraught relationships among a psychoanalyst (the narrator), her patient (Dan), a prostitute (Kim Lee) with whom the patient is involved, and a father and son (Jay and Paul Minkoff) who had parallel affairs with the prostitute before she met the patient.[2] Through the mediation of the analyst (who must trust to what she hears from her patient) and of the narrative itself (the reader cannot verify the truth of the analyst's inferences), McGrath articulates the ways these inscrutable relations can be read as a "domestic" allegory (to use Richard Gray's term) of the historical 9/11 trauma. By way of this transference, McGrath ultimately seeks to reach through to the unmediated core of world-historical trauma as such. While DeLillo, Spiegelman, and Schulman zero in on the ethical experience as mediated by visuality, McGrath shows that therapeutic practice, while prohibiting face-to-face intimacy and therefore hampering the ethical act, in fact re-creates the premises of this act and complicates our perception of what constitutes viable therapy (how sexuality, for instance, shapes analytic rapport and transference), viable ethics (as opposed to streamlined Aristotelian morality), and viable reading (itself a form of analysis that allows the ethical to shine through).

My own investigations into the September 11, 2001 Response and Recovery Project at Columbia University's Oral History Archives have shown that in a post-9/11 context the correspondence between narratives originating in literature and in therapy is more easily demonstrable than McGrath himself may realize, which makes his approach all the more significant. The purpose of the 9/11 Oral History Archives was to gather individual narratives on the impact of September 11th, outside the frameworks of official media and government accounts,[3] a project that recalls Spiegelman's efforts to attain a subjective voice in narrating the events and accurately reflects the dichotomy between the personal and the political on which my analysis in this chapter is based. Importantly the personal responses included in this archive are hardly idiosyncratic, especially since they appear to resonate with literary representations of the same event.

Consider, for instance, the uncanny resemblance between the post-9/11 dreams of a patient suffering from posttraumatic stress disorder (PTSD) as described to her analyst and the plot of an unrelated short story about one woman's experience of the attacks. In an interview for the September 11, 2001 Response and Recovery Project, the psychologist Ghislaine Boulanger recounts the dreams of a female PTSD patient, a resident of Battery Park City. In a recurring dream, the patient is trapped alone in her apartment on the morning of September 11, and her ties with the world are completely severed: the TV is not working and the phone lines are down. She hears the rumble of the towers collapsing but cannot discern what is happening. When a cloud of dust and debris envelops the building, she fears that she is the sole survivor of a nuclear explosion and will inevitably die. There are other dreams as well, yet Boulanger focuses on this one in particular as a small, faltering first step toward symbolization, which also marks a step forward in the patient's treatment by paradoxically revealing what the analyst calls "the absolute meaninglessness of the event" (31).

The scenario of this dream is repeated with astounding accuracy in

SEX AND SENSE

Joyce Carol Oates's short story "The Mutants" (in *I Am No One You Know*), whose female protagonist takes shelter in her apartment located on the thirty-sixth floor of a high-rise in Battery Park and remains stranded there until shortly after 2 p.m. on September 11. She slowly realizes that the TV, the lights, and the telephone are down, and she interprets what she can see—or rather, *cannot* see due to minute particles of ash and dust obscuring the view through the window—as possibly a cyclone, "a ghastly accident" (282), a great fire, a solar eclipse, an earthquake, or chemical warfare. Aside from the (rather improbable) possibility that Oates was in fact Boulanger's patient and the writer decided to paraphrase her own dreams in "The Mutants," there seems to be no apparent explanation for this unusual coincidence. Yet in the process of reading other reports by New York psychiatrists interviewed for Columbia's 9/11 Oral History Archives, it has become clear to me that the language of psychotherapy and that of narrative after 9/11 are replete with overlapping imagery. Throughout my psychoanalytic discussion of post-9/11 fiction in this chapter, I refer periodically to the 9/11 Oral History Archives, not as an authoritative body of psychological knowledge, but as a rich and complex reservoir of impressions leading to a deeper insight into the layers of 9/11's impact on actual individuals, and ultimately into character analysis as well.

Through a close reading of "Ground Zero," which dwells on trauma as a concept endemic to both narrative and psychotherapy, I argue that McGrath articulates the idea of transference in both psychoanalytic and hermeneutic terms. Using the dynamic of the analytic encounter on the one hand and narrative unreliability on the other, "Ground Zero" stages the personal mediation of public events in the literary representation of 9/11. Importantly in the context of my ethical approach to 9/11 writing, the story enacts its psychoanalytical model of transference not only through an oscillation between world-historical trauma and personal affect, but also in relation to questions of morality and guilt after 9/11. In opening up this model of transference to account for the dynamics of projection and blame triggered by the attacks, I discuss moralistic forms of scapegoating at work in the text and conclude by asking how McGrath's thematic concerns are reflected in his narratological decisions. The final section of my analysis thus addresses the role of the reader within the transference model outlined and unmasks the narrative mechanisms by which she too becomes entangled in the chain of mediation set in motion by the story.

Yet beyond its direct treatment of how individuals experience the shock inflicted by the 9/11 attacks, "Ground Zero" also helps retrace the broader links among world-historical trauma, psychotherapy, and literary expression by exposing the transference of punctual shock into systemic trauma as closely entangled with the sublimation of psychic experience and libidinal drive into the writing (and the reading) of fiction. Both uses of the term by Freud—transference as constitutive of the relation between patient and analyst, and as the displacement of psychic material through a chain of conscious and unconscious signifiers—are in evidence here. The whole story is thus played out in the aporetic interstice between analytic and narrative transference, between the sexual seductions that fuel the shifting erotic triangles and the mediation of 9/11 as image and memory, in a complex rhetorical transfer whose undecidability establishes the story's ethical stakes.

Trauma, Transference, and the Recognition of Evil

By charting the dissolution of the barriers between the analyst's personal and professional lives—a dissolution as gradual as it is unstoppable—McGrath points to the transference of world-historical trauma into the minor-scale trauma of a love quadrangle (and the analyst's response to it). As I argue in this section, this transference leads each of the story's protagonists to understand evil in new ways against the backdrop of 9/11. The unnamed psychiatrist prefaces her account of a patient's case by admitting, "Danny Silver was like a son to me, and as a childless woman who never married I do not say this lightly" (175). The problems that Dan discusses with his therapist originate in what she refers to as "a suffocating maternal relationship which created conflicts that ran like fault lines deep in his psyche, becoming visible only when he tried to sustain intimacy with a woman" (175). The intimacy that Dan develops with his psychiatrist will prove, however, much more knotty and turbulent than any of his relationships with other women. By acknowledging that she is "mothering" him (whether obviously or through subterranean manipulation), the therapist prompts the suspicion that she might be responding to Dan's problematic motherhood issues by assuming an overbearing and emotionally controlling role, a suspicion that the text will confirm.

Both actions—Dan's investment of the analyst with mother-like features, or transference, and the analyst's ready appropriation of this image, or countertransference—are well-known components of the analyst-patient relationship. In 1925 Freud summarized his concept of transference as "an intense emotional relationship between the patient and the analyst which is not to be accounted for by the analytic situation. It can be of a positive or of a negative character and can vary between the extreme of a passionate, completely sensual love and the unbridled expression of an embittered defiance and hatred" (*An Autobiographical Study* 42). One could also say, with Otto F. Kernberg, that "patients hang the fabric of their transference onto the protuberances of the analyst's personality" (51), so it is more likely that a therapist with a penchant for domineering manipulation will revive a mother complex in her patient. The therapist responds in keeping with her own unresolved neurotic conflicts, which gravely hinder her therapeutic effectiveness. In the most seminal and widely quoted statement on countertransference, Annie Reich describes this phenomenon as comprising "the effects of the analyst's own unconscious needs and conflicts on his understanding or technique. In such cases the patient represents for the analyst an object of the past on to whom past feelings and wishes are projected" (26). McGrath's opening gambit thus reveals the nature of his protagonists' analytic relationship, the form of the patient's transference onto his female therapist, and her reverse transferences onto her patient. The rest of the story serves to deepen the "fault lines" set forth in this dense preamble.

Although the analyst's reaction is a common one among psychotherapists, it may have been exacerbated by the precarious psychological condition to which many therapists were reduced in the wake of the terrorist attacks, a condition partly attributable to a lack of professional training. As Randall D. Marshall, director of the Traumatic Stress Studies Unit, the

Anxiety Disorders Clinic, and Columbia's Psychiatric Institute, admitted in an interview for the 9/11 Oral History Archive, "After 9/11 . . . only a handful of clinicians in the greater New York area had been specialized enough to really learn these very new treatment approaches [to trauma], and had come up with a way to integrate them into their everyday practice" (3). In some cases the terrorist attacks sent New Yorkers back into therapy after long hiatuses, leaving it to the analysts to decide whether 9/11 itself or some other underlying motive had been the catalyst for the change of heart. The experience of Eric R. Mendelsohn, a screenwriter and Columbia University faculty member, is pertinent in this regard: six months after the attacks, Mendelsohn returned to therapy, seemingly as a means to overcome what appeared to be a case of writer's block. His analyst was convinced, however, that the feelings of vulnerability triggered by the terrorist attacks were the true cause of his inability to write. Mendelsohn describes his predicament by imagining his psychological defenses as a door to insecurity that 9/11 opened up, yet this "was never a solid door, it was probably always a screen door, and it's open or waving in the wind" (40). The analyst in "Ground Zero" discovers that Dan's emotional defenses are quite permeable as well. She is in fact the first person to whom Dan turns after 9/11, the events of that day having "disturbed him profoundly" (175).

Even though the text never states this unequivocally, the therapist herself is undergoing psychic transformations as a result of the attacks; her responsibility as a clinician, as Dori Laub formulates it, is to watch over these transformations and shape the analytic relationship to factor in their effects. "The listener," Laub states, "is also a separate human being and will experience hazards and struggles of his own, while carrying out his function of a witness to the trauma witness. While overlapping, to a degree, with the experience of the victim, he nonetheless does not become the victim—he preserves his own separate place, position and perspective; a battleground for forces raging in himself, to which he has to pay attention and respect if he is to properly carry out his task. . . . The listener, therefore, has to be at the same time a witness to the trauma witness and a witness to himself" (58). Laub writes here about a generic "listener" figure, whose presence is essential in the creation of knowledge necessary in working through trauma. Awareness of the traps of oral testimony is even more important for an analyst, whose function exceeds passive listening and requires an involvement in the act of testimony that the psychoanalytic alliance entails.

However, while the analyst does claim to be "vigilant," she soon loses sight of herself and of her own vicarious involvement in her client's affairs—an involvement that any competent therapist should have expected and attempted to neutralize. In his interview for Columbia's Oral History Archives, Claude Chemtob remarks that "in the context of disaster, people's personal boundaries are automatically made ... less vigilant," which in turn renders therapy work "more intense because the boundaries are softer" (29). In "Ground Zero" the analyst's intense scrutiny of her client softens the boundaries between his life and hers. From her sheltered position as impersonal observer, the analyst watches her client and his lover traverse a period of trauma and emotional upheaval, thinking that she will remain exempt from such turmoil yet actively intervening, through her very watchfulness, in the undoing of both the love affair and the analytical relationship. The elephant in this particular room is thus not the analyst's bias—a frequent and in itself uncontested phenomenon—but the pervasive and insidious trauma caused by the 9/11 attacks, an event that, in McGrath's estimation, marks one of three threshold moments in the cultural history of New York.

Just as in the previous two stories in McGrath's *Ghost Town* broader historical traumas are encoded in the idiom of individual psychology, so do pointed slippages between the characters' traumatic circumstances and a larger, ambient trauma abound in "Ground Zero." It appears, for instance, that the terrorist attacks have triggered a traumatic syndrome to which Dan's personal circumstances have already predisposed him: "He was finding it difficult to work. It brought back everything he has suffered after his mother's death: the same disabling grief, the same leaching of joy and purpose from projects which had previously given meaning to his life. The same sudden debilitating waves of anger and wretchedness and despair" (178). Easily identifiable here is what Claude Chemtob calls the "neon effect" of trauma: "Whatever was going on before, in a trauma tends to be heightened and brought to the floor more intensely" (4). The neon effect operates not only chronologically, illuminating prior blockages, but also transversally, paving the way for a reciprocal contamination of personal and collective traumas. This collusion is hinted at when Dan looks on as an acquaintance covered in gray ash enters a building on the opposite side of the street and opens his mailbox—a routine gesture that symbolically indicates the infiltration of trauma into Dan's own daily life.

In passages that anticipate the prevalence of moral racialization in later 9/11 narratives, McGrath pairs Dan with a prostitute of a different race, dramatizing the insidious transference of posttraumatic animosity and confusion from the political realm into the sphere of affect and sexuality. To be sure, even before she finds out that the prostitute is Chinese, none of what the analyst hears about Kim Lee arouses her sympathy, and although Dan emanates profound contentment, the analyst sees waste and deception in his affair rather than emotional gestation and the promise of true love: "I nodded, I smiled, I wanted to reassure him. But I was not at all happy about this relationship. He thought he was falling in love, and he may have been right, but he was falling in love with a prostitute. This was not appropriate for a man who, in emotional terms, was only just beginning to learn to walk" (192). Naturally the analyst deludes herself into thinking that her antagonism toward the prostitute is based on a cool assessment of her character, yet it is shot through with the resentment of a rival. McGrath reveals little of the therapist's personal circumstances, but it is clear that, through therapy, she develops a sense of fusion that seems to set her and Dan apart from the rest of the world, so the prostitute can be regarded only as an intrusion, irrespective of her race.

The discovery that the lover is Chinese shifts the antagonism between the two women into something with even greater potential for maliciousness and harm. The prostitute's racial difference, although not directly resonant with the War on Terror, releases in the therapist the pent-up energies of an indiscriminate racist feeling prompted by the terrorist attacks. A prime symptom of this sentiment is her endorsement of Attorney General John Ashcroft, a Patriot Act supporter, in his attempt to run roughshod over civil rights to preemptively detain suspicious foreigners. Likewise the therapist fails to confront (or even register) her own rather worrying propensity to regard Kim's moral failures primarily as a function of her race. As a civil rights lawyer, Dan is particularly sensitive to the infringement of civil liberties in the aftermath of the attacks, and his first post-9/11 conversation with his therapist in fact circles around these troublesome issues. When she rebukes him for concealing the fact that his lover is Chinese, Dan responds by defending Kim against the therapist's veiled discrimination: "She's called Kim Lee. And she's as American as you or me though I shouldn't have thought that needed saying!" (207). Yet even he fails to recognize to what extent the analyst's resentment of Kim originates in racial fear.

Nor does Dan surmise the extent to which the analyst is haunted by the attacks, or realize that in her mind professional interest and personal trauma—converging in her relationship with Dan—are dangerously co-extensive. In an account of his pro bono work as a civil rights attorney for people who lost loved ones or property in the attacks, Dan mentions the wife of a 9/11 victim who yearns for closure but is unable to achieve it because there is nothing left of her husband, no body that can be buried and mourned. In the last paragraph of the text, the therapist invokes this story again and wonders whether the woman has managed to find closure—a veiled metaphor of her own desire for emotional resolution after losing a dear patient. This conflation may suggest that the analyst regards the loss of her patient as coterminous with the destruction wreaked by the terrorist attacks. And in many ways Dan does seem to embody the towers themselves. As Kim confesses to Dan, her dissatisfaction with men lies not in their infidelity but in their tendency to "buckle" under emotional pressure. The analyst concurs: "Poor Dan. He had buckled often, he was seriously structurally flawed" (219). "Buckle" is precisely what the towers did, and the images of the horrific buckling and its aftermath (buckled girders being trucked away from Ground Zero) are clearly meant to serve as parallels to Dan's own fragile psyche: Dan was always already traumatized (by the death of his mother as well as by two failed marriages) in the same way that the towers had been ever since the 1993 bombings. Thus not only is our image of Dan mediated (through sex and psychotherapy), but he himself constitutes the channel of transference from crumbling buildings to crippled psyches and from world-historical to personal trauma—the two poles between which "Ground Zero" constantly oscillates.

Finally, in a graver case of transference than I have described thus far, the therapist associates the evil perpetrated by the terrorists (evil she sees embodied in the ruins at Ground Zero) with her immediate professional circumstances and especially with Kim's morally reprehensible behavior, as if she were "working through" her own trauma by redirecting its shockwaves toward her nemesis. Seeing Ground Zero provokes in her sentiments that she has not experienced before, sentiments that alter her moral understanding of the world. Ground Zero is the mast supporting the text's moral master narrative, now crumbled, as the analyst's story is, after she has directed and controlled it into a monstrous cul-de-sac overwritten by her own unconscious, the duper hoist with her own petard. "I am a psychiatrist," she remarks, "I do not believe in evil, I believe all human experience can be traced to the impress of prior events upon the mind—But this. As I began to walk back uptown I attempted to find a few sticks of thought with which to build a structure that might explain why those men had done what they had to us. To us. But I could not, and all at once I felt what was, for me, a most rare emotion, I felt rage—the sort of blind primitive destructive rage which I imagine drove those men to attack us as they did" (196).

The analyst's sudden outburst of rage codifies the tensions at the heart of her profession's ethical project, which rests on the accessibility of experiential meaning. As Lacan writes in *Seminar VII* in *The Ethics of Psychoanalysis*, "Analysis progresses by means of a return to the meaning of an action. That alone justifies the fact that we are interested in the moral dimension. Freud's hypothesis relative to the unconscious presupposes that, whether it be healthy or sick, normal or morbid, human action has a hidden meaning that one can have access to" (312). The attacks and the scale of destruction in Lower Manhattan remain impervious to clarification and thus shatter the analyst's belief in the determinism of human psychology, which leads her to freely associate minor events of less catastrophic proportions—or what she calls "episodes of peripheral insanity"—with the fallout of the terrorist attacks. Such "random bits of evil" (211) accumulate into a worldview that begins to color her perception of not only pathologically aggressive people (such as terrorists and cold-blooded murderers), but also of her own patient's lover, a woman whom she has never met and whose mental condition she glimpses only furtively and from afar.

Especially her understanding of 9/11 as a pivotal moment marking an abrupt transition from paradise to apocalypse betrays the analyst's proclivity for stark moral boundaries: "September 11, a date which was rapidly becoming a watershed in all our lives, a line of demarcation, or a point in time, rather, before which the world seemed to glow with a patina of innocence and clarity and health. And after which everything seemed dark and tortured and incomprehensible, bearing nothing but portents of a greater darkness to come" (212). In line with this Manichaean perspective, the analyst projects rather than recognizes evil, jubilating as Dan recounts Kim's unethical behavior toward her former lover, Jay Minkoff, and claiming that the Chinese woman is "the devil" (234). Naturally, projecting evil onto the Other leaves her in a position to claim goodness for herself. At no time does the therapist deviate from her firm belief that she alone can provide succor and support to a deranged Dan and protect him from the wiles of Kim the prostitute. "He could not abandon me," she self-righteously proclaims, "to abandon me would be to cast himself adrift upon towering seas with no raft, no lifejacket even save his own confused and fragile psyche" (214). She also dismisses as "pedestrian psychology" (228) the reasonable hypothesis that Kim is being haunted by her dead lover because she is repressing guilt about her infidelity with his father. Instead the fact that Kim is "rocked to her foundations by a ghost" (228) suggests to the analyst that it is not guilt and regret, but all-out *evil* that lies at the core of Kim's emotional collapse in the aftermath of the terrorist attacks.

Considering its malleability in the text, it is difficult to define McGrath's understanding of evil. On the one hand evil appears to be the root of extremism and extremity. The "exquisite tension" (238) caused by the presence of both Minkoff men in the same apartment as Kim waits for scandal to erupt qualifies, in the analyst's eyes, as evil. What also counts as evil is Dan's refusal to confront his own moral failure, as evidenced by his indulgence of Kim and her self-flagellating confessions of immoral behavior. In both instances evil behavior occurs against the background of severe emotional numbness and is motivated by an irrepressible desire for sensation. Set against a metaphorical Ground Zero of affect, emotional pyrotechnics such as stress, guilt, and masochism assume gigantic proportions. "But at what point does one say—this is evil?" the therapist wonders. Her confession sheds light on the permeability of conventional boundaries between abstract ethical judgment and the transgressions of ordinary life: "I am a psychiatrist. For my entire professional life, until, that is, I went down to Ground Zero, I had rejected the concept of evil. . . . Not anymore. And now, hearing Dan's account of two adults taking pleasure from a third party's ignorance of their actions, a third party with whom they were both on terms of intimacy, and whose knowledge of those actions would prove utterly devastating—for them to run this risk, and for one reason only, their own pleasure—was this not evil? I am inclined to think it was" (232). That the world took an evil turn after the 9/11 attacks is an untenable claim, not least because the analyst makes no effort to support it; rather a transference is at work here that imbues her posttraumatic sensibility with a spirit of moral decrepitude and deceit. And what leads the analyst to castigate as evil the extreme and indefensible behavior of Kim Lee and Paul Minkoff is not the act itself, immoral as it may be, but the aftershock of witnessing the crime scene.

Ground Zero gives away little that might help the reader in pinpointing the evil so effusively invoked by the therapist. The "slender gothic arches" that mark the place where the towers used to be are unusefully compared to "the wreckage of some vast modernist cathedral" (195). Rather it is the effects of the collapses on the neighboring buildings (in another symbolic image of transference) that reveal to the analyst the scope of the destruction, again establishing a line of equivalence between evil and extremity but also reinforcing the transposition of architectural into corporeal structures: "I saw a high building torn open, its innards sheared off and spilling out, twisted beyond recognition and starkly illuminated by that unearthly blue light; at the sight of it I was viscerally awoken to the magnitude of the violence that had occurred there. When the towers came down, corkscrewing as they collapsed on themselves, they spewed out steel girders which tore open the walls of adjacent structures, and what I saw now was physical evidence of forces of an almost unimaginable destructive power" (195). In comparing the private transgressions of a woman (and a sex worker, at that) on the one hand and the destruction of the Twin Towers on the other, McGrath does convey a palpable sense of evil, in that both deeds can be associated with some form of (physical) immorality; the problem lies in its calibration. Paradoxically Kim's mundane infidelities appear to have affected the analyst's life in a much more conspicuous way than the devastating terrorist attacks. They are, in fact, the only means by which the analyst's trauma can be manifested at all. Yet beyond fueling the analyst's rage in her guise as stand-in for the evildoers of 9/11, Kim also serves as an agent of sacrifice and purification, a dual role that invites closer investigation.

Procuring the Scapegoat

Taking my cue from René Girard's theory of scapegoating, I want to argue that Kim Lee fulfills the role of both victim and perpetrator as she comes to absorb the moral resentment of those who have been traumatized by the attacks and are searching for a third party on which to project their collective fears. "Ground Zero" illustrates several of Girard's core theories, particularly his view of "acquisitive mimesis" or "appropriative mimicry" as a basic human trait and primary trigger of conflict.[4] Girard defines mimetic desire as a drive provoked by the acquisitive intentions of the Other. Once a person seeks to take possession of an object, Girard proposes, those around her will also begin to covet it. Likewise in the process of competing with each other over Dan's affections, the analyst and Kim mimic each other's desire, fighting not only for Dan himself but also for the prestige of snatching him from the clutches of the other desirous woman.[5] More important for the present argument, however, is Girard's invocation of the scapegoat figure as lightning rod for the aggressive tendencies of two or more parties engaged in bitter conflict with each other.

Although Dan and his analyst clearly grapple with some communication problems and with a fraught analytical alliance, they easily and self-evidently converge to repel and strike down one and the same adversary, the Chinese prostitute Kim Lee. Dan may appear less enthusiastic about pinning his own frustrations on his lover, yet he repeatedly admits that his feelings for her are tinged with fear and resentment. Kim thus emerges as a scapegoat figure both in the conflict consuming analyst and patient and in the more encompassing clash between good and evil, the people of New York and the terrorists, Homeland and Rageland.

Kim also embodies the traits employed by Girard to classify scapegoats into a homogeneous group. In *The Scapegoat* he names as common victims children, elderly people, the disabled, women, members of ethnic or racial minorities, and the poor, as well as some other potential "outsiders." Kim is a woman, she is Asian, and she is an artist (and not a very successful one, at that); the fact that she has turned to prostitution is an indication that her income is probably lower, more variable, and less secure than either Dan's or the therapist's. Dan and the analyst choose Kim as a scapegoat for the evil that invaded their post-9/11 lives partly because the object of their projection, in Girard's formulation, already "bears the signs of a victim" (*The Scapegoat* 21). In other words, the rationale for persecuting Kim is that she has already been victimized: by the attacks, by the death of her lover, by her sordid life circumstances, by her promiscuity. It is her promiscuity that Dan and his analyst condemn most pointedly as a cardinal sin, and the strength of this condemnation almost seems to suggest irrationally that Kim, through her inherent evilness, was to blame for the retaliation of September 11; the attacks were indiscriminately directed at an entire city (and nation) when only Kim herself should have been struck.

Revealing the ethical affinity between the transference enacted through psychotherapy and the ritual of the transfer of evil associated with scapegoating, the text thus completely transfers responsibility for the 9/11 attacks from the terrorists who perpetrated them to Kim, the duplicitous lover caught both figuratively and literally between two men, father and son, as one emerges from her bedroom and the other sips coffee at her kitchen table: "three figures frozen in space as they await the sickening impact of whatever it is that is coming at them at unimaginable speed" (238).⁶ In case the evocation of a "sickening impact" of something "coming at them at unimaginable speed" didn't draw a parallel to the 9/11 attacks explicitly enough, the very next sentence begins "Ground Zero has now shrunk" (239)—as indeed it has, from the enormous pile of debris in Lower Manhattan to the kitchen of a Chinese prostitute who entertains two simultaneous affairs, even while working for an escort agency. It almost seems as if the planes were plunging not into the Twin Towers but into Kim's bedroom, in direct retribution for her villainous acts.

Kim's contradictory qualities cement her role as a scapegoat figure. She is "passionate and possessive" (220), features that tend to smother her lovers, provoking their anger and abandonment. Yet this pattern also teaches her "caution and detachment" (220). She may seem vulnerable to Dan, but to his therapist she appears caustic and irreverent, her patina of urban sophistication barely concealing the depths of indifference underneath. She thus conforms both to the prototypical "unhinged lover" figure and to the stereotype of the uninvolved sex worker. Her dominant personality traits may well exclude her from the ranks of average women, but what the analyst perceives as her "enlightened self-interest, the American way" (221) reintegrates her into some semblance of normality. The analyst in fact cannot reach a consistent verdict concerning Kim's character, vacillating between a neutral view of the woman as "cold and selfish" (224) by nature and a harsh condemnation of her aloofness as "the emotional emptiness of a sociopath" (225). Other accusations display similar contrasts and contradictions. Kim, the analyst argues, is merely *using* Dan to cleanse herself of corrupting memories. This assertion bears more than a hint of irony in light of the analyst's exploitation of Dan to fill her own psychological void, and of the common view of prostitutes as women *being used* rather than employing their partners for their own psychosexual satisfaction.

And Kim is indeed procured—on more than one level—to fulfill several functions. The analyst is no less a "client" and recipient of Kim's services than Dan. Not only does the analyst indirectly employ Kim as therapeutic aid in her treatment of Dan, but she herself serves in a capacity very similar to Kim's: Dan pays both his prostitute and his analyst for a service centered on the idea of release and cleansing—physical and psychological, respectively. On the other hand both the analyst and Kim *use* Dan as a distraction from their own traumas and as a projection screen for the symptoms they develop after 9/11. Both perceive the other woman as an impediment to Dan's recovery and as a threat to themselves. And in both cases their reaction helps to mediate their responses to the world-historical event that Dan, the two women's buckling pillar of strength, represents.

When the analyst senses that Dan is "pathologically obsessed with his Chinese prostitute" (212), she looks for a credible setup that would help explain his condition (a condition that, ironically, she shares). The context, she concludes, is the gloomy backdrop of the terrorist attacks, the disagreements and tensions between people like Dan and Kim being mere shadows or reflections of this larger catastrophe. The analyst is "forcibly reminded of an image that [she] had once seen of two actors engaged in a furiously complicated drama in front of a screen on which were projected enormous indistinct shadow-figures performing obscure destructive actions which mirrored and at the same time grotesquely distorted the drama going forward center stage" (212–13). Both the terrorist attacks (as large-scale projection) and the dealings of ordinary human beings (introspection, infidelity, indifference to the projection itself) are witnessed not only by the analyst but also by the implied reader, who cannot remain immune to the text's overlapping circuits of transference.

Trauma and Narrative Unreliability

Unlike the analysand-narrator on which Peter Brooks predicates his account of narrative "transaction" derived from the Freudian model of psychoanalytic transference, McGrath's story appears to present us with an *analyst*-narrator. Yet in the process of recounting her experience with Dan, she effectively assumes the position of analysand as she gradually reveals past desires and fantasies (about Dan and especially 9/11) that she aims to render "closed and legible," in Brooks's terms (106), and thereby achieve the transition between what the story frames as the present reality (her life after Dan) and the tale within the tale (life after 9/11). Here as in Brooks, "the story unfolds ineluctably from the removal of the mediator" (in this case, Dan as a temporal and emotional medium) and marks "the failure of transmission" (107)—although in McGrath the mediation continues on the level of narrative focalization and authoriality. What emerges is a hermeneutic triangle that implicates the reader in the narrative situation and emphasizes the necessity of narrative transferability. In order to succeed, the narrative must cajole the reader into "contracting" (with the implication of both agreement and contagion) the trauma into which the analyst's memories of 9/11 have congealed. The narrative's transgression of its frame to encroach upon the naratee is, I would argue, an ethical act, confirming the pertinence of the psychoanalytic model of transference for the study of reader-response in narrative ethics. I propose that the interplay between an underlying world-historical trauma and center-stage individual distress is replicated in the act of reading through a form of hermeneutic transference supported by the analyst's narrative unreliability and by the ways McGrath deliberately offers her as a scapegoat figure meant to imbibe the reader's post-9/11 anxieties.[7]

Importantly in this context, Girard's theory of the scapegoat is founded on what he calls persecution texts, "accounts of real violence, often collective, told from the perspective of the persecutors, and therefore influenced by characteristic distortions" (*The Scapegoat* 9), a phrasing that unmistakably points to the authorial unreliability of these narratives. Any discussion of the scapegoat principle within a text, Girard remarks, should first distinguish between "a scapegoat *of* the text (the hidden structural principle) or a scapegoat *in* the text (the clearly visible theme)" (119). He classifies persecution texts, which are "entirely subjected to the representation of persecution from the standpoint of the persecutor" (119), as applicable only to the former category. Haunted by the specter of a scapegoat it does not acknowledge as such and permeated by the illusion of her false culpability, "Ground Zero" can be read as a persecution text, one in a long series of post-9/11 retributive fictions centered on morally ambivalent (and highly seductive) narrative voices.

A key distinction organizing my argument (and one that corresponds to Girard's separation of hidden and overt scapegoating in narrative texts) is that between unreliable narrators and unreliable narratives. The unreliable narrator's value system departs from that of the implied author, thus relaying a message to the reader that the speaker cannot be trusted.[8] By contrast, an unreliable *narration* confronts the reader with irreconcilable oppositions between the world of the text and the reader's own reality, which prompts the reader to dissolve this tension by discrediting the author's trustworthiness. In this scenario the narrator falls prey to the reader's desire to see her preconceptions reinforced and to place blame for any textual discrepancies onto the narrator's deliberate attempts to occlude facts that the reader takes for granted. Unreliable narratives can be recognized primarily in situations where the text is set against a larger factual reality upon which the narrative depends for its significance and which the reader also invokes in her attempts to reintegrate the text into her own cognitive horizon. As Heinz Antor has persuasively argued, in his novel *The Grotesque* McGrath employs an unreliable narrator who distinguishes himself as such through "internal contradictions in what the narrator tells us, inconsistencies of a kind that make the reader suspect that Sir Hugo wants to present himself at a given moment in a favorable light and then unwittingly gives himself away" (16). The reliability of this narrator is further weakened by his explicit references to the considerable excitement he experiences at the moment of narration, as well as by countless attempts to compensate for his mental volatility by justifying his actions in order to secure the reader's trust.

Precisely because the analyst makes no such effort to legitimize her position and authenticate her claims, McGrath leads the reader to doubt her insights, if not the method she applies to arrive at them. While an unreliable narrator produces a sense of disorientation and uncertainty in the reader, the analyst achieves quite the contrary: a coherent and at least superficially compelling account that disguises the confusion of the romantic quadrangle beneath a veneer of logic and predictability. If Sir Hugo "pathetically fails to provide epistemological clarity in a fictional universe that seems to have fallen apart" (Antor 20), the analyst offers *too much* clarity. This clashes violently with the reader's expectations that

9/11 has undermined feelings of safety and certainty, including the reliability of narratives. Disoriented by this clash, the reader seeks resolution through a process of scapegoating that closely resembles the analyst's own scapegoating of Kim Lee. Because, as I suggested earlier, the analyst gradually assumes (through her verbose defensiveness) the position of analysand, McGrath's implied reader automatically takes over the role of analyst, as well as its attendant countertransference. By seeing in the analyst a disturbed, secretly traumatized person, the reader in effect rewrites the story in more intelligible ways while mediating the damages she herself has incurred.

The analyst's final reference to "closure" marks her identification of Dan's departure with the massacres of September 11, a transference that proves pivotal to the text's incorporation of scapegoating as a structural principle. To the extent that the analyst and the reader disavow personal guilt to accede to a state of innocence by symbolically sacrificing both Kim and the narrator, they also enter into an ethically charged relation with their own potential victimization. The closing sentences summon the overdetermined semantic chain "funeral-coffin-closure," brutally drawing our attention to the story's circular transference and recontainment of trauma. In the process of scapegoating, both the analyst and the reader become aware that they too have been or may be sacrificed, that the coffin and the funeral are to some extent their own. Conditioning this final transference is a sense of naked exposure to trauma in its unmediated form, once the interpersonal entanglements have evaporated. The narrative and hermeneutic opportunities for healing and purification that Kim and the analyst open up in becoming scapegoats are thus suspended: despite the text's appropriation of the two women for symbolic ends, the story remains unconcerned with the possibility of personal redemption. Like Dan and like the towers themselves after having been dealt traumatic blows, the narrative eventually buckles, exposing its singed core—a mirror image of the crippled architectural structures to which the towers themselves have been reduced.

McGrath's allegory of world-historical trauma, I have been arguing, involves a complex transference encoded in the double gesture of scapegoating that attributes guilt to both the racialized Other and to the analyst herself as unreliable narrator. In carrying out this multifaceted mediation, the narrative reveals the unmediated core of trauma by inscribing the sacrificial death of the terror victims into the symbolic sacrifice of Kim and of the therapist. Without entirely disputing Richard Gray's pronouncement cited at the beginning of this chapter, "Ground Zero" complicates it by suggesting that an immediate event such as 9/11 does not always lack mediation. Rather it acquires its world-historical impact precisely through discursively sophisticated forms of mediation and transference that defy what Gray dismisses as the ineffectual "confusion of feeling, the groping after a language with which to say the unsayable" (132) in post-9/11 fictions concerned with interpersonal and domestic affect.

Beyond its relevance to a study of post-9/11 writing, in foregrounding transference as a mode of encountering social and historical trauma, McGrath's story reflects theoretical debates that are central to the broader field of trauma studies, which has recently been faulted with a "difficulty accounting for those forms of trauma that are *not* punctual, that are more mundanely catastrophic than such spectacular instances of violence as the Holocaust" (Forter 260) or, for that matter, the 9/11 attacks. What "Ground Zero" demonstrates is the sublimation of punctual trauma into more systemic patterns of behavior, such as racial scapegoating and a malady of suspicion the reader contracts in the very process of reading. The mundanely traumatogenic psychology mobilized in this story exposes trauma less as a trope of post-9/11 fiction than as a truth or condition of the post-9/11 literary experience itself, while providing an intriguing emendation to the dyadic model of transference. Significantly the transference model proposed in this story is not dyadic but a quadrangle, later expanded to include the reader(s), and as such better suited to reflect the systemic dimension of 9/11 trauma. The preceding novellas in McGrath's collection already establish a dynamic of triangulation to investigate how the same event impacts on the lives of several characters (usually a victim, a victimizer, and a group of bystanders experiencing various degrees of guilt). In "Ground Zero" McGrath recasts the impact of the terrorist attacks in personal terms without, however, disengaging the initial shock from its most prominent features: its social content and collective structure. In its psychotherapeutic take on post-9/11 scapegoating, the text spells out the imbrication of social motives and psychic motivations, providing an ethical epidemiology of trauma—the first story in the collection fittingly refers to its protagonist's guilt-ridden trauma as a form of "contagion" (62)—which ultimately usurps the divide between the social and the narrowly personal. Evil resides partly in resisting the pervasive nature of trauma, a resistance that manifests itself in the characters' attempts to stigmatize and exploit each other's posttraumatic condition. The ethical task of literature, McGrath suggests, should be the opposite of such accusatory practices: to provide an understanding of each other's traumas and to help articulate the historical forces that endlessly replicate our shared anguish.

Race, Sexuality, and Moral Liberalism after Abu Ghraib

To pursue the ethical implications of scapegoating further, I turn to Claire Tristram's novel *After*, a controversial book that remains the author's only fictional work to date. Unlike McGrath, who enlists scapegoating on a symbolic level, Tristram depicts the scapegoat as subjected to physical and psychological torture, inflicted in ways that signal this author's more daring approach to rendering post-9/11 racial tensions. The novel describes a casual sexual encounter between an American Christian woman and an Iranian Muslim man—an encounter that degenerates into sexual violence perpetrated, unconventionally, by the woman. Following on its provocative premise, the ethical stakes of the novel rely on the enforced conjunction of sexuality, race, and psychoanalysis, which opens up urgent questions in the context of the present study and makes the novel easy to pair with McGrath's somewhat more oblique if no less potent insights into post-9/11 racialization. In addition, it is worth noting that both McGrath and Tristram showcase the ethics of literature in relation to feminine sexuality, which seems significant in light of Lacan's conceptualization of the ethical act as in itself feminine, and of woman as the embodiment of being's "not-all," that is, of being's fundamental insusceptibility to assemblage into a whole. The fact that in both narratives the female focalizers are single, emotionally isolated, and unnamed enhances the anonymity of their being and their proximity to its present truth.

I will return to an explicit Lacanian interpretation of the two texts in the final section of this chapter; for the time being, in focusing on Tristram's novel, my first intention is to discern how the moral implications of the book resonate beyond the perimeter of intimate relationships across a wider cultural and political spectrum. Due to its publication on the heels of the Abu Ghraib scandal, *After* is a unique book, despite the plot elements it shares with "Ground Zero" and with the texts I discuss in chapter 3.[9] The ethical valences of my approach certainly resonate with this kind of timely, audacious, open-ended novel awash in desire and psychological disturbance, whose workings are no clearer at the conclusion of the narrative than they are at the outset. And yet in a world where the aftereffects of 9/11 yield new insights every day, the moral responsibilities of topicality come sharply to the fore, inviting a juxtaposition of the novel with its grotesque political enactment at Abu Ghraib.

After has been translated into eight languages (an impressive feat for a 9/11 debut novel), yet no studies of the text have been published so far, partly because a critic's first impulse might be to shirk engagement with a novel whose historical embeddedness is so evident and unsettling. In what follows, I do not advocate a value-driven argument against or in favor of the novel, but instead outline a critical strategy that demands a rethinking and rearticulation of post-9/11 racial discourse at the confluence of trauma, sexuality, and psychoanalysis. Above all I am interested in the role this novel could play in elucidating what ethical implications the domestication of world-historical trauma (through scapegoating or deviant sexuality) might have in public and political terms. This question has led me to consider carefully the argument proposed by Gary Wihl in a 2001 essay on D. M. Thomas's *The White Hotel*, a Holocaust narrative similarly concerned with morality, sexuality, and psychoanalysis. Wihl suggests that this novel's dramatic exposure of cruelty is best understood as an ethical strategy that underpins liberal thought and constitutes its chief moral responsibility. He deplores the failure of literary studies to apply theories of liberalism to the interpretation of literature, and formulates an injunction whose urgency the 9/11 attacks, occurring the same year his essay was published, have finally brought home: "The question for further moral reflection is the role of these literary works in a liberal public sphere. If liberalism is the articulation of autonomy and a criticism of tyranny and cruelty, then we are obliged to compare the moral gravity of novelistic descriptions to the descriptions produced within the spheres of law and politics" (483).

In reading Tristram's *After* with this injunction in mind, I want to test the ethical validity of Wihl's theoretical yoking of literary and liberal discourses in a way that not only clarifies the novel's contribution to the post-9/11 literary canon, but also retraces a conceptual genealogy for its imbrication of trauma, sexuality, and race. Specifically my argument is that the novel focuses much less on the explicit racial dynamics that characterize political discourse after 9/11 (both internationally and domestically) than on articulating practices of cruelty that help define liberalism's long-term agenda. To glean the relevance of political theory in examining the novel, I use Judith Shklar's work on moral psychology and liberalism as a theoretical grid helpful in revealing how *After* resonates with the broader political climate of post-9/11 America. One of the Central European intellectuals the Nazis drove to the United States, Shklar is my guide in examining victimization and cruelty after 9/11 for two reasons: first, she is interested in literature as a source of narratives about human vices and moral conflict, topics whose absence in philosophical discourse she emphatically bemoans; and second, she stresses the centrality of moral psychology for the conception and study of politics. While most American liberal theorists argue about rights and virtues, Shklar focuses on wrongs and vices, pointing toward an ethical interpretation of cruelty as the main concern of liberal societies. My analysis similarly singles out cruelty as the main impetus of Tristram's narrative.

I propose three avenues for exploring the novel's treatment of cruelty: its traumatic topographies (especially the isolated hotel that provides the central setting); its discussion of sexuality, gender, and torture's feminizing component (particularly in the context of the Abu Ghraib photographs); and the discourse of racialization that wields a destructive force throughout the text. I take seriously the novel's extremes of cruelty as well as the excessive inhumanity of the real torture images that retroactively illustrate them. No complete ethical diagnosis of post-9/11 literature can be reached without squaring the political implications of the terrorist attacks and of the Abu Ghraib revelations against the sexual and moral atrocities described in this novel.

Judith Shklar: Rethinking Moral Liberalism and Contemporary Fiction

With her focus on immoral behavior—rather than, say, the heroic dimension of the 9/11 experience—Tristram addresses cruelty from the perspective both of the 9/11 victim (embodied here by the bereaved woman) and of the perpetrator (misrepresented by the Muslim lover, Changiz),[10] though the roles are never entirely clear-cut. "Victimhood," Shklar proposes, "happens to us: it is not a quality.... Victimhood may have become an inescapable category of political thought, but it remains an intractable notion. We are often not even sure who the victims are. Are the tormentors who may once have suffered some injustice or deprivation also victims? Are only those whom they torment victims? Are we all victims of our circumstances? Can we all be divided into victims and victimizers at any moment? And may we not all change parts in an eternal drama of mutual cruelty?" (*Ordinary Vices* 17). What unites Shklar and Tristram is their awareness that in talking about victims and victimhood one runs the risk of making "unfair, self-serving, undignified, untrue, self-deluding, contradictory, or dangerous" statements (22–23). Both "put cruelty first," in Shklar's memorable phrase, while admitting that however attentive to evidence and ethically scrupulous, the project of putting cruelty first is, above all, an incentive, both in political theory and in literature, to which Shklar often turns to illustrate her points. Despite the confusion surrounding its intent and politics, Tristram's novel may be productively situated within the discourse of cruelty in the liberal sense defined by Shklar. "Her essential point," Wihl writes, "is that somewhere at the core of genuine liberal thought there is a profound respect for the autonomy of the individual; fear, or the infliction of cruelty, harms or demolishes that autonomy" (469). Both Shklar and Tristram not only portray the effects of cruelty on ordinary lives, but also attach ethical importance to the act of exposing cruelty. Wihl associates this ethical task with "a larger commitment to liberalism" (477), a commitment to which literature must subscribe in order to prevent "the loss of moral reflection in the face of extreme brutality" (483).

I use the term *liberalism* with broad reference to the political tradition governed by the individual's fundamental right to liberty and inaugurated by theorists such as John Locke and Jean-Jacques Rousseau. While Shklar's argument—that liberalism's overriding aim is to "secure the political conditions that are necessary for the exercise of personal freedom" ("The Liberalism of Fear" 21)—abides by this tradition, she departs from mainstream liberal thought when she locates its deepest grounding in the conviction that "cruelty is an absolute evil, an offense against God or humanity" (23). Significantly for my purposes she voices the opinion that "public cruelty" (of the kind instantiated by the Abu Ghraib transgressions) "is not an occasional personal inclination. It is made possible by differences in public power, and it is almost always built into the system of coercion upon which all governments have to rely to fulfill their essential functions" (29). Shklar insists that we must therefore place constraints on public power and suggests that this can be achieved by limiting the opportunities for physical cruelty that emerge in everyday human encounters. This is why she devotes considerable interest to the moral psychology of individuals, resting on details of character and context (however contingent or irrational) that can inspire human beings to harm themselves and others. She ultimately comes to the conclusion that we should not distinguish between personal and public cruelty (*Ordinary Vices* 2) but extend the experience of victimization to both realms, which leads Bernard Yack to regard her position as a dialectical one: "We bear the source of public cruelty within us even when we live in relative security within the protections provided by the liberal state" (5). It is the interrelation she envisages between personal and public cruelty in the sphere of liberalism that makes Shklar's thoughts particularly instructive in my discussion of Tristram.

Reading Tristram after Abu Ghraib

Not every abuse at Abu Ghraib was "motivated by a clear-headed and rational desire to obtain information that could not be obtained in other ways," Karen Greenberg writes. Instead the historical record "suggests that American torture policy was motivated, at least to some extent, by a *cruelty* that Americans must eventually explain to themselves and to one another" (43, my emphasis). This cruelty, as Shklar might have expected, is both personal and public, both an individual gesture belonging to the sphere of privacy and sexual intimacy and a generalizable act within the moral paradigm of contemporary liberalism.[11] Before I consider the novel in detail, I wish to clarify the mutual refractions at work between this narrative and the photographs published by CBS news and the *New Yorker* in April 2004. Their visions of cruelty reflect larger questions about the state of liberalism in post-9/11 society, particularly since the Abu Ghraib revelations, which have so far given rise to intense ideological discussions in which the links between sexuality and violence, perversion and politics are formulated and interrogated.

To begin with the most tangible link between Tristram's narrative and the familiar torture images, three of the seven U.S. soldiers charged with abuse at Abu Ghraib (i.e., "softening up" prisoners for interrogation in ways that violated the Geneva Conventions and the federal antitorture statute) were women: Specialist Megan Ambuhl, Private First Class Lynndie England, and Specialist Sabrina Harman. Many insightful readings of the photographs pinpoint the ethical tensions mobilized by the pictures in ways that are congruent with my own approach to Tristram's novel. The photographs, Philip Metres argues, "ride the tension between inviting our subjective identification with the tortured and demonstrating our own position as complicit witnesses to a war crime" (1598). Far from merely recording the abuses, the images themselves were used as a weapon of shame, as Seymour Hersh notes in his investigative report. "The photographing of prisoners," he writes, "seems to have been not random but, rather, part of the dehumanizing interrogation process" (38), and he cites a former inmate's testimony that the cameras aggravated his humiliation. In ways that help explain why a novel like Tristram's could be written before Abu Ghraib became a household name, Hersh points out that the susceptibility of Arabs to sexual humiliation had already been a conservative talking point prior to the invasion of Iraq in 2003, and drew in turn on a frequently cited study, Raphael Patai's *The Arab Mind* (1976), which argues that the tabooization of sex in Arab culture has resulted in a perception of sexuality as fraught with shame and debasement.

Interestingly, both for the general population and senior Pentagon officials such as Donald Rumsfeld, what brought home the horror of the abuses was not their formal description in administrative documents but the photographs and videos, which cumulatively portrayed a program run amok. Susan Sontag pushes Hersh's argument further to suggest that the sexual component of the abuses may itself have been a function of the imperative to record the prison experience. "An erotic life," Sontag writes, "is, for more and more people, that which can be captured in digital photographs and on video. And perhaps the torture is more attractive, as something to record, when it has a sexual component" ("Regarding the Torture of Others" 27). Sontag appears convinced that the abuses and the photographs in some ways emulated "the vast repertory of pornographic imagery available on the Internet"—a contention that might be seen to occlude and normativize some of the images' gendered transgressions. For Sontag, the pictures put cruelty first in a literal sense, as they dramatize the "reigning admiration for unapologetic brutality" (29) of a violence-driven culture in which we have all become complicit.

Also complicit in the abuses, even though they carefully shun association through their restrained body language, are the male guards. Responding to this aspect of the images in an interview for *Art Review*, Judith Butler stresses the "sexualisation of the punishment, the coercive sodomy for instance, or fellatio" (L. Gray 51), focusing on homosexuality as a specific site of offense. Although they might be said to have contrived homosexual scenarios through the emasculation of the male prisoners, the images featuring Lynndie England and other female soldiers stage forms of domination and submission within a markedly *hetero*sexual matrix. In a study of the photographs' pornographic subtext, Laura Frost compellingly shows (against Sontag) how interpretations of the Abu Ghraib setup have taken recourse to pornographic themes to mask the difficulty of imagining a woman as torturer. Frost avers that "a reading of a woman as sexualized is more accessible than a reading of her as powerful, whether abusively or responsively" ("Photography/Pornography/Torture" 141). It is this disturbing power—leaning on sex yet exceeding it—that Tristram bestows on her protagonist.

I would contend that in the aftermath of the abusive conduct at Abu Ghraib, Tristram's novel redeems the notion of sexuality as a female authority trope and as a form of power that verges on reprehensible abuse. In so doing the novel intervenes in, manipulates, and ultimately critiques post-9/11 stigmatizations of the racial Other, particularly of the Iranian Muslim male seen as both racially and sexually conspicuous. The novel testifies that sexuality in fact sustains the libidinal economy of the War on Terror and other contemporary forms of racialized and anti-immigrant violence, in which Slavoj Žižek detects an elementary "relationship between pleasure and *jouissance*, between the circle of the pleasure principle that strives for balance, for the reproduction of its closed circuit, and the ex-timate foreign body" (*The Metastases of Enjoyment* 70). There is much that the sexual treatment of Changiz shares with the torture of prisoners at Abu Ghraib: feminization, shaming, submission, hooding (the prohibition of the gaze). The novel's sexual explicitness powerfully confirms strategies of dominance that the (frequently censored) photographs only intimated. Embedded in this fraught image-novel interaction are the ways military and domestic torture seem to reinforce and validate each other, painfully dismissing the fantasy of post-9/11 racial cruelty as merely an individual, isolated impulse. Clearly it can also degenerate into the systematic, large-scale pursuit of revenge among soldiers and prison guards—or a form of militaristic fringe extremism. As the novel shows, it can also corrupt interracial heterosexual dynamics among ordinary Americans (just as in McGrath's "Ground Zero" political and psychological manipulation go hand in hand).[12]

Sexual cruelty in particular underpins the power relations galvanizing the War on Terror. What the Abu Ghraib photographs and their cultural mediation have revealed is that sex is generally inseparable from power, as Peter Morris's play *Guardians* demonstrates. By juxtaposing the monologues of an unscrupulous journalist ("English Boy") and a female soldier ("American Girl") evidently modeled on Lynndie England, Morris sets out to explore the premise that "an ordinary person's experience of power is invariably centred on its sexual manifestations" (22). Power and sex, though interrelated, are attached to two distinct categories of authority and agency: political leaders on the one hand and the everyman (woman) on the other, whereby an implicit sexualization within the former category filters down and takes explicit shape in the latter. While exposing the "mindless concupiscence" (43) of the War on Terror across all ranks, Morris dramatizes two ideas eloquently formulated by Leo Bersani in 2008: that in post-9/11 America "the rulers' nonsexual sadism has been sexualized in those who are ruled" (Bersani and Phillips 69) and that aggression, irrespective of its target, is sexualized by the pleasure of its satisfaction, which implicitly and retroactively encodes aggression within the sphere of the sexual. "The pleasure of war is pain," Morris writes. "Our sexual conquests are military conquests" (54)—an idea that unmistakably resonates with Bersani's eroticization of post-9/11 U.S. imperialism. By suggesting a new, impersonal key in which sexual relations can be reinscribed, Bersani undertakes a revision of power relations toward a more rewarding (and safer) ethical accord between enemy factions, in bed and on the battlefield. Morris anticipates Bersani's intervention by testing the potential of deviant sexuality to contain and reorder networks of aggression and empathy. In staging an Abu Ghraib scene featuring his submissive gay lover, English Boy takes the phrase "I feel your pain" literally and looks beyond the gruesome images to *perform* cruelty and suffering on the aestheticized border between public and private, politics and intimacy: "Less like sex, more like—Guernica" (42).

The moral distortions of power relationships also inform Eve Ensler's play *The Treatment*, which opened in New York in the fall of 2006 and is thus a decidedly post–Abu Ghraib work. Through the aggressive and erotically charged relationship between a military psychologist and an Iraq War veteran, *The Treatment* teases out the issues of accountability and morality around which discussions of torture rotate in ways reminiscent of (though far less subtle than) McGrath's psychoanalytically themed "Ground Zero." Like Tristram's *After*, *The Treatment* reenacts the brutal interrogations at Abu Ghraib by featuring the humiliation of a man by a woman, although a more clear-cut, unproblematic morality emerges from the much greater proximity of Ensler's characters to the actual scene of crime: he a soldier involved in prisoner abuse, she a woman on a mission to discover how far up the chain of command the responsibility for the abusive tactics lies. Much less of a feel-good, redemptive story than Ensler's, *After* provokes confusion partly as a result of what Karen Greenberg diagnoses as a "split screen syndrome" since 9/11: "The nation is both vulnerable and powerful, both victim and victimizer, both aggressor and defendant. Confronted with competing realities, the public has chosen to live with cognitive dissonance rather than try to resolve the contradictions" (40). Tristram isn't convinced that the contradictions can or should be resolved, as it is in the cauldron of such conflicting passions (both erotic and choleric) that the new ethics of 9/11 literature are forged.

Trauma Hotel

Part identity thriller, part erotic romance, *After* resonates with several events in recent memory, despite its taut, evasively allegorical format. The plot revolves around the nexus of grief, race, and sexuality in a minimalist, pared-down, almost journalistic style aiming at universality, as if to testify both to the novel's historical relevance and to its capacity to transcend history. In brief, *After* recounts an eventful one-night stand between a nameless, recently widowed (white) woman and the Muslim man she has chosen to be her lover. The two meet and consummate their illicit passion (he is happily married, with two daughters on the honor roll) in a secluded, nondescript hotel on the Pacific coast against the indistinct background of a postapocalyptic America whose post-9/11 condition is only obliquely suggested. They have sex, go out for dinner, engage in physical and psychological torture, and finally separate twenty-four hours later. Although the woman's decision to take a Muslim lover is clearly part of a broader redemptive longing for an act that is "unexpected, so clearly outside the role that she had been forced into by her circumstances" (29), her encounter with this particular man is accidental, like a random collision, "as sudden as a knife edge, dividing him from the monotony of his days" (85). Foreshadowing the obsession of post-9/11 literature with issues of risk and preemption, this encounter provokes the widow's reconsideration of how and why her life defies or assimilates contingency. Prior to the 9/11 attacks, she "lived in a world where every event was connected in some lucky and happy way with what had come immediately before, in an unbroken string leading all the way back to early childhood . . . a way of ordering the world that works quite well as long as nothing comes along to challenge it" (12), but the attacks had severed the sense of moral justification and order she had come to take for granted.

Despite sharing a sense of exhilaration about the immorality and fortuity of their tryst, the lovers spend most of their time together puzzling over what they should do or say next. Although some of their thoughts come into focus by the end of the book, their actions seem hesitant and impulsive throughout, to some extent because the characters' biographies remain inconclusive. Both are defined in terms of a crucial experience yoking the personal and the political in ways that mirror their present situation. The woman's husband was publicly murdered by Muslim extremists a year previously—and the wound of this loss is still tender—yet she ensnares the man in a trap by withholding this information from him. Echoes of Daniel Pearl's well-publicized death in early 2002 are clearly in evidence, as are elliptical references throughout the novel to a barely fictionalized 9/11. To reinforce the postcatastrophic atmosphere, during the lovers' tense cavorting in their hotel room, an unspecified incident occurs that involves ambulances and low-flying planes, provoking macabre jokes from both about potential nuclear threats. This and other specters of doom haunt the widow, who cannot shake off "the ugly and uncompromising beat of a distant war drum, warning her of some chaos or terror to come" (93). She harbors both the fear of an event that might disrupt her existence in the same way that the 9/11 attacks did, and the desire for disaster to irrupt, thereby inflicting on everyone the anxiety and longing that have already plagued her for twelve months: "Alternatively she wished for a disaster ... after which all that had come before would be erased in a brilliant white light, rendered irrelevant from one searing moment to the next, so that all the world could experience the same dislocation that she had.... In this way they would all be equal, just as this man lying next to her had become her equal" (177).[13]

In his turn the Muslim man struggles with memories of unrest in Iran in 1979, especially of a demonstration during which a good friend was shot in the neck and killed (185), an event that precipitated his decision to leave Iran and emigrate to America. Another significant detail is a brief scene in which the widow receives posttraumatic counseling from a professional who—absurdly, from the widow's perspective—"expected her to become clay again, when she was air" (29). The widow defiantly tests the therapist's patience by insulting her and rejecting her advice. Clearly this patient prefers to take matters into her own hands, and the rest of the narrative shows how the widow "treats" herself to all sorts of psychosexual cures. The sensualism of her self-prescribed therapy is prefigured in the novel's first pages, which portray the widow's obsession with sexuality as an extension of her bereavement: "Day by day, month after month, without her attending to it, her grief had subtly changed its shape, until what was left was not quite grief at all, but something she could only describe as desire. She ate with her fingers. She slept naked. Grocery boys aroused her" (4). Her Muslim lover later identifies this sensual propensity as "the nature of her attraction: her stark emotionality, her willingness to feel" (71).

Tristram weaves her plot from the two bare threads of the lovers' distinct traumas, as each sees in the other a potential for rehabilitation and rebirth. The widow's knowledge of the man with whom she is about to have sex is limited to his appearance—"the face you might see these days in the pages of any newspaper. The deep-set eyes. The youthful, fawn-colored skin. The skin of a martyr" (8)—which is racially and morally marked in the aftermath of September 11. Over the few hours of their encounter, even this sketchily defined face, more imagined than observed, begins to fade. Hardly has the man left the hotel room (for a few minutes, at her request) when the widow "felt the coldness of the sheets, and felt the terror of his absence, and it dawned on her that she had forgotten his face entirely" (16). In turn the man remembers the woman's face from a television appearance in the aftermath of her husband's death, but this memory does not prompt any suspicion on his part. On the contrary, he interprets their experience as a meeting of kindred souls and wonders "whether this widow had sensed in him also a gap, a hole, a tragedy in need of resolution and healing, just as he had somehow sensed it in her" (20). Despite his initial uncertainty about her "morbid need" (82), he drives to the hotel, runs out of gas on the way, buys some at bootleg rates from a farmer who eyes him suspiciously, and finally arrives to find the widow wandering along the beach, lost in the desolate landscape. The tenuous relationship takes off slowly, oscillating between oppressive silence and mindless verbosity, budding sexual chemistry and small talk. It is never entirely clear whether the lovers seek talk therapy for their respective traumas or believe "that too many words would get in the way of complete understanding, an understanding beyond words, the result of their lovemaking and the tragedy they had both known in their lives" (67).

The lovemaking begins with role-play: the widow performs the part of sacrificial victim, "spreading herself out like a bower, like a sacrifice, her arms languid and restless above her head" (73). The sexual act appears at times to reveal the man's desire to "touch her original self, before she had been so damaged by events" (130); mostly, however, it is mired in misunderstandings and distrust. After the opening erotic session the lovers go out for dinner, spending most of the evening in the company of an unpleasant age-differentiated couple. The male half initially mistakes the Muslim man for a Mexican and erupts in anger upon hearing that he is a "towel head" from the Middle East, his resentment fueled by his nephew's death in the Gulf War (121). The widow does little to protect her lover; indeed the episode appears to release in her a surge of negative, destructive energies that redirect the course of the evening as soon as the lovers return to their room. Unexpectedly the widow confesses that she has been plagued by fantasies of revenge against "a man of your sort" (134). To his surprise, the admission prompts a swell of desire in the lover rather than shock or anxiety. It is in this atmosphere of pleasurable confusion—"a masterpiece of subtle shadings combined with violent and saturated splashes of color" (137)—that the novel's final act begins. A hush settles over the text, projecting the sounds and, above all, the silence of what happens in the hotel room against the readers' stunned attention.

The Muslim man's status as "undesirable alien" (151), albeit violently desirable to the woman, is enhanced by the fact that he forgets his billfold and thereby all identification at the restaurant; his "nakedness" in the bedroom is thus at once physical and ontological. After forcing him to close his eyes, the widow becomes the "voyeur" (142), though previously her gaze had been repelled by the man's searching looks. She carefully selects ordinary objects lying around the hotel room and proceeds to torture her lover with delicate then brutal gestures meant to recall the 9/11 attacks and the fate of Daniel Pearl, gestures that uncannily predict the torture of Muslim prisoners at the hands of the Abu Ghraib guards. During these proceedings the widow meditates on evil as mundane and accessible— "The inherent cruelty of ordinary things, she thought. A wire. A piece of string. A box cutter" (144)—while the unrepeatable nature of the sexual encounter (which she perceives as an event beyond censure, reality, or consequences) invokes for her the recklessness of suicide bombers who "will never be held responsible for their final acts" (145). Like the 9/11 terrorists, before sexually abusing the Muslim man the widow meticulously shaves her entire body, her "ritualistic cleansing" (147) mimicking theirs and injecting into their act a "self-referential eroticism" (90) that cements the novel's understanding of sexuality as part of a broader, politically inflected sacrificial ritual.

The man tacitly accepts this treatment, even though "some part of him was alarmed and startled and wholly unprepared for the passive way the rest of him accepted her desire to dominate him" (149). The widow even emboldens herself with the self-deluding belief that "if he had given any overt sign of protest she would have stopped, stricken and contrite" (159); as soon as she dials his wife's number on his cell phone, the lover does protest, yet instead of stopping, she forces him to leave a message on his home's answering machine, dictating to him incriminating words meant to confuse his wife and endanger his marriage. Sometime during the night her menstrual bleeding sets in, staining the sheets and prompting so much disgust in the man that he leaves immediately, without touching her again, despite her baffling suggestion that the night they spent together has left "in its wake only a great tenderness" (183). This detail substantiates another connection between the novel and the Abu Ghraib torture rituals that it increasingly resembles: the Iraqi prisoners at Abu Ghraib recoiled from (fake) menstrual blood, which was reportedly employed by guards during their "enhanced interrogations."[14]

The widow is left alone in the hotel room, yet instead of melancholia or remorse she feels absolutely nothing. She packs her bags and leaves the hotel. On the beach she makes out a woman in a red scarf, an image of herself, rushing toward her much the same way that she had rushed toward her Muslim lover upon his arrival, hungry for relief. The novel ends on this purgatorial note of hope before the two women can blissfully merge—or slaughter each other, as the case may be. Nothing in the novel helps the reader imagine the outcome of this final confrontation. The flatness of the closing is indicative of the state of consciousness the story as a whole describes, a state that has at its center a profound discrepancy between the narrative's clinical attention to the characters' mental meanderings on the one hand, and their detachment from themselves on the other. In ways that provide a flawless example of Butler's and Hale's ethical visions of the novel genre, the ending's overall effect is not to clarify the significance of what occurs as much as to deepen one's sense of its ambiguity.

Both in this final image and throughout the novel, the basic binary of victim/victimizer is blurred, leaving readers with a moral dilemma, which strengthens my view that what Tristram seeks to achieve is a representation of cruelty as such—free of agency and culpability. Significantly all communication is expressed in the language of sexuality and bodily sensation. Trust and pleasure are visibly lacking, partly because the woman idealizes her late husband, partly because the traumas she and her lover have suffered at different moments in their lives render them unfit for emotional intimacy. Clearly both the woman and her sexual partner are dealing with the aftermath of trauma, yet a full recovery from this trauma is precluded by the fact that neither of them is a direct survivor: both are witnesses who seek to understand the impact of terrorism on their lives. Both strive for accountability and a sense of cathartic release that never eventuates. Their material and affective exchanges occur at the bodily level, viscerally, although the two occasionally engage in dialogue about subject matter to which they encounter emotional barriers. They bristle at each other's statements, and their language is saturated with an ideology unfavorable to their sexual project. Their failure to assimilate each other's experiences only reproduces their trauma: the man feels "brushed with the darkness of her grief, which seemed to curl into his mouth like old smoke that he wanted to expel" (70). When he recognizes her grief, he not only detects its origins and nature, but also the ways it mirrors his own: "He was stunned to realize . . . that he was no longer thinking of her as widow, or victim, or failed actress, or partner in an illicit tryst, but as someone very much like himself. A victim of random violence" (122). Both parties are thus reduced to their basic common denominator: the experience of cruelty, gradually tilting toward a retributive form of posttraumatic empowerment.

Particularly the state in which the woman finds herself while "recovering from her loss" (73) testifies to the delay in response that is a fundamental feature of the traumatic experience.[15] Traumatic victimization also determines the specific terms in which the widow codes her fantasies. Power and powerlessness form the axis around which her ego congeals.[16] The widow thus needs to see herself as capable of exerting power, ferociously resisting the victimized position into which the attacks and her husband's death have forced her. Yet despite the empowerment seemingly implied by the situation, the potential outcome and inherent logic of her sexual arrangement unsettles the woman—she worries that her plan might be too "elaborate," "sordid," and "pointless" (7)—betraying her fragile state of mind and an instability that extends beyond the arena of sex to the general realm of expression, both physical and linguistic.

Beyond its occasionally strained notes and the taxing reading experience it offers, compared to other post-9/11 fictions this novel does not gloss over the psychological fragmentation and indeterminacy that set in after 9/11, both in individual minds and in the psyche of the nation.

Like Schulman's haunted ballerina, Tristram's protagonist derives creative strength from her precarious position, yet in this text the transformation is also marked by severe formal torment. The ever-present sense of pain and schism is rendered in the book's style: languid, divorced from affect, at once subdued and strangled, driven by a rabid desire for more (more sex, more truth, more violence). Underneath its limpid style, the narration as a whole has the quality of a sketch. The distant narrative voice absorbs into its surface all the emotional edges we might expect from even the most callous story of pleasure-oriented (or rather pain- and ennui-inducing) sex. Initially the novel revolves solely around the woman's experience. We share her perspective and listen to her voice for most of the twenty-eight chapters (a number that might be taken to suggest the length of the average menstrual cycle). In some chapters we get the man's account, often as a retelling of the same events we witnessed through the widow's eyes. In the sections that describe sexual intercourse, the alternating point of view shifts the focus from the spectacle of sexualized bodies to the reader's role in the creation of the scene. When we read the same episode twice, the brutality of the act increases by dint of its mere repetition, which captures on a textual level the cruelty of the sexual scuffles taking place on the hotel bed.

The claustrophobic effect of these repetitions is enhanced by the fact that the novel is set almost exclusively within the confines of the secluded hotel (with the exception of dinner, which takes place at a nearby restaurant, and the ending on the beach). On one level the confinement of the plot to this setting ties in with the novel's aesthetics of detention, linking the hotel room and the torture chamber as locations of intimate abuse and humiliation. And like a torture cell, the hotel room contains objects that participate in the annihilation of the prisoner. The isolation of the characters simultaneously carves out an atemporal location—a realm of "exception"—for the plot of the white woman as torturer. The suspended nature of this nonplace also helps the protagonists and the reader to gain some distance from the larger post-9/11 narrative, thereby proposing the hotel as the ideal locus of escape from remembered horror in a way that has become a near commonplace. In Liliana Cavani's *The Night Porter*, for instance, an ex-Nazi officer finds in a large Viennese hotel a sanctuary in his attempt to bury all traces of his past. D. M. Thomas's Holocaust novel, *The White Hotel*, revolves around a very similar trope of the hotel as a literal hotbed of libidinal fantasies. In Tristram's *After* the inherent escapism of the hotel setting also prepares the reader for the transgression and cruel undecidability of the sexual encounter about to unfold. Nicolas Royle sees in the hotel a perfect metaphor for such liminality. "Is there not perhaps some sense in which every dream is a 'hotel dream,'" he asks, "a not-at-home place that is nevertheless not the same as homelessness, a funny form of temporary accommodation in which the 'I' is away, undecidably for business or pleasure, business *and* pleasure?" (4). The spatial rhetoricity of the hotel also chimes with the connotations of casual eroticism. Desire is enhanced by the lovers' sense of dislocation, by the semiotically open, unmarked, unarticulated "somewhere" of the hotel (no town or city is specified).

Yet the pleasure ensuing from desire is only implied rather than overtly stated, because it strays so far from conventionality. Here pleasure hinges on scarcity and temporal condensation rather than emotion and occurs mostly against the lovers' wishes, more like an accidental hemorrhage than a natural outcome of intercourse. As soon as the sex results in concrete enjoyment, the widow panics. She had intended to resist orgasm, yet "her body had gone galloping off of its own accord with this satyr, this troll. It could only mean that she harboured feelings for him. She felt her anxiety beginning to mount" (88). These pockets of unanticipated and unwelcome pleasure notwithstanding, most of the encounter unfolds in a cool, mechanical fashion. It requires no overt preparation and occurs without preamble—and it is precisely this inimitable instantaneity that precludes any expectation of future trysts between these two characters. As a result the intensity of their encounter relies to a great extent on an unspoken awareness of their lovemaking experience as expendable—not only on the larger timescale of their lives, but even over the course of the single night they spend together. The secluded hotel is thus a perfect setting for their meeting, whose location on the ocean shore perfectly accommodates the spillages, ebbs and flows, and final retreat of sexual desire. To the man, the hotel feels like "a liquid place as wide as the sea where waves and waves of thwarted desire rose up and threatened to engulf him, but the waves at the last moment would inexplicably dissipate, and he would find himself in waters flat and unmoving, where he was becalmed, where all desire left him" (75). What also dissipates amid these ebbs and flows, with their subtext of "menstruous" femininity, is Changiz's sexual identity.

Cruelty and Sexual Torture

Discourses of racial suspicion after 9/11, Anjali Arondekar has argued, were "accompanied by a concurrent and visible remasculinization of American culture as strong, turban-less, aggressively heterosexual, and refuelled with a newer, more bellicose version of the colonial *mission civilisatrice*" (243). In her landmark study *Terrorist Assemblages*, Jasbir Puar also makes a compelling case that "at this historical juncture, the invocation of the terrorist as a queer, nonnational, perversely racialized other has become part of the normative script of the U.S. war on terror" (37). Puar identifies an American sexual exceptionalism that coheres against Muslim sexualities regarded as improper and deviant. Tristram turns this counterterrorist agenda on its head. She locates deviance at the core of heterosexuality, embedded in the conventional and familiar imagery of casual sex containing the ingredients of countless Hollywood films. She also "queers" the sexual act itself (she describes various forms of sodomy, rape, and torture) and, by extrapolation, "queers" also the forms of expression into which the sexual act is contained. The narrative style and structure are clearly meant to daze, confuse, and generally "deviate" from what we might expect from a post-9/11 novel. Tristram further complicates this picture by ascribing sexual deviance to a woman whose past embodies the melodramatic narrative of counterterrorist propaganda. Heteronormativity, Puar writes, is "indispensable to the promotion of an aggressive militarist, masculinist, race- and class-specific nationalism" since 9/11, citing the "grieving white widows of corporate executives" to illustrate the heteronormative fantasies with which TV viewers were bombarded after the attacks (40). Tristram's female torturer clearly belongs to the imaginary of this enforced collusion of sexuality and nationalism: she has been widowed by Muslim terrorists and has appeared on television programs to commemorate the 9/11 attacks.

In engaging with the sexualized discourse of the War on Terror so early on, long before Puar and others joined the conversation, Tristram provides a fascinating vocabulary in which the obsessive concern with gender trouble at Abu Ghraib may be framed. The issue of gender featured prominently in media coverage of the abuses, mainly for the sake of prurient scandal, yet was willfully ignored as soon as discussions of the female soldiers' conduct threatened to move beyond the pornographic images circulated by the media. Marita Gronnvoll has perceptively noted how "gender and sex are discussed and not discussed in the media reports regarding the women and men implicated in the Abu Ghraib abuse scandal" (372). Gronnvoll also detects the "stark visibility of gender in media reports of England and Harman" in contrast to the "invisibility of gender markers in the male soldiers also charged with abuse" (373)—an inexplicable oversight, especially if we consider that what the female guards aspired to achieve was precisely to disturb and unbalance male gender markers.

Tristram's widow provides a spectacular illustration of this gender revolt. Like England, she is "over-sexed, rebellious, and not at all inclined to behave as a woman should" (Gronnvoll 378), let alone one recently and publicly widowed. Also like England, she is a "woman who victimizes with sex" (381). In much the same way that the Abu Ghraib guards were trying to feminize their victims—a transgression felt by the prisoners as particularly humiliating—the widow seeks to interpret her sexual encounter in terms of a gender reversal: "His touch was almost feminine" (*After* 79), she observes, and she yearns for a physical mutation that will allow her to fully inhabit the masculine role: "She watched his hips rise and fall and wished fervently for some hard thing rising up out of her body so she could thrust it into him" (159). The Muslim man, whose sensations we can only vaguely and chillingly intuit, claims to feel "like a woman" (160), which also accurately reflects the Abu Ghraib prisoners' interpretation of their guards' intentions; in the words of a former prisoner, "They wanted us to feel as though we are women, the way women feel, and this is the worst insult, to feel like a woman" (qtd. in Kaufman-Osborn 610).

This complex gender dynamic contributes to the novel's dramatization of sexuality and sexual cruelty within a broader pattern of cruelty of the kind that can, according to Gary Wihl, serve a "moral function" (483).[17]

Yet the pornographic explicitness of the text, which invites us to interpret the widow as merely an embittered, wanton dominatrix, almost entirely overshadows the subtler sexual dynamic I am articulating here. Interpretations of the Abu Ghraib photographs featuring female guards harassing male prisoners have been similarly oversimplified. As Laura Frost aptly observes in relation to the photographs of Lynndie England, despite media discussions of female sadism that began soon after the publication of the images, sadomasochism does not describe the dynamic between the petite woman and the prisoner she holds on a leash. "There are no snarls, leers, or postures of intimidation," Frost remarks, "and none of the slack-jawed ecstasy, eye-narrowing cruelty, or lip-licking excitement of female pornographic types" ("Photography/Pornography/Torture" 138). As the widow herself declares, to characterize her excitement as "arousal felt cheap. The colors of her feelings ranged so far beyond the sexual" (*After* 146). But even though the range of emotions depicted here may exceed the strictly sexual, it is on the foundation of sexuality that the novel is built, in ways that are unique in post-9/11 literature. Of course *After* is not the first post-9/11 novel to speculate on the links between sexuality and death; see, for instance, the sexual interludes at Ground Zero in Jay McInerney's *The Good Life* or the short-lived affair between two WTC evacuees in Don DeLillo's *Falling Man*. But Tristram uniquely locates sexuality in the rifts between race, moral nationalism, and identity formation.

An important reason why the sexuality manifested in this novel represents more than mere sex is, paradoxically, that it also represents quite a lot less. The lovers feel nothing of the stimulating verve and pathos usually distinguishing sexual intercourse, nor do they experience intimacy. The man passively succumbs to the woman's attacks, without demur but also without enjoyment, and the woman fails to emerge as either an empathetic or thoroughly despicable character. Far from liberating, the revenge she tries to enact is enslaving and unsettling, and it infuses the narrative with an ambiguity of both intent and expression. Partly this ambiguity stems from the intoxicating, undisguised imbalance of power between the two characters, the widow rejoicing in the plight of her lover "at the mercy of her beneficence" (126). Yet it is also the upshot of her profound refusal to feel and of her conviction that emotion would signal a betrayal of her late husband. As a consequence the sexual act degenerates into a series of inhibitions and denials: "I want to be sad, she thought. I should be sad. These love acts should mean nothing more to me than memories of the grave. I will not be moved. I will not be confused. I will be calm. I must never be moved again. If I am moved again I will forget my husband, which I must never do" (59). The man experiences a similar self-imposed prohibition. He perceives the incipient sexual attraction between him and the widow as not only metaphorically entwined with death, but also linked to the deaths at the root of their respective traumas. Ultimately, then, the attraction between the two indicates not only a propensity for self-flagellation but also a fragile emotional connection that is constantly in danger of either not starting or of disappearing unexpectedly: "Something was going to happen here. Something he didn't understand. We are poised on the edge, he thought. A moment like this comes just before taking vows. Just before dying. Committed, but not yet set in motion" (56).

Another reason why sex in this novel is never simply about the physical act emerges from the widow's refusal to separate her pleasure from her pain, and *his* pain from her pleasure. Whether the Muslim man is "the instrument of her destruction, or her salvation" matters little to her: "What division could be made between the two, after all? What difference between suffering and ecstasy, civilization and savagery, brutality and tenderness?" (156). The boundaries between erotic contact and sexual torture are extremely tenuous here. In making love to the man, the widow reaches toward an interior space where sexual desire and the desire for cruelty are coterminous: "She dove more deeply inside herself and touched the idea of violence, lightly, in her mind, and saw how attractive violence was to her, how she longed to be above this man, to have him crouched below, compliant, barely murmuring" (58–59). Casual sexuality, which often implies pain without foregrounding it, thriving as it does on the cruel negation of attachment in oneself or in the other, may also be seen as the focal point through which the experience of terrorism is communicated. As minor aftershocks to 9/11, the sexual acts described here fold the cruelty of terrorism within the anonymous, ordinary cruelties of eroticism.

A third reason why sexuality in *After* provokes reflection on issues extending far beyond physical desire lies in the novel's unperturbed refusal to talk about anything *but* sex. "The one characteristic by which a 'Freudian reading' is generally recognized is its insistence on sexuality, on its crucial place and role in the text," Shoshana Felman writes ("Turning the Screw" 103). Even without closely following a Freudian interpretive pattern, sexuality in this novel is impossible to overstate. Yet what prompts a psychoanalytic reading, Felman suggests, is not so much the sexual content of a novel as its ambiguity. All three solicitors of psychoanalytic questioning identified by Felman (erotic vocabulary, abnormal happenings, and elliptic narrative) are in evidence here. Felman also acknowledges that sexuality, ambiguity, and narrative incompleteness are in fact related and mutually enhancing. The point of Tristram's narrative is thus not that the story "won't tell . . . not in any literal, vulgar way," as Henry James puts it in *The Turn of the Screw*, but that literality and sexual explicitness in particular are essential ingredients of what "telling" means. In Felman's words, "The question here is less that of the meaning *of* sexuality than that of a complex *relationship between sexuality and meaning*; a relationship which is not a simple *deviation* from literal meaning, but rather, a *problematization of literality as such*" (110). Knowledge itself as the ultimate purpose of reading (knowledge of the Other and from the Other) is therefore both epistemological and carnal (158). Tristram's widow performs her "reading" of the Other through sexual torture and interrogation, meticulously questioning the interlocked dynamics of violence and power through what may be seen as a silent (albeit intensely communicative) enactment of the talking cure.

Far from overwriting a Freudian reading, to analyze this novel ethically, as I do here, in fact confirms Felman's diagnosis of the ambiguity of sexuality, even in its most literal, "vulgar" forms. The ambiguous paradox of *After* is that sexual intercourse remains so inscrutable despite being so overtly described. The novel is a crushing rebuke to the kind of psychoanalytic criticism that limits narratives with a sexual subtext to "simply sex" in much the same way that it is a rebuke to scholarship that simplifies post-9/11 literature to "9/11 novels." "Sexuality," Felman writes, "is precisely *what rules out simplicity as such*," containing instead "the violence of its own division and self-contradiction... experienced as anxiety and lived as terror" (111). An ethical and a psychoanalytic reading thus share an investment in the text's structural desire for fulfillment and its constitutive failure to attain it. If Felman is right and sexuality indeed denotes "meaning *as* division, meaning *as* conflict" (112), then the ethics of *After* are virtually indistinguishable from its sexual plot—the *sex* preventing the text from making *sense*, engendering instead a deeply ethical conflict of interpretations.

By embedding the sexual plot within a larger racial and political context I want to show exactly how the sexual "meaning" of the novel becomes ethical in ways that emphasize the divisiveness and contradiction of post-9/11 literature as well as the provisional nature of reading literature for the "9/11 plot"—as conflicted and discordant a trope as sexuality itself. Even though sex is so prominent in this novel, it never manages to obscure the other themes that timidly attach to it: the abuses of the media cashing in on the widow's public pain, terrorism, and racial discrimination after 9/11. There is even a suggestion that the two lovers exploit the cruelty of terrorism as a means of heightening their own sexual pleasure. After their adventurous dinner in the company of an outspoken American racist, they even appear to dismiss the racism around them as part of their own sexual play, a rejuvenating force that stirs their excitement, thus subtly denaturalizing post-9/11 revenge discourses and exposing their captivating sexual underpinnings in ways that the Abu Ghraib abuses have emphatically reinforced. If the sexual rituals do not erase the pain of racialization, they at least transform it from endured suffering to *inflicted* suffering, from posttraumatic working-through back to the moment of violent impact—in Shklar's words, from misfortune to injustice. This transitive kind of cruelty becomes constitutive of post-9/11 racial issues and of the (white) American construction of self.

Sexuality and Racial Formation

The widow initially strikes the reader as a privileged white woman, insulated from the realities of race and unwilling to consider them until her husband is brutally murdered. Even after the encounter with the Muslim man, for a long time this protective sheath around her remains intact. Yet the sexual dynamic between the two clearly hinges on their racialized identities. Indeed the greater the widow's resentment of the Muslim man as abject Other, the more intense her physical attachment to him. What surfaces here is a Freudian principle of overcompensation: when "the hostile attitude has no prospect of satisfaction," Freud writes in *The Ego and the Id*, "it is replaced by a loving attitude for which there is more prospect of satisfaction—that is, possibility of discharge" (42). The man recognizes the widow's skewed self-image as a destructive trait, one that signals her belonging to what Shklar calls "unjust people," who "suffer from disordered psyches and are tormented by driving desires and rages that they are unable to satisfy or control" (*The Faces of Injustice* 29). His submissive attitude stems, in part, from a desire to expose this cruel streak in her (putting cruelty first by sacrificing his own body to the performance of cruelty) and to help her overpower her racial prejudices and misconceptions.

Yet the widow doesn't perceive it as in the least unjust or unsettling that race should determine her physical attraction to this man. As "the only man of his kind who had ever touched her," the Muslim lover allows her to imagine "that she could glimpse a kind of primitive and barbaric beauty in his features, a fierceness, and it exhilarated her to be so close to its source. It helped not to look at him too closely, or to think about her motives too directly" (99). She is convinced that the man is not only Muslim but an Arab, and falls asleep when he begins to explain that he is Persian and "not particularly religious . . . the most secular sort of Muslim you're ever going to meet" (81). Certainly the man has suffered racial discrimination after September 11 and openly resents the way many of his fellow citizens "collapse all differences and hurts into a single feeling, which could flare up and consume any innocent in its path" (121). Since the attacks he has tiptoed through life "shrouded in a sense of profound apology, careful with his words and deeds" (52). Aware of his precarious position and of the undirected anger raging around him, he is initially surprised that even though "he could walk through crowds and feel the bodies shy away from him," the widow, "she of all people" (69), would want to touch him after "he had lost his mystery and his aura of the forbidden and had become bland, unattractive, sexless" (18) to most other women due to his racial appearance.

The widow senses his surprise and realizes that her approach to the affair is racist and blatantly unethical. To her friends—even to the most promiscuous and undiscerning of them—she would "need to say the Muslim was a German or a Brazilian, to avoid the shock of it, the perversity of it, . . . she was doing something so dishonest, so questionable, that she couldn't speak of it with even the least morally demanding of her friends" (100). Yet she preserves a veneer of authenticity and outspoken guilt about being "an ugly, bigoted woman" (128), reiterating this assessment in such a way that the man can only politely disagree (to humor and soothe her). In response to her simplifying racial calculus, he encourages her to ignore his racial alterity and regard him as "an individual" (132) rather than as the emblem of a politically disreputable group, even if only for one night. To the widow, however, "it's the context that matters" (133): in the absence of racial and political markers, her adventure would be far less transgressive, ethically innocuous, and therefore not worth her time. Selecting a secluded hotel as the location for their tryst might suggest her willingness to break away from context, yet the widow (literally) tethers the man to his context as a means of escaping her own. The cruelty of her behavior thus resides in her unwillingness to free her partner from such contexts, a refusal that may be traced back to the death of her husband, who lost his life not as an individual but as a Jew, a racial scapegoat.

Treating the Muslim man as if he were not Muslim would have amounted to what Shklar terms the democracy of everyday life, a form of egalitarianism that does not arise from sincerity but from the morally correct "pretense that we must speak to each other as if social standings were a matter of indifference in our views" (*Ordinary Vices* 77). What the

Muslim man requires of the widow, then, is nothing but a "formal" appearance of respect, to which all victims of discrimination and scapegoating after 9/11 are entitled. The entire sexual ritual described in the novel appears from this perspective as an aborted attempt to shore up moral pretenses and anchor them physically in a way that temporarily resolves cultural distinctions and mimics a liberal disposition. The failure to uphold this respectful indifference is the source of cruelty, the *summum malum* that suffuses, according to Shklar, all of collective and individual human life. In much the same way that Shklar is concerned with avoiding evil rather than fostering good, Tristram focuses on the ordinary victims of terrorism, on cruelty and its avatars in daily life. Beyond a post-9/11 hint, little historical specificity is conveyed by the novel's title, yet the events of Abu Ghraib situate the novel's thematic and formal cruelty on the border of private and public victimization, as a relation between history and the body in ways that reveal the ethical potential of literature as at once enabled and circumscribed by historical context. *After* does not provide a conceptual solution to the problem of cruelty, nor does it offer much consolation, but it does take the measure of this predicament much more courageously than any other work of post-9/11 fiction. It is to the circuits of transference through which political and libidinal cruelty is simultaneously situated and deferred, in Tristram as in McGrath, that I now turn.

Power Politics

After is a novel without guaranteed meaning, a novel that might have attracted much less attention had it not been for the complex mediation network of which it has now become a part. This is not to diminish the value of the narrative on the level of individual pathology as much as to insist that the text is best understood within the broader dynamics of post-9/11 politics and power. It is not merely that the widow's sexual power over her lover makes her cruel, nor that her power is accompanied by or even requires cruelty. Quite simply her cruelty, her willed amorality, *is* her power, *is* the means by which she selects her victim, seduces him, and greets him after a night of confused sexual interplay with the conjecture that all she feels for him is tenderness—a statement as absurd as it is cruel, bespeaking not merely her detachment from reality but also a callous indifference in her selection of words, feelings, and actions when the situation might require more discernment. Similarly the shock provoked by the Abu Ghraib images, especially those of Lynndie England, resides in the cruelty of the woman and that of the camera, above and beyond questions of gender or pornography.

In Patrick McGrath's "Ground Zero," cruelty attains a level of psychological refinement unmatched in Tristram's novel, the latter exploring the etiology of cruelty as an ordinary vice rather than assessing its more abstract, allegorical subtleties. To span a bridge between the scapegoating ethics of McGrath's narrative and Tristram's story of unbridled and ill-conceived desire for revenge, I have framed the novel within the ideological mode of liberalism and its emphasis on exposing and denouncing cruelty. Not incidentally in both texts this cruelty is overtly sexual. The two narratives are clearly in tune with each other and linked by their reliance on subtle interplays between sexuality, politics, and psychoanalysis. At first glance the balance in "Ground Zero" seems weighted in favor of the psychoanalytic, whereas *After* appears most concerned with the tensions and ambivalence of sexual relations. However, a detail that shouldn't pass unnoticed is that McGrath locates Kim Lee's sexual escapades and the 9/11 attacks within the same temporal node and squarely at the heart of the analyst's concerns. And although her novel is sustained almost exclusively by a sexual act, Tristram does imply the psychoanalytical relation, albeit by exclusion. "Psychoanalysis is about what two people can say to each other if they agree not to have sex," Adam Phillips writes (Bersani and Phillips viii), and *After*'s agreement is obviously not psychoanalytic. While "Ground Zero" engages its implied reader as "working through" both the content of analytic transference and her own use of this transference as a form of resistance to trauma, Tristram's racy narrative strikes an extrapsychoanalytic chord ultimately inspired by psychoanalysis as a general mode of exchange. Tristram in fact confirms and completes a new relationality of which McGrath reveals only the merest soupçon, thus dramatizing the use of analysis as a "disposable catalyst" (Bersani and Phillips 10) on the path toward a physically intimate yet ethically impersonal human rapport, whose primary responsibility lies not with the Other but with intimacy itself.

The widow's racial experiment and, by extrapolation, the novel's ethical investment are thus best understood as a dramatization of Lacan's ethical question "Have you acted in conformity with the desire that is in you?" as the opposite pole of traditional ethics, which demands an Aristotelian "cleaning up of desire, modesty, temperateness" (314). "The morality of power," Lacan writes, "is as follows: 'As far as desires are concerned, come back later. Make them wait'" (315). Tristram inverts this tidied-up, ideal order to reveal the violent topologics of desire and the obligation of not giving ground relative to this desire, no matter what irresponsible forms our fidelity to desire might take. "There is no other good," Lacan insists, "than that which may serve to pay the price for access to desire" (321); Tristram's novel examines this accessibility through the prism of sexual longing, placing desire at the heart of the mental and physical economy of ethics. While McGrath's analyst is left confused by her inability to access the meaning of the terrorist attacks and the meaning of Dan's actions as the metonym of the attacks' broader significance, Tristram's widow undergoes a visceral experience that renders Otherness tangible by enlarging the pores of her own sensorial communication with her own libidinal self.

From this perspective the widow and her lover endure "the drama of misaimed desire endemic to the sexual relation . . . to emerge on the other end of the sexual" (Bersani and Phillips 27) and affirm what Bersani calls "the indispensable concept of an *im*personal narcissism" (56). Rather than merely dramatizing the sinister exploitation of an innocent person through the benignly normativized one-night-stand plot, *After* interrogates and redirects the dualism of aggression and sexual intimacy through which the Abu Ghraib abuses can be encoded as a symptom of sadistically motivated and sexually satisfying imperial narcissism. This self-destructive narcissism, Bersani argues, is "never more visible than at those moments when a nation or empire appears to be at the height of its power—for example, at the current moment of American power" (68). Without engaging explicitly with imperialist power, Tristram imagines the ego "hyperbolizing itself" (Bersani and Phillips 70) and explores how its destructive rage might be forestalled not by the rational guard of a moral superego, but by what Bersani calls "a nondestructive eroticizing of the ego" (72) as a precondition of love—not in the romantic sense, which the novel evidently disdains, but as a new form of ethical relation.

Part of the problem with romantic love and its conventional morality is that we are expected to love others "for themselves," that is, for their Otherness. Yet the assumption that in love we are more open to Otherness has been disproved by psychoanalysis (by both Freud and Lacan). And whereas love doesn't automatically make us more responsive to the Other, sex, paradoxically, might. Through sex as imagined by Tristram and Bersani, the ego establishes an impersonal relationship in which the Other is divested of Otherness (in other words, taken out of context, as both Kim Lee and the Persian man are by their respective lovers) and embraced, however briefly or precariously, for their sameness—that is, their ability to satisfy or play out the ego's impersonal desires. This is a risky narrative gesture sustained by the formal devices of both McGrath's and Tristram's texts, whose cool self-awareness—a kind of impersonal narcissism in itself—is a vicious retort to the optimistic attempts in a large segment of post-9/11 writing to manufacture naïve empathy and sentimentalism as a response to the brutality of the attacks and of the War on Terror. To some extent the model of transference subconsciously informs other post-9/11 narratives that have little to do with psychoanalysis, as in Pat Barker's *Double Vision*, where vicarious trauma is used to develop an analogy between ethics and the process of falling in love (see chapter 4). Yet McGrath and Tristram add astounding nuance to the idea of what *counts* as love, and how love originates in—is indeed unimaginable in the absence of—a substratum of hyperbolic and self-consuming narcissism.

In *Narcissism and the Literary Libido* Marshall Alcorn contends that "the central focus for rhetorical study should not be language exclusively, but should include the relations between language and libidinal structures" (4). In its crudest sense, libido denotes sexual involvement, a component that infuses the psychodynamics of *After* and "Ground Zero," where the ethical stakes of writing are entwined with an erotics of literature. Supporting a wide array of libidinal investments is narcissism or self-love, a concept that seems especially interesting to ethics and cannot be divorced from the self-image presupposed or created by the ethical act. "Apparently the most private and individual of psychological forces," Alcorn writes, narcissism "is also the most social, because it marks the self's most fundamental response to an image of otherness. It is the primary force working at the cutting edge of the self's differing from itself" (16). Despite its attachment to self-identity and its implicit resistance to change, it is often the libidinal force of narcissism that emerges as a form of infinite desire to sustain the ethics of impersonal solipsism proposed by Bersani and Tristram. The desire of the woman and of the narrative that struggles to contain this desire "may be in excess of any object's capacity to satisfy it" (Bersani and Phillips 104), yet this insatiability is precisely what binds it to an ethical demand. The ethical subject, since Levinas and Critchley, has shaped itself in relation to an imperative that can never be adequately met. Likewise Tristram's novel seems to grope desperately for the sort of climax that its priapic excitement, by definition, cannot offer.

This excitement begs recognition (and even identification) through transference, which directly implicates the reader as impersonal witness to a spare narrative whose actants have been pried loose from the contexts in which a human life is normally embedded. What ensues is an overpowering feeling of shame that evacuates the self and, with it, the widow's power over her perverse plot, as well as our own control over the narrative and over the set of expectations in which we are tempted to frame it. "In shame the personal is beginning to give way," Phillips writes, and the abjection, the mortification, the humiliation is a literal form of self-holding" (Bersani and Phillips 115). The consolidation of selfhood through its dissolution, what Dorothy Hale refers to as self-binding, also defines the ethical project of Tristram's novel. Its spareness, remoteness, and hypersexualized mechanics are not the story's formal envelope but its very essence. After setting out to have sex with an Arab man (who turns out to be Persian), the widow attains a degree of intimacy with her lover that renders personal identity, both his and hers, entirely superfluous.

The political consequences of such intimacy on the geostrategic macro level are, Bersani avers, "enormous" (Bersani and Phillips 124), yet neither he nor Tristram offers any clues as to what they might be. Indeed the very process of reading literary texts as easily apprehensible symptoms of the political—as, in Žižek's words, "the point of emergence of the truth about social relations" (*The Sublime Object* 26)—is controversial and has recently been criticized as "an ethical problem because it eradicates dimensions of alterity particular to art, making any encounter with the difficulty and strangeness of aesthetic experience seem beside the point" (Dean 23). In many ways, despite its willed racial and political brazenness, Tristram's novel succumbs to, even extols an ethics of equivocation, as if rebelling against the notion that post-9/11 literature must inevitably respond to the sociocultural conditions of the post-9/11 age. *After* remains enigmatic, so enigmatic in fact as to appear indifferent to its own status as a work of literature on a highly politicized subject, conceding that the various alterities depicted in the book remain untranslatable and largely impervious to an accurate political decoding. I have tried to honor this hermeneutic enigma by reading the book from a perspective that is partial and nondefinitive, prioritizing cruelty (the "form" of the political rather than its content) in ways that only deepen the mystery of this text.

As Tim Dean observes, "Otherness is a property of discourse, and the enigmas of otherness are exacerbated by art. We might even say that art's purpose lies in intensifying those aspects of alterity that otherwise remain dormant in everyday discourse and conventional intersubjective communication" (38). To align aesthetic and intersubjective alterity from within a culture that is not politically alien (we identify with the storyteller, or at least aren't stumped by a jarring unfamiliarity in her voice) is the hallmark of this text's centrality to the post-9/11 canon. From this perspective the political importance of Tristram's novel is secured precisely by the random, morally inexplicable cruelty dramatized in this book (and later literalized at Abu Ghraib) by an author we encounter for the first time and by a protagonist whose sexual desire to "put cruelty first"—that is, above the personal and the self—we might be tempted to dismiss as a frustratingly absurd scenario on the psychological "unmaking" of torture and trauma. *After* takes huge risks (as do the fictions I discuss in the next chapter), above all by inviting the accusation that its sensationalized sexuality might mitigate the reprehensibility of racialized violence. Rather, through its reckless engagement with cruelty as ordinary vice and with the impersonal narcissism of desire, *After* offers guidance on literature's transference of world-historical trauma into the personal realm, on how an ethical hermeneutics might countertransfer the personal into the political, and on the ways we can work through this aesthetic trauma by depersonalizing the opposition between self and Other and by becoming more attuned to the situational connectivity by which they might become intimately strange bedfellows.

3. MORAL CRUSADES

Race, Risk, and Walt Whitman's Afterlives

The changes wrought by the terrorist attacks of September 11 to our collective understanding of race, risk, and their correlation have been dramatic. In the immediate aftermath of those events, a nationwide system of social control was put into motion, aimed largely at racial, ethnic, and religious outsiders in ways that fed on and further fueled the confusion and the desire for retaliation of the American population at large. Fear of and the need for protection against outsiders of all kinds were on everybody's minds as all struggled to make sense of what the attacks would mean for the future of the nation and for their own personal lives—two discrete realms that suddenly became deeply interconnected. Central to this post-catastrophic climate was a sense of perplexity and disorientation about the structural failures that had led to such a major fissure in the social system, resulting in frustrations that were ultimately channeled into the War on Terror. In the previous chapter I examined the ethics and aesthetics of retributive fictions and racial scapegoating in texts whose perspectives were signally white and, as such, governed by moralistic idioms of innocence and victimization. In this chapter I seek to offer a fine-grained analysis of racial perceptions as they manifest themselves across a range of post-9/11 fictions that trouble the ethics of victimization from the opposite end of its racial binarism: the perspective of the stigmatized Other. Once investigated, I believe, these underexamined works, particularly those by ethnic American writers, can help unpack the role of literature in responding to the erosion of human rights and civil liberties in the War on Terror.

A chief limitation of post-9/11 fiction, Richard Gray has convincingly demonstrated, resides in its failed or absent "encounters with strangeness." According to Gray, writing since September 11 hasn't yet risen to the important challenge of "facing the other, in all its difference and danger," a challenge that needs to be met "not just because of obscene acts of terrorism committed by a small group of people, but because the U.S. has become, more than ever, a border territory in which different cultures meet, collide, and in some instances collude with each other" (135). Yet to project an insular worldview onto post-9/11 fiction as a whole would be to overlook what may be called "the second wave" of post-9/11 novels, which clearly attempts to deal with America's liminal position between historical borders and cultures. Specifically these novels are more intently focused on the racial fear and anxiety sparked by the attacks (and by the official response to them) in the lives and minds of people previously inured to the domestic repercussions of distant international affairs.

In the aftermath of the terrorist attacks, a national rhetoric fueled by misconstrued patriotism rushed to vilify and marginalize persons of an allegedly suspicious racial makeup through what I call moral racialization, a strategy that informs the first three novels I examine here: Chitra Divakaruni's *Queen of Dreams*, Ken Kalfus's *A Disorder Peculiar to the Country*, and Laila Halaby's *Once in a Promised Land*. I argue that American literature after 9/11 has replaced the moral discourse around race with a more ambivalent ethical approach that coheres around risk as key to the cultural animosities of late modernity. Significantly racial profiling is folded within and partly defused by this conceptualization of risk. My approach assumes a difference between morality (referring to the set of values prescribed by a particular community or situation) and ethics (the broader philosophy that investigates the principles behind moral judgment), a distinction that establishes the moral as a subset of the ethical (B. Williams 6). I want to use this partial distinction between morality and ethics to define the problematic overlap between racial profiling and discourses of risk.

While Divakaruni's and Halaby's novels only obliquely invoke accident and coincidence to mitigate racial determinism, the novels I discuss in the second part of this chapter—Gayle Brandeis's *Self Storage* and Michael

Cunningham's *Specimen Days*—more clearly stage the transition from racial formation to risk as a way of harnessing and defusing post-9/11 social tensions. This second section lays out my understanding of an ethics of risk in more detail, a concept that I regard in a broad political context as well as from a narratological perspective. In linking the two sections I turn to Mohsin Hamid's novel *The Reluctant Fundamentalist*, in which I discern a form of reverse racial profiling that adulterates the threat emanating from race and helpfully flags corporate policy as a model for the kinds of risk management mobilized in the War on Terror.

Interestingly both Brandeis and Cunningham invoke the works of Walt Whitman as an axis around which national (and occasionally nationalist) discourses rotate. *Self Storage* and *Specimen Days* use Whitman as a historical springboard to pinpoint the dangers that average Americans encounter in their daily lives, outlining a post-9/11 riskscape that complicates what the German sociologist Ulrich Beck refers to as the "risk society" of late modernity (9). Yet these two writers' interest in generalized risk is at the same time part of a denial strategy that ignores the more specific dangers associated with the use and abuse of racial profiling. This lends support to my claim that post-9/11 fiction is not simply cognizant of the racialization of the War on Terror, but to some extent is also complicit with its strategies, reinforcing the subliminal influence of race on counterterrorist practices through a paradoxical, tacit neglect of this influence. It is its complicity with the workings of contemporary culture that advances our understanding of post-9/11 literature, incites us to examine its ethical function, and singles these novels out from among other racially informed fictions making up the "second wave" of the 9/11 genre.

Other novels than the ones discussed here address racial issues in twenty-first-century America, while not explicitly scrutinizing the ways post-9/11 fiction is entangled with the discourse of the War on Terror.[1] Joseph O'Neill's *Netherland* celebrates a multiracial post-9/11 New York "overrun with South Asians" (78), where the idea of a Cricket Club promises to "start a whole new chapter in U.S. history" (211). In his response to Richard Gray's assessment of post-9/11 literature, Michael Rothberg in fact proposes *Netherland* as precisely the kind of fiction Gray would like to see more of, one that "places earlier stories of American self-invention . . . in a fully globalized terrain" ("A Failure of the Imagination" 156). Yet even in this world astir with dreams and possibilities, where persistence equals success, the 9/11 attacks instill in the protagonist "an awful enfeebling fatalism, a sense that the great outcomes were but randomly connected to our endeavors" (O'Neill 30), which strongly resembles the kind of risk perception and powerlessness described by Brandeis and Cunningham.

In Lorrie Moore's *A Gate at the Stairs*, a novel more broadly concerned with race in twenty-first-century America, the issue of post-9/11 racial fear that cuts both ways (Americans and Arabs are equally fearful of each other) looms subterraneally as a sort of narrative sleeper cell. The novel unspectacularly exposes the suspicious "Brazilian" whom the protagonist has been dating as an Islamofascist whose repetitive anti-American diatribes sound like "Gertrude Stein speaking from inside a burka" (210): "Do you believe an entire country could embark on a spiritual mistake? . . . Do you believe an entire country could *be* a spiritual mistake?" (191). Hardly has this revelation taken place when the plot moves on to the challenges of biracial adoption in America. Post-9/11 paranoia and racial stigmatization are treated here as merely a local flare-up on the larger map of U.S. racism.[2] In other words, rather than mark a milestone in the national history of racial formation, in Moore's novel the post-9/11 War on Terror merely crystallizes deeply entrenched regimes of political differentiation based on moral binarisms of the simplest kind, the kind that the novels I discuss here seek to interrogate.

By examining these novels I aim to show how they juxtapose a moralistic understanding of post-9/11 racial fear on the one hand and an ambiguous ethics of risk (supported by narratives of contingency), which obscures a more easily condemnable moral racialization, on the other hand. A more general feature of the ways post-9/11 fiction addresses race should be noted here, a feature that characterizes most of the texts discussed in this chapter and inevitably inflects the tenor of my analysis. The authors of these novels tend to display a barely inchoate awareness of race as a major component of the War on Terror; their fictions are not always in full control of the race subject, occasionally obfuscating or marginalizing it. Yet these failings are significant for what they imply about the nature of the War on Terror itself: hesitant, operating with what Lorrie Moore would call "energetic adhoccery" (184). When classic forms of racism are reworked into less clearly defined plausibility principles, risk rather than race becomes the currency of suspicion, and the fictions discussed here appropriately lean in this direction. The purpose of my analysis is to delineate this development and articulate some ethical concerns about its modus operandi on a narrative and cultural level.

Moral Racialization and the War on Terror: Divakaruni, Kalfus, Halaby

In 2007, after several years in which Arab Americans and Arab-looking individuals were indiscriminately rounded up and detained, often without evidence or due process, the international security scholar David Mutimer trenchantly concluded, "The discourse of the war on terror ... is extensively racialized. It has articulated its enemy as people identifiable not just by their religion, as important as that obviously is to their representation, but more particularly by their (racial) appearance" (173). What further reinforces the salience of visible ethnicity in an examination of Arab American identity after September 11 is that prior to the attacks, the Arab American community was largely, in Nadine Naber's words, "the 'invisible' racial/ethnic group" ("Ambiguous Insiders" 37) of the United States. The Palestinian American scholar Lisa Suhair Majaj aptly summarized this ambiguous categorization shortly before the 9/11 attacks: "Arab Americans occupy a contested and unclear space within American racial and cultural discourse. Although classified as 'white' by current government definitions, they are conspicuously absent from discussions of white ethnicity, and are popularly perceived as non-white" (329). This situation was fundamentally changed by the 9/11 events and the panic they generated. As the critical race scholar Steven Salaita has noted, with the beginning of the War on Terror, "Arab Americans evolved from invisible to glaringly conspicuous (whether or not the conspicuousness was welcomed)" (74) and often became the victims of racial violence.

Violence motivated by hate, especially aimed at innocent Middle Easterners and South Asians, indeed represents one of the earliest and most vivid manifestations of the War on Terror. Propelled primarily by tremendous and unchecked outrage over the 9/11 attacks, this wave of violence included the murder on October 4, 2001, of Vasudev Patel, a forty-nine-year-old Indian, at his convenience store in Mesquite, Texas. The perpetrator, Mark Stroman, who unrepentantly located his deed in the context of a generalized "war" and confessed to having murdered the Indian "in retaliation," was also responsible for the murder of a Pakistani in Dallas and was ultimately convicted and sentenced to death (Welch 63). His victims were selected "solely because they shared or were perceived as sharing the national background or religion of the hijackers and al-Qaeda members deemed responsible for attacking the World Trade Center and the Pentagon" (Human Rights Watch 3). As the criminal justice scholar Michael Welch observes, the FBI recorded a seventeen-fold increase in anti-Muslim crimes nationwide during 2001 (66–67), with the worst crimes occurring in the months immediately following 9/11. Significantly for my purposes in this discussion, such racial crimes ranged from vandalism and arson to verbal taunting, employment discrimination, and hassling at airports, to assault and murder, and were often perpetrated against Arab-*looking* American citizens rather than genuine Middle Easterners. Each of these crimes, barring murder, features in the novels by Chitra Divakaruni, Laila Halaby, and Mohsin Hamid.

The division of the world into good and evil as proposed by the Bush administration in the days leading up to the invasion of Afghanistan and the start of the War on Terror culminated in what may be called moral racialization, that is, the articulation of a racially suspicious enemy figure propagated through the visual media and intended to absorb and redirect as much public resentment as possible.[3] Moral racialization as I understand it relies on the group dynamics of moral panic, amplifying already entrenched patterns of racial intolerance.[4] While in the previous chapter

I outlined the psychosexual mechanisms underpinning the vilification of racial scapegoat figures, in reading stories narrated from the perspective of these ersatz villains I want to understand the perception of racial profiling and counterterrorism within the targeted communities themselves.

But before I proceed to read Divakaruni and Halaby as voices of dissent and warning against the erosion of civil liberties, I must first point out that even though scholars described the War on Terror as "a form of racial, civilizational knowledge" (Puar and Rai, "Monster, Terrorist, Fag" 122) at a fairly early stage, literature was initially slow to accept that practices of mass scapegoating (rather than, say, individual revenge fantasies) were worth narrative investigation. And even though the images of prisoner abuse at Abu Ghraib inflected the reception of post-9/11 fiction (such as Claire Tristram's novel *After*, as the previous chapter has shown), they had little impact on other narratives, at least until the publication of Ken Kalfus's *A Disorder Peculiar to the Country*. This novel about the violent death throes of a marriage that has lost its savor and turned hateful goes off at a tangent in its final section, where it establishes a parallel between private and political conflict through a shocking sexual reenactment of racialized spectatorship in the context of torture at Abu Ghraib.

I am not the first to observe that the Abu Ghraib images recall the pictures snapped at public lynchings in the American South from the 1880s through the 1930s, typically featuring the naked, mutilated bodies of black men dangling from trees.[5] These images usually also show townspeople milling about, grinning or pointing, just as the pictures taken at Abu Ghraib include American soldiers in jarring dispositions ranging from boredom to downright amusement. Writing about how the Abu Ghraib photographs were discussed in the media, Steven Salaita rightly notes that "the racism of the abuses was hardly mentioned." His plausible suspicion is that "most politicians and media commentators kept silent about the possibility of a racialist dynamic in Abu Ghraib because it would have meant at least tacitly acknowledging a racialist dynamic in the American decision to invade Iraq" (190). The racial symbolism that was almost universally overlooked in the media—that of a brown prisoner subdued on a leash and dehumanized by a white captor—appears for the first time in

Kalfus's blaxploitation scene. Kalfus also reenacts the more specific feminine symbolism inherent in the Lynndie England episode, which features a female master as an emblem of colonial discourse, thus echoing Salaita's estimation (also resonant with Cunningham's approach, as we shall see) that "the invasion was a nurturing expression of concern for those whose future is too important to leave in their own hands" (191).

The shocking party episode plays out between a young white male, Nick—wearing a vaguely fascist sunglasses-and-leather-jacket outfit and, as the text specifies, working "in corrections" (210)—and his purported girlfriend, Miss Naomi, who at the moment is sexually abusing "a young guy in a sweatshirt, his hood still up" (211–12). Significantly the victim is black and sports a "supple and unmarked" body, "fine as a piece of statuary" (214), which touches both the aesthetic and sexual sensibilities of the white youngsters witnessing the scene and raucously cheering on Nick's attractive girlfriend, who promptly and expertly fellates the black youth at Nick's request. In the meantime one member of the audience produces "a Bloomingdale's shopping bag" and places it over the boy's head. Now able to focus on the physical reactions of the youth's body rather than being distracted by the contortions (and racial significance) of his face, the audience responds, not unlike some of the guards at Abu Ghraib, with "general laughter, good, easygoing, unironic laughter, the kind of sweet laughter you might hear on a playground" (216). When someone starts to take pictures of the proceedings, enraptured by what might be described as slack-jawed interracial pornography with a voyeuristic, political-bondage twist ("His mouth was open like a gash. A blister of spittle floated at the edge of his lower lip" [217]), Miss Naomi nonchalantly returns the camera's gaze and repeats Bush's much criticized "Mission accomplished" caption for the benefit of the camera and of the live viewers.

Kalfus himself seeks to accomplish here a rather daunting mission: to shift attention from a clinical interest in the deviant sexuality of this act of torture toward its racial aspects. What we see in the War on Terror is the expansion of racial profiling techniques that were perfected on black populations, which is why Kalfus invokes racial echoes after 9/11 that are more likely to elicit a reaction from his readers than contemporary anti-

Arab sentiment. Whether these readers pause to reflect on the black-to-brown genealogy of racialization—considering the marginal significance of the scene for the plot as a whole, as well as the book's worrying use of sarcasm in dealing with the terrorist attacks—is an entirely different matter. But whether literature in general can or is willing to advance an antiracialist agenda is a resonant, if complex question, one that requires us to move beyond the mainstream (white) canon of post-9/11 fiction.

Describing the "major intention" behind her post-9/11 novel *Queen of Dreams*, Chitra Divakaruni confesses that she aimed to "touch people, to have them think about issues they haven't considered before, to make them more compassionate towards other people." This heartfelt statement accurately characterizes the tenor of her book while charitably overestimating its aesthetic effect—if not its moral ambitions, seemingly modeled on a utopian vision of literary ethics. "If I could make the pain and the hope powerful enough in the book," Divakaruni explains, "then maybe I might stop some of the prejudice out there, and have some sort of countereffect to what followed 9/11" (Hong 6). The prejudice she describes refers to rampant racial violence in a post-9/11 America where merely "resembling the enemy literally became a threat to one's life" (Hong 6). Divakaruni's novel outlines the daily pre-9/11 life of Rakhi, a young divorced mother, painter, and coffee shop owner who considers herself Indian in name only and feels more deeply bound to the culture of northern California, which is where she has lived all her life. A second plot strand revolves around her mother's past in Calcutta and the mysteries of her work as a professional interpreter of dreams. A third narrative moment, which intervenes in the book's closing pages, is the hunt for surrogate Arab-looking evildoers even in liberal California in mid-September 2001.

Divakaruni's tale of mistaken identity and racial profiling in post-9/11 America is all the more resonant and, at the same time, problematic in light of the exceptionalist discourse of the "model minority" favored by Asian American immigrant communities and often applied particularly to Southeast Asian Americans. According to Puar and Rai, "This model minority construct is predominantly a reference to economic exceptionalism, upward class mobility, and educational excellence" ("The Remaking"

77). Racial profiling is arguably more evident and disruptive in a community that enjoyed a privileged status before 9/11 and was suddenly subjected to unchecked discrimination after the attacks. Especially because they wear garments that visibly signify their ethnic and cultural belonging (particularly turbans), Southeast Asian Americans attract the attention of a panoptical gaze that fetishizes the insignia of racial identity as tools of surveillance and social discipline. As Puar and Rai have noted, "Since the very first post-9/11 arrest of a turbaned Sikh man, Sher Singh, who was pulled off an Amtrak train in Providence, Rhode Island, turbaned Sikh men have become substitutes for an elusive Osama bin Laden. As this substitute embodiment, Sikhs are a sanctioned hate-crime target" (82). Divakaruni's Asian American protagonists indeed suffer everything from deturbaning to verbal invective, barely managing to escape the crosshairs of grassroots counterterrorist power.

Throughout the novel the protagonist's subconscious obsession with hues of whiteness and the racial ambivalence of diasporic identity informs and energizes her art, particularly two paintings, one produced before the terrorist attacks and one immediately after. The first depicts a man whom she regularly observes (from a distance) in the park; he is dressed, significantly enough, in white, and his fleeting appearances punctuating important events in Rakhi's life lead her to believe he might hold the key to some of its mysteries. Previously "most of her paintings had been about India—an imagined India, an India researched from photographs, because she'd never travelled there" (10)—and the stranger's appearance inevitably makes her wonder whether he might himself be Indian. The challenges she faces in drawing this person ("His body seems stiff and posed; there's something fake about the angle of his neck. And his face—she's been unable to draw it at all" [67]) accentuate her preexisting inability to locate her own identity within the context of her family's cultural heritage. Importantly Rakhi has not inherited her mother's gift for interpreting dreams, a fact that makes her own waking life even more difficult to elucidate.

When she finally gives up on her introspective project, she paints over the man in white completely, leaving only "trees and grass, fallen bark, hanging branches—and behind them, a man-shaped gap of darkness you wouldn't even see if you weren't looking right. A man with his left arm arced high over his head, at once in the picture and absent from it, the final element the painting needed" (90). Having the man's face obstructed from view signals that Rakhi's search for her own identity is still ongoing, albeit temporarily blocked, and in the course of the novel he will make further appearances as the plot of his identity begins to thicken: a witness describes him as "Mediterranean, or maybe Middle Eastern" (100), and Rakhi begins to suspect him of having indirectly caused the car accident in which her mother dies—by (again mysteriously) seducing her mother into following his car into the night and off a highway bridge at full speed. The mysterious stranger's identity and her own appear to be one and the same thing: initially white, then effaced, and finally invisible. After September 11 the man disappears completely, leaving Rakhi to undergo a personal rebirth in the aftermath of total artistic and personal blockage.

The painting she produces after the attacks reveals the shift from a consciously defaced identity to one that ramifies and multiplies. It is an almost lurid, congested representation of post-9/11 hate crimes worthy of Hieronymus Bosch and informed by Rakhi's own experiences after the attacks: the obligation to put up American flags to deflect potential resentment (264); the inexplicable hatred contained in the word *terrorist* in red letters over the name of her store (274); people crossing over to the other side of the street as she walks by, making her feel both "frightening" and "vulnerable" (275); an attack on her coffee house, recently renamed Kurma House International, which leaves her family terrified and wounded (275). The painting helps clarify for Rakhi the cultural particulars of her artistic style, which isn't merely imitative of classic Indian art but is nonconformist and eclectic. The wide social canvas of the image facilitates for her a deterritorialized self-image as both American and foreign, an identity energized by a vague sense of victimization and outrage that, paradoxically, quiets her emotional turmoil:

> She takes out her easel, the first time since September. She closes her eyes and doesn't fight when the images deluge her. . . . She starts

painting them in: a Sikh man shot at a gas station because someone thought he was Middle Eastern; terrified women peering from behind curtains that look like burkhas; Jespal's turban unraveled like a river of blood.... The background is a collage of faces striped red, white and blue. A fist waves a flag so mammoth that if it falls, it'll suffocate them all. The birds have disappeared, their places taken by airplanes. Some crash into buildings. Some drop bombs as easily as insects drop their eggs.... When she stands back to look, the colors and shapes come together in a rush that makes the hairs on her arms stand up. She gives it the only name possible: *You Ain't American*. (279)

The title of the painting originates from an offensive remark directed at Jespal, the young Indian man dating Rakhi's best friend, Bella; it is a remark that the enraged patriots attacking Kurma House International explicitly direct at Jespal on account of his physical appearance. Racially ambiguous faces are clearly no longer an artistic challenge for Rakhi, not since they have become politically salient, demanding rather than resisting representation. If Rakhi's daughter inherited her grandmother's occult abilities—the girl dreams of people trapped in burning buildings before the September 11 attacks (212)—Rakhi herself uses her art to *see* reality more clearly instead of *fore*seeing it. Through this subtle renunciation of pre-viewing and preemption in favor of critical self-analysis and social awareness, *Queen of Dreams* interrogates post-9/11 conceptualizations of vigilance based in violent prevention rather than long-term, introspective therapy. Dreams, premonitions, and statistic profiles that anticipate reality are ultimately useless, Divakaruni suggests, if the problems triggered by real events that we cannot stop (even when we "see" them coming) have the power to overwhelm us.

Like *Queen of Dreams*, Laila Halaby's *Once in a Promised Land* portrays racial profiling and hate crimes, but ultimately develops different and more nuanced conceptualizations of race, visual profiling, hate, and crime. For one thing, at the core of this book is an Arab American couple who are closer to their native Jordan than Rakhi ever was to India and therefore are more likely to stand out as potentially suspect Middle Easterners after 9/11 (they live in Tucson, Arizona). Not quite at home in either Jordan or the United States, Jassim and Salwa struggle to find a place for themselves, and for much of the novel they remain confused and stymied by their mixed identity. Their confusion is further compounded by the "patriotic breathing of those around them" and by what Salwa in particular comes to resent as "those red, white, and blue fingers flapping at her, flicking her away" (184–85). He a hydrologist, she a banker and trainee real estate broker: these are upwardly mobile overachievers living the American Dream who suffer a spectacular downfall when suddenly branded as outcasts.

Halaby prefaces *Once in a Promised Land* with the statement "Salwa and Jassim are both Arabs. Both Muslims. But of course they have nothing to do with what happened to the World Trade Center. Nothing and everything" (viii). And the novel gradually reveals that even though Salwa and Jassim did nothing to provoke the attacks, when they did occur the attacks had a powerful impact on the couple's lives. Because their appearance invites mistrust, a friend of Salwa's offers them American flag decals to announce their patriotic inclinations to any American sufficiently rattled by the terrorist attacks to attempt an act of vengeance (57). In the end both Jassim and Salwa come under personal scrutiny by citizens galvanized by Bush's call to act as the eyes and ears of the government. Salwa, for instance, is verbally assaulted by a bank client, "a native Tucsonan, American born and raised," who prefers to discuss her bank account with someone she can "understand better" (114). With astounding presence of spirit, Salwa offers her the option of a Mexican colleague, an American lesbian teller, or their Chinese director. Yet the point Halaby makes is that after September 11 Arab Americans have fallen one step further behind other social outsiders, being branded not only as second-rate citizens but also as social hazards, "Mahzlims who are just waiting to attack us" (56) and whose plans must be foiled at any price.

This anti-Arab backlash "attempted to urge Arab Americans, before 9/11 generally anti-assimilationist and radical, into total assimilation" (Salaita 78), a strategy that Salaita sees reinforced by the discourse of what he terms imperative patriotism. "Drawn from a longstanding sensibility that nonconformity to whatever at the time is considered to be 'the national interest' is unpatriotic," this repression tactic "generates its strength most consistently at the level of morality" (82–83). It is easy to see how this crucial and discomfiting feature of imperative patriotism—the negotiation of morality—is played out in Halaby's novel: Salwa becomes involved in an affair with Jake, a younger coworker; her husband comes perilously close to having an affair with a waitress; by emigrating to the United States and marrying there, both appear guilty of having dashed the innocent hopes of Hassan, Salwa's childhood sweetheart, for a modest future that rejects America's alluring but destructive promise of wealth. The isolation and condemnation of this couple as foreign and immoral in fact form the gist and main engine of the narrative, which describes a long string of catastrophes culminating with Jassim's termination from his job despite his excellent record with the firm. Of course, Jassim's termination is purportedly based on something other than his racial profile; after all, as Salaita has stated, "imperative patriotism relies on a perceived pragmatism in order to command moral legitimacy" (90). In this case the pragmatism comprises the manager's concern that the suspicion evoked by Jassim in his clients, coupled with Jassim's neglect of his duties as a result of personal troubles, would greatly endanger the position and profitability of his business. These personal troubles consist in Salwa's secret pregnancy and miscarriage, as well as an accident in which Jassim runs over and kills a young boy on a skateboard. As a result of these misfortunes, both of which Jassim could have done nothing to prevent, he begins to neglect his professional duties, thus endangering his position and making it easier for his employer and even for the FBI to single him out as a potential danger to the community.

Salwa similarly strays from what may be considered decent, professional conduct, yet her transgressions carry much more symbolic weight than Jassim's. In her second profession as a real estate agent, she seems complicit in the image of the United States as an agent of territorial infringement and occupation. As Salaita contentiously argues, rather than regard anti-Arab racism as a function of the geopolitical interaction between the Arab and the American worlds, "we are better served looking at that racism as being on a continuum with America's roots in settler colonialism. A correlative settler colonialism in the West Bank, after all, accounts for much of the tension among the United States and Arab nations—and, by extension, Arab Americans" (87). As soon as Salwa breaks explicit professional and marital rules—she sleeps with her young American lover in the pristine bedroom of one of the properties she has been assigned to sell—the metaphor is reversed: the Palestinian woman has entered territory from which she had been excluded and betrayed her status as tolerated guest, both in her native Jordan and in the United States. Tragically for Salwa, her lover feels rebuffed when she fails to abandon her marriage for his sake (opting instead for a provisional return to Jordan), so in a drugged stupor he hurls invective at her, even attacking her physically, seeing in her trip home a return to the "pigsty" (320) from which she came. Coincidentally his own apartment at the moment these words are spoken looks and feels much more like a pigsty than any home of Salwa's, but in Jake's mind at this point in the narrative, race, femininity, and moral power are knotted together. After taunting his desire, Salwa awakens in him only disgust by being unfamiliarly despicable—as an Arab, a woman, a portent of his own moral failure—in ways that Jake cannot begin to untangle.[6]

Appropriately in the atmosphere of squalor and moral defilement that permeates the novel, Jassim arrives at his local gym for his daily swim, "a morning ritual as close to prayer as he could allow" (3), only to have the receptionist inform him that "someone pooped in the pool" (101). Although at this point Jassim hasn't yet attracted the attention of federal authorities, the contamination of the pool seems related to his suspicious presence at the gym, where he is under constant surveillance by a former U.S. marine (with a personal grudge against Jordanians) who seeks to make himself useful to his country again through hypervigilance and racial profiling (173). So although Jassim himself is not responsible for the defilement of the pool, symbolically the stigma attached to that defilement also applies to him. The visit he pays to the mother of the boy he has killed—a visit that places him in a working-class environment where he appears incongruous and ill at ease—presents another opportunity for

Halaby to line up a series of morally abject metaphors, comparing Jassim's invasive presence to germs and malign tumors: "Jassim, child of Jordan, whose feet learned to walk on holy soil, was a beautiful cancerous growth in his pressed dress pants, Armani tie, olive skin, holding a bouquet of lilies to mourn the dead, penance for his enormous sin" (194). In fact as one among several features of the War on Terror, Michael Welch invokes "the need for purification that goes beyond ridding the world of terrorists deemed not only dangerous but also morally tainted" (42). Nor is such a connection between fecal impurity and a morally racialized War on Terror unusual or far-fetched in public discourse. On September 17, 2001, U.S. Representative John Cooksey explained to a network of Louisiana radio stations that anyone "wearing a diaper on his head" should expect to be interrogated as a possible suspect in the investigations of the 9/11 attacks (qtd. in Puar and Rai "Monster, Terrorist, Fag" 137).

The general climate of suspicion percolating through the novel soon acquires criminal and juridical urgency. After his car accident and several tense run-ins with his manager, Jassim is interrogated by two FBI agents who blow things out of proportion and create scenarios whose only purpose is the unequivocal attribution of guilt. Jassim's interrogation takes place in a restaurant, a tightly circumscribed yet public space. The conversation is dominated by the white FBI agents, who confront a racially and socially ambiguous figure as simultaneously a possible terrorist and an ordinary traffic delinquent. The ritual of interrogation is thus acted out with a subject who must both behave normally and effectively defend himself. By imposing a "plot" on Jassim's "story"—teeming with random incidents and unlikely coincidences—the FBI agents effectively reverse the normality/deviance opposition, seeing causality in inexplicable events and failing to find an explanation for occurrences that Jassim considers logical and related. "The FBI is trying to get information on every Arab in the country right now. Our government is at a loss, so they're grasping at straws. Jassim is a straw," Jassim's employer observes with what strongly resembles common sense (269). His ability to view the situation so reasonably does not prevent him, however, from firing the Arab scientist and feeling that he has received confirmation of his suspicion when an article entitled "Engineering Mistakes in the Building of the Twin Towers" (298), of the kind millions of Americans would have read after the attacks, is found on Jassim's desk.

As a result of his unjust marginalization, Jassim begins to regard his surroundings with renewed candor and interest. Suddenly feeling "like a ghost who might vanish at any time without being noticed ... a visitor to this country, to this woman, to this life" (153), he perceives the world from an increasingly detached perspective that grants him insight into aspects of American life to which he had previously given little thought. In contrast to his wife, who can expertly hide her identity as "Palestinian, Muslim, recent mother of buckets of blood" (160) partly by virtue of her deft deployment of sexual exoticism coupled with a strong dose of American-trained professional charm, Jassim feels exposed, as if an eager surveillant eye opened right in front of him, with no possibility of circumvention. If prior to the terrorist attacks he could live his American life "bulldozer style, an Arab in a Mercedes, oblivious of the sizzling around him, the words tossed his way, the puddles of fear and loathing he skirted and stepped through," after September 11, "his diorama sufficiently shaken, he began to see, slowed down, and looked at those looking back. And for the first time he felt unsettled in his beloved America" (165). The massacre of thousands of Americans in the Twin Towers and the Pentagon not only peels "the safety film from people's eyeballs, allowing in what is really there rather than the filtered view through the comfort of routine" (217), but encourages Jassim to return the fearful, loathing gaze of anti-Arab racism and respond not necessarily in kind but in the same style: looking at himself through a hate-tinted lens, he internalizes the racist profiling to which he is outwardly subjected. His work standards slacken, his sense of morality declines steeply, his hitherto balanced and empathetic vision of America suddenly degenerates into a lugubrious view that diagnoses a (largely nomenclatural) social apartheid with "unwelcoming" neighborhoods on one side and "more liberal streets where fear and hatred were disguised" (201) on the other.

Similar images of the racially profiled subject partly internalizing the suspicion, partly gazing back into the oppressive eyeball, structure the perspective taken by Changez, the narrator of Mohsin Hamid's novel *The Reluctant Fundamentalist*, which follows a young Princeton-educated Pakistani from his privileged position as a member of the New York business elite to his transformation into a radical anti-American protester in his native Lahore. In ways that reverse the dynamic of moral racialization summoned by Divakaruni and Halaby, Hamid's novel can be read as a study of how racial profiling can boomerang back to compromise those who perpetuate it. After September 11, whose symbolic political impact he perceives with secret glee (73), Changez suddenly elicits looks of concern from Americans and feels "uncomfortable in [his] own face" (74), which corresponds to "the CNN version of what a terrorist looks like" (Naber, "Look, Mohammed" 296). He thus suddenly becomes visible, though not in the meritocratic sense to which he would have aspired, so he refuses to embrace this visibility, instead fearing, deploring, or using it as a tool in his struggle for retaliation. Even more, he turns the strategy of racial profiling against those who force it on him, which suddenly prompts him to regard as "foreign" the "fair hair and light eyes" of one of his colleagues at the Underwood Samson valuation firm (67).

Significantly Changez's impression that post-9/11 New York has regressed into a backward-looking community—"a set that ought to be viewed not in Technicolor but in grainy black and white" (115)—carries a barely concealed racial subtext. Yet beyond attaching a moral stigma to one color or another, the novel suggests, racial profiling is, above all, an instrument whose utility depends primarily on the intent of whoever happens to apply it. Whether in the hands of the "white" or of the "black," its importance lies less in its content than in its contrast. "I resolved to look about me," Changez remarks, "with . . . the analytical eyes of a product of Princeton and Underwood Samson. . . . Seen in this fashion I was struck by how traditional your empire appeared. Armed sentries manned the check post at which I sought entry; being of a suspect race I was quarantined and subjected to additional inspection" (157). The result of such scrutiny remains constant (moral quarantine), irrespective of who the scrutinizer may be. Back in Lahore, where he finds himself under the circumspect eye of an American who may or may not be following him, Changez warns his pursuer, "It seems an obvious thing to say, but you should not imagine that we Pakistanis are all potential terrorists, just as we should not imagine that you Americans are all undercover assassins" (183). Put differently, suspicion can be turned on Americans just as easily as it is aimed at "dangerous-looking" foreigners, residing as it does primarily in the eye of the beholder, as well as in a highly ambiguous conceptualization of danger. Since guilt may be assigned to both camps, race does not decisively inflect the discourse of suspicion. What matters is the awareness and management of *risk*, irrespective of its color.

Race and the Ethics of Risk: Brandeis and Cunningham

The distinction between moral panic, which singles out and vilifies specific scapegoats from among the wider population, and more general risk factors is particularly germane to the study of post-9/11 American society.[7] Risk as a site of social anxiety, Michael Welch has argued, entails worries that "are side effects of industrialization and modernization," contributing "to the perception of a catastrophic society taken hold by a disaster mentality" (22). Yet the ambivalence and malleability of racial profiling suggested by Hamid's approach are in line with the concept of risk as a "way of seeing" the world rather than a demonstrable moral paradigm rooted in catastrophic reality. In insurance parlance, risk does not designate an event but "a specific mode of treatment of certain events capable of happening to a group of individuals.... Nothing is a risk in itself; there is no risk in reality. But on the other hand, anything can be a risk; it all depends on how one analyzes the danger, considers the event" (Ewald, "Insurance and Risk" 199). Similarly, in their study of risk management in the War on Terror, Louise Amoore and Marieke de Goede refer to risk as "performative" in the sense that "it produces the effects that it names" (9). Elaborating on the social motivations behind this idea, the anthropologist Mary Douglas and the sociologist Aaron Wildavsky have similarly interpreted risk as a social construct emerging from the prevailing subjective consciousness of a society rather than as a reflection of objectively verifiable danger. The selection of certain risks over others for conscious public awareness, they contend, helps shape the values of a community and ensures the perpetuation of its social structure.

Seen in this light, racial profiling denotes a particular form of risk at a specific historical juncture and reflects, as Mita Banerjee has persuasively demonstrated, culturally entrenched sites of distinction in American society. "Under extreme psychological duress," Banerjee argues, "any culture will activate the particular manifestation of difference which is most genuine to it: in the U.S., this distinguishing marker, which seems to prove salient above all others, seems to be the distinguishing marker of race" (15). Post-9/11 fictions of risk and security extend, however, beyond an explicit concern with race, devising a rhetoric of devastating coincidence to illustrate the consequences of absurdly diligent counterterrorism policies within the domestic sphere and particularly in the lives of innocent (white) citizens.

Halaby adumbrates the collusion of racial suspicion and indefinite risk by having a hate-crazed youth who adorns his skateboard with the sticker "Terrorist Hunting License" (76) and the Arab American protagonist of her novel converge fortuitously as a result of a traffic accident.[8] If terrorism threatens the larger community, such accidents—where the distinction between the morally reprehensible "foreigner" and the victimized white American is no longer clear-cut—signal the presence of hazard even in the privacy of the domestic realm among people whose lives do not permit a neat moral categorization. Certainly Salwa pursues Jake in spite of warnings about him from her coworkers, while Jassim deliberately withholds information from his boss and mentor. Yet the consequences of these missteps are disproportionately disastrous. It is mainly as a result of racial profiling and sheer coincidence that Jassim and Salwa lose control of their lives, entering a downward spiral that sees them unemployed, alienated from each other and from their adopted country, and increasingly inclined to suspect that the decision to come to America compromised their happiness. This narrative development appears in line with the assessment of the sociologist Frank Furedi that "the pessimistic view of humanity that is implicit in the precautionary principle is reflected in the representation of the individual as helpless or sick" (10), hopelessly delivered to forces beyond her agency and control.

The two novels I consider in this section, Gayle Brandeis's *Self Storage* and Michael Cunningham's *Specimen Days*, contradict this view, proposing ways of redefining and consolidating narrative agency that make use of (rather than being at odds with) an aesthetics of coincidence and risk. They do so by deftly substituting the types of moral racialization that interest Divakaruni and Halaby with an ethics of risk, which I interpret less as a neutralizer of racial prejudice than as camouflage for a new type of racial politics so insidious that it pervades even those aspects of the text that appear most antithetical to racialization. By focusing on their narrative form, we will see how the two novels bring into play intriguing questions about the relationship between the cultural textuality of risk and its formal aesthetics.[9]

On the surface, and not unlike *Once in a Promised Land*, Gayle Brandeis's *Self-Storage* is premised on a dynamic of racial othering in post-9/11 America. Members of a small American community are united in this novel by their suspicion of and perverse interest in the affairs of their Afghan neighbors, further stoked by the mystery of the Afghan wife, Sodaba, who wears a burqa that conceals every inch of her body. Yet the unfortunate accident by which Sodaba runs over the daughter of the novel's protagonist, Flan, serves to sharpen an otherwise vague notion of the dangerous Other and simultaneously to defuse it by subordinating it to an environment of undifferentiated risk. In doing so, the novel replaces fear of the Muslim outsider with a close scrutiny of what it means to live with the threat of imminent hazard in a chaotic world that defies conventional morality. Brandeis thus transgresses race as a site of social paranoia, supporting Welch's suggestion that "America's war on terror is better understood in the context of a 'risk society' rather than in the traditional realm of moral panic" (15).

Certainly this story of a small student family housing community in Riverside, California, turning against an Afghan couple after a series of unfortunate and highly fortuitous events, does seek to show how misplaced aggression has marred communities across America since the War on Terror. The settler colonialism that Salaita describes resurfaces in the politically uncouth question voiced by one of Flan's friends as to whether he and his wife may move into the Afghan couple's house once the owners have been deported (139). More important, however, the sense of perverse contingency that permeates the novel demonstrates that post-9/11 racial fear is embedded in a broader discourse of safety and risk. Unexpectedly, and with a sleight of hand shared by Cunningham's *Specimen Days*, the lynchpin of Brandeis's plea for an ethics of risk is, as we shall see, the work of Walt Whitman.

Unlike moral panic, which inevitably results in the allocation of blame, the perception and acceptance of risk encourages efforts to determine how the hazard can be contained and the self shielded—in other words, the central activity of a risk society is "self storage" and self-preservation rather than apportioning blame. What structures risk ethics is an implicit consensus about selfhood and solidarity, the latter largely derived from the former (one cannot imagine or empathize with the Other without a solid foundation in the self). The complex rapport between the self and the Other is precisely what preoccupies Brandeis in her novel, which promises to supplant the ethic of American individualism with a more sustainable, community-based lifestyle. "I think our cultural focus on the individual and self-reliance can be inspiring in terms of people wanting to find their own voice and trust their own vision," Brandeis comments in an interview, soberly adding, "but it can also be very isolating. Such a focus makes it easy for us to forget how interconnected we are; we can forget to reach out to a larger community that can nourish us" (279).

To dramatize this vision of social solidarity, *Self Storage* takes the "good Samaritan" ethics to the extreme: Flan, a white American homemaker, threatens to draw toward herself and her family the outrage of the community and the suspicion of the authorities by helping her innocent Afghan neighbor, Sodaba, evade a federal investigation and possible deportation after Sodaba's husband has already been detained, presumably at Guantánamo Bay.[10] To be sure, at least in its underlying message of support for fellow citizens and celebration of human compassion, this scenario is statistically more realistic than the stories of discrimination and racial profiling recounted by Halaby. As Salaita has noted, "For every racist comment and report of harassment there were ten stories about 'average' Americans going out of their way to make their Arab neighbors feel safe and welcome" (78). Yet in focusing an entire novel on this act of kindness against all logic (after all, Sodaba almost killed Flan's small daughter), Brandeis implies that Americans should be proud of their mortified response to the erosion of human rights after 9/11, for this outrage is proof of their exceptional values and superior moral credentials.

The morality of Flan's gesture, however, is questionable. Her "encounter with otherness," as Richard Gray would put it, ultimately folds back into the self (though in a gesture far removed from the ethically enabling impersonal narcissism illustrated by Tristram's *After*), parodically cementing the differences between the white American woman and her Afghan protégée. Flan and Sodaba are initially united by the value they bestow on motherhood—Flan as a mother of two children, Sodaba as a survivor of several miscarriages and a stillbirth—as well as by a very similar concern with gauging the meaning of their lives in an environment that has yet to give them a chance to excel. In this sense the novel may be said to propose ways of storing and connecting individual selves at a remove from a national self that is splintering out of control. Yet the idea of selfhood becomes contested, residing somewhere on the fault line between the personal and the political, the singular and the plural, categories whose friction both emits emotional warmth and creates tension. The novel opens with a poem by Marge Piercy that includes the lines "Sometimes I find no self in me / but a hungry multitude demanding the use / of my body. Self storage? Is that all / poems are?" The self as nation, besieged by multiple intruders, its body endangered by their colonizing claims, suggests uneasy connections between this novel's discourse of selfhood and the larger nationalist rhetoric of the War on Terror.

As Puar and Rai have noted, in this war the media are using the figure of the Muslim woman in what are often racist and chauvinistic representations of the Middle East as part of a colonial tradition that Gayatri Spivak once characterized as "white men saving brown women from brown men" (qtd. in Puar and Rai, "Monster, Terrorist, Fag" 127). In *Self Storage* it is white women who are saving brown women from white men. This "Western savior" rhetoric limits Sodaba to the status of oppressed victim inspiring both compassion and disavowal. Like Salwa's, her concealed identity intrigues and incites violence. She is, at the same time, utterly helpless: socially and linguistically isolated, but also physically vulnerable. As Jasmin Zine has written concerning the women of Afghanistan and their representation in the War on Terror, "They are invested with freedom and agency only by the grace of the American military complex" (34). Or, as Cynthia Peters notes, "Afghan women are now showing up as 'pregnant,' 'fleeing,' 'starving,' and 'widowed'"—Sodaba is all of these—which reduces them "to the sum of their most desperate parts" (122–23). One cannot help noticing the similarly ambivalent rhetoric employed by Brandeis in establishing Flan's rapport with her protégée: she is continually tempted to murder her ("I wanted to shake Sodaba, to hug her, to rip her veil off her head and slap her across the face. Or kiss her. Maybe kill her" [135]). Her docile body reminds Flan of a caged animal ("I felt horrible thinking that way, but it was kind of true. This was her new cage, and I was her keeper" [178]). Last but not least, whereas Sodaba cannot survive without Flan's help, Flan herself is perfectly capable of saving herself when her own situation as accomplice to a terrorist suspect becomes precarious.

Brandeis's is undoubtedly a feminist stance, but it is centered less on rights than on righteousness. She may even be said to succumb to the fallacy of many Western liberal feminists who have been invoking Afghan women as an "'easy icon' in need of feminist rescue" (Puar and Rai, "Monster, Terrorist, Fag" 127). Krista Hunt calls this practice "embedded feminism," defined as "the incorporation of feminist discourse and feminist activists into political projects that claim to serve the interests of women but ultimately subordinate and/or subvert that goal" (53). Hunt's phrasing aptly circumscribes Flan's inward narrative trajectory. Throughout the novel Flan seeks not only to "embed" her own life into a larger political context that carries the promise of personal redemption, but also to "embed" Sodaba's plight into her own, absurdly laying claim to the Afghan woman's persecuted condition. Flan achieves this in two distinct steps: first, she manipulates Sodaba's image into a blurred impression that she can handle at will; and second, she uses Sodaba to fill a void within her own self, an emotional cavity whose treatment is more beneficial to Flan herself than it is to Sodaba, who can only crouch inside and wait to be released. The title phrase "self storage" thus gains the added significance of a self forcibly stored within another or trapped within an unwelcoming milieu.

Indeed Flan perceives Sodaba not as a woman but as an opaque entity uncomfortably ensconced in the local community. "I had never talked with her," she laments, "had never even made eye contact—I didn't know if it was even possible to make eye contact through the mesh window in her veil" (18). Flan's son, Newton, likens the "burqa woman" to a "black ghost" (75); Flan herself looks at Sodaba and sees "an oil spill in the water, or a giant sea mammal" (76), images that relegate her to the inanimate and animal realms. The hand that tries to completely rub off Sodaba's existence (with greater resolve than what Halaby's Salwa described as "flicking away") grows increasingly insistent. The sense of Sodaba's physical solidity continues to diminish until her race and identity are entirely bleached out for the benefit of Flan's own purification and self-empowerment. "She almost didn't seem like a person," Flan comments with astounding naturalness, as if she were merely observing the plant pathogens studied and cultivated by Sodaba's microbiologist husband. "She was more an idea of a person. An approximation of a person. A mound of fabric with some breath underneath" (173).

When the Afghan woman retreats to the bathroom of Flan's friend, in whose remote lodgings she is now temporarily quartered, Flan imagines her "invisible under the burqa, invisible in the bath other than her hands and feet and the side of her cheek, her body clear as the rushing water" (194). An interesting parallelism emerges when it turns out that Flan's friend, an aspiring Zen nun, has painted an image of Flan wearing a pair of overalls "shaped like a body was inside of them, rounding them out, but the body was invisible; it was just the overalls, standing, legs about shoulder-width apart, the fabric rippling as if in the breeze. Light shot out of all the holes, like divine shafts of sun" (195). Compared with Sodaba's invisibility (heavy, dark, and toxic like a secret contaminant), Flan's strikes the reader as infinitely more benign and luminous. It certainly looks as if Brandeis were carving out a blankness within Flan's self where the uncanny Other may be housed, probably to compensate for Flan's inability to reach *out* toward the Other in Sodaba. Yet no meaningful "encounter with otherness" is forthcoming.

After the traumatic experience of their daughter's accident, gradually Flan and her husband decide to defy fortune and embrace risk as they leave Riverside and go into hiding, possibly forever. By now the racial plot has been neatly absorbed into a narrative of personal redemption pitted against randomness. While the novel does revolve around an unstable axis of fortuity until the very end, it ultimately projects empathy and compassion as definitive solutions to both racial fear and the uncertainties of risk society. And although the novel is sprinkled with unexpected developments and symbolic narrativizations of risk (such as the wannabe Zen nun's attempts to make life-changing decisions on the basis of randomly placed YES and NO cards, "a Zen practice in itself" [59]), gradually the protagonists' actions lapse into the transparent, risk-free behavior of soap opera characters, known primarily for the almost mechanical predictability of their actions. No wonder, then, that Flan's husband, Shae, spends most of his time watching soaps and starts working as a professional screenwriter for soap operas by the end of the novel. The risky adventure of leaving Riverside thus lends gravity to Flan and Shae's humdrum existence, reinvigorating the plot of the soap opera their lives have become. "This could be our chance to break out of our patterns," Flan muses (*chance* here meaning both opportunity and the courting of danger), "fling ourselves into Whitman's great Unknown together" (231). This is the first in a series of references to Whitman's work, which provides, through its textured ethical implications, an ennobling subtext to the plot finale.

At the close of her novel, Brandeis extends her gratitude to Whitman for "giving [her] such gorgeous and expansive words to play with" (253). The game with Whitman's words entails witty linkages between the life situations in which the characters find themselves and apposite citations from Whitman's "Song of Myself." It is not only Whitman's poetry that

Flan constantly conjures up but also generic aspects of the poet's personality and image. Even Flan's occupation (she makes a living by purchasing the contents of unclaimed storage units and reselling them on eBay and at garage sales) demonstrates a Whitmanesque circulation of objects. The suspicion of ownership implied in this trade anticipates Brandeis's use of Whitman to revise narratives of American proprietary individualism, although it is not altogether clear to what extent the novel endorses or condemns Whitman's ideas, as Flan's admiration for the poet is boundless to the point of absurdity. Throughout the novel italicized snippets of Whitman's poetry are enlisted as intertextual ciphers around solidarity and selfhood, pointing in several directions at once.

First, building on the poet's egalitarian vision that makes the business of one man the business of all mankind and vice versa, Brandeis uses Whitman as shorthand for the vigilant paranoia that befell even categorically "blue" California after the 9/11 attacks. "I don't know if it takes a village to raise a child," Flan marvels upon seeing the gaping crowds gathered outside her house after her daughter's brush with death, "but that village certainly turns out when a child is hurt. To help and to gawk, both. *Whatever interests the rest interests me*" (124). Later she answers her son's question as to what God's eyes look like by offering the panoptical hypothesis "Maybe all our eyes are God's eyes" (143). Her statement implies that the collectivity of vision is what makes it divine, so one cannot help wondering whether the corporeal invisibility she attributes to her friend and arch nemesis Sodaba doesn't by now begin to resemble an existential rejection: not only is she foreign, needy, and utterly helpless, but her failure to reveal herself to the eyes of others (i.e., the eyes of God) places her in the realm of whatever is the opposite of or impervious to divinity. Ironically Sodaba finally takes shelter in a Zen monastery—an establishment that we imagine to be operated by modern-day Whitmans—where she remains a hidden and indigestible human enclave.

Second, *Self Storage* evokes the inflationary empathy that Whitman's work, taken at face value, seems to propagate. In Flan's mind—a mind increasingly frustrated with the physical apathy and emotional disinterest of a husband who lives to watch TV—this empathy translates into the inexplicable desire to bestow kisses (on the mouth) on anyone who crosses her field of vision, from Afghan men to toddlers. At least in the case of Sodaba's husband, this bizarre behavior can be made to appear as a wholesome cure for the racial suspicion that the Bush administration irresponsibly sowed in everyone's minds (with echoes of Tristram's emplotment of perverse, conciliatory, or retributive desire): "Isn't that who the news told us to be scared of, angry Middle Eastern men? Isn't that who all those color-coded alerts were supposed to warn us about? All I could think about, though, was kissing him" (83). In fact Whitman's outward attention to the world and its inhabitants is used here to gloss over the transcendental self-attention practiced by this book's protagonist. The narrator starts out as a moderately cultured ingénue eager but as yet unable to put on the mantle of self-confidence and defiance worn by Whitman: "*I celebrate myself*. Sorry. I just can't do it. Walt Whitman starts 'Song of Myself,' the greatest poem in the world, with those three words. I wish I could follow his lead, start the same way, but I can't. The words sound tinny in my own voice—arrogant, wrong" (3). Flan sets out to overcome this incapacity in herself by first "celebrating" the selves of others, her identity paradoxically gaining in solidity and strength through her selflessness, much the same way Whitman leans on the multitudes of his surroundings to define and consolidate his own vision. Sometimes these multitudes harbor a sense of racial and cultural otherness, from which the Whitmanian persona seeks to distantiate itself.

Third, it could therefore be argued that what Brandeis most immediately associates with Whitman is an inflated Americanism that leads the novelist to take recourse to the poet whenever the moral purity and preeminence of the United States are at stake. "To me," Whitman noted, "the United States are important because, in this colossal drama, they are unquestionably designated for the leading parts, for many a century to come. In them History and Humanity seem to seek to culminate" (*Prose Works* 742). As a representative of American preeminence, Flan too plays the leading role in *Self Storage* and seems to embody the common humanity that Brandeis intended to highlight in her book. This humanity is hardly "shared," however, as none of the supporting characters can match Flan's humane intervention, instead revolving around her like mere satellites to reflect and better showcase the blinding light of her compassion. The "air of defiance, radical egalitarianism, unabashed individualism, almost jingoistic Americanism" (Reynolds 66) attributed to Whitman thus apply to Flan herself. Admittedly both Whitman and Brandeis's heroine merely react to external circumstances that force them to go on the defensive. Flan careens down the path of extreme patriotism in response to the violent national shudder following the September 11 attacks. And Whitman inserted his inflated sense of individuality and personal strength into the gaping space left behind by a series of events propelling the United States into political disarray. As David Reynolds explains, "Into the vacuum created by the dissolution of the nation's political structure rushed Whitman's gargantuan 'I,' assimilating images from virtually every aspect of antebellum American structure in a poetic document of togetherness offered to a nation that seemed on the verge of unraveling" (67).

This is not to say that Whitman would have accepted the post-9/11 rhetoric and unconstitutional civil rights infringements of the Bush administration without question or skepticism. After all, the poet believed that any effort to disregard the U.S. Constitution, which he reverently referred to as "the work of the wisest and purest statesmen ever assembled," would be "worthy only of a madman and a villain" (qtd. in Reynolds 69). Nonetheless even though *Leaves of Grass* appeared in a period of relative progressiveness, Whitman later reverted to racial conservatism as a reaction to rampant and radical abolitionism; even prior to this development he had expressed doubt that the races could be successfully integrated (Reynolds 71), voicing both southern and northern perspectives in his works. The great bard, who liked to use messianic metaphors to describe his own poetic mission and regarded *Leaves of Grass* as a new Bible (a perspective with which Flan would certainly concur), went as far as stating that America's digestion was strained by the "millions of ignorant foreigners" coming to its shores (*Prose Works* 762).

Whitman has been a familiar comfort figure for a number of commentators looking for models of national community after 9/11, and Brandeis usefully reminds us of the less appealing aspects of the poet's legacy. She does so, however, not through direct exegesis of the poet's views, but through a creative declension of those views as perceived by Flan and dramatized in her increasingly self-serving actions. Seduced by Whitman's teachings in the aftermath of national disaster, Flan applies his indiscriminate ideas indiscriminately: in trying to consolidate her sense of self by liberating it from countless misconceptions, she whittles it down to its fully depersonalized bare essentials. To that extent Whitman's influence does not so much revitalize the self as impoverish it. As Wai Chee Dimock has brilliantly argued, the self seen by Whitman "is increasingly stripped bare, put through an increasingly rigorous set of refinements, until it is purified into no more than an idea, an empty form, but for that very reason, a form of transcendent dignity" ("Whitman, Syntax" 71). Likewise *Self Storage* initially insists on the virtues of connection and community building but ultimately favors the rewards and promise of the dream of freedom pursued *independently* of the community that had seemed to nourish the protagonist.

When she realizes that by saving Sodaba from deportation she has drawn the ire of federal authorities, Flan escapes with her family to build a new home away from Riverside. She makes this momentous decision entirely by herself (without consulting her husband) and with a frenzy probably intended by Brandeis as a paean to the American Dream, with post-9/11, counterterrorist thrills thrown in. Yet even this selfish, unsympathetic decision follows Whitman's script. To quote Dimock, "as much as it is a poetry of accumulation, 'Song of Myself' is also a poetry of divestment, a poetry that spins out an endless catalog of the self's many attachments only to distinguish the self from all those attachments" ("Whitman, Syntax" 70). Indeed not only does Flan abruptly break her attachments to her friends and to her community, but she also abandons all of her possessions, except some family photographs, a painting, and, naturally, *Leaves of Grass*. Ultimately even this book—a rare, valuable edition—is sold for ten thousand dollars, despite the fact that it contains the precious scribblings of Flan's late mother, who left nothing behind apart from these penciled notes. With this money, however, the family will be able to survive wherever they decide to settle, so the mere coincidence by which Flan manages to quickly sell her copy of Whitman at such an exorbitant price eases the consequences of the earlier accident that left her daughter injured and bleeding under the tire of Sodaba's car.

This unequivocally happy ending (and the blanket distribution of happiness) excludes, however, the Afghan couple, who exits the narrative as soon as Flan's virtue and compassion have been sufficiently underlined. In other words, although the novel's plot was initially triggered by racial marginalization, later replaced by a sense of generalized risk (as Sodaba's accident has shown), in the end the outrage with which Flan responded to the racial profiling of Sodaba is forgotten in favor of an individualist starting-over scenario—rather than, say, an active engagement on Sodaba's behalf against the injustices of the War on Terror. Flan's narcissism thus builds on Whitman's self-consuming ethics (self-consuming because he is cognizant of the Other without properly recognizing the Other) and suggests that mere outrage at the injustices of the War on Terror does not mean that the premises of American individualism have been entirely overcome in favor of an indiscriminate (i.e., unreflected and nondiscriminating) transcultural empathy.

Similarly employing Whitman's words to contextualize post-9/11 racial suspicion and the vagaries of chance that help disguise it, Michael Cunningham's novel *Specimen Days*—in fact a triptych of linked novellas—maps the broader historical embeddedness of the terrorist attacks (an issue I explore at length in chapter 4), at the same time envisioning their impact in the distant future. The dawning machine age in 1870s New York is the setting of the first tale, "In the Machine," which describes a community riven by ethnic and class differences. The Irish boy at the center of this story recites Whitman's lines partly as a symptom of the posttraumatic disorder caused by his brother's death, and in a further hallucinatory twist even appears to meet Whitman on the streets of New York. The third tale, "Like Beauty," imagines a world "after the meltdown" (236), a national disaster only evasively described. Earth is shared here by humans and a socially repressed alien race known as Nadians. Whitman's function in this story is to provide moral guidance to the protagonist, a humanoid robot who mechanically recites disjointed lines at random moments, and whose maker sees in poetry a means to forestall or defuse life's contingencies. "I wanted to give you some moral sense," he confesses. "To help you cope with events I couldn't foresee. I thought that if you were programmed with the work of great poets, you'd be better able to appreciate the consequences of your actions" (281). In this imaginary, risk-aversive world, Whitman's ethical vision thus lies in his comprehensive knowledge of human mores and his perceptive profiling of human behavior. It is in the second story, "The Children's Crusade," a neo-noir piece set in post-9/11 New York, that race, risk, and Whitman's sublimation of selfhood converge in a way that makes this narrative interesting to juxtapose with *Self Storage*.

Cat, a black female police investigator in New York who takes the calls of people threatening to carry out acts of massive and public violence, fails to tag as dangerous and credible the threat of a young boy who ends up killing himself and a wealthy banker at Ground Zero. A second, very similar attack occurs (also after prior warning), this time against a poor burger-flipper, as if to prove that "you're not safe if you're a real estate tycoon, and you're not safe if you work for minimum wage" (154). By the time the third young caller is put through to Cat, we know the young perpetrators are part of a domestic terror cell coordinated by a woman who goes by the name of Walt Whitman and indoctrinates the children with the poet's teachings. As in *Self Storage*, Whitman's textual relevance is made up of small, orchestrated moments that require the reader to fill out narrative interstices with intertextual adhesive. But while Brandeis uses the broad, undiscriminating ecstasy of Whitman's vision as shorthand for hedonistic compassion, Cunningham (clearly more suspicious of Whitman as a national icon) invests it with the moral ambivalence of the post-9/11 era, cannily acknowledging Whitman as a useful if slippery interlocutor in exploring the pitfalls of contemporary patriotism.[11]

Whitman, insists the NYU academic whom Cat consults in investigating her case, was not (simply) a patriot, since that would imply "a certain fixed notion of right versus wrong" (146). Key to Cunningham's evocation of Whitman to encode the moral morass in which a nation haunted by memories of terror finds itself is not the "motivating hopefulness" of

American foreign policy (D. Brooks) but the ambitious line of equivalence the poet draws between his own moral makeup and that of his country. "I make the poem of evil also," Whitman proclaims in "Starting from Paumanok." "I commemorate that part also, / I am myself just as much evil as good, and my nation is" (54). This slippage from personal to national investment lies at the core of Cunningham's narrative, which enacts the transference of national paranoia onto personal risk.

In contrast to Brandeis's extended citations, Whitman's presence in "The Children's Crusade" is at once more elliptical and more intense. For one thing, the poet's hubris-ridden diction (which Cunningham assumes but never quotes at length) insistently recalls to contemporary readers the post-9/11 rhetoric of national self-reliance. "There are moments in Whitman," Jacqueline Rose writes in her review of Cunningham's *Specimen Days*,

> that tip over into something more troubling: we will build "an enlarg'd, general, superior humanity," he writes in *Specimen Days*. In "Salut au Monde!," his most translated poem, he moves across the globe "in America's name." At what point does a nation's exuberance start to obstruct its vision? "Sharing," as we have seen only too clearly in relation to Iraq, can be a form of domination, and being lavish with one's own values can be a cover for taking power. "As nature, inexorable, onward, resistless, impassive amid the threats and screams of disputants, so America," Whitman wrote to Emerson. "Let all defer." (25)

Yet Cunningham's America is far from impassive before the threats of those who resist its expansion, instead "bombing other countries simply because they make us nervous" (171). This sense of impending threat, whether justifiable or not, ensures that Americans "live constantly in the shadow of the future" (D. Brooks 33)—though not with the messianic hopefulness the poet envisaged. Paranoia, not ambition, forms the narrative nucleus of "The Children's Crusade" and results in the ambient fear that "you could easily, at any moment, make your fatal mistake. That we all humped along unharmed because no one had decided to kill us that day. That we could not know, as we hurried about our business, whether we were escaping the conflagration or rushing into it" (105). The precise nature of the danger is equally mysterious: from full-on terrorist attacks to small-scale murders perpetrated by youngsters who strap rudimentary pipe bombs around their chests, embrace total strangers in parks and along avenues, sacrificing themselves and their victims in the explosion.

The unknown is thus twofold: not only when and where we could encounter risk, but also exactly what could befall us any minute is cause for concern and permanent anxiety. As Ulrich Beck has argued, risk awareness is informed not only by personal and secondhand experience, but also by "second-hand non-experience," in other words, by the expectation of a risk that has not yet been experienced (72). Or, in the chilling terms proposed by former U.S. secretary of defense Donald Rumsfeld, it depends on so-called unknown unknowns, that is, the threats we don't know we don't know, and as such serve as ideal justification for preemptive action.[12] Faced with such overwhelming insecurity, Cat and her colleagues at the police department desperately hope that the killings are not random (100), because "cause and effect [are] always comforting" (107) and certainly more conducive to the illusion of safety that she and her coworkers are professionally obliged to secure. Their desire for clarity—"I hope there's something there to see. I hope it's not just . . . randomness. Chaos" (155)—pits the visibility of perceptible danger against the chaos of blank risk.

References to race and racial profiling illustrate the kind of visible danger that Cat and her coworkers can tackle more easily. Cat especially appears to have resigned herself to being a victim of racial profiling; she summons "a regal bearing" upon entering an antique shop—"I have no intention of slipping any of your sorry shit into my handbag" (159), her posture means to signify—and even accepts without demur the exoticism that her white, yuppie boyfriend demands of her as "stern black goddess of law enforcement" (165). Yet as soon as she slips out of character by betraying her emotional vulnerability, their relationship already dims into a generic memory, the memory of an "older black woman" (165), a "colorful character" (166), cherished but utterly replaceable. When she leaves the city with the third little terrorist boy, whom she has decided to adopt, Cat bitterly observes the other passengers on the southbound train as they make "a little extra room for her, unconsciously, the way New Yorkers do when they sense the presence of someone strange. Black woman with a compromised white child. Crazy" (193). The second boy, who blew himself up in Central Park, had been black, but neither Cat nor he was able to discern their shared race simply by speaking on the phone. "Funny," Cat concludes. "Two black people, cop and killer, each assuming the other must be white" (154). As in Hamid's *The Reluctant Fundamentalist*, racial profiling (here even literally, Cat being a "profiler") does not attach to a particular race, feeding instead on the cultural intensity of racial contrast.

Indeed the child's race contributes nothing to the case. In effect "The Children's Crusade" not only reverses racial stereotypes (the policewoman is black), but appears to dismiss the notion of race as a risk factor to the point of complete disregard. Even though Cat herself clearly does not consider the color of her skin to be immaterial and enjoys shocking people who mistakenly expect her to be poor and uneducated, she refuses to factor in race as a potential hazard. Everyone, without exception, looks suspicious to her: "The guy nervously unloading boxes from a bakery truck, the jogger in Princeton sweats, even the blind man tapping along with his cane—they all seemed like potentials. They were, in fact, all potentials. Everyone was. The trick was to keep living with the conviction that almost everyone was actually harmless" (127). Even a (white) colleague who expresses exaggerated enthusiasm about capturing and punishing the amateur terrorists provokes her sense of alarm with his "pure, shining conviction" (140). Just as Whitman envelops everyone in sympathy and compassion, so too is Cat suspicious of everyone she sets eyes on, yet derives from this a sense of common humanity similar to the "shared heart" Brandeis repeatedly invokes in *Self Storage*. Precisely because danger is so meticulously concealed, suspicion cannot alight on any single individual. If everyone is a suspect, no one truly is.

To that extent, even though she cannot help examining everyone she meets for signs of danger, Cat occasionally exonerates everyone and voices a distinguishably Whitmanesque, all-encompassing acceptance: "Just about everyone, or everyone who was at least minimally functional, had to get up and get dressed. Even the ones who were going to call her and tell her about their plans to shoot or stab or ignite somebody. Even the ones who were going to strap a bomb to their chests and blow up a businessman on the street. Here we are, all of us, going through this daily miniature rebirth, and doing it together" (114). (Color-)blind solidarity finally prompts Cat to flee with the orphan terrorist, seeking a purer life, for she is as out of place in post-9/11 New York as the riderless horse she sees running up Broadway and causing her world to momentarily tip on its axis (160). "With a sense of vertiginous recklessness, a queasy and light-headed plunging" (192), she leads the child away from the city as she would have ridden the white horse away, absorbing some of the child's own recklessness—just as Flan had soaked up Sodaba's fear and gone into hiding in that novel's final act of flight.

Contributing to Cat's sympathy with the child is her remorse for the death of her own son, Luke, as a result of a misdiagnosis that could have been prevented had Cat decided to consult a second doctor. Traumatized by this earlier misfortune partly caused by her own failure to meet and neutralize risk, she overcompensates in the present by sacrificing everything and assuming the ultimate risk of obtaining nothing in return: "She and the boy were hurtling toward the day when, with milk on the table and a dog browsing for scraps, her adopted son, her second Luke, the boy she had rescued, would decide that he finally loved her enough to murder her" (196). In behaving so foolishly, at least by conventional (and legal) standards, Cat responds to risk with risk, embracing hazard in both its negative and positive dimensions, not only as danger but also as opportunity, as the voluntary and redemptive acceptance of uncertainty. The boy may well be an inveterate criminal, yet Cat "might still want to be his mother even if it proved fatal" (196), in an attitude that casts motherhood as an antidote to terror and calls to mind theories of terrorist psychology that attribute such deviance to inconsistent mothering.[13] The story is ethically and politically problematic in this sense, to the extent that it might lead the reader toward a subliminal acceptance of the notion that terrorists and those who harbor them are deranged but ultimately savable as long as we agree to "mother" them (which in this case, despite Cat's best intentions, also means interrupting the course of their lives and carrying them away to a place where we think they will be happy and under control).

Yet it is through its textual features that this story's ethical and social relevance becomes most apparent. "To die is different from what any one supposes, and luckier" (196), one of the boys had written on a wall outside Cat's apartment. This is a Whitman line, so open and baffling that one could go at it, as the NYU scholar would put it, "from just about any angle and find something that seems to support some thesis or other" (147). The angle I would like to explore here results from the convergence of three separate issues: the ways the narrative form of the text mirrors the story's theme of uncertainty and risk; Whitman's "noncontingent" poetics (Dimock, "Whitman, Syntax" 77) as it applies to Cunningham's text; and the conceptualization of what may be called an ethics of risk as the opposite of what I referred to earlier as moral racialization.

Brandeis and Cunningham clearly choose different paths in narrativizing risk. The structure of *Self Storage* suggests that whatever risks the characters may encounter, the readers can rely on the guidance of the first-person narrator. The shock and disorientation caused by the fallout of 9/11 and the accidents befalling the protagonists are thus absorbed and neutralized by a narration that consistently restores context and control. Cunningham, however, plays his hand with much more energy and relish, partly because *Specimen Days* constitutes a departure from his previous novels in terms of character dynamics and plot sequencing, both of which generally pivot on a pattern of buildup, release, and expectancy. The plot of "The Children's Crusade" evolves gradually, each character receiving his or her time in the spotlight, while revelations and reversals abound: one boy is black, and Simon, Cat's boyfriend, turns out to be a superficial thrill-chaser. Some of these are clichés of the police procedural genre, which Cunningham is reworking here, and yet—like the concept of risk itself—ultimately the narrative relies not on these concrete events but on the anticipation and anxiety created by their tenuous linkages.

Cat herself, while clearly a product of cliché blending, transforms almost surreptitiously from a kind woman who makes a living by being compassionate into an irresponsible individual whose empathy is as impartial as it is impersonal. Although she does leave everything behind in order to offer the little boy a chance at a normal life, it is this very act that seems to betray as much flippancy as generosity. Her boyfriend vanishes inexplicably from her memory; the office worker with whom she has been having a casual affair is dignified only with a terse farewell note; and her commitment to her job (which she must have considered at least honorable if not virtuous) is not strong enough to keep her from leaving. As for the little boy, even Cat admits he will play the (merely derivative) part of a second Luke.

In a twist on the neo-noir genre, the female protagonist (at once femme fatale and detective) unravels at this point, her character distorted by a series of contradictions. Cat may choose to embrace the risk of being killed by her adopted son, or she may opt to stay behind and protect New York from murderous children, but if "dying is luckier," then the whole structure of illusions distinguishing life and death, safety and risk, morality and transgression becomes flawed or even invalid. If Whitman's hypothesis is accurate, then the reason Cat fearlessly leaves the city with a potential criminal in tow is not that she has bravely decided to face risk, but simply that she no longer believes in risk at all. By enveloping the world in a mantle of goodness, Cunningham's narrative suppresses any potential for danger, not because this doesn't exist but because Cat decides not to perceive it; if risk is nothing but the perception of risk, then lack of perception will result in an effectively risk-free world. "The Whitmanian self," Dimock explains, "is thus always lucky, he can only be lucky, whether he lives or dies. And he is just as lucky as everybody else. In being so assured of that fact, in having so little room for surprise, let alone for complaint, he might also be said, paradoxically, to be beyond luck.... What does it mean for a self to be beyond luck? Martha Nussbaum has argued that an ethical life that aspires to be noncontingent is also one that is necessarily impoverished" ("Whitman, Syntax" 77). Indeed Nussbaum values the openness of human existence created by chance, which lies, she says, beyond human control and does not happen through an individual's agency, "as opposed to what he does or makes" (*The Fragility of Goodness* 3). Chance, then, cannot be fully controlled by an autonomous self, but that is not to say that it cannot be tampered with at all. To reiterate Douglas and Wildavsky's contention, risk is less a matter of individual perception and more the result of social enforcement, which indicates those aspects of life we see as threatening or destabilizing. What Whitman withholds from us, Dimock claims, is what she calls "an ethics of preference" ("Whitman, Syntax" 78), which I understand as a moral system that assists in discerning between one option and its opposite, a system that can be used to counter what Douglas and Wildavsky call the social "risk portfolio" (8), which emphasizes certain risks as more urgent than others.

Whitman is content to be "just as much evil as good" and equally lucky whether or not he makes a moral choice. Yet unlike Whitman, I would argue, Cunningham *longs* for an ethics of preference. In fact he appears to suggest that coming in to fill the space left behind by a vacuous ethics of risk is an arbitrary morality that may in the end revert to racial difference as its principal site of distinction. It does make a difference to New Yorkers that a black woman is the sole caretaker of a helpless-looking young child. Whether she admits it or not, Cat will be haunted by this discrepancy wherever she decides to get off the train and start a new life. "We'll have books and no television, and I'll do the best I can with the boredom and racism" (155), she hopefully declares, without realizing, perhaps, that the boredom of moral nihilism is precisely the niche into which racism will settle. Her mistake is to believe that if nobody is safe then risk itself becomes superfluous and, with it, the important mechanisms through which a society will determine its sites of danger. Seen in this light, Cunningham's novella might be said to endorse assertive action for the purpose of risk management after 9/11 by offering the instructive scenario of a passive world, hurtling toward disaster, in which people decide to confront risk simply by refusing to perceive it or by relativizing its constraints.

I have suggested two ways to think about the intersection between narrative, ethics, and the racially informed discourse of counterterrorism. First, I have shown that Chitra Divakaruni's *Queen of Dreams* and

Laila Halaby's *Once in a Promised Land* productively assess the overbearing moralism of racial profiling in the War on Terror, especially in relation to its most vulnerable targets: citizens of Arab American descent. Second, with appropriate variations I have looked at the category of risk to elucidate the attempts of Brandeis, Cunningham, and to some extent Halaby to connect the threat of the racialized Other with a more generalized sense of insecurity that pervades contemporary society. Yet far from disappearing altogether, racism and racial profiling in these texts transmute from explicit to tacit. I hope these readings have also pointed the way toward some of the implications that racial profiling might have not only for a thematic study of post-9/11 literature but, beyond that, for a consideration of narrative and literary form as expressing an aesthetics and ethics of social risk. In their intertextuality and revisionist formal choices, these fictions are no longer conscripted to the posttraumatic imagination of earlier 9/11 novels. Their generic ambiguity, their uneven concern with racial fear in a climate of generalized menace, and their collapsing of moral categories create a milieu where race and risk, visual profiling, and faceless threat interfere with each other. And this is suggestive of the ambiguities of the War on Terror itself, which cannot easily be situated on either side of the moral dividing line that upholds its aims.

4. THE INTERNATIONALIZATION OF CONSCIENCE
Hemon, Barker, Balkanism

The growing interest in racial profiling since the 9/11 attacks has led to a flurry of fictions concerned with the contemporary Muslim experience in the United States. Some of these fictions have more in common with Hamid's *The Reluctant Fundamentalist* than with Halaby's *Once in a Promised Land* in that they adopt a transnational perspective, even when the setting doesn't extend beyond New York. H. M. Naqvi's *Home Boy*, for instance, opens with a conversation between three hip Pakistanis, with "their fingers on the pulse of the great global dialectic" (1), about America's chummy relations with the Mujahideen, the subsequent civil war with the freedom fighters, and the radicalization of their progeny, the Taliban (13). Rarely has 9/11 writing showcased characters that are so "privy to the imperatives of wild men and the goings-on in far-flung arenas of the world" (14). Naqvi's Pakistanis do get assaulted with "A-rab" invective—the word "like a dagger thrust and turned" (30)—yet they seem more concerned with the violently deterritorialized condition of New York's multicultural underclass than with the abuses of the War on Terror. The moral implications of this war are squared against jihad, "the struggle within—the struggle to remain moral and charitable" (67), a contrast that has otherwise remained outside the purview of post-9/11 literary ethics. After being detained for forty-eight hours on suspicion of terrorist intent, in order to put things in perspective one of the Pakistanis begins to discuss the Japanese internment, although it was precisely his historical expertise (especially on terrorist and insurgent conduct, from Sarajevo to the Tamil Tigers [147]) that aroused his interrogators' suspicion in the first place.

Naqvi's is only one in a series of novels that have shifted the focus of post-9/11 literature from debates on American domestic affairs to a set of questions by which writers attempt to locate the post-9/11 experience in space and time. The issue of racial formation as a determining cultural marker in U.S. history has come sharply to the fore in these fictions, as has the transnational shape of post-9/11 discourses and the ways the terrorist attacks can be understood through the lens of other historical events of similar importance. Kazim Ali remarks in his lyrical novel *The Disappearance of Seth* that "history is written in stories one on top of the other," forming an uneven palimpsest in which certain episodes "press their vision down on everything that came before" (60). In Ali's narrative the 9/11 attacks reshape the legacy of the first Persian Gulf War (1990–91) and the missile attack against Baghdad.

Yet it is the Bosnian War (part of the Yugoslav dissolution wars, 1991–95) that has emerged as the most significant moment in this move toward contextualizing the 9/11 attacks, for a number of reasons.[1] For one thing, the events in Bosnia have informed the idiom and imaginary of post-9/11 discourse partly due to the stylistic resemblances between visualizations of the Bosnian War and of the 9/11 attacks, both of which have been photographed by the same photojournalists and have reached the public through the same media outlets. Widely considered to have marked a turning point in the radicalization of Muslims in Europe, the Bosnian War also provides a frame of reference for studying the effects of peacekeeping missions and UN interventionism on a global scale, and thus facilitates a critical understanding of U.S. intervention in Afghanistan and Iraq in response to the 9/11 attacks. Additionally a growing body of literature has examined the immigration waves set in motion by the Bosnian conflict, as well as the media scrutiny that brought that conflict to international attention by putting a face, as it were, on the violence on the ground and providing the most comprehensive debate on the ethics of media witnessing since Vietnam.[2] This chapter examines two novels that largely turn on the explicit and ethically charged juxtaposition of September 11 and the Bosnian War to probe the deeper phylogeny of moral dogmas mobilized in the War on Terror, as well as their entwinement with paradigms of sympathy and rescue whose scale of aggregation is no longer the nation but the world.

In *The Lazarus Project* Aleksandar Hemon addresses practices of scapegoating and racial profiling in ways that link his novel with the narratives analyzed in the previous chapter, although the ethical import of Hemon's writing coalesces more forcefully around the characterization of evil. While Brandeis and Cunningham do undertake a historical repositioning of the War on Terror through intertextual references to Walt Whitman's work, Hemon opens up a much broader vista of documented racialization that aligns the terrorist attacks and their aftermath with the long durée of racial fears in America. *The Lazarus Project* proposes perplexing connections between the experience of immigration and atavistic cultural perceptions of evil. In ways that recall McGrath and Tristram but weave a larger chronotopic canvas, Pat Barker teases out the cataleptic effects of the terrorist attacks around the transnational and transhistorical plot of her novel *Double Vision*. While representations of global war effect an internationalization of empathy, Barker looks into how the individual fails to internalize sympathy in the realm of personal relationships. The terrorist attacks of 9/11, which Barker places in the broader world-historical context of war atrocities and crimes, mark the point where the internationalization of empathy precipitates its domestic failure. The fears mobilized by terrorism in the twenty-first century, Hemon and Barker suggest, are "memories of other fears" (*The Lazarus Project* 68) revived by an increasingly globalized theater of war and sympathy.

Aleksandar Hemon and the Balkanization of 9/11: Exile, Evil, Nostalgia

Aleksandar Hemon's work carries out an important intervention in literary debates about how the 9/11 attacks should be contextualized in both time and space. The narrator of his short story "The Conductor" (in *Love and Obstacles*), who finds himself on an airplane to Washington DC on the cloudless morning of September 11, links the attacks with his own defining biographical experience, the Bosnian War. "While America settled into its mold of patriotic vulgarity," he remarks, "I began to despair, for everything reminded me of Bosnia in 1991" (76). In another story the same narrator mentions his "family history and the war crimes of the Bush regime" (150) in the same breath, suggesting a kinship between Bosnian ethnic feuds and the Muslim scare in post-9/11 United States. It is consistent, then, that while having dinner with his parents in Sarajevo, he is watching news footage of the Iraq War, which his war-weathered Bosnian family takes in "sideways" with an attitude that bespeaks a mixture of complacency and boredom. While in *Love and Obstacles* it is never entirely clear how the Bosnian narrator himself responds to the War on Terror and the invasion of Iraq, we sense that his guilt at having left besieged Sarajevo in 1992 makes him especially sensitive to the political volatility of post-9/11 America. *The Lazarus Project*, a narrative specifically organized around the parallels between the Bosnian War and September 11, more forcefully interrogates the ways the attacks are embedded within broader spatial and temporal frames. Balkan history becomes the underlying force that shapes all histories, those to which the Bosnian narrator and protagonist can lay claim by bloodline as well as others.

These "others"—or, more broadly, the concept of Otherness—are what *The Lazarus Project* is truly about, which is unsurprising for a novel by a Bosnian American writer who once stressed his double Otherness by observing, "Bosnians are not a big audience, so I fit into this loose category of '*other* cultures'" (Blazan 259, my emphasis). Indeed *The Lazarus Project* cleverly positions the War on Terror within the historical contexts of "other cultures," ranging from the Kishinev pogrom of 1903 through the anti-anarchist paranoia of early twentieth-century Chicago to the siege of Sarajevo in 1992, in what the notoriously self-deprecating Hemon would describe as "one of those brainy postmodern setups everybody likes so well because it has something to do with identity" (*Love and Obstacles* 151). The narrative dramatizes this setup both in its structural composition and in its eclectic, almost haphazard historical layering: the novel doesn't argue or evolve, it accumulates. With the attacks of September 11 at its center, it ramifies along avenues such as mass murder (pogroms, concentration camps), systematic xenophobia, ethnic conflict, and the

War on Terror, allowing these separate narratives to shade into each other and sketching the tentative framework of a diasporic ethics rooted in memory and nostalgia.

Like Hemon himself, the protagonist of *The Lazarus Project*, Vladimir Brik, grew up in Sarajevo and came to Chicago on a visit in 1992. When the war broke out and his native city came under siege, Brik was forced to stay in the United States, where he has never felt entirely comfortable. His marriage to Mary, a successful and serene American neurosurgeon, only serves to highlight his own disaffection as his journalistic work and English-as-a-second-language teaching fail to provide him with a sense of achievement or spiritual sustenance. Upon receiving a major grant to pursue a transnational project (Hemon himself was awarded a MacArthur Foundation "Genius" Grant in 2004), Brik—accompanied by his photographer friend, Rora, whose blurry images adorn the narrative—starts investigating the life and death of another immigrant, Lazarus Averbuch, a young Jew who survived the 1903 Kishinev pogrom and came to Chicago, only to be murdered by the chief of police in a brief (and mysterious) scuffle. Brik suspects that the incident probably occurred as a result of a misunderstanding inflamed by the pervasive xenophobic paranoia characteristic of those times. In the aftermath of the anarchist Haymarket riots of 1886, in which several police officers died, and fearing an insurgency stoked by the mayor's cancellation of a speech by the anarchist leader Emma Goldman, Chicago gradually succumbed to public hysteria about anarchists emerging from the ranks of immigrants and union workers.

Retracing Lazarus's steps and his own, Brik embarks on a trip to Kishinev, Bucharest, and Sarajevo. Parts of this Bosnian story are already familiar to the reader of Hemon's other books; at stake here, as in Hemon's writings generally, is the narrator's attempt to cobble together some cohesive meaning from disparate episodes in order to close up the intolerable void—a mixture of nostalgia and moral malaise—opened by his immigrant experience. The Lazarus metaphor introduced in the title helps fuse the fragments of his story: the biblical figure is himself an immigrant, an exile from death hurled back into the world and forced to confront the challenging task of finding a home for himself. The Lazarus image also conveys the survivor's guilt that plagues the Bosnian American narrator, who sees little difference between Lazarus's postresurrection blues and his own post-Sarajevo existence. But most of all Lazarus offers an apt symbol for the restlessness of the past, its tempestuous resurrections throughout space and time.

Because it foregrounds the thresholds and transgressions implicit in Lazarus's ambiguous, somewhat anticlimactic resurrection, *The Lazarus Project* is more of a post-9/11 novel than it cares to acknowledge. What impels Brik to uncover the story of Lazarus, and Hemon to explore "the sumptuous palette of American fears" (47), is the desire, further inflamed by the War on Terror, to curb a sense of growing moral turpitude tinctured by nostalgia (both personal and political) in the aftermath of the 9/11 attacks. The solution proposed in and through this novel is a contextualization—in a different sense than Tristram's—of post-9/11 paranoia against an incredibly vast historical canvas. Like Barker's *Double Vision*, Hemon's narrative is a test case for whether and how post-9/11 literature envisages the relation between the terrorist attacks and distant historical events (such as the Peninsular War of 1807–14 and the Chicago anarchist riot in 1886) or, more recently, the long aftermath of the cold war. But what does Hemon's novel reveal about the ethical importance of inscribing the 9/11 attacks within the deep historical and transnational imagination? Crucial to a reading of the novel from a post-9/11 perspective is the precise nature of this inscription, which ultimately resides in the infernal recurrence of evil across histories and memories lived and imagined, a concept that I analyze through the critical lens provided by Alain Badiou. In summoning Badiou's criticism of goodness and Otherness as ethical cornerstones, I argue that Hemon opens up the ossified imaginary of evil that attaches to the War on Terror in much the same way that Badiou pushes beyond the limits of an ethics based primarily on victimhood. Not only does the novel encode ethics as the product of specific sociocultural environments, aspects of which may resurface over time, but it also imagines the racialized ethics of the War on Terror as inseparable from a transnational dynamic in which evil is both contextual and deterritorialized.

THE INTERNATIONALIZATION OF CONSCIENCE

Bookends to the American Century: 1908 and 2001

Lazarus Averbuch, the subject of Brik's research, is a young Jew living in Chicago during the first decade of the twentieth century, a *"slim, swarthy young man... that could send a shiver of distrust into any honest man's heart"* (7).[3] Lazarus sets out to deliver a letter to George Shippy, the chief of police, yet when he arrives at Shippy's residence the maid instantly decides that the young man must be up to no good: "She cannot place his accent; she is going to warn Shippy that the foreigner who came to see him looked very suspicious" (1). While waiting to be admitted into Shippy's home, Lazarus spends some time buying candy in a shop whose owner "glares at him; for all he knows the foreigner might have a gun in his pocket" (5). The trials and tribulations that Lazarus faces in a country where he is met with unfounded suspicion occupy a large part of the narrative, which is punctuated by leaps into the present time. These flash-forwards reveal the ways contemporary America strangely mirrors the anxieties of 1908 Chicago, which is, of course, why Brik takes an interest in Lazarus's story in the first place. Mary, on the other hand, finds her husband's "idea of a Lazarus who struggled to resurrect in America a tad pretentious" (41), part of his general propensity to take refuge from the pressures of the here and now (with its attendant commitments) into the "wilderness of elsewhere" (46). In this respect Brik again resembles Lazarus, who "was always prone to fantasies, always with one foot in some other world" (60).

Resemblances between Brik and Lazarus allow Hemon to compare the historical periods against which the two main strands of the narrative are set: the war on anarchist conspiracies in Chicago and the War on Terror initiated by the Bush administration. The hapless Lazarus is explicitly described as *"a Russian Jew of the terrorist type"* (137), removing all doubt as to how his plight relates to the contemporary context. Brik draws the link between contemporary racial profiling and the vilification of allegedly anarchist behavior without equivocation: "The war against anarchism was much like the current war on terror—funny how old habits never die. The immigration laws were changed; suspected anarchists were persecuted and deported; scientific studies on degeneracy and criminality of certain racial groups abounded. I had come across an editorial cartoon depicting an enraged Statue of Liberty kicking a cage full of degenerate, dark-faced anarchists bloodthirstily clutching knives and bombs" (43). Many details of the Chicago story are meant to echo discourses of suspicion with which the reader is doubtless familiar. Although the alleged anarchists engaged only in localized crime, it is clear to the authorities "that their failed plot had well-hidden, deeper-than-usual, possibly worldwide roots" (61). Upon reading a melodramatic, first-person book manuscript written by Lazarus, the assistant chief of police inevitably concludes that "the narrative has all the earmarks of a confession of a double crime committed in Russia, exhibiting Averbuch's cunning, murderous proclivities and foreshadowing a life of anarchism and crime in Chicago" (61–62). Averbuch's "disappointment and murderous anger . . . are almost palpable" (62), the assistant chief remarks with near certainty, of the kind that routinely draws the ire of civil rights advocates opposed to the War on Terror.

The anarchist witch hunt in early twentieth-century Chicago is an especially convenient peg on which to hang a critique of counterterrorist tactics taken to the extreme, partly because the concept of anarchism itself—even though it appears quite unrelated both to Brik's Bosnian profile and to the book's transnational themes—speaks to the moral implications of the novel in its broader historical context. Not only is the novel's subject position governed by a unique brand of cosmopolitan relativism (uniting relativity of values with a sense of universal humanity distilled in the phrase "the Other is just like me because he is unlike any Other," expressing a universalism of difference); at times it appears entirely ungoverned. In this sense it is not surprising that the subject of Brik's meditations should be a suspected anarchist. More important, this anarchist is an impoverished immigrant with whom Brik easily sympathizes. What mattered in 1908—"lousy jobs, lousier tenements, the acquisition of language, the logistics of survival, the ennoblement of self-fashioning" (41)—still has purchase almost a century later. And some of the pronouncements that fueled the hunt for anarchists still resonate today, although they do clash with Brik's post–American Century perspective. For instance, the view that the United States "naturally strive[s] toward liberty and excellence, toward the greatness that would dwarf all the sanguine accomplishments of the past empires" (273) has an embarrassing ring to it, especially after the much publicized Abu Ghraib and Guantánamo Bay fiascos. The sense of injustice that attaches to these names bolsters Hemon's decision to investigate the world of Chicago's anarchists, whose trial "has been recognized as one of the most unjust in the annals of American jurisprudence . . . the first 'Red Scare' in American history, sparking a campaign of radical-baiting and repression that has rarely if ever been surpassed" (Avrich xi, xii). The same acute anxiety swept the nation both after the terrorist attacks of 9/11 and in the aftermath of the anarchists' violent encounter with the police. In 1908 unbridled hatred and fear echoed in "cries of 'Hang them first and try them afterwards'" (Green 9), as well as in the citizens' demand that the state punish "not only the 'dynamite orators' responsible for the bombing, but also *those who sheltered and encouraged them*" (9, my emphasis), a phrase that George W. Bush would later employ to morally stigmatize the so-called Axis of Evil and consolidate the coalition of the willing assembled against Saddam Hussein.[4]

Yet even before revealing his interest in the formation and manufacture of political evil, Hemon establishes Brik as the subjective beholder in whose eyes notions of right and wrong, good and evil will be refracted or disguised. In fact the novel first reveals its ethical concerns by proposing Brik's research trip as a life-shaping moral quest: "The book would make me become someone else," Brik hopefully muses; it could "go either way: I could earn the right to orgasmic selfishness (and the money required for it) or I could purchase my moral insurance by going through the righteous process of self-doubt and self-realization" (133). Nor is he alone in hoping for moral enlightenment: his wife, Mary, "from her high position of surgically American decency," witnesses his "moral waddling" (133) and secretly awaits his recovery. To some extent Vladimir and Mary's moral incompatibility is only a particularly virulent symptom of a total mismatch: he is an introspective "global soul" (to borrow Pico Iyer's phrase), living *across* several countries rather than inhabiting any one of them; she is a down-to-earth professional woman who both anchors and frustrates him while she invisibly and unwittingly nourishes his self-flagellating instincts. Like America itself, Mary has no time for "useless metaphysical questions" and "parallel universes" (205). She is translucent and, to Brik, utterly irritating, partly because her lack of depth prevents her from noticing or appreciating his own multilayered persona. "She did not know what my life in Bosnia had been like, what made me, what I had come from; she could see only my American face, acquired through failing to be the person I wanted to be," Brik laments (106). Not knowing of his distant past, neither can she perceive *what lived invisibly* (234–35) inside him, waiting for a spectacular resurrection—an ignorance that provokes Brik's concern that their children would grow up to be "too American" for his transnational tastes, "miserable mongrels undoing their foreign deadbeat father in themselves" (254).

Yet Brik's ethical struggles reveal themselves most clearly through his interest in the Chicago anarchist movement. As a political concept, anarchy is founded on ideas of moral conditioning. It has been described as a system that "(perhaps optimistically) believes that people are fundamentally good and will voluntarily act in an ethically and morally appropriate way for the betterment of all" (Nicholson 4). Complementing this ethos of an a priori morality is a series of intriguing moments that occur during Brik's trip to Eastern Europe, and that likewise posit a soul-soothing, utopian humanism. Brik's empathy with the people he meets ("That's me," he often exclaims) verges on a vague sort of substitution that helps dispel his fear of death: "Everybody was me, and I was everybody, and in the end it didn't matter if I died" (262). Throughout, however, his "self" is only further unmoored by his ready identification with strangers. "The only one who was not me," he confesses, "was myself" (235). Brik certainly does appear to possess a solid sense of self, yet this self takes shape not as the essence of a single person—differentiated from its peers—but only when thinly spread over a large number of individuals. It is so pluralized that it outstrips the bounds of the first-person possessive; it is not the image of the world distilled in one mind, but something like a moral chromosome, evenly distributed among people and nations. Politically this understanding of selfhood serves as an antidote to the morally essentialist vision of the War on Terror, which appears intent on separating the American self from evil others for the betterment of all. Hemon's suspicion of an American desire to monopolize moral judgment seems central to the novel as a whole, and we understand it a good deal better if we bring the ethical skepticism of the French philosopher Alain Badiou to bear on the narrative.

Ridding the World of Evil, for Good: Alain Badiou

What unites Hemon and Badiou is a concern with the abuse of "goodness" both in personal relationships and in the realm of politics. By the end of the novel Brik concludes, like Badiou, that "the Good is the Good only to the extent that it does not aspire to render the world good. Its sole being lies in the situated advent of a singular truth. So it must be that the power of a truth is also a kind of powerlessness" (Badiou, *Ethics* 85).[5] Also like Badiou, as we shall see, Brik is not concerned with Aristotelian virtue ethics largely because it emphasizes happiness and well-being, states that are deeply alien to him. Overall *The Lazarus Project* criticizes the understanding of the individual (irrespective of nationality) as possessing natural and perfectible goodness, which inadvertently leads to a view of nations as intrinsically "saved" and in need of America's good intentions to recognize and fulfill their inherent potential:

> I recalled Mary, her strained, half-assed Catholic innocence, her belief that people were evil due to errors in their upbringing and a shortage of love in their lives. She just could not comprehend evil, the way that I could not comprehend the way the washing machine worked or the reason the universe expanded into infinity. For her, the prime mover of every action was a good intention, and evil occurred only if the good intention was inadvertently betrayed or forgotten. Humans could not be essentially evil, because they were always infused by God's infinite goodness and love.... I deigned to suggest ... that it was also the American thing—America was nothing if not good intentions. (187–88)

THE INTERNATIONALIZATION OF CONSCIENCE

From the assistant chief of police, who "talks, rather poetically, *about the world that resists disorder, about all that needs to be done, now or never, to rid it of evil for good*" (115), to George W. Bush's conviction that the United States "can overcome evil with greater good" (State of the Union Address, January 29, 2002), for Brik U.S. history seems imbued with an endlessly self-replenishing reservoir of goodness, ready for export. Mary's ignorance of this moral imperialism also manifests itself in her reaction to the Abu Ghraib photographs, in which she sees "essentially decent American kids acting upon a misguided belief they were protecting freedom, their good intentions going astray." By contrast, what Brik sees is "young Americans expressing their unlimited joy of the unlimited power over someone else's life and death," Americans who feel "alive and righteous by virtue of having good American intentions," intentions with whose "tortured corpses" he is mentally burdened on his trip to Eastern Europe (188–89). Not only does Brik disdain the overbearing U.S. doctrine of good intentions, but he clearly also bemoans the damage it inflicts on America's international standing as moral arbiter of political and military might.

America's moral hegemony coheres in fact around a principle of evil as an objective category that remains constant in space and time. Far from selflessly pursuing ideals of goodness, in Brik's mind the ethics of the War on Terror rely on the identification of evil, which in turn is produced and experienced, as Sherene Razack has argued, "*in relation* to the subordinate other" (*Casting Out* 63). Engagement with Otherness is thus a precondition for the formation and banishment of evil. That evil is so surprisingly easy to pinpoint recalls Badiou's observation that "according to the modern usage of ethics, Evil—or the negative—is primary: we presume a consensus regarding what is barbarian. . . . Good is what intervenes visibly against an Evil that is identifiable a priori" (*Ethics* 8). This is a pessimistic, indeed nihilist, form of ethics that places goodness at the heart of a subjectivity under constant ontological threat. Like Slavoj Žižek, who denounces contemporary biopolitics as "ultimately a politics of fear" that "focuses on defense from potential victimization or harassment" (*Violence* 34), Badiou sees in ethical thought a debased understanding of the human subject centered on its vulnerability. "Ethics subordinates the identification of this subject to the universal recognition of the evil that is done to him," Badiou writes, and concludes that "ethics thus defines man *as a victim*" (*Ethics* 10), an assessment that leads him to reject the current ideological framework of ethics as unfavorable to a positive formation of the human subject.

Importantly in the context of post-9/11 literature, Badiou defines world-changing events and evil as deeply interrelated. "At the heart of every situation, as the foundation of its being, there is a 'situated' void" (*Ethics* 68), he writes, and, in ways that help establish the significance and impact of the 9/11 attacks, he suggests that "the fundamental ontological characteristic of an event is to inscribe, to name, the situated void of that for which it is an event" (69). September 11, by the same token, doesn't signal a reordering of the world as much as it exposes the order that preceded it and which the attacks violently disrupted. *The Lazarus Project* thus seems written with the purpose of describing the "void" (a "truth" that becomes visible only in retrospect) to which the terrorist attacks ultimately gave a name: the long history of American racial fears, as well as the moral polarity of the cold war era. The subsequent War on Terror can be seen as evil to the extent that instead of aiming to correct this history, it reinforces and exacerbates its impact on the present. In Badiou's words, evil is "to believe that an event convokes not the void of the earlier situation, but its plenitude," resulting in the disaster of identifying "a truth with total power" (71). The evil instrumentalized by the War on Terror, then, ultimately turns on its historical amnesia. And this is a powerful reconfiguration of post-9/11 ethics, whose central mandate, Hemon suggests, is not a responsibility to the Other as much as fidelity to the past.

"Fidelity" to the history of an event, in Badiou's work, signifies the process by which that event is used to reorganize existing knowledge by opening up a void—historical and moral—that conceives the possibility of new subjective and political formations. In Brik's case this reorientation (encompassing both the past and the future) is a journey, which provides an opportunity for lived rather than disembodied reflection. To Brik, good and evil are defined and delineated by national boundaries and geographic coordinates, even though his own journey transgresses these barriers. Like Terry Eagleton's, Brik's ethics is "a lived relationship to truth, not a question of speculating on what one should do" (*Trouble with Strangers* 265), a question divorced from sociocultural and psychological contexts. Within this inconclusive process, for which the novel's inchoate-sounding title provides an objective correlative, what guides the fidelity is, in Badiou's terms, "something like a trace, or a name, that refers back to the vanished event" (*Ethics* 72). For Brik, a set of images fulfill this role: pictures of the Abu Ghraib tortures juxtaposed with the photograph of the dead Lazarus Averbuch (reproduced in the book). Hemon sees in this parallelism the ethical impetus of his novel: "The most painful thing to live through in the last administration was how we became complicit in the crimes the administration committed. It interested me how we were suddenly torturing people and taking photos of them. I conceived of *The Lazarus Project* before the invasion of Iraq and before Abu Ghraib but then the picture of Lazarus being held up by the police captain—a dead immigrant that was suspected of something and killed just in case—was structurally identical to the Abu Ghraib pictures.... It was one of the lines of ethical, philosophical, narrative inquiry in the book" (Reyn n.p.). In an extension to this visual collage of murder and mayhem, his dreams, the narrator notes, begin to resemble a "who's who" of international war crime: "Milošević, Mladić, Karadžić, and, lately, Bush, Rumsfeld, and Rambo figured in them" (*The Lazarus Project* 257).

Explicit comparisons between Balkan War atrocities and abuses in the War on Terror recur throughout the book. The Bosnian gangster named Rambo, who among other things capitalizes on people's despair by helping them escape besieged Sarajevo disguised as corpses, recalls less the entrepreneurial idealism of a George W. Bush than the purposeless cruelty of the guards at Abu Ghraib. And like the torture poses caught on camera at Abu Ghraib, Rambo's self-fashioning as the embodiment of evil and coolness is visually iconic: "Here he was sitting on top of a corpse of one of our soldiers, some poor sap who stood up to him in front of the wrong audience—the boy's eyes were glassy and wide open in surprise, Rambo on his chest with a cigarette in his mouth, as if he were in a commercial for a vacation in Iraq" (183).⁶ Rambo's pictures with the dead evidently recall the images of American guards at Abu Ghraib posing alongside the piled bodies of Arab prisoners, and we can reasonably assume that Rambo experienced the same thrills and motivations as his American counterparts. Brik's friend Rora describes these emotions as Rambo's "big dick, his absolute power: being alive in the middle of death" (189). The stigma attached to these pictures ultimately rubs off on image making itself, which takes on a transgressive, evil aura. Rora, for instance, recalls a time in Sarajevo when he was asked to photograph "children running away from snipers, ducking and hiding behind garbage containers, even though there was heavy sniper fire," children who were paid "to run back and forth under fire so [he] could take a perfect picture" (255). To aim a camera at these children is to become another sniper, so photography of this kind not only exposes, but sometimes actively facilitates the historical recurrence of evil by reproducing its morally unchanged avatars.

Hemon's transversal attempts to contextualize evil on a historical and geographic map implicitly seek to counteract the established understanding of evil as purely unmotivated and beyond comprehension. And it is precisely such deterritorialized obfuscation that has facilitated the rhetoric employed in the War on Terror to vilify citizens whose actions allegedly admit no explanation other than their inherent evil. In Terry Eagleton's words, in its "disparagement of rational analysis" such indiscriminate apportioning of blame "reflects something of the fundamentalism it confronts" (*Holy Terror* 116). The more assiduously we proclaim the incomprehensibility of evil, the more incomprehensible our reasoning is bound to become.⁷ In *The Lazarus Project*, particularly those sections that deal with anarchist terror, evil is identified as such precisely through its inscrutability: "*Despite all the encouraging success, we have yet to learn about the evil among us that needs to be exterminated.... It is almost impossible,* Assistant Chief says, *to pick up a man and determine whether or not he is an anarchist. We know, however, that such men are generally half-crazy individuals of foreign descent and of considerable degeneracy. We must follow them and learn their habits from the moment they reach this country so as to pre-empt their atrocities*" (60). "There is no context," Eagleton notes, "which would make [evil] explicable"; on the contrary, "the less sense it makes, the more evil it is" (*On Evil* 3). And the less sense evil makes, the more inscrutable the crusade on behalf of goodness. By attempting to decipher right and wrong as ingrained in the imperatives of an era, Hemon does not impose an explanation on atrocity, or suggest that to combat evil we must espy its underlying sense. While he denounces the inscrutability of post-9/11 moral crusades, his critique isn't directed against inscrutability as such. Rather the question posed by *The Lazarus Project* is how rationality—especially the kind of rationality (or causality) mobilized by narrative—may be instructive in decoding and deterring the maleficent mechanics of violence.

The disparagement of rational analysis may in fact have contributed to the apparent reluctance of post-9/11 literature to ask trenchant questions about evil: what it is, how we know what it is, how it can be used to facilitate politically expedient vilifications. The silence of literature about these questions may have something to do with the fact that evil as an ethical "grand narrative" induces a conceptual blockage, functioning as "a way of bringing arguments to an end" or "an end-stopping kind of term, one which forbids the raising of further questions" (Eagleton, *On Evil* 8).[8] Where evil is invoked, as in Patrick McGrath's novella "Ground Zero," the protagonist, a psychoanalyst trained in the psychological determinism of human behavior, cannot accommodate the terrorist attacks within her cognitive frame. In her unreliable narrative terrorist evil is therefore circumvented or obfuscated through various forms of transference. Hemon takes a similar approach, working *around* the term in an attempt to place it historically and philosophically, yet his overt interest in the "sense of futility or meaninglessness" (Eagleton, *On Evil* 13) commonly associated with evil cuts to the core of the concept and betrays Hemon's intention to retool this meaninglessness into an effusive ethical ambiguity. In "its uncanniness, its appalling unreality, . . . its assault on meaning, the fact that it lacks some vital dimension, the way it is trapped in the mind-numbing monotony of an eternal recurrence" (Eagleton, *On Evil* 49), evil comes to represent in this novel everything that Brik's consciousness experiences as unrepresentable, from his own adulterous proclivities to the image of the biblical Lazarus himself, from turn-of-the-century Chicago to post-9/11 New York, echoing Žižek's statement "Evil is something which threatens to return forever, a spectral dimension which magically survives its physical annihilation and continues to haunt us" (*Violence* 56). Far from inhibiting moral judgment, this haunting testifies to the resilience and malleability of the rational mind as a fundamental premise for an embodied ethics as frail and indeterminate as the human condition it regulates.

Aesthetically Hemon's subtle recalibration (and, in a way, vindication) of evil as a timeless, complex condition manifests itself in the narrative's transgressive visual strategies and the supreme pointlessness of its many digressions. The form of the novel, one could argue, is coextensive with its moral outcome. The futility mobilized by Brik's journey is a product of the novel's meanderings through a realm beyond belonging and nationhood, where past and present intersect, emotions ebb and flow, responsibilities wax and wane. In this realm the magic séance with ancient evil can be held and recorded, while Rambo, Bush, and Brik exchange notes without qualms or remorse for their transgressions. The narrative voice consequently suffers from a severe attention deficit disorder evident in the novel's shifting plot development and uneven dedication to characters. Many relevant episodes trail off unexpectedly; other episodes never become relevant at all. As the epigraph to his earlier novel, *Nowhere Man*, reveals, Hemon has always been interested in what he calls, borrowing from Bruno Schulz, "events that have been left in the cold, unregistered, hanging in the air, errant and homeless"—events that would otherwise pass unnoticed on the radar of history. Yet Brik's errant homelessness cannot be imagined outside his immigrant condition, so it is worth asking to what extent his exilic consciousness shapes his ethical dilemmas and his interest in transnational axes of evil.

A Theodicy of Exile

Ethics and transnationalism have been two exciting fields of study in recent years, each enlivened by vast scholarship. Despite their many distinctions, Hemon's novel suggests some unexpected overlaps between these fields, asking questions that illuminate the conceptual trajectory

I am retracing in this book: from the moralistic rhetoric of the War on Terror on the domestic front to the increasingly transnational forms of contemporary ethics and its narrative emplotment. Eagleton defines evil in terms of its liminality: it is "a transitional state of being," he writes, "a domain wedged between life and death, which is why we associate it with ghosts, mummies, and vampires. Anything which is neither quite dead nor quite alive can become an image of it" (*On Evil* 123). Lazarus's condition fits this image, as does the novel's broader concern with exile and migration, exposing the concept of evil as a link between ideas that are rarely grouped together, particularly, as I suggest here, those of immigration, exile, and nostalgia.

The self as fluctuating, deterritorialized sum rather than stable entity is Brik's chief obsession as he travels, finding it difficult to "return" to a world he never "leaves" in any definitive sense of the term. The American Dream, once based on a sharp separation between the promised land and the country one chose (or was forced) to leave behind, has little purchase in a time of transcultural bigamy. As Hemon observes in an interview, "You don't have to choose anymore. . . . The former homeland, which became a nostalgic dream because the connections were lost, doesn't exist anymore. The American Dream became completely obsolete in this two-way situation" (Blazan 261). Thus unmoored from a fixed notion of homeland, Brik feels that "there is nowhere to go," and uses the absence of locality as a positive index of the increasingly porous geography of the contemporary world: "Nowhere is the biggest place in the world—indeed, nowhere is the world" (*The Lazarus Project* 182). Free from direction and purposefulness, he and Rora travel "mindlessly from one place to another" (228), seeing nothing beyond what presents itself at any given moment, then moving on to the next fleeting impression.

Yet even though he appears at peace with being "a reasonably loyal citizen of a couple of countries" (11), Brik often sounds very much like someone who has been painfully severed from his past. This sense of loss transpires most clearly in his speculations on how the biblical Lazarus may have reacted to his resurrection, disguised as a blessing yet concealing depths of loneliness and nostalgia. "Did he remember being dead," Brik wonders, "or did he just enter another dream of another life by way of Marseille? Did he have to disremember his previous life and start from scratch, like an immigrant?" (127). Although Brik's self is centered around his American passport—a "bounty of American life" (177) he carries with him—other identities also revolve around it, and though nothing is lost, nothing is gained either. Like the protagonist of *Nowhere Man*, Brik oscillates between an enjoyment of this confusion as "being in mid-chapters of one's own Bildungsroman" and frustration with the "lonesome climbing up the steep, craggy cliff of self-knowledge" (*Nowhere Man* 82). The novel seems to vibrate with the masochistic pleasure Brik reaps from his exiled condition, yet for the most part the suffering is deeply felt and unwanted. While his trip may have been intended as a homeopathic gesture of self-healing, it ultimately leaves him languishing in all manner of twilight regions, where forms of belonging and citizenship slither and tangle, further sapping his already defeatist morale. Ultimately his multiple locations amount to a sense of permanent *dis*location: "I am not here and not there. I am in both places at the same time" (Blazan 263).[9] Even though he is ambivalent about distinguishing between home and adopted country, Brik is a permanent human "contact zone" (to borrow a phrase from Mary Louise Pratt), a deterritorialized site constituted not necessarily along the fault line between Western discourses and non-Western formations (a fault line that is almost soothing in its moral familiarity), but with reference to multiple, overlapping allegiances and ethically contingent discourses, the most predominant of which congeals, again, around the arbitrary and exclusionary formation of evil.[10] So in addition to explicitly political discussions of evil in times of war, Hemon criticizes the abuse of moralism more generally in contemporary discourse. He does so by defusing the self/Other binary in favor of a capacious notion of "sameness," a concept to which I now turn.

Debbie Lisle has persuasively argued that contemporary travel writing stages "the complex rearticulation of Western authority within the most liberal and cosmopolitan gestures" (261). By contrast, Hemon's novel has the ability to focus on forms of authority and expression that are separate from a Western paradigm. As a result of Brik's label-free identity, his journey does not conform to traditional, apolitical encounters with difference, as recounted in travel writing. While on the surface the narrative relies heavily on the logic of identity and difference, its primary concern is the formation of selfhood in the face of *sameness*—not a glib, cosmopolitan uniformity, but a structure of identity and coincidence that contains as much potential for responsiveness as the preferred interlocutor of Levinasian ethics, the Other. To some extent this revision of the self/Other binary is facilitated by modern means of communication and the ease of travel, which the novel stresses by indirectly comparing Averbuch's experience of exile with Brik's contemporary journeys.[11] Hemon in fact often speaks of the global communication system as a game changer in the history of immigration, allowing migrants to inhabit two or more worlds at once. Yet in investigating Lazarus Averbuch, he interrogates an ethics of exile that this new media dynamic has repressed: Does the person toward whom we feel morally responsible need to be accessible or still alive? Does moral responsibility presuppose or even require the inaccessibility of the Other? And to what extent does Hemon's "sameness" defy the self-binding "honoring of Otherness" in which Hale, Spivak, and others see the key ethical function of the novel?

Badiou's ideas on ethics and evil are again informative in this respect. Like Hemon, Badiou is suspicious of alterity as the primary basis for encountering the Other, who "always resembles me too much for the hypothesis of an originary exposure to his alterity to be *necessarily* true" (*Ethics* 22). Instead Badiou locates the ethical imperative in "*recognizing the Same*" (25). In a way that Hemon's narrative helps to illuminate, Badiou trenchantly claims that "no light is shed on any concrete situation by the notion of the 'recognition of the other'" (27). The alternative is not vapid universality but a subjective operation in which the Same is recognized in relation to a constructed truth very much resembling the process by which Badiou explains the "fidelity" around a historical event: even though both Other and event might appear alien in a given situation, they help to focus their opposite (the Self, the void) not by distinction—which, as Badiou rightly claims, tends to block discussion—but by assuming common features. In *The Lazarus Project* these features often appear to be the lowest common denominator of all mankind, the ultimate Sameness of death and dying as well as the imagination of the afterlife, images to which the novel returns with obsessive regularity, and sometimes with delectable humor: "Death must be pleasant, the pain and shock of its infliction notwithstanding.... Never mind Mr. Christ's eschatological circus—there must be the postorgasmic moment of absolute peace, of coming home, the moment when the fog of life floats away like gun smoke and everything is finally nothing. Perhaps that was what Mr. Christ deprived Lazarus of. He may have been okay dead; it was all over, he was home.... Once Lazarus was thrown out of the comfy bed of eternity, he wandered the world, forever homeless, forever afraid to fall asleep, dreaming of dreaming" (179).

There is much play in the novel on ideas of death and other forms of ontological homelessness, what Badiou would call "nostalgia for the void" (*Handbook of Inaesthetics* 132). The black pages that separate the chapters (black on both sides, the second including a black-and-white photograph) recall the black pages in Laurence Sterne's *Tristram Shandy*, where the device is used to convey, among other things, ideas of death and disappearance. The return of Averbuch's sister, Olga, to the house she shared with Lazarus after having identified his corpse encapsulates the entire novel's monochromatically despondent mood: "Her home will be cold and empty. Night will be falling, dense and boundless. She will not light the lantern, blind to the shadows. She will sit at the table, say nothing to no one, let nothing settle all around her like falling snow" (274). As with Olga and Lazarus (and many other immigrants to America, we are asked to imagine), the location of subjectivity both within and outside the spaces of life suggests that there is a touch of the depressive about Brik. His dedication to his research project, while certainly a source of energy for the otherwise unemployed and unmotivated writer, is infused with emotional and cerebral nihilism. What's more, Brik becomes morbidly fascinated with his own dissolution, crawling off to live or die in his native Sarajevo as a final flourish to his peripatetic life. His slide toward death parallels his move toward the Same: Lazarus, Sarajevo, past friends and memories, his past self—a move that is ethical and sinister at the same time. "Only the good are capable of dying," Eagleton remarks, seeing in death "a form of self-dispossession which must be rehearsed in life if it is to be successfully accomplished.... Being-for-others and being-toward-death are aspects of the *same* condition" (*On Evil* 24, my emphasis).

The nothingness encroaching upon Brik is bound up with the novel's recurrent themes of misrecognition and unknowability. Brik is inscrutable to himself. He can never fully grasp his own nature because there is nothing stable or determinate about it to be securely known. Echoing back to McGrath's and Tristram's scrutiny of psychosexual deviance, Hemon is concerned with the instability of selfhood as a precondition for ethical insight and response. "He had always been complete," Brik jealously remarks of his friend Rora. "He had finished the work of becoming himself, long before any of us could even imagine such a feat was possible" (30). The fluidity of his self-image engulfs the whole world in a terrifying state of ambiguity. Everything around Brik appears sinister and unruly. His marriage steadily falls apart at the seams. In order to pluck order from chaos, he sets out to unravel the intricate text of his own existence through that of Lazarus, yet the dissolute nature of both writer and protagonist infects the narrative itself.

Despite his transgressions (romancing the grant giver, leaving his wife), the novel nevertheless does not reject its hero, harboring a view of evil (including Brik's own misdemeanors) that is perfectly in line with his contextualizing approach. To the idea of Otherness within the text the novel adds the text *as* Other, a narrative whose main feature is its tantalizing incomprehensibility. This textual strategy is not new, of course. Writing about Henry James's *The Golden Bowl*, Robert Eaglestone remarks, "The characters are simply not characters in a recognizable sense.... Just when they seem to have become settled, to be *heimlich*, they change. It is not simply a question of 'behaving out of character': the change interrupts the understanding of the character right from the beginning" ("Flaws" 84). Staging this experience of Otherness is, according to Eaglestone, the fundamental task of literature: "It is this sense of unease, this sense that it can never quite be encapsulated that seems to give literature its most significant appeal to the ethical" (85).

The ethical appeal of Hemon's novel ultimately rests in its injunction that the spatial and temporal coordinates of the post-9/11 era should not be too swiftly demarcated or ignored. The provocatively incoherent plot of *The Lazarus Project* thus exemplifies the advantages of coming at the already established "9/11 plot" from unfamiliar, unsettling angles. The anarchist insurrections in Chicago and the Bosnian War supply a wider frame that reveals Hemon's concern with anteriority in gauging the implications of the 9/11 attacks. This is, in part, a reaction to the exclusion of anteriority in the War on Terror—that is, the refusal to examine the history of racial prejudice in the United States and the transnational overlaps it secretly contains. *The Lazarus Project* problematizes moral discourses in the War on Terror by recruiting the concept of evil as an ideological hinge in conjoining past and present. Ironically enough, as I have shown, the novel's notion of evil contextualizes events throughout history and across national borders, despite the fact that evil, as it has hitherto been defined, resists contextualization. To be sure, Brik's efforts to reconstitute Averbuch's past and his own hybrid heritage involve forms of misunderstanding and—to use a term I have already discussed at some length—*mediation*: through historical documents, photographs, museum exhibits, secondhand reports, and plain narratorial subjectivity. Yet the elusiveness of knowledge, Hemon suggests, should not obviate the value of attempting to understand more fully the occluded cultural history and circuitous global framework that continue to shape the post-9/11 era.

Representing Ethics in Pat Barker's *Double Vision*

Seen in a global context, not only can the terrorist attacks be productively juxtaposed with other acts of political violence, but even the Ground Zero site in the aftermath of the collapses may be understood as one of the most photogenic war zones of modern times, despite its densely populated, urban setting.[12] While certainly not a typical military combat zone, characterized as it was by a largely civilian death toll and a striking imbalance in the level of preparation and foreknowledge of the parties involved, the site of the terrorist attacks does display similarities to international conflict zones covered by modern war correspondents. As Alex Thomson, chief correspondent of Britain's Channel 4, aptly points out, "Wars are less and less based on a battlefield. If you want to see a good old-fashioned frontal war happening now, probably the only place you'll see it is Eritrea, Ethiopia and nobody covers that. More and more it's happening in towns, in villages, Chechnya for example, and largely against civilian populations" (qtd. in McLaughlin 13). Phillip Knightley also identifies a "trend that has shifted the danger of dying in war from soldiers to civilians—at the beginning of the century, ninety per cent of casualties in war were soldiers; at the end of the century ninety per cent of casualties in war were civilians" (505).

Images taken in Lower Manhattan during the attacks similarly qualify as *war* photography, with the significant distinction that unlike war photographers who enter a combat zone with previous awareness of its existence and perils, photographers at Ground Zero had no inkling of immediate danger until the towers eventually collapsed. "The first on the scene," *Time* magazine's photographer Christopher Morris explains, "were shooting the burning tower, with people jumping out of the building"; to most witnesses at that point, the plane impact appeared to be an unfortunate accident. "And then they found themselves in a war situation when the second plane hit because of all the debris. Shrapnel can just as easily be a piece of steel or a piece of glass; it can all decapitate you. Debris like that falling on you is the same as somebody shooting at you, especially when the buildings collapsed" (qtd. in Howe 37). Indeed many combat-experienced photojournalists lost their lives on that day, doomed by their professional desire to get as close as possible to the flaming buildings in order to obtain the most powerfully descriptive shots. The renowned war photographer James Nachtwey, who lives in the vicinity of the towers and witnessed the impact of the first plane, admits that the beauty of the scene, coupled with the danger of taking pictures from up close, forced him to face a dilemma otherwise specific to more conventional war zones. "In a fraction of a second," Nachtwey reminisces, "I recognized what an incredible sight it was—that it actually looked very beautiful as well as terrifying, that it would make a brilliant photograph, and that if I took even a moment to raise my camera I would not survive" (qtd. in Howe 189).

The centerpiece of Pat Barker's novel *Double Vision* is precisely the experience of the 9/11 attacks from the perspective of a seasoned war correspondent. Coincidentally the attacks occur on the same day that the marriage of its protagonist, Stephen Sharkey, virtually ends after he calls his wife—probably to dispel her anxieties about his well-being—only to find her in bed with another man. Symbolically, then, the destruction of the towers amplifies the shock of his personal disappointment. Long after the attacks, images of that day witnessed directly or mediated by television still come back to Stephen with astounding clarity and insistence: "When he closed his eyes, Stephen's brain filled with images of shocked people covered in plaster dust. Grey dust blocking their nostrils, caking their eyelids. Gritty on the floor of the hotel lobby, trampled up the stairs and along the corridor to his room, where the television screen domesticated the roar and tumult, the dust, the debris, the cries, the thud of bodies hitting the ground, reduced all this to silent images, played and replayed, and played again in a vain attempt to make the day's events credible" (96–97).

Whereas in Schulman and DeLillo the images build up into an emotional blockage, here they explosively evoke a series of catastrophic conflicts and their representation in art. The muted images of dust-choked Manhattan appear to suppress muffled cries, something they share with Francisco de Goya's ghoulish representations of war and massacre in etchings that Barker's narrative repeatedly invokes.[13] Like the soundless footage of the burning towers, Goya's paintings quietly "roar" at the viewer (*Double Vision* 154), a paradox that anticipates the tension Barker sets up between visualized suffering and its depiction in words. Complicating its transnational and cross-historical view of war atrocity, the novel's counterpoint to the iconic representation of September 11 is a memory fragment that Stephen carries with him from the Bosnian War, congealing around the image—and later the photograph taken by his friend Ben Frobisher—of a rape victim in Sarajevo. Stephen periodically rehearses this memory flash only to realize that he has not managed to assimilate it properly despite the lengthy passage of time. "Nothing else had ever affected him in the same way," he concedes, "though he'd seen many worse things. She was waiting for him, that's the way it felt. She had something to say to him, but he's never managed to listen, or not in the right way" (55)—the "right way" implying both visual acuity and ethical responsiveness.

In ways that shed doubt on exceptionalist discourses of 9/11 as unprecedented, unrepeatable, and impossible to describe, Barker repositions post-9/11 literary ethics within the larger international context of war representation (which also constitutes the topic of a book Stephen Sharkey is writing). My argument singles out two aspects of Barker's novel that crystallize debates around the ethics and aesthetics of representing terror: on the one hand, the responsibility to assuage the suffering of war, a duty that may be fulfilled through the relentless representation of atrocity (whether in a sympathetic or impersonal manner) and, on the other hand, the deeper intricacies of "representing" (i.e., detecting, expressing, and reciprocating) emotions in the equally embattled realm of private life. This dual focus—or indeed "double vision"—is what motivates the book's compartmentalized narrative structure, making up an ensemble piece that brings characters together without necessarily helping them commingle in emotionally significant ways. Drawing on the affective alienation of these characters and on their efforts to transgress it, Barker's investigation into the disasters of war scrutinizes the international scope of human empathy, of trauma, and of war itself, waged across expanses of space and a range of timescales, but also on the domestic front.

The alternative to "the promiscuous voyeurism a visual culture makes possible," Michael Ignatieff has stated, is to regard the global mediation of atrocity "as a hopeful example of the internationalization of conscience" (10). While the transfer of world-historical trauma into personal crisis of an erotic nature is certainly common in other post-9/11 narratives (as the previous chapters have revealed), Barker explicitly examines the role of art in this mediation and regards the erotic not merely as the end product of this transference but as one of its essential ingredients. Love, Barker suggests—and this is an argument that runs parallel to Felman's and Tristram's insights into the sexualization of "meaning"—is not only *what* but also *how* we represent, thus inviting an ethical reading of the novel in the idiom established by Martha Nussbaum in her classic work *Love's Knowledge*. Far from being peripheral to contemporary ethical discourse, Nussbaum's work strikes me as indispensable in understanding narratives that dramatize not only the mechanics of empathy but also the temporal investment of opening up to the Other (in ways adumbrated by DeLillo, Schulman, and Hemon through a decelerated narrative pace), as well as in charting the galvanic chrono-erotics by which the ethical contact between the domestic and the remote comes into being.

The Ethics of Representation

Barker's fictional world is dominated by significant historical events, especially World War I, which casts long shadows over the *Regeneration* trilogy, *Another World*, and *Life Class*.[14] Barker often retraces the reverberating long-term effects of these events, so to a reader who comes to the book expecting this writer's by now familiar interest in war and its aftermath, 9/11 might appear as a disingenuous pretext for her more intense engagement with the Balkan wars of the 1990s and with the bombing of Afghanistan in October 2001.[15] Yet even though the terrorist attacks are described only in passing, the reader does retain a sense of their catalytic function throughout the novel. They could even be seen as precisely the kind of conflict toward which a writer like Barker would naturally gravitate, defined as they are primarily by their aftermath and long-term impact rather than by their own (brief) duration. Like *Another World*, which keenly observes the cognitive and emotional life of a World War I veteran less for what his war experiences may suggest than for what may be called his "memory management," *Double Vision* moves beyond the terrorist attacks as they happened, engaging instead with a post-9/11 international panorama marked by political volatility and paranoia.[16]

In order to capture the far-reaching consequences of the events in New York, Barker locates the plot of her novel as far from the madding crowd of urban terror as possible, in a village near Newcastle, England, plagued by the hoof-and-mouth disease epidemic of 2001–02. Even against this seemingly peaceable backdrop, echoes of the 9/11 attacks persist: the carcasses of farm animals are burned, setting off "clouds of foul-smelling black smoke," "a stench of rotting flesh," and "scraps of burnt hair and skin" whirling into the air (31). Barker subtly reconstructs the aftermath of the 9/11 attacks in this passage, so Elizabeth Swanson Goldberg is right to emphasize the symbolic connotation of the singed cowhide that falls on Kate's lip and "resonates with testimonies from New Yorkers regarding the horror of breathing the air in Lower Manhattan for weeks after 9/11, the way in which they experienced the ingestion of death and violation with every breath" (169). John Brannigan detects further echoes of post-9/11 urban disaster: "The images of a dust-filled city are also ghosted in the novel by other images of snow, fog, the whiteness of Kate's studio, and the impenetrable sea mist which endangers Stephen and Justine in their boat trip to Holy Island, images which recurrently figure the problems of seeing" (*Pat Barker* 154).

Such correspondences notwithstanding, the geographical contrast between urban terror and a rural milieu helps to establish the ethical duality of the book, starkly signposted in its title and intimated by Barker herself in a revealing interview. Distinguishing between the *Regeneration* trilogy and her more recent novel *Life Class*, Barker juxtaposes "the ethics of representation" with "the ethics of action," the former energizing her later work (*Double Vision* and *Life Class*), the latter guiding her more direct engagement with the reality rather than the image of war in earlier fiction (Brannigan, "An Interview" 370). Barker delineates the stakes of her inquiry in simple yet trenchant terms: "I wanted to capture . . . the ethical dimension of people having to think about what they represent and how. How much can people take? How far can you go in showing it as it actually is? On the other hand, can you afford to be so anodyne in your representation that people lose a fresh sense of the horror and of the price that is being paid?" (qtd. in Smith 48).

Double Vision's main contribution to an ethics of representation inflected by a post-9/11 sensibility lies in its oblique discussion of how war reporting—through both presence at the scene of violence and visual or verbal narrativization—brings into focus the horror and disasters of warfare. In glimpsing humanity at its worst, war reporters more or less consciously and consistently intervene in the chain of destruction, so the ethics of representation cannot be entirely divorced from an ethics of action.

Barker's only caveat to this otherwise essential correspondence between two categories of ethical engagement is voiced in the critique of visual consumerism expressed by Justine, a nineteen-year-old with whom the recently divorced Stephen is having an affair (her name a clear indication of her starring role in the novel's ethical parable). Rather than indiscriminately absorb the media's deluge of information, Justine divides atrocities into those to which she can respond (and which she chooses to watch) and those whose alleviation exceeds the range of her interventionist abilities; these she refuses to ingest, as they arouse in her moral sentiments at the same time that they reinforce her political paralysis: "I don't see the point. There's nothing I can do about it. If it's something like a famine, OK, you can contribute, but with a lot of this there's nothing anybody can do except gawp and say, 'Ooh, isn't it awful?' when really they don't give a damn. It's all pumped-up emotion, it's just false, like when those families come on TV because somebody's gone missing, or thousands of people send flowers to people they don't know. It's just *wanking*" (141).

Barker shares Justine's view, which she commends as reasonable temperance in a world of media gluttony. "I'm very tempted by Justine's point of view," she confesses, "because it has a kind of austerity to it. You could argue for it as a religious point of view: you restrict your seeing of horrors unless you can actually do something to relieve them; otherwise you turn away. There's a kind of wisdom in that" (qtd. in Smith 48). Stephen's disabused relationship to his own profession is similarly predicated on questions about the ethical and practical viability of intervening in global atrocities. Ultimately, admits Michael Nicholson, a former ITN senior foreign correspondent, despite the ambitions of correspondents starting out to redress the evils of the world, their sole achievement is to "advertise its ills" (qtd. in McLaughlin 14). Particularly in the Bosnian conflict, war reporting notoriously failed to outbalance the compassion fatigue that had set in despite (and partly due to) the steady stream of horrific images, whose impact was further weakened by the political consensus that the conflict was irresolvable.[17]

Barker complicates her discussion of representational ethics by proposing analogies between Ben Frobisher's landscape photography (in which he dabbles when not on assignment) and Goya's early works. The similarities are not only intriguing but also integrative to the novel as a whole. Ben's resolutely antipastoral rural photography encloses a coiled potential for explosive violence, just barely visible from the corner of one's eye: "Fenland, waterland, brown tarns in gorse-covered hills, snow light, water light—all with the same brooding darkness in them.... You always knew, looking at these empty fields, these miles of white sand with marram grass waving in the wind, that somewhere, close at hand, but outside the frame, a murder had been committed" (*Double Vision* 64–65). Goya's early works similarly contain barely hidden traces of the darkness flaunted without restraint in his later productions. In a seemingly lighthearted painting of a small child holding a bird by a string, two cats hover in the background, watching the bird with deadly concentration, as if awaiting the propitious moment to ambush their frolicking prey.

Such is, of course, the nature of the terrorist threat as well, a menace masked by the aura of familiarity and ready to reveal itself only when it is too late for an effective interception. Such is also the charm of the novel's rural setting—feisty in its frequent gatherings, yet ominous in the secrets everybody seems to harbor and in the acts of violence that shake the village. The darkness of the surrounding forest gnaws away at the safety and coziness of warm, well-lit homes, "pressure building behind the thin membrane of everyday life like matter in a boil" (89). For such a starkly underplotted novel, the death count in *Double Vision* is indeed quite disturbing: two animals are killed, and their remains provide the topic of a morbid conversation between Stephen and his nephew Adam; Ben is killed on assignment in Afghanistan; the Sarajevo rape victim revisits the text at regular intervals; Ben's painter wife, Kate, hires a temporary assistant, Peter Wingrave, who seems to have slaughtered several women (or at least relishes inventing fictional plots along these lines). Near fatal experiences abound: there is a car accident, a burglary, and one episode of near drowning.

Beyond this sense of lurking menace, Goya's centrality to Barker's narrative is already announced in its epigraph "*No se puede mirar*. One cannot look at this. *Yo lo vi*. I saw it. *Esto es lo verdadero*. This is the truth," later invoked by Stephen in a conversation with Kate: "It's that argument he's having with himself, all the time, between the ethical problems of showing the atrocities and yet the need to say, 'Look, this is what's happening' . . . and I thought, My God, we're still facing exactly the same problem. There's always this tension between wanting to show the truth, and yet being sceptical about what the effects of showing it are going to be" (119).[18] Stephen's interest in these ethical concerns do not, however, originate with Goya but emerge indirectly from viewing the documentary footage filmed by the Naudet brothers in New York on September 11. "Something [Jules Naudet] said haunted me," Stephen remarks. "At one point he turned his camera off—he wouldn't film people burning—and he said, 'Nobody should have to see this.' And of course immediately I thought of Goya" (118–19). Naudet himself does, of course, see the horror, but he is able neither to intervene nor to look away.

Yet by overstressing the question of whether a situation of crisis can be helped through its visual representation, the novel overlooks the extent to which the eye of the spectator (painter, photographer, filmmaker, and so on) may be damaged in the process of witnessing, or how such damage might impregnate the resulting representation. Many of Ben's war photographs depict conditions of global squalor and misery whose image is meant to galvanize the viewer into humanitarian action: "an old Serbian woman surrounded by icons, scraps of food on the table in front of her; a queue of women and children waiting their turn at the tap; an old Muslim woman, tottering down the street with a milk bottle full of water, the only container she was strong enough to carry" (121). The very last image Ben takes, however, does not depict war victims, but a field of deterritorialized desolation sprinkled with shadows and abandoned tanks: "This mass of military debris filled most of the frame, so that from the viewer's angle they seemed to be a huge wave about to break. Behind them was a small white sun, no bigger than a golf ball, veiled in mist. No people. Hardware left behind after the Russian invasion of Afghanistan: the last war. But the composition was so powerful it transcended the limits of a particular time and place, and become a *Dies Irae*. A vision of the world as it would be after the last human being had left, forgetting to turn out the light" (123). Representation itself, in an aesthetic sense uncoupled from ideas of territory and nation around which wars are usually waged, prevails here over Ben's sense of humanitarian responsibility, leading him to believe that mere witnessing—of a condition that cannot be changed—has an inherent value over and above moral action.

The futility of visual interventionism becomes palpable, however, in the circumstances of an execution that Ben witnesses and captures on film:

> A man on his knees staring up at the men who are preparing to kill him. But Ben had included his own shadow in the shot, reaching out across the dusty road. The shadow says I'm here. I'm holding a camera and that fact will determine what happens next. In the next shot the man lies dead in the road, and the shadow of the photographer, the shadow of a man with a deformed head, has moved closer.
>
> This wasn't the first execution recorded on film, nor even the first to be staged specially for the camera, but normally the photographer's presence and its impact on events is not acknowledged. Here Ben had exploded the convention. (123)

Despite this minor transgression of photographic framing rules, the presence of the camera emphatically fails to determine the course of events or to avert the prospect of death. The only one on whom spectatorship has an impact is the photographer himself, his "deformed head" having absorbed the shock of the murder without deflecting its traumatic potential. *Double Vision* shows that such professional deformations have a lasting effect on war reporters' capacity to distinguish between ethical and opportunistic behavior while weakening their ability to intervene in domestic situations that they would otherwise be quite readily equipped to change.

Journalism, Globalization, and the Pain of Others

Coined by the former BBC correspondent Martin Bell, the term *journalism of attachment* has divided the profession between those who support morally engaged reporting that takes sides and is partial to the human catastrophe of war and those anchored in the tradition of objective and dispassionate journalism (Bell 102–09). Bell dismisses objective reporting as "bystander journalism" bound to miss the real story, which can be accessed only through emotional investment. The damages of war inevitably rub off on reporters who choose to make this investment through a form of affective contamination quite similar to trauma transference. Witnesses of war thus become attuned to the pain they observe and record, yet without setting their indirect experience on par with immediate victimization. Barker invokes the myth of the returning soldier in her description of Stephen's arrival in the countryside (201) precisely to suggest that the distinctions between war correspondents and military combatants have become blurred. By acknowledging the moral ground on which it operates, Bell's ethical journalism as practiced by Barker's protagonists aims to prevent the terrors of war from dissolving into an empty spectacle and places these terrors within a framework that distinguishes right from wrong, even if this discernment might take a heavy psychological toll and provide only a contingent, temporary placeholder for an elusive sense of absolute justice.

However, particularly in conflicts where moral standards are bloodily contested, to define the rights and wrongs of a conflict is often to mischaracterize its stakes. In a way that reinforces this sense of moral ambivalence permeating the novel's transnational plot, I perceive a productive thread connecting the ethical ambiguity of the Bosnian War with the equally murky Peninsular War featured in Goya's works—an ambiguity that Barker explicitly sets against the moralistic idiom of post-9/11 conflicts in the Middle East, conflicts that increasingly take place on television screens and are, as such, susceptible to the same ethical challenges encapsulated by Goya and Balkan photojournalism. Julia Blackburn describes the Peninsular War as depicted by Goya in terms that are strikingly redolent of the Bosnian conflict: "It was a war of random slaughter and terrible confusion in which as many soldiers were killed by hunger, disease and exhaustion as by gunshot and the sword. It was a war in which the women in the towns and villages could expect to be raped by their English allies as well as by their French enemies. . . . Savagery was answered by even more savagery and the land was littered with grotesquely mutilated corpses. . . . It hardly seems to matter which side you are on since there is no way of disentangling right from wrong, the just from the unjust; there is only cruelty answered by more cruelty" (100–101).

In such cases it is advisable, Stephen believes, to "put cruelty first," in Judith Shklar's words, namely to adopt an understanding of journalism as "giving people the raw material to make moral judgments" (Barker, *Double Vision* 227) by acting on viewers in ways that bear only indirectly on the judgments that these viewers form about the war. Such moral relativism was clearly not required in the aftermath of the September 11 attacks.[19] Within hours the consensus emerged, briefly punctured by Sontag, that the victimized view condemning the perpetrators (individuals and entire nations) as unequivocally evil was not only acceptable but mandatory. Likewise, as McLaughlin writes, the Bosnian conflict "was reported as a titanic battle between good and evil in which journalists in general adopted a sustained anti-Serb narrative. Atrocity stories were reported with scant regard for their veracity—no checking, no official confirmations or denials, just the rush to instant judgment" (167).

Yet in Barker's novel the discovery of the raped woman and the photographs of her body, which Stephen rejects as too invasive and simulacral, provides an ideal opportunity to showcase cruelty, unattached to moral judgment, in the representation of violence. The incident polarizes the two friends in terms of how they prize veracity, whether they choose to express or withhold their response to cruelty. After he discovers Ben's photograph and realizes that his own attempt to cover the woman's genital wounds was reversed by the photographer, Stephen sees in the demeaning exposure of the woman's suffering yet another act of violence perpetrated against her, in conditions of even greater vulnerability than those of the rape itself. By returning to the raped woman and restoring her initial position, Ben subjects her to the camera's voyeuristic gaze, thus staging, if not the photograph itself, then at least the circumstances of its reception: "Stephen was shocked on her behalf to see her exposed like this, though, ethically, Ben had done nothing wrong. He hadn't staged the photograph. He'd simply restored the corpse to its original state. And yet it was difficult not to feel that the girl, spreadeagled like that, had been violated twice" (121). Although Ben's gesture isn't, in itself, immoral, his repetition of the initial cruelty subordinates violence to the aesthetic success of its representation.

Deepening this guilt-inducing sense of violation, the image haunts Stephen as sensory experience, the exact smells and textures of the crime scene revisiting him with the same insistence as his vision of the woman in her harrowing pose. The memory of her body is organic as much as it retains the indeterminacy of hallucination: "Her head was beside his on the pillow, and when he rolled over on to his stomach, trying to get away from her, he found her body underneath him, as dry and insatiable as sand" (55). His position on top of the woman replicates the act of violence that killed her in the first place, yet the sexual connotations of the image become more benign as the narrative proceeds, particularly through the understated analogies (but also wholesome differences) between the raped woman and Stephen's nubile lover, Justine. In the peaceful cottage his brother Robert offers him to accommodate his writing and help assuage the trauma of divorce, Stephen defines his blissful location in contrast to his painful memories of Sarajevo: "No skulls in the grass, no girls with splayed thighs and skirts around their waists revealing, even in the early stages of decomposition, what had been done to them before they died. No smell of decay clinging to the skin. Just a square of window fringed by dark leaves" (49). Justine's presence is appreciated precisely because she replaces the remembered "other woman" in Stephen's bed.

In fact Stephen seems incapable of perceiving Justine as anything other than an extension of his suppressed Bosnian memories, which lure him into an acute fascination with female victimization as such. It is, then, quite significant that among all the crimes Stephen has witnessed, it is the rape victim who stands out as an iconic image of inhuman cruelty, recalling the fact that rape was indeed the most notorious and hyperbolically overhyped crime of the Bosnian conflict, exaggerated by all sides who sought recourse to war photography to substantiate their contradictory claims. Historically, as Caroline Kennedy-Pipe and Penny Stanley have pointed out, rape has been an inescapable by-product of war. Yet "the conflicts in the Balkans during the 1990s," they note, "produced 'visible' evidence of the phenomenon of rape in war" as well as "showed the historic problem of providing accurate data on rape, revealed tales of rape for propaganda, and demonstrated repeatedly the difficulties of finding appropriate legal and political mechanisms for dealing with the abuse of women" (73). Rape was used in Bosnia not only as a supplement or alternative to genocide—often in rape camps where women were held in custody over several weeks and repeatedly assaulted—but also as an effective propaganda tool, revealing how the representation of atrocity, beyond triggering aesthetic debates, joins the visual arsenal of media as a weapon of war.

Considering the extent to which his memories of war revolve around the spectacle of ravaged female bodies, it is hardly surprising that Stephen should become romantically involved with Justine—the young woman whose innocence threatens to be violently defiled by burglars—rather than with the mature, sophisticated Kate, who overcomes random violence (her car accident) with resolute elegance and refuses to be intimidated by the invasive surveillance of her deranged assistant (the same man who seduces and callously abandons Justine). Amplifying Stephen's fascination with female vulnerability is the recurrent representation of animals mutilated in acts of violence that evince a close analogy between natural and human cruelty. First a badger then a fox are run over by cars at decisive points in the novel, the crushed animals recalling the image of the Sarajevo rape victim: "The badger was sprawled on his back, legs splayed, a trickle of black blood running down from one side of his mouth. His fangs were bared, snarling at the car he'd seen too late" (40); "He'd almost reached the car when he saw [the fox]: a red mess of spiky fur and splintered bone" (92). The badger mimics the pose of the dead woman, while the fox pictures a distressing image of her genital wounds. Moreover the fox is killed by the car carrying an enthralled Stephen and the sleeping Justine, whom the valiant journalist proceeds to seduce—yet not before the skin of the girl's neck is scratched in the bushes around which they seek the remains of the roadside casualty. Justine's light wound emanates the vapors of victimization that Stephen, again, finds impossible to resist.

Not only on this occasion but throughout their courtship, it is Justine's "elusive expression of pain" that sweeps Stephen most effectively off his feet: "What did it say about him that it was her capacity to feel pain that aroused him?" (165). Indeed what does it say about Stephen that he becomes serially captivated by women who bear evident stigmas of victimization? Is his emotional response a manifestation of sympathy, and if so, why did the suffering of his own wife during the long months he spent away from home leave him cold? And how does his personal life relate to the kind of war ethics he advocates? The answer, I suggest, lies in his fascination with the unfamiliar pain of *others*, adulterated by the remoteness of time and space. Stephen *wants* to see the Sarajevo woman in Justine and cannot conceive of a role for her that doesn't entail suffering on her part, suffering that he regards with interest and restraint. What Ignatieff welcomed as the "*internationalization* of conscience" disguises here a reporter's failure to *internalize* conscience. Not until she threatens to become as bloodied and splintered as a rape camp victim abroad does Justine finally secure Stephen's affection at home. Barker makes this resounding point by juxtaposing domestic and transnational affect in ways that are consonant with the post-9/11 tension between international conflict escalations and domestic trauma. Of course, the "domestic" nature of Stephen's troubles is especially relevant because it is his wife, at first, for whom he cannot muster much sympathy, despite his susceptibility to the plight of strangers—a discordance that is a function of his profession as much as of a larger national crisis.

Catalepsis after 9/11

As Barbara Korte has shown in her investigation of the war correspondent in contemporary fiction, the image of the battle-fatigued seeker of truth oscillating between a personal life in shambles and a theater of ethnic and genocidal destruction is becoming increasingly central to current representations of military combat.[20] Critics such as Korte and war correspondents themselves have diagnosed not only a profound schism between duty and personal life, but also a deep-seated egoism at the heart of this profession, whose practitioners are permanently engaged in regarding the pain of others. So absorbed are they in observing the misery of strangers and in finding verbal or visual channels for expressing it that they lose all ability to recognize their own. The ethics of empathy that preside over the activities of war correspondents in the line of duty often seem to have little or no purchase on their own family life—or even in the context of the conflicts they photograph. What we are witnessing here is a kind of unethical spectatorship: arguably, as with the aestheticization of the WTC jumper's image, the act of turning violence into art (as happens when a camera is lifted to frame a shot of catastrophe) is always mediated. The event is no longer "real" or happening in "real time." A distancing element intervenes, which later translates into emotional distance in the photographers' personal lives.

Stephen Sharkey (his name carrying a hint of cruelty as "key" to his professional experience) is no exception. Not only does he become estranged from his wife during his journeys to Bosnia and Rwanda, but he even fails to notice the extent to which his conjugal life has been ravished by his experience of war. Christopher Morris, a journalist who covered conflicts in some of the same war regions, sheds light on the isolation that is intrinsic and even necessary to the profession of a war reporter, whether as writer or photographer. Morris identifies selfishness—an ego-driven rather than ethical obsession with the horrors of war—and an ingrained inability to juggle personal and professional lives as the features that set war reporters apart, as creatures armed with a semiheroic disposition who squander it on a scavenging mission. "I know photographers working today who continue simply because when they get back to their regular lives, they can't cope with the normality of existence," Morris writes. "They're always looking for the next dangerous assignment because, honestly, it's an escape.... The only things you have to worry about are your survival and taking pictures. You forget everything about the modern world. When you fly back into the real world, you feel separate from everything else" (qtd. in Howe 171).

Yet despite the perceived opposition between domesticity and violent combat, the two realms intersect at the close of *Double Vision*. Justine is attacked after walking in on a burglary, incurring serious wounds as Stephen looks on from a nearby hill, too far away to intervene. Not unlike the attacks of September 11, this act of random violence comes unexpectedly and produces a seemingly pointless narrative rupture. Barker herself admits that the device just barely stops short of being a narrative failure, and she justifies its use as a symbolic reenactment of the terrorist attacks rather than as a plot point integral to the novel: "I think the whole mood of the time we live in at the moment is that we're all trying to incorporate a random act of violence. And arguably we have been a lot more thrown by it than we should have been" (Brannigan, "An Interview" 370).

Taking my cue from Nussbaum's theory of the cataleptic experience espoused in her influential essay "Love's Knowledge," I want to argue that the insight precipitated by the sudden episode of violence in Stephen's life (marked by the attack on Justine in the house the two of them are temporarily sharing) replicates what Nussbaum identifies as a frequent literary trope of knowledge gained in *compressed* emotional time, while the subsequent period of intimacy with Justine pertinently illustrates Nussbaum's alternative understanding of emotion gained through a ritualistic experience *over* time. In the subtext of both moments lies, I suggest, the shadow of September 11 as a cataleptic shock followed by the decelerated aftermath of mourning. Nussbaum traces the notion of cataleptic knowledge back to Stoic literature and demonstrates how it emerges from primal impressions, constituting not only a route to knowing but knowing itself. The ethics of *Double Vision* is similarly "created" by the violent final episode rather than revealed through its epiphanic moment. For the first time in the text, representation and action coalesce into the image of the violated war victim abruptly embodied in Justine. Barker's understanding of ethics is thus conspicuously close to Nussbaum's and amounts to the pressing need (which surfaces explosively in the novel's climax) to put an end to self-deception and refuse to give ground, in Lacan's formulation, relative to one's desire (see chapter 2)—a desire that is less sexual here (despite Stephen and Justine's undeniable chemistry) than the erotic impulse of other narratives I have examined so far. As we shall see, the emotional component of this relationship is partly a function of its complex temporality, comprising both punctual insight (sexual or otherwise violent) and lengthy introspection.

Robert Fox, a correspondent reporting for the *Daily Telegraph* during the first Gulf War, described his combat experiences as a quest for what he called "the moment when things come together" (qtd. in McLaughlin 7). For Stephen, now forced to contemplate from a distance the prospect of his lover's being raped and mutilated like the victim of a gruesome war zone, things *do* come together, and what he experiences at this moment— love for Justine, commitment to their relationship, and disavowal of his predatory profession—suddenly acquires the timbre of truth and the ring of plausibility that they previously lacked: "We live our whole lives one step away from clarity, he thought. That moment, careering down the steep hillside, knowing that however hard he ran he wouldn't get there in time, had taught him more about his feelings for Justine than months of introspection could have done. All along in the back of his mind he'd been aware of his priorities in life rearranging themselves without any conscious effort on his part. You thought you cared about that? Don't be silly. The girl. She's what matters" (265). While his earlier statements on the future of his affair with Justine seemed barbed and skeptical, the burglary is as emotionally momentous as it is materially damaging to the house, the intruders sweeping objects off the mantelpiece and thoughts from Stephen's mind without leaving any trace or memory of their existence. Prior to the attack, in his strained conversations with Justine's father, the vicar Alec Braithewaite, and in several tense exchanges with Justine herself, the reader could sense the vacillation Stephen was undergoing. He was profoundly interested in Justine, yet willing to let things take their course one way or the other, without any interference on his part. So in what way does the burglary affect him, and why does Justine suddenly become both essential and strangely dissociated from this emotional cataclysm that binds him securely to a relationship he had taken so lightly only moments earlier?

In "Love's Knowledge," an essay that should count as one of the most profound and enduring statements on the crystallization of feeling in modern fiction, Nussbaum distinguishes two paths toward emotional insight. The first she derives from Proust by analyzing Marcel's anguish at the news of Albertine's departure as a cataleptic event rooted in a discrete moment of suffering. Marcel's pain overthrows his intellectual approach to matters of the heart and convinces him that he is madly in love with this woman—the same woman he only recently decided he did not love. "The shock of loss and the attendant welling up of pain show him that his theories were forms of self-deceptive rationalization," Nussbaum elaborates, citing as particularly apt Proust's description of the insightful knowledge as "hard, glittering, strange, like a crystallized salt" (*Love's Knowledge* 164–65). The essential aspect of this epiphanic theory lies in the coextensiveness it establishes between the route to insight and insight itself—or, stated differently, love resides *in* knowing, rather than being something extraneous and preexisting that is suddenly exposed. As Nussbaum meticulously explains, "We find that knowledge of our love is not the fruit of the impression of suffering, a fruit that might in principle have been had apart from the suffering. The suffering itself is a piece of self-knowing. *Through* responding to a loss with anguish, we are grasping our love. The love is not some separate fact about us that is signalled by the impression; the impression reveals the love by constituting it. Love is not a structure in the heart waiting to be discovered; it is embodied in, made up out of, experiences of suffering" (267–68). If any rational understanding can be wrought from such a cataleptic experience, it is that genuine understanding is not, by necessity, rational.

Applying Nussbaum's theoretical construct to Stephen's sudden acceptance of his love for Justine as he attempts to save her life begs the question of whether this random surge of affect can indeed be trusted. Or does it, borrowing from the violence of the event that precipitates it, apply a rather coarse and blunt instrument to the delicate matter of feelings? Instead of gracefully disentangling the Gordian knot of his affections for Justine, Stephen seems to be simply cutting it, taking a shortcut that points to deep-seated frustrations regarding his own inadequacies, rather than to love. Running down the hill toward the house that Justine is about to enter, a house that is being burgled, Stephen feels a blow to the heart that focuses his attention initially on the girl, but ultimately swings back toward himself—*his* war obsessions, *his* anger over not having intervened more often and more effectively to stop or prevent the pain of others: "All the way down the hillside he'd had flashbulbs exploding in his head. So many raped and tortured girls—he needed no imagination to picture what might be happening to Justine. It would not have surprised him to find her lying like a broken doll at the foot of the stairs, her skirt bunched up around her waist, her eyes staring" (250). By the time he enters the house, Justine has become a pretext; at this point Stephen's actions are determined primarily by his war trauma as he brings a "hard, glittering" object down on the head of one of the burglars with the intention of killing him.

Nussbaum's portrayal of Marcel is helpful in understanding Stephen's sudden altruism and the streak of self-involved introspection it conceals. Marcel "is a suspicious man who can be content with nothing less than full control, who cannot tolerate the other's separate life," which is why "he demands cataleptic impressions and a certainty that the other can never give him. It is because he wishes not to be tormented by the ungovernable inner life of the other that he adopts a position that allows him to conclude that the other's inner life is nothing more than the constructive workings of his own mind." His conclusion is at once self-evident and disheartening: "that love is not a source of dangerous openness, but a rather interesting relation with oneself" (*Love's Knowledge* 271–72). In using a cataleptic model, Barker may be suggesting similarity to the aftermath of the 9/11 attacks, as America turned its startled gaze toward the Middle East in a gesture that signaled—or at least mimicked—the desire to understand, only to turn its eye inward once again, comfortably redefining the attacks as a test from which the country had emerged triumphant. If catalepsis in Nussbaum's sense was indeed involved in the aftermath of September 11, it had a short-lived effect that even at its highest pitch of intensity did not manage to wrench the country away from its cherished individualist illusions. The flash-like presence of international war zones in *Double Vision*, along with competing explanations for Stephen's post-9/11 career change as a result of either global conscience or self-absorbed obsession, confirms the novel's concern with the inward trajectory of cataleptic experience, both personal and collective.

THE INTERNATIONALIZATION OF CONSCIENCE

Once the emotional unrest generated by Justine's brush with death has settled, Stephen takes her on a trip to the Farne Islands off the coast of Northumberland in what may be taken as the first concrete materialization of his cataleptic decisions. What follows is a soporific account of time spent in untroubled intimacy, alternating with unexpected sequences that describe, for the first time in the novel, the circumstances of Ben's death in Afghanistan, followed by the book's subdued finale: the two lovers skimming pebbles over the calm surface of the sea. After haunting the novel without finding an appropriate place of submersion, the image of Ben's death finally sinks here and is swallowed up by the peaceful scene of romance. Stephen appears to have finally opened up to Justine; although verbally nothing of any significance is communicated between them, he subliminally frees himself from two obsessive figments of his past: the memories of the raped woman in Sarajevo and Ben's death.

To return to Nussbaum's terminology, Stephen might be "learning to fall," exercising a controlled yielding to love, born of repeated patterns of closeness to the loved one rather than of the momentary revelation of pain. He is tender and attentive toward Justine, responding to her with a sense of abandon that he had not displayed before, caught up as he was in his own obsessions. And this is where the novel at once acknowledges and breaks with the legacy of suffering—caused by war or terrorism—by redirecting the energy of affect into a kind of personal program geared toward increased emotional fitness: intimacy practiced with the religiosity of physical training, aiming to get the heart back into shape. In her essay Nussbaum establishes a cogent opposition between cataleptic knowledge on the one hand and love gained through steady relational interchange on the other, yet *Double Vision*, despite the duality of its title, does no such thing. The bliss of the domestic ending necessitates and presupposes the global violence that precedes it—from Bosnia and September 11 to Afghanistan and the local burglars—and for that reason it remains hazy and half-hearted. Seen in this light, Elizabeth Swanson Goldberg's conclusion that "the novel's surprise is the significance at the heart of this relationship" seems somewhat reductive. Stephen's commitment to Justine, Goldberg proposes, "fulfils all the novel's hints that human desire, nurture, love, and care can override the empty violence lurking at every turn" (171). Sarah Ross offers a similar diagnosis, construing the novel's tidied-up ending as ethical resolution. "*Double Vision* is also Barker's most positive of novels in its conclusion in relation to evil," she writes (140).

Yet Barker's historical contextualization of evil, like Hemon's, results in a morally ambivalent sense of homecoming: Brik returns to Sarajevo and decides to stay partly because his friend Rora is brutally murdered in an act of random violence (and another coded 9/11 reference), whose narrative impact very much resembles the plot twist of the accidental attack against Justine. Similarly, had he not been brutally awakened from the stupor of "playing house" with Justine, an anodyne coexistence that lulls them into an advanced intimacy pejoratively resembling marriage, Stephen would probably have allowed the relationship to shape itself into the classic image of a short-lived, middle-age affair. The reunion enacted in both novels, then, does not override or transcend violence, but relies instead on a violently catalyzing emotional crisis. The denouement of Barker's novel does take place on a beach—a setting evocative of peace and reconciliation—although, very much like Schulman's maritime ending in *A Day at the Beach*, this is a highly ambivalent conclusion. It is only through external intervention, Barker suggests, that the individual can shed the carapace of passive self-contentment and respond to the Other. Victimization thus becomes not only the means through which we see the Other but an opening that allows us to partake in each other's fate; it is, in the words of Judith Butler, "a way a primary human vulnerability to other humans is exposed in its most terrifying way, a way in which we are given over, without control, to the will of another, a way in which life itself can be expunged by the wilful action of another" (*Precarious Life* 28–29). Butler doesn't simply extol victimization as an ethically enabling loss of control—an approach that Badiou vociferously condemns. Once again the key to unlocking access to Otherness is to "put cruelty first": not by fetishizing victimhood as a self-binding condition (although it does reaffirm the limits of the self) but by interrogating the "hard, glittering" objects and cataleptic impacts by which emotion and judgment come into being.

THE INTERNATIONALIZATION OF CONSCIENCE

As I have sought to show, *Double Vision* poses the question of how a globalized conscience can be changed into a personal ethics, to what extent this change is generated individually or imposed from the outside, and how a writer, a photographer, and a painter artistically reflect on this phenomenon. Ultimately—and against Barker's unequivocal distinction—there is no genuine opposition between the ethics of representation and the ethics of action; ethics itself arises only if the two are brought to bear on and inform each other. Barker can be said to regard international and internal forms of conscience as based on reciprocal dynamics of exchange, one side of the equation always engaged dialectically with the other. Far from attempting to resolve this oscillation, she writes *around* the issues rather than addressing them head-on, devoting only a few paragraphs to an explicit investigation of representational dilemmas in the guise of Stephen's musings on the topic of his book.

We learn about Goya's *Disasters of War*; the Naudet brothers' self-censorship on September 11; the "bloodless precision" (241) of the bombardment of Baghdad in 1991, which effectively removed all visible traces of collateral damage. Throughout, these conflicts are connected by a sense of transnational ethics enveloping a more tightly circumscribed narrative of personal conscience. And while it is clear that Barker positions her novel squarely at the metaphorical core (if not the spatial center) of a post-9/11 world, the novel's approach to the attacks is diffused by its structure as an ensemble piece of multiple characters and geographically far-flung political subplots. Dealing with the issue of representation after 9/11, Barker seems to suggest, involves not only a sudden, cataleptic illumination of the "hard, glittering" kind about morality, sympathy, and the internationalization of conscience (as the novel's deterritorialized erudition initially suggests), but also using this punctual violence to invest in an ethical agenda that leads, in the novel, to an internalization of conscience, and to help establish, in broader aesthetic terms, a type of 9/11 writing decelerated by the tentative practice that Nussbaum dubs "learning to fall"—that is, quietly rehearsing the art of representation and waiting for the insight that is bound to arise if one patiently and authoritatively pursues it.

5. READING FOR THE PATTERN

*Narrative, Data Mining, and the
Transnational Ethics of Surveillance*

In the four-page chapter titled "Singularity" at the center of William Gibson's *Pattern Recognition*, the protagonist Cayce Pollard—whose father disappeared in Manhattan on September 11 and is presumed dead—witnesses the collapse of the Twin Towers concomitantly with the micro event of "a single petal fall, from a dead rose, in the tiny display window of an eccentric Spring Street dealer in antiques" (135). The episode eloquently exposes the singularity of the personal and intimate act of witnessing against the backdrop of global terror. Unlike the masses glued to their TV sets on September 11, Cayce is the "sole witness to this minute fall" (135) that replicates or, more precisely, anticipates the collapse of the towers on a reduced but all the more poignant scale. The falling petal exists in the realm of small, manageable objects (rather than that of national symbols of glass and steel), objects that Cayce has learned to cherish and observe closely. What the peaceful, slow-motion fall of the rose petal signifies amid the chaos of the city, with its blaring sirens, suicidal jumpers, and general anguish, is "the loneliness of objects. Their secret lives. Like seeing something move in a Cornell box" (136).[1]

More ominously, I would suggest, Cayce's scrutiny of the micro world contained in the display window symbolically encapsulates the panoptic obsession triggered by the terrorist attacks. Gibson's novel, along with a number of other post-9/11 fictions, describes a world riddled with suspicion and encompassed by a tight system of surveillance. Like *Falling Man*, *In the Shadow of No Towers*, and *A Day at the Beach*, these are novels about spectatorship, but with a key difference: while the recognition of the Other in DeLillo, Schulman, and Spiegelman revolves primarily around seeing and responding to images of pain, these novels are all about being seen, about "visibility" as the barometer of belonging and citizenship in a post-9/11 "culture of control" (Garland). Beyond identifying spectatorship as a key constitutive element of modern subjectivity, they point toward the specific problems that this panoptic focus poses for the ethics of narrative.[2] I argue that surveillance—whether as visual panopticon or postoptic data-mining system[3]—can be used as a thematic and structural heuristic to interpret how post-9/11 literature dramatizes the ethical challenges posed by increased securitization to the public's privacy rights. To illustrate this dynamic of discipline and suspicion, I investigate five narratives that portray and critique surveillance policies after 9/11: Walter Kirn's *The Unbinding*, Jonathan Raban's *Surveillance*, William Gibson's *Pattern Recognition*, Richard Flanagan's *The Unknown Terrorist*, and Lorraine Adams's *Harbor*, in addition to Barker's *Double Vision*, which I briefly revisit.

I should begin by noting that the panoptic impulse in fiction is by no means a recent development. From Charlotte Brontë to Muriel Spark, disciplinary aesthetics have not only emerged as a recurrent trope in fiction, but have also infiltrated narrative technique and literary form. Surveillance fictions are almost always sensitive to the technological and political implications of the vigilant processes they describe, as well as to the specificities of historical context.[4] The most frequently invoked forerunner to contemporary fictions of surveillance is, of course, George Orwell's *Nineteen Eighty-Four*, summoned and discussed with renewed urgency since 9/11 partly because, as David Brin remarks, "Orwell's metaphors have been expanded beyond his initial portrayal of a Stalinist nightmare-state to include all worrisome accumulations of influence, authority, or unreciprocal transparency" (225). Despite the frequent adulteration of his themes—especially through the adoption of Big Brother as a quasi-mythological entertainment figure—Orwell does anticipate several aspects of the current war against terrorism, including permanent surveillance, unlimited and unwarranted detention for potential crimes, and torture. In Orwell's Oceania "endless purges, arrests, tortures, imprisonments, and vaporizations are not inflicted as punishment for crimes which have actually been committed, but are merely the wiping out of persons who might perhaps commit a crime at some time in the future" (181). Central to the novel is the technology of the telescreen, a piece of broadcast equipment that permanently streams propaganda content at an ambient level—the audience paying only scant attention as they perform their daily tasks—while monitoring the viewers: "You had to live—did live, from habit that became instinct—in the assumption that every sound you made was overheard, and, except in darkness, every movement scrutinized" (8). The asymmetrical interchange allows those at the top of the political pyramid to fully control the flow of information with unidirectional accountability.

In its secondary focus on writing as a means of countersurveillance, *Nineteen Eighty-Four* also gives preliminary confirmation to my vision in this chapter of how fiction may be conceived as a monitoring practice, in terms of both its production and its reception. The control over language in this novel is a formal manifestation of its surveillance plot, especially in the structure and diction of Newspeak, an artificial idiom that banishes indeterminacy, abolishes exceptions, homogenizes and welds grammatical categories in a leveling discourse in which nothing catches the eye. The post-9/11 fictions discussed in this chapter similarly entwine surveillance aesthetics and narrative form.

That the politics of the surveillance novel are in fact inseparable from their narrative emplotment is a point that has already been successfully made. From D. A. Miller's influential study, *The Novel and the Police*, to more recent readings of realist surveillance fiction, critics have persuasively revealed the extent to which surveillance infiltrates the textual operations of fiction, and how shifts in these operations map onto political chronology.[5] "The realist and naturalist novel," Mark Seltzer observes, "appears on the scene at the same time as the disciplinary society takes power" (527). Yet technological advances in the post-9/11 world have rendered surveillance ubiquitous and inescapable to an even greater extent than in the societies described by twentieth-century fiction. As a result the contemporary surveillance novel accentuates the global expansion of surveillance culture in terms that vastly exceed the capabilities of political watchfulness in the era preceding the War on Terror. Paradoxically—and this is where a post-9/11 approach becomes truly rewarding—this expansion leads to a diffusion or democratization of watchfulness, to which post-9/11 surveillance fiction responds by representing disciplinary control as divorced from power and susceptible to subversive counterforces.

The broken bond of surveillance and authority also redraws the moral demarcations that organize panoptical society, exposing it to leveling forms of surveillance that affect all hegemonic ranks (rather than emanating from a single sovereign power) and to the pressures of an increasingly global panoptic network. In reading fiction that integrates (and advances) this phenomenon, I argue that the ethical purchase of the post-9/11 surveillance novel resides in its formal and conceptual emplotment of the transnational connectivity facilitated by surveillance and counter-surveillance circuits. The boundaries that are policed in these fictions no longer correspond to established moral categories, but are seen as entirely arbitrary. The novel re-creates this volatility on the level of narrative structure. Plotwise, what the post-9/11 surveillance novel has relinquished, in contrast to the detection techniques promoted by the realist novel, is a sense of solvability (and intelligibility) with regard to the phenomena that are described and supervised, frustrating the expectation of a conclusive outcome. Supervision is therefore dispersed, weakening authorial control over character and action. Narrative and ontological omniscience are permanently questioned, even from within a single character's perspective, with fundamental ethical consequences. Authority itself is held up to scrutiny and indicted. This sense of uncertainty is also an effect of narrative temporalities that often swerve out of the reader's grasp. Further disrupting the linearity of these narratives are conspicuous gaps in logic and continuity, but also more subtle strategies of ethical disorientation interpretable in the mode suggested by "new ethics." What these fictions add to a "new ethical" paradigm is their ability to recuperate surveillance—now decentralized and inconclusive—as an effective form of data mining in the practice of reading. The novels can thus be said to explore what Lewis MacLeod calls the "liminal ground between data and narrative" (591).

They do so by narrating unfocused stories and abjuring the obligation to create a meaningful world, reflecting instead an unlimited, unknowable global society that challenges not only the impoverished ethics of the surveillance economy, but also the world-making abilities of fiction.

Surveillance Ethics

According to David Lyon, surveillance "refers to routine ways in which focused attention is paid to personal details by organizations that want to influence, manage, or control certain persons or population groups. It occurs for all kinds of reasons, which can be located on a continuum from care to control.... Surveillance societies emerge wherever such practices begin to touch daily life at every point" (*Surveillance after September 11* 5). Usually attending episodes of militarization either within a nation-state or in the context of transnational warfare, surveillance is part of a more generalized biopolitics initially articulated by Michel Foucault in his discussion of governance strategies that "brought life and its mechanisms into the realm of explicit calculations" in the nineteenth century (143). Specifically Foucault theorized surveillance within confined, fixed spaces as exemplified in Jeremy Bentham's panopticon. Yet his disciplinary societies, ordered by a system of observation and correction—which in turn supplanted traditional societies based on sovereignty through enclosure (in the form of schools, factories, and prisons)—were soon superseded by what Gilles Deleuze has characterized as "societies of control" (5), systems of domination based on passwords and other coding procedures that regulate movement and access to information. Previously analogical sites are now paralleled by new digital technologies. The resulting modes of vigilance juxtapose a macropolitics of social security with the micropolitics of personal insecurity, producing two significant modes of securitization: of the Other and of the self. The novels I discuss in this chapter illustrate both the machines of capture that encode bodies and spaces (camera devices, wiretapping techniques, electronic tracking tools, and so on) and the lines of flight through which surveillance subjects manage to escape these machines.[6] Oscillating between larger narratives of social control and a focus on the individuals under the vigilant eye of surveillant devices, they reveal how individuals react subversively to surveillance in ways that can no longer be fully orchestrated by official policing stratagems.

The ethical problems associated with surveillance narratives (and I focus here on only three of these problems) originate in the conundrums raised by the rapid proliferation of surveillance itself. First, we assume that the surveillant eye discerns between the acceptable and the morally transgressive, yet surveillance after 9/11 has its own ethical underpinnings, provided by the "just war" doctrine. In ways that clarify the links between surveillance, ethics, and security, Paul Virilio clads his suspicion about the justice of the War on Terror in terms that relate vision to religion and watchfulness to divine persecution as punishment for moral transgressions: "After the eye of God pursuing Cain all the way into the tomb, we now have the *eye of Humanity* skimming over the oceans and continents in search of criminals . . . opening up the possibility of *ethical cleansings*, which now seem set fair to replace the *ethnic cleansing* of undesirable or supernumerary populations" (*Strategy of Deception* 21–22). This hyperoptic society also challenges our ability to act as witnesses to the world around us, an ability that would allow us to pass moral judgment on what we perceive. In this context, what Virilio calls "the ethics of common perception" are profoundly inflected by the "overexposure of the visible" and by the "development of sightless vision machines" (*Open Sky* 91). To rectify the deficient insight of vision, paradoxically caused by its extreme proliferation, is to observe an "ecology of images" (97) that would retain their visual power and ethical appeal despite the increasing acceleration of perception.

Second, surveillance practices impugn basic principles of morality by threatening the integrity of human personhood. Panoptic architecture atomizes and isolates the individual, preventing individual resistance while constructing a collective moral purpose that infringes on each individual's ethical independence. The emphasis on privacy and personhood in the novels discussed here counterbalances the tendency of surveillance studies toward "the pole of stressing the role of the 'system' rather than the 'self'" (Lyon, *Surveillance Studies* 91). The post-9/11 surveillance novel is at pains to regain a sense of morality and selfhood by mapping out the global and domestic circuits of surveillance, interrogating the strategies used to embed individual perception within an overarching scenario of objective vigilance, or to expunge the individual altogether from the realm of an increasingly digitized citizenship.

Third, as Lyon briefly points out with reference to Levinas, despite the technological progress of face-recognition devices, the face of the Other—in which Levinas recognizes the touchstone of ethical thinking—remains hidden. Levinas maintains that ethics begins with the impossibility of being indifferent to the Other, and that "the approach to the face is the most basic mode of responsibility" ("Ethics of the Infinite" 189). As it is sometimes based on an ethics of care, surveillance may be seen to facilitate a Levinasian approach to the face by rendering it visible and allowing for a humane response to it.[7] However, in using proxies such as fragmentary data from fingerprints or transaction records, surveillance since 9/11 has become removed from the face-to-face encounter facilitated by optical monitorization.[8] The novels by Kirn, Raban, Gibson, Flanagan, and Adams dramatize this shift from visibility and spectatorship as the primary engines of surveillance toward forms of ubiquitous monitorization that are integral to a social system rather than attached to it. Their interest in the systemic workings of surveillance allows these texts to look beyond the manifestations of the Patriot Act that are specific to North America and to use panoptic data mining as a touchstone for ascertaining the ways the novel (itself a hybrid, international genre) is adjusting to the infinitely wired, hypervisible post-9/11 world.

The constraints of growing securitization for counterterrorist ends clearly inflect the life cycle of international terrorism, from its well-camouflaged points of origin to the media through which we experience terror or the channels we use to disrupt its circuits. Yet surveillance also invites an ethically charged remapping of global space predicated on the fluid boundaries between domestic and international hypersecurity narratives. The source of ethical ambiguity in both political and fictional surveillance plots can be found not so much in the distinction between self and Other as in the movable separation of the national and global arenas in which the War on Terror is being waged. As Michael Shapiro writes, "The current security and intelligence policies dissolve many of the former distinctions between domestic crime fighting and global warfare" (27). These distinctions appear especially permeable in the aftermath of September 11, and the growing domain of surveillance literature since 2001 testifies to the fruitful conjunction—which may hold sway for years to come—between fiction in the transnational mode and the more established topos of panoptic society.

Surveillance, Trauma, and Self-Control: Pat Barker

Post-9/11 surveillance fictions illuminate the tension between the centrifugal forces activated by global security on the one hand and the centripetal forces sustaining the domestic ethics of safety on the other. To understand this tension, it is necessary to consider surveillance after 9/11 as rooted in a concern with individual safety before examining the ways such private anxieties spill over into the more volatile space of international securitization. Pat Barker's *Double Vision* (already discussed from a different viewpoint in the previous chapter) is one novel that explores the paranoia engendered by the 9/11 attacks in the personal realm and probes the ethical underpinnings of surveillance as a form of self-scrutiny. Despite Barker's apparent focus on the individual, subtle links have been proposed between the uncanny stalker in *Double Vision*, the ominously named ex-convict Peter Wingrave, and a broader sense of evil and violence in the international arena. "Wingrave's mysterious criminal tendencies," Elizabeth Swanson Goldberg writes, "lurk menacingly over the mise en scène of the novel as another figure of unnameable threat, the kind that plagues the sureties of the privileged parts of the first world in its capacity—shared with illness or accident—to materialize at any moment and quite literally wreck everything" (167). As his writing reveals, Peter is interested in psychiatry's acknowledgment of stalking as a pathological manifestation of human behavior after centuries of ignorance about its destructive potential. Although to some extent Peter's representation of surveillance in his fiction does reflect the ambivalence and guilt surrounding evidence-gathering and monitorization strategies in the War on Terror, more importantly it complicates the relationship between observer and subject within the panoptic paradigm. Peter's short stories strike Stephen as having "no moral center," partly due to the "ambiguity in the narrator's attitude to predator and prey" (164). Nowhere is this ambiguity more apparent than in Barker's own scrutiny of Peter and his temporary employer, Kate Frobisher.

In her absence Peter wears Kate's clothes and pretends to be working on her fifteen-foot sculpture of the risen Christ. Once aware of his intrusions, Kate responds with similar acts of invasiveness and secrecy. For some time before Peter joins the cast of characters, Kate already feels stalked by a pursuer, yet there is little reason to assume that this entity might be more than a phantasm of her own troubled psyche, shaken by the loss of her husband, the loneliness of country life, and the stress of having to accomplish large amounts of work in record time. Once she has witnessed Peter's clearly pathological and menacing masquerade in her studio at night, however, the danger takes a material form and Kate balks under the terror of having a potentially disturbed individual inhabiting her house and her mind at the same time, while the War on Terror continues unaffected by her husband's work and sacrifice. As a hostile agent, Peter is thus both internal and external to the mind of the woman he is silently persecuting. As Timothy Melley has argued, drawing on John Berger's perception of female identity as divided between its surveyed and surveying parts, "Such self-divisions begin to indicate how a sense of being watched might be linked to pathologies of self-fragmentation, dissolution and loss of bodily control" (76).

Crippled by her accident and the death of her husband—Ben's absence is not "an illness she would recover from" but "an amputation she had to learn to live with" (*Double Vision* 32)—Kate does display a gradual diminishment of her physical and psychological integrity. Her feeling of being stalked results partly from an abnormally zealous process of posttraumatic self-surveillance rather than external monitoring. Marooned in a forest and surrounded by wilderness, made even more austere by the gloomy weather, Kate is engaged in routine domestic activities as she lives her life in slow motion and with painstaking exactitude, paying attention to the minute rituals of loneliness and the quick, fluttering rhythms of the mind left to its own devices. Barker conveys this exacerbated self-awareness through attentive descriptions of Kate's activities throughout the day, lingering especially on atmospheric details, but also on lengthy sequences of self-observation, with Kate regarding the familiar settings of her life as if from a great distance, zooming out, as it were, on the daily grind of her secluded existence: "There she stood looking back at the house, empty again now . . . seeing the lighted windows and reflected firelight almost as if she were a stranger, shut out" (1).[9] Yet strangeness seems to reside within the house as well, which appears self-sufficient and cozy even in the absence of its sole occupant, pulsing with warm life like a large, tame organism. So intense is Kate's effort to accurately register her surroundings that after Peter's arrival she begins to suspect that objects in her studio have been moved around ever so slightly. This sensation prevents her from securely locating herself and her artwork in a familiar setting upon whose precise cartography her entire existence seems to depend. After she musters enough courage to dismiss Peter, Kate attributes the watching gaze to the discreet malevolence of the Christ, who emerges from her hands as a scaly, reptilian creature, more dragon than human being and not even remotely a conventional holy figure. While her sense of entertaining an invisible witness persists, this time it is clearly linked no longer to a corporeal spectator but rather to what Melley calls a "spectator function"—built both into her own identity and into the narrative itself in ways that are at once ubiquitous and impossible to pin down.

This spectator function is given material shape in a group of statues on which Kate has been working. The statues represent the 9/11 hijackers as a surveillant lynch mob engaging the viewers, through their blank stares, in a subliminal war of visual attrition. Unlike the Christ figure, these figures may be imagined to possess malicious motives: "They were part of a sequence she'd started after 9/11, not based on Ben's photographs, or anybody else's for that matter, because nobody had been there to photograph what chiefly compelled her imagination: the young men at the controls who'd seized aeroplanes full of people and flown them into the sides of buildings. There they were, lean, predatory, equally ready to kill or die. She thought they might be rather good in the end. They certainly frightened her" (65–66). Even Stephen, the war correspondent well versed in the detection of danger, begins to suspect that something is lurking beyond the white surfaces of the huddled forms, which he describes as "extraordinary figures: frightened and frightening" (122). Such "figures of utter ruin" (29) are now ensconced in Kate's studio, imperceptibly shifting their position, either of their own volition or under Peter's guidance. The uncertainty they create translates political insecurity into domestic unease, in a reminder that the familiar image of terrorist threat betokens a pure, ballistic hypermasculinity infiltrating the feminized perimeter of homeland safety.

Yet Kate's fear of a male persecutor is clearly also coupled with her anxiety about completing the Christ figure in time and about the quality of her work. Ultimately the Christ evolves into a towering and all-consuming obsession—her amulet in warding off the evil emanating from the hijacker figures—absorbing all the blows that Kate has been dealt in the recent past and accumulating the negative energies around her. Oddly, though, the Christ himself conforms to the idea of surveillance. His menacing exterior masks a core of comforting strangeness of which both Kate and Peter are aware and to which they respond by treating the lifeless figure with utter familiarity, as if in the presence of a third entity. The entire narrative in fact operates on the principle of a third presence capable of the damage wrought by the 9/11 hijackers, whose single-handed power is equal only to that of Christ. This lurking presence inspires a constant concern for personal safety and urges the protagonists to permanently police the borders of their selves lest they should be illicitly infiltrated. The third presence from which the novel draws its haunting power—a domestic correlative to the larger issues of global surveillance—is felt repeatedly in post-9/11 literature. Barker's understated analogies indicate that political or institutional surveillance and excessive self-awareness in the aftermath of terror are equally damaging to an ethics of selfhood. Whether the surveilling eye is turned inward or outward—whether we are focused on the evil at home or abroad—mistrustful vision distorts our perception and the narratives in which it is couched.

Plotting Surveillance: Walter Kirn

Walter Kirn's *The Unbinding* deplores the plight "of what people used to call 'the self' in an age of high-tech snooping, political paranoia, identity thievery and Internet exhibitionism" (viii). Although it hinges less on nuanced psychology than Barker's, Kirn's understanding of surveillance retains the notion of a hovering presence generally accepted as an uncomfortable, if almost natural appendage to everyday life. Though it does not explicitly refer to the War on Terror, the novel encapsulates both the advanced technology of post-9/11 surveillance and the prevalent anxiety propagated by (and in turn propagating) panoptical practices of visual control. In ways that reinforce the formal ethics I am delineating in this chapter, Kirn's focus on surveillance shifts with unprecedented clarity from the thematic to the structural, revealing the extent to which post-9/11 fiction incorporates intelligence gathering and selection as a fundamental paradigm in the aesthetics of writing itself and in the reading strategies it invites.

The novel's protagonist, Kent Selkirk, works for a personal protection system known as AidSat, an online monitoring database that compiles complete files on its clients and offers to remotely coach them through hundreds of so-called Life Challenges, then continues passive coverage without the client's permission if something causes the operator to be concerned. Physical data communicated by surveillance devices—data that do not suggest anything explicitly offensive but are only deemed to harbor a potential threat that should be "looked into"—prompt operators' suspicion in ways reminiscent of what Orwell calls "facecrime," that is, a trivial visual distortion that renders an individual suspect even in the absence of any concrete proof of misdemeanor or hostile intention (*Nineteen Eighty-Four* 52). In contrast to Orwell's totalitarian telescreens, Kirn defines AidSat as one among many "seamless life-assistance interfaces" (*The Unbinding* 54) competing with a similar platform more transparently named "MeNet," a term that recalls contemporary social networking sites rather than online surveillance and interception of data (although social networks can, of course, also be sourced to collect and use personal content). As an operator for AidSat, Selkirk indeed manages a wealth of information that he can use to monitor subscribers' vital signs, track their locations, and insinuate himself into their lives.[10] Because the purpose of observation is to foresee and preempt the unexpected through the codification of normative behavior, AidSat uses an algorithm to translate simple suspicions into actionable intelligence, calling to mind what Virilio lamented as "the automation of perception" that underlies contemporary surveillance and its sightless "capacity to analyze the ambient environment and automatically interpret the meaning of events" (*The Vision Machine* 59). This precautionary logic implies that decisions are made "not in a context of certainty, nor even of available knowledge, but of doubt, premonition, foreboding, challenge, mis-trust, fear, and anxiety" (Ewald, "The Return of Descartes's Malicious Demon" 294).

Its context of uncertainty also determines the form of Kirn's novel, which turns on a close affinity between surveillance and fiction, both of which are concerned with "sifting the chatter to find the plots" (*The Unbinding* 10). By distinguishing the plot behind the commonplace, AidSat separates the normal from the abnormal, and thereby prevents the unintelligible narrative unfolding on the screens from thickening into a plot that might, in turn, lead to a violent denouement.[11] The prospect of a "plot" finale animates the writing of fiction, the process of reading, and the strategies of surveillance itself. Fittingly Kirn's plotless novel turns on Selkirk's attempts to preempt or disrupt a permanent threat that must remain incomplete as a plot—otherwise he has failed his mission. Here, as in other post-9/11 surveillance fictions, an incomplete plot does not signal the absence of danger but inevitably invites the suspicion of concealed threat. The more uncertain a potential development, the greater the range of options as to its outcome. The fragmentariness of Selkirk's persona (which is either a prerequisite of his position or a quality that renders him particularly suitable for the job) shores up this sense of inconsistency and mutability in the novel.

In sections that are diegetically signposted with the tag "MyStory.com," the novel recounts Selkirk's own autobiography as he sifts through not only the numerous life stories that the AidSat service makes available to him, but also his own life-plot. In his frantic search for a sense of identity, he seeks to isolate his "soul" from the overpowering static of countless other souls upon whom he begins to encroach as he becomes more deeply involved in AidSat's invasive practices:

> Before AidSat I had no self, no soul. I was a billing address. A credit score. I had a TV, a phone, a car, an apartment, some furniture, and a set of leather-bound Tolkien novels. . . . Then AidSat hired me and gave me life. And not just one life. Hundreds of them, thousands, attached to mine by fine, invisible cords that I can still feel on my skin when I leave work. It's one of the reasons I'd rather walk than drive these days—it doesn't shred the tender hooks and loops that fill up what most folks regard as empty space. There's no such thing, though, I've learned. The air is dense. The "nowhere" from which people think their troubles appear—the cars in their collisions, the tumors on their X-rays, the letter bombs in their corporate mailrooms—is, if they'd just pay attention, packed solid with soul. (15)

The "soul," then, is a form of narrative that can deliver the unexpected in its most abstruse and nefarious guises: accidents, illness, or terrorism. As a transparent medium through which entities and events float—the medium of surveillance itself—the "soul" gives rise less to full-blown identities than to occurrences that may create selves or destroy them. Selkirk ultimately represents the sum of the events that he helps to prevent, make happen, or coordinate, which is why Kirn describes him as "**a holographic data-ghost** composed of appropriated biographies and incompatible sensibilities" (102).[12] As an operator of other people's lives, Selkirk isn't a fictional character as much as a data-mining filter in which the detritus of surveillance traffic is evaluated and entrapped.

There are other reasons why Selkirk is an unstable narrative figure. Defined by the unequal balance between observer and observed, his dalliances with his surveillance subjects are never conducive to stable emotional relationships, turning him instead into "a line of walking code programmed to seek attention electromagnetically" (153). By adopting a philosophy of "revolutionary incoherence" (153), he seeks to achieve an "unencumbered freedom" (153) that promises to relieve him of burdensome human attachment while also unmooring him from the stability of real (as opposed to real-time) communication. A virtual presence feeding on the existence of others, Selkirk is "cross-referencing himself to life" (154) to the point that his own identity no longer stands apart from the collective hum of the subscribers whom he purportedly protects while secretly working to ensure the protection of his own unraveling self. His failed struggle to isolate and affirm his own identity as separate from his panoptic role bears the shifting weight of the novel's oscillation between traditional narrative and the increasingly disorganized, cumulative formations of new media and surveillance culture.

But the operator with full access to a database of souls is not the only one to suffer a de-substantiation of personality: all participants in the system, including subscribers to the protection service, find themselves adrift as a result of tension caused by permanent surveillance and the fragmentation of discourse into what gets said, what is heard, and what is *over*heard. As Selkirk puts it, "Every word that I speak, every message that I write, and every action that I perform (with certain sacred exceptions) is partly addressed, or in some way conscious, of a hovering third party—if not an infinite host of them" (151). Beyond the blanket surveillance that the protagonist (and everyone else) takes in stride, the post-9/11 world imagined in this novel is imbued with a vigilance that seems to accompany daily existence with unquestionable self-evidence: "People his age have new assumptions. They've grown up believing in the orbiting eye, the subdermal microchip, the circling drone, and they're no more afraid of them than they are of moonlight. Perhaps that's because they're born onstage, these creatures, and the first thing they see is the snout of Daddy's Handycam. Their first steps, their first words, their first Little League at-bats are all directed toward the lens. In time, they have nothing inside them that hasn't been outside. No depths, no interiors" (140).[13]

The novel emulates this depthlessness in its textual form. Indeed this isn't merely a novel *about* surveillance, but a hybrid text whose production and reception are already corrupted by surveillance media. Originally written for the web and updated weekly with a new section, *The Unbinding* was prompted, as Kirn himself admits, "by a surge of naive faith in the capacity of cyberspace to do for long-form fiction what it has done already for journalism, music, gaming, and the graphic arts" (vii). Thematically and structurally the novel embodies the challenges of relocating a work of fiction from its established medium into one that transforms not only its modality of reception, but also textuality itself. The "unbinding" of the title, an image of cyberspace as "a realm of forking paths, of endless choices and alternatives" (ix), could also function as a metaphor for the dismemberment of the print medium itself. Just as an "unbound" book would be helpless to enclose its content, so does *The Unbinding* refuse to be constricted by the traditional groundwork of novels, such as plot, character, subjectivity, and narrative time. The form of the text evacuates characterization, reducing narrative figures to avatar models or surveillance data-doubles (i.e., the information package corresponding to each existing individual in the surveillance network). Surveillance thus becomes the condition and signature of the narration itself.[14]

The reading process inevitably mirrors the surveillance circuits described in the book, with readers having to track down the temporal sequence of the various sections and follow the characters on the meandering map of their online journeys. To read *The Unbinding* is thus to flounder through several narrative plots that start and stop at short notice, slipping under the surface of the text to emerge again from one of its (hyperlinked) fissures. To read this novel means, in other words, to perform an act of data mining that mirrors the way security agencies sort through disparate fragments of information. The reading vigilante is compelled to operate a system of mass observation very much like Selkirk's own AidSat. Ethically the novel baffles without sketching normative paths of response to the dissolution of narrative. It establishes and names the challenges of surveillance for post-9/11 literature but stops short of developing a recipe for ethical reading, devoting all its energies to the practical illustration of how fiction might adapt to the panoptic age.

Personal Privacy and Foreign Relations in the War on Terror: Jonathan Raban

If post-9/11 fiction teaches us to screen and investigate subversive plots, it also emplots surveillance as an ingenious frame for an overt critique of America's War on Terror. This politicized approach denounces permanent surveillance both as an instrument of state oppression and for its role in the design of modern communication and interpersonal relationships. Kirn already adumbrates this latter aspect, but it is Jonathan Raban's novel *Surveillance* that most clearly envisions a wired post-9/11 world where government-sponsored and peer-to-peer surveillance are rampant and interconnected, borrowing each other's methods and enveloping their overinformed participants in a haze of paranoia and suspicion. Raban probes not only the concept of surveillance but also its practical application and the ways the surveillance method itself can be "supervised," and all these are concisely encoded in the novel's epigraph, a citation from Gaston Bachelard's treatise *Applied Rationalism*, which explains the so-called surveillance of the third degree: "In order that self-surveillance be fully assured, it must somehow be itself held under surveillance. Thus, there come into existence forms of surveillance of surveillance to which, for the sake of brevity, we shall give the exponential notation (surveillance)^2. We shall, moreover, set out the elements of a surveillance of surveillance of surveillance, in other words, of (surveillance)^3."[3] Insofar as Bachelard is concerned with forms of epistemological vigilance rather than concrete practices of political watchfulness, he prescribes a system that scrutinizes not only the application of a method but the method itself, pointing to the subjective positionality that underpins all scientific work. Raban accordingly demands increased self-awareness in the implementation of surveillance, presenting his own text as a cipher for the kind of self-vigilant surveillance that could help keep other forms of containment and control in check.

To set up his indictment of surveillance society in instantly recognizable terms, Raban taps more explicitly than Kirn does into a post-9/11 world afflicted by a climate of fear amid a new landscape of checkpoints, red alerts, and evacuation drills. Set three or four years in the future in

Seattle—which, like Virilio's "overexposed city," is presented here as a "world without hidden sides, a world in which opacity is no longer anything but a momentary interlude" (Virilio, "The Overexposed City" 23)—the narrative summons many of the 9/11 attacks' psychological and political remains. In particular Raban divulges the dysfunctional activities of an administration suddenly and recklessly amenable to testing "all the new bells and whistles of its fright-machine" (*Surveillance* 143) at the expense of privacy rights. The vexed relationship between knowledge and conjecture transpires in the countless simulations meant to prepare the population for a pending (albeit invisible) threat. The government sustains a perpetual state of fear by staging elaborate drills in which professional actors portray the victims of imagined terrorist attacks, and whose performative aesthetics clearly exceed their strict necessity: "The administration was in the business of manufacturing fear and methodically spreading its infection from city to city. The lengths they went to—setting fires, showing make-believe corpses to the cameras—surely went far beyond what was needed to test the emergency services" (15). Similarities to DeLillo's *White Noise* and Kirn's *The Unbinding* are obvious here, but even more apparent are the resemblances between Raban's vision of a futuristic surveillance vortex and the forms of social control deployed in the War on Terror.[15] Raban discloses, as Kirn does, the transition in surveillance practices from the reporting of accidents, crashes, and incidents during or after an event (where the protagonist provides eyewitness evidence or hindsight) to post-9/11 anticipatory surveillance, where sight becomes foresight: "homeland security" comes to mean "keeping the homeland in a state of continuous insecurity" (15).[16]

From the vernacular surveillance of ordinary people subscribing to Google Alerts on each other's names or undercover marshals intending "not to observe but to be observed, the watcher watched" (218), Raban's novel registers a gamut of surveillance forms enabled by fairly recent technological advances, some of which have become so common that their ethical implications are elided or disavowed. "We're all spooks now," one character opines. "Look at the way people Google their prospective dates. Everybody does it. Everybody's trying to spy on everybody else" (226).

Peer-to-peer surveillance, Raban points out, is a miniature instantiation of mass surveillance by national authorities and, as such, an impediment to a full-fledged reproof of a political system whose unethical stratagems we are duplicating in the "privacy" of our homes: "We're all dataminers now," he writes in an essay for the *Guardian* published in 2006. "Just 10 or 15 years ago, it would have taken days in libraries and record offices, along with the full-time services of a private detective, to get the kind of hard intelligence on my prospective dinner date that I can now retrieve in a few idle minutes; and if I can do that, I tremble to think of what governments, equipped with massive financial and technological resources, are capable of doing" (Raban, "We Have Mutated" n.p.).

Official programs such as Echelon consequently appear less as rogue systems of inadmissible intrusion than as the natural extension of grassroots trends toward a securitization of personal relationships through digital espionage, trends that *Surveillance* engages on multiple levels.[17] A landlord delegates one of his employees to watch over the others and report to his boss in cases of disobedience or misdemeanor (156), at the same time as he rifles through his female tenant's underwear drawer. A character whose mantra is "Just because you're paranoid does not mean they're not out to get you" (160) deems himself a victim of vast surveillance mechanisms conspiring to expose and censure his own subversive activities as a defender of humanist causes. Deeply distrustful of the government, he believes the War on Terror is designed merely to keep the public in a state of constant pliability: "Datamining was Tad's current obsession. Someone, somewhere, was watching as he tramped from site to site in cyberspace. . . . Tapping out email, Tad had the sense that his messages were being scanned by an anonymous eavesdropper. Paranoia? No. Internet service providers were required by law to render up complete records of their clients' every digital move if they were sent a 'national security letter' by the FBI" (161–62). In his obsessive drive to research and uncover whoever might be uncovering him, Tad is both a victim of surveillance and a dissident performer or agent provocateur whose online activities are motivated primarily by a desire to be exposed. The murky pleasures that Tad-like subjects derive from being monitored, pleasures that consolidate citizenship as well as a vague sense of personal security and belonging (as Adams's novel *Harbor* confirms), complicate Raban's emplotment of surveillance as a frame for ethical edification.

Nor is Tad the only suspicious and ethically indeterminate presence in *Surveillance*. At the opposite end of the novel's ideological spectrum we find the Holocaust survivor and retired history professor August Vanags, author of the best-selling memoir *Boy 381*, whom the novel's protagonist, the journalist Lucy Bergstrom, sets out to interview by employing a discreet surveillance procedure. Her photo sessions and conversations with the writer highlight the startling contrast between his current life in the United States and his plight as a child in Poland during World War II, the two identities seemingly irreconcilable. After extensive research in the field, including reading Wladyslaw Szpilman's *The Pianist*, Lucy is struck by substantial overlaps between events narrated in those books and Vanags's purportedly autobiographical narrative—overlaps that Vanags dismisses as traceable to the rituality of evil irrespective of its historical contexts. "In war brutality gets to be fun," Vanags explains, invoking the Abu Ghraib torture images to make his point; by 1942, he insists, the Nazis "could do the unconscionable because they'd worked it up into a whole series of rituals" (182). Not yet fully convinced of Vanags's authorial legitimacy, Lucy investigates reviews of the book posted by readers on Amazon.com and predictably discovers one that exposes Vanags as a fraud. The incriminating evidence—a photograph that bears a striking resemblance to the one reproduced in Vanags's book—leaves enough room for reasonable doubt, however, so Lucy's search, like many counterterrorist investigations lampooned in the book, ultimately remains fruitless.

Even more suspicious than the authorship of the memoir is Vanags himself, not only a Holocaust survivor and best-selling memoirist, but also an adjunct fellow in international affairs at the Council on Foreign Relations.[18] His policies are distinctly and disturbingly imperialist with regard to America's cultural and political leadership in the world, which he views as preoccupied less with territorial and ideological expansion than with the recognition of an already existing transborder "Americanness" inherent in most societies (whether or not it is acknowledged as such). "Every poor sap living under a dictatorship," Vanags hazards to explain, "when he dreams of being free he dreams of being an American. Most probably he doesn't know that. He doesn't say to himself 'I want to be an American,' but it's our freedoms that he's dreaming of. . . . We got to open that guy's eyes to what he's really feeling" (197–98). Given that Vanags seeks to unveil the formally abjured democratic desires of nondemocratic peoples and nations, and to incorporate those desires into a broader American "liberation" project, his vision clearly partakes of the same suspicious invasiveness that coheres the agenda of global surveillance and securitization.

Giorgio Agamben's remarks on the international reach of the War on Terror are instructive here. Notably revising Foucault's notion of disciplinary power, Agamben suggests that the conventional defense of territories is being replaced by an aggressive securitization that dissolves the traditional (internal and external) boundaries of law. "While disciplinary power isolates and closes off territories," Agamben explains, "measures of security lead to an opening and globalization; while the law wants to prevent and prescribe, security wants to intervene in ongoing processes to direct them. In a word, discipline wants to produce order, while security wants to guide disorder" (n.p.). Vanags's appetite for hypersecuritization grounded in a concept of transnational, pro-American liberation ultimately testifies to the increasingly global reach of surveillance and to the international impact of morally polarizing security discourses. That said, other post-9/11 fictions juxtapose discipline and security to excavate the implications of global surveillance not (or not merely) as the expression of political climates but from the more elaborate standpoint of its circuits and media infrastructure—an approach that dovetails with a renewed concern about the repercussions of visual archiving and control for the ethics of narrative.

The Ethics and Aesthetics of Global Surveillance: William Gibson

One is tempted to ask at this point to what extent the recruitment of surveillance as a narrative strategy is underwritten by a keen awareness of how September 11 and the War on Terror have laid bare the permeable boundaries of nations and national identities. I take this question to be fundamental to the production of literature after 9/11, as it analogizes the global scope of surveillance (personal, corporate, and political) to the transnational range of contemporary fiction. It is thus hardly surprising that a transnational surveillance novel, William Gibson's *Pattern Recognition*, was the first to incorporate the events of September 11, partly due to the fact that Gibson was "about 100 pages into the book on September 10."[19] Gibson's speculations about an increasingly digital environment, couched in the fast-paced idiom of a detective story and freshly minted technological jargon, applies the trope of "pattern recognition" to correlate the image-making techniques of the advertising industry on the one hand and the forces harnessed by global networks of commodification, consumption, and control on the other.

In the wake of September 11, having recently relocated from Britain to New York on a work assignment, Cayce Pollard "feels as though something huge has happened, is happening but she can't define it" (292). In ways that resonate with many of the post-9/11 fictions contemplated in this study, she senses "life shift beneath her, rearranging itself according to a new paradigm of history" (340). Cayce is sensitive not only to historical upheaval but also to the semiotics of cultural mapping, and in her profession as freelance "coolhunter," she tries "to recognize a pattern before anyone else does" (88) within the "immaterial labor" regime of global capitalism.[20] While the novel extends her sensitivity to comprise reactions to large-scale events such as 9/11, Cayce's expertise lies primarily in fashion and commodity design, where she acts as a surveilling eye to judge a design's potential efficacy as well as predict successful new fashions emerging from the sartorial energy of street style. Her premonitory sensitivity is best deciphered as a logo-reactive nausea—or, in Fredric Jameson's words, "commodity bulimia" (*Archeologies of the Future* 390)—that borders on the pathological, mimicking the structure of an allergy. Yet Cayce's responsiveness is not conscripted to fashion development and marketing, instead marshaling more broadly aesthetic reactions to the attacks. Emphasizing the versatility of her talent is her quest for the creator of a mysterious film footage posted bit by bit to an Internet website known as F:F:F:—Fetish:Footage:Forum. "Footageheads" around the world follow the postings and exchange e-mail speculations about what the footage might signify and who its author might be, constructing in their enthusiasm the "site of a collective production of meaning" (Wegner, "Recognizing the Patterns" 191) that incurs its intersubjective, ethical relevance from what Paul Virilio calls "the globalization of the collective imagination" ("The Visual Crash" 111). The web-based cult vacillates between admiration of the footage as high art and dismissal of it as advertising campaign, yet irrespective of their views the devotees never cease to question and discuss each other's positions.[21]

Essentially the footage consists of a series of short videos featuring different characters in mundane circumstances that cannot be placed historically or geographically. Yet even while it vivifies montage aesthetics through detailed discussions of the footage, *Pattern Recognition* remains one of Gibson's most conventionally linear novels, eschewing the jump-cuts characteristic of his earlier work. Surveillance is, accordingly, only partly a structural concern (especially evident in Gibson's use of technological language), but it emerges forcefully on the level of plot design, which indirectly affects character construction and reader response by enabling parallels between the footage community and literary readership. Around the divergent surmises as to the source and authorship of the video, a community forms consisting of regular posters and so-called lurkers (i.e., those who merely read what has been posted without writing any contributions of their own). Cayce experiences this confined community as a mutable, virtual home that supersedes other, more palpable locations in geographic space, which is to say that the forum becomes "one of the most consistent places in her life, like a familiar café that exists somehow outside of geography and beyond time zones" (4). What sutures together this community is not only fidelity to the footage itself but also the concurrent loosening of competing, more material social and emotional links. As Phillip E. Wegner argues, the novel thereby suggests that a "weakening of older national and regional borders, coupled with the explosive growth of new instantaneous communication technologies, has made possible the emergence of original forms of cultural, or more precisely subcultural, belonging" ("Recognizing the Patterns" 190).

The footage inevitably attracts the attention of an ambitious entrepreneur, Hubertus Bigend, founder of the advertising agency Blue Ant, a company that has internalized the fluid and fluctuating structures of the global marketplace: "relatively tiny in terms of permanent staff, globally distributed, more post-geographic than multinational . . . a high-speed, low-drag life-form in an advertising ecology of lumbering herbivores" (6). Bigend, who refers to the footage as "the single most effective piece of guerilla marketing ever" and "the most brilliant marketing ploy of this very young century" (64, 65), seeks to harness its viral power into advertising capital and decides to invest unlimited funds in tracking down its maker. Unsurprisingly his professional ideal is a "country without borders," "a world where there are no mirrors to find yourself on the other side of, all experience having been reduced, by the spectral hand of marketing, to price-point variations on the same thing" (341). No wonder, then, that Bigend can see the footage only as a harbinger of a single, boundaryless surface-world that entraps claustrophobically interreflecting objects.

Much as Kirn's addled figurines, in piecing together the puzzle of the footage through repeated screenings and investigations, Gibson's characters become overseers of a visual narrative that they replay and rearrange in an act of more or less conscious surveillance.[22] Here, as in the foregoing texts, a metalevel of narrative emerges to the extent that readers are supplied with techniques of intelligence gathering and reconnaissance that sanction their own investigations on the margins of the plot. It goes without saying that the detective search for the godlike master of filmmaking on a surreally global production set is nothing but a classic MacGuffin, which occasions a parallel line of inquiry into the broader aesthetics of detection (narrative and investigative). Yet despite the titular "pattern," the central organizing trope of narrative data mining is absent here, eclipsed by a shift toward an indeterminate visual aesthetics and the circulation of objects. It is this last concern that I want to summon as critical to understanding how *Pattern Recognition* anticipates the hyperkinetic montage structure of later surveillance novels. The relatively intact structural coherence of Gibson's narrative only drives surveillance inward and renders it more acute, in ways that expose surveillance as integral to any creative endeavor, visual or otherwise.

It is thus significant that the creator of the footage is discovered when intelligence agencies carrying out surveillance on information traffic retrace a visual steganographic watermark on the segments of video. The footage turns out to have originated in surveillance cameras, "mere scraps of found video" (305) manipulated by the damaged consciousness of a young Russian artist who has been injured by a bomb fragment lodged in her brain. The paradox here is that the footage—described in the novel as timeless, bland, impossible to locate chronologically or spatially—should originate in CCTV material, which is, by definition, attached to a particular time interval that determines its value as data, information, and intelligence.

The universal appeal of Gibson's mysterious surveillance footage thus rests not on its ability to convey concrete intelligence, but on a lack of specificity that renders it impervious to factual inquiry, driving home the slipperiness and malleability of surveillance material deployed in the War on Terror (a line of argument continued in my analysis of Richard Flanagan's *The Unknown Terrorist*). The footage manifests a timeless, unidentified Otherness so generic that it becomes unique, in much the same way that Cayce's sartorially brandless existence transforms the woman into her own brand, each item of clothing partaking of a fetishistic, commodified aura; the garments are known as CPUs (Cayce Pollard Units), which "ideally seem to have come into this world without human intervention" (8). Even as its "absence of stylistic cues suggests a veritable Barthesian 'white writing'" (Jameson, *Archeologies of the Future* 389), the footage thus divulges the deeper subject of *Pattern Recognition*, namely the semiotic neutrality and systematic effacement of context on which the aesthetics of global surveillance patently depend. Deprived of such contextualization, the narrative devotes inordinate attention to the surface circulation of things, zooming in on their technological and aesthetic objecthood.

Indeed the novel furnishes a prism for conceiving an intersubjective ethic that is deeply shaped and haunted by an unalloyed cultural obsession with objects, gadgets, and technological paraphernalia. Gibson is fully attentive to the many registers in which the texture of surfaces and our addictions to them can be described. Yet only seldom does he detect emotional bonds between his characters and the objects they use, wear, or carry, partly because the brand names with which they are associated convey "both instant obsolescence and the global provenance and neo-exoticism of the world market today in time and space" (Jameson, *Archeologies of the Future* 386), a multidimensionality that makes emotional rapport next to impossible. Instead of focusing on things as material objects, Gibson accordingly foregrounds their immateriality, their "secret," virtual lives, implicitly pointing to the aura of signification that surveillance devices seek to tease out of ordinary things (and ordinary people). Likewise, although certainly a material concoction in its early stages, the footage assumes a shadowy existence emblematic of this virtuality, much the same way that the petal Cayce watches while the Twin Towers are coming down symbolically registers the larger rearrangement of the world at a moment of extreme tension. What Gibson tries to uphold, in other words, is not the life of things but the poetry of their deadness, the surprise caused by their movements in a world that expects them to stay put—vis-à-vis both the unexpected petal fall and the collapse of what had seemed unassailable, the Twin Towers.

While in Tokyo retracing the steps of the surveillance artist who created the footage, Cayce is assaulted by countless references to the now defunct World Trade Center. Sprinkled in between commercials and billboards, these images confirm Gibson's claim that the terrorist attacks were essentially "an experience outside of culture" (137), one that remains unassimilated, uncanny, and perpetually out of place: "There's a small, cheap-looking television behind the bar, just at the periphery of Cayce's vision. It's made of transparent plastic and shaped something like a football helmet. On its six-inch screen she sees a screaming human face attempting to thrust itself through a sheet of very thin latex, then a quick clip of the South Tower collapsing, then four green melons, perfectly round, rolling along on a flat white surface" (151). As an object of endless reification and consumption, the image of the burning and crumbling towers converts into a postmodern logo, a brand name of universal recognition and traumatic effect. At the end of the novel, stranded in Russia waiting to eventually meet the maker of the footage, Cayce confronts further crude reminders of the 9/11 attacks in the unlikeliest places: "There's a plastic Garfield atop one monitor, other signs of workplace personalization. She picks up a square of clear acrylic: laser-etched in its core are the Coca-Cola logo, a crude representation of the Twin Towers, and the words 'WE REMEMBER'" (302–03). Not unlike the generic footage, these synecdochic 9/11 miniatures have become ordinary and impersonal as a result of their sheer ubiquity. The logos into which the terrorist event has hardened soak up the toxicity of this kind of global omnipresence and visual commodification, which transforms objects and images into portable replicas of themselves, publicly owned across national borders.

The unexpected fall of the petal that had seemed parched into its position, defiant of gravity and random violence, reinforces Cayce's impression of the terrorist attacks as both a site of communal remembrance and "some vast and deeply personal insult to any ordinary notion of interiority" (137). It is through their ability to cut to the marrow of private fears and expose them that the terrorist attacks destabilize the ethical formation of interiority in the novel. Cayce's experience of the contained petal fall—perhaps a metaphor for the equally contained world of fiction and its symbolic miniatures—counterbalances this effect. The private glimpse of the petal within an environment otherwise sequestered from the vicissitudes of the outside world may be seen as an attempt to replace the surface aesthetics of surveillance with an ethical understanding of watchfulness as an interior, intimate act. *Pattern Recognition* thus indicates that even as the 9/11 attacks and the ensuing global insecurity have triggered the preemptive surveillance strategies currently deployed under the Patriot Act, the same event also invites a rethinking of transnational spectatorship as *not* distanced, dispassionate, or easily commoditized. Gibson posits these forms of spectatorship—private yet global, both interior and exposed, material and disembodied—as ethically viable alternatives to the mechanical vigilance of the counterterrorist or corporate surveillance screen.

Death by Media: Richard Flanagan

In his analysis of Australian fiction after 9/11, Nathanael O'Reilly probes Richard Flanagan's novel *The Unknown Terrorist* for its potential to "interrogate the interdependent relationship between governments, the media, and terrorism, while critiquing the use of terrorism by governments and the media to exert, maintain, and increase power" (296). O'Reilly reads Flanagan through the lens of Jean Baudrillard's theories of terrorism as self-referential spectacle fundamentally subsumed to its own visual imagery. "The image," Baudrillard writes, "consumes the event, in the sense that it absorbs it and offers it for consumption" (*The Spirit of Terrorism* 27), and images of the 9/11 attacks indeed reify and multiply that event in *The Unknown Terrorist*. Widely transmitted on multiple screens (from TVs to commercial billboards) after an unsuccessful terrorist attack in Sydney, piecemeal images of terror—of the collapsing Twin Towers, children's bodies being laid out after the Beslan school massacre, bombed-out trains in London and Madrid, bin Laden, Bush (159–60)—instill general panic, which the media and the authorities rush to exploit for commercial and political gain. Though intriguingly analyzed by O'Reilly, this self-evident idea seems too easily amenable to the potboiler genre of conspiratorial thrills, and it strikes me as the novel's secondary or tertiary focus, used merely to set the stage for its central trope of morally abusive surveillance and manufactured justice.

When the stripper Gina Davies, who goes by the name "the Doll," becomes a terrorist suspect after surveillance footage associating her with a putative Islamic extremist is picked up by the media, the story gains momentum deriving less from the surreal machinations of Richard Cody (a news anchor of declining reputation who tries to frame Gina) than from the disastrous role of surveillance, which ultimately seals this woman's fate. Quite distinct from Gibson's footage yet equally contagious in effect, surveillance shots of the Doll, provocatively embedded within more generic terror imagery, are disseminated publicly in segments that support Cody's narrative and reinterpret virtually every aspect of Gina's life. Spectatorship in this case implicates a power play aptly intimated in Gina's profession as a stripper, a woman who earns her living from exposure. Rather unfortunately bolstered by the Doll's stripping act as the "Black Widow" (involving a long black dress and hijab, crotchless black knickers, and a data projector with Arabic lettering), the scenario of the Doll as feral homegrown terrorist is, of course, preposterously contrived. The pattern that Cody nudges viewers to recognize has no basis in reality beyond the inherent family resemblance of the terror-themed images themselves, which are fused by an aesthetic rather than causal continuity. Clearly these images do not sum up into a compelling narrative, yet instead of inciting alarm, their arbitrary association only enhances the viewers' expectation that one comprehensive image or solution will eventually elucidate all, "as if there were a logic in their ordering that demanded a yet unknown conclusion; as if they were the opening quick cuts summarizing a series' shows prior to its cataclysmic finale" (139). In this sense Flanagan questions surveillance not merely as a strategy for deriving portentous clues from trivial information, but also as a component of narrative expectation and sequence.

Cody, who appreciates journalism as the art to "use the truths you could discover to tell the story you believed to matter" (181), uses surveillance footage to tell the story he wants people to see (in order to indirectly inject some blood into his own career), a story "produced" (in the cinematic sense) by himself and his collaborators from standardized data and uninformed speculation. When Cody's preferred talk-show psychologist hears the outline of the Gina Davies plot, his mind hums "like a hard drive booting up" (182), ready to draw the dots that will fit the predetermined lines of connection. "It's like Sudoku," the psychologist proclaims. "You just have to make the numbers fit" (184). Once they do fit, the product will likely become more marketable in the "spirit of free trade, of this great globalised world" (193) in which the ultimate aim is to cut a deal that will maximize profit. The tenuousness of his argument provokes not a glimmer of doubt or remorse in Cody's mind; on the contrary, he maintains, "the fact of something missing could be used to prove the idea of it actually existing" (256). Meanwhile, beset by this incessant surveillance and angered by the erotic domination implicit in Cody's persecution, Gina

Davies as a woman ceases to exist. By manipulating the surveillance footage and its pre-attached narrative, Cody succeeds in "turning her from a woman into cartoons, headlines, opinions, fears, fate" (261), and the novel is itself (quite self-consciously) complicit in her degradation. This debasement creates, in the face of apparent subjection, an unprecedented degree of freedom for Gina. She eventually retaliates by shooting Cody point-blank with a stolen gun once used in the arsenal of NATO troops on a mission to defend the Bosnian Muslim town of Srebrenica, in an act that seems intended to avenge the deaths that were so quickly forgotten by the media, which are now being held symbolically responsible for the massacres—hers and the Bosnian Muslims' alike.

In subtle ways the narrative itself shifts and mutates to imitate Flanagan's inconclusive image of terrorism, from the mildly absurd preface defining Jesus as the first suicide bomber to Gina's obsession with playing the role of Devil or scapegoat for an enraged, bloodthirsty community. (Here as in McGrath, the scapegoat is an easily vilified, sexually promiscuous woman.) As David Lyon has remarked, the "rise of surveillance has everything to do with disappearing bodies" ("The Search for Surveillance Theories" 15), namely the bodies of the observers themselves. Yet in becoming visible as a panoptic presence (his face is, of course, all over the news), Cody precipitates an imbalance of power whereby the surveillance image itself (rather than an omniscient surveilling eye) assumes ultimate authority, wielded through wily narratorial practices. The narrative often evinces a sentimental and puppet-like tenor (hence "the Doll"), while the characters are caricatures of cultural types (such as the evil media scammer and the virtuous prostitute). With the release of the surveillance footage, the novel takes an even sharper turn to the surreal, signaled by a narrative style that, on the one hand, allows Gina no textual privacy or interiority (every sentiment and thought process is exposed) and on the other hand mimes the commercial, libidinally exploitive agenda to which Cody and his ilk subscribe. The plot itself is sensationalized to the hilt, including a raunchy sex scene and a public murder, as if already training to be a screenplay, borrowing equally from the breathlessness of the news cycle and from the ethical binarism contained in its structure of feeling—both of which are implicitly maligned in the novel.

Inevitably, because the Doll internalizes the prejudice against her, she sifts through her own past thoughts and deeds for something that will justify the world's persecution. Her own complacency with regard to the War on Terror now strikes her as a "way of agreeing with what the world was, one more attempt at getting on with that very power that was now turned on her. On her, *who had never questioned the right of those who made the judgments to be the judges!*" (291, my emphasis). Tragically Gina learns the ethical value of withholding judgment only when the media and the public alike unleash their fatal judgment upon her. Holding a mirror to her past self-righteousness and present moral compunction is the surveillance footage, mingled with images of terror (so "the Doll felt as if she too were in that school in Beslan as body after body was laid out" [148]) and with a wall of plasma screens stacked together to form the image of the burning Twin Towers. One is not quite sure where the screen ends and reality begins in this theater of interreflecting gazes, where the 9/11 attacks, Australian counterterrorism, and the power of global media commingle into one menacing eyeball. What Flanagan does delineate, and clearly so, is the power of surveillance material disembedded from circumstance to attract and nourish hasty moral judgment. Compounding the moral sharpness of his critique is the novel's narrative simulation of the guilty pleasures of surveillance, of its libidinal drive, and of the textured mechanisms of watching in order to condemn, of scapegoating a human subject reduced to a set of images "stacked together" to suit expedient preconceptions.

How to Do Things with Intelligence: Lorraine Adams

Drawing on similar tropes of mistaken identity and unwarranted suspicion, Lorraine Adams's novel *Harbor* melds terrorism, surveillance, and diaspora in ways that resonate with several of the foregoing texts. The parallel deployment of surveillance as both theme and formal procedure is more sophisticated here, as it is set against a broader canvas on which transnational and historical vectors are mapped out. *Harbor* revolves around an Arabic-speaking, mainly Algerian, immigrant community in Boston that comes to the attention of a counterterrorist investigation about one year *before* the 9/11 attacks. Despite this unexpected temporal setting, *Harbor* explores counterterrorist surveillance in greater depth than any of the narratives discussed so far.[23] Although Adams has FBI investigators explicitly connect Algeria to the U.S. global War on Terror ("Algeria has a problem with these sickos.... They've got ties to Al Qaeda. Lots of the Afghan vets were Algerian, went back home, viva Allah" [285]), which boosts the novel's post-9/11 relevance,[24] Algeria's wars had in fact already been a matter of concern to the United States for half a century. One of Senator John F. Kennedy's most significant speeches on foreign affairs, delivered before the Senate on July 2, 1957, refuted President Eisenhower's claim that Algeria was exclusively a French problem, urging instead that the rebellions in Algeria be seen as a matter of international concern. Kennedy's address may be regarded as a turning point in America's involvement with issues of international terrorism and democratic revolution in ways that anticipate American support of local liberation movements in Afghanistan and usefully contextualize the current War on Terror.[25]

Once this historical parallel has been implicitly drawn, first among the novel's revelations is the incompetence and inefficiency of the intelligence agencies in charge of foiling terrorist plots—agencies that Adams exposes as mutually suspicious, territorial, and woefully underprepared. Quite hilariously, members of the Joint Terrorism Taskforce need to be reminded that they must actually read the intelligence reports prior to their meetings and be gently assured that their "first exposure to names of a Muslim or Arabic type" (205) will seem less traumatic once they have familiarized themselves with the suspects. Unsurprisingly, then, in conducting surveillance on the illegal Algerian immigrants and their mysterious storage locker outside Boston, the task force assembles a shockingly inaccurate picture that allows the instigators to trade their knowledge for a quick release, while the innocent are caught and deported. But for a long time the reader, like the investigators, has no clue as to who might be involved in what. Anchoring the narrative around a sympathetic face and a moral center is Aziz Arkoun, a young Algerian refugee who enters the United States illegally as a stowaway in the hold of a tanker and finds shelter in an apartment crowded with fellow Algerians, petty criminals involved in various kinds of fraud, constantly trying to dodge the authorities. Downtrodden and penniless, what soaks up their energies is not jihad but the struggle to make ends meet. And although it is a commonplace that living a threadbare existence in the West will help stimulate radicalization among Muslims, Aziz and his fellow Algerians evince no Islamist sympathies whatsoever. In fact they are pleased to have escaped the Islamist groups that forcefully recruited them at home. Throughout the novel a series of flashbacks reveals the horror from which Aziz has managed to flee: the Islamist militias and corrupt Algerian military brutalizing the civilian population, as well as the particular atrocity of passively witnessing the murder of the woman who had been (sight unseen) betrothed to him. Yet even though he has abjured allegiance to fundamentalism, America is no safe harbor for Aziz: the Boston field office of the FBI becomes convinced that these destitute Algerians are conniving to form a dangerous sleeper cell. Soon their suspicion snowballs into a full-fledged counterterrorist operation: microphones, microcams, surveillance vans, the full intelligence paraphernalia are aimed at the loose Algerian group, which soon dissolves as its members leave the city or the country and the number of globally scattered dots on the FBI's conference boards rises exponentially.

Like the FBI agents tapping the phones of the Algerian expatriates, ultimately the reader herself becomes an eavesdropper struggling to make sense of their unwieldy alliances, memories, and conversations. The sprawling ensemble cast ensnares the reader in a network of stories whose permutational possibilities are orchestrated by Heather (the FBI's most puzzling surveillance target), an American woman around whom several of the Algerians gravitate—dating, loving, or abandoning her. Adams amplifies this confusion, as do Kirn, Raban, Gibson, and Flanagan, on the narrative level. While other surveillance fictions rely quite heavily on technoconcepts (such as AidSat or Footage Forum), the prose often serving merely as delivery device, *Harbor* deftly weaves into its language the alienation, discomfort, and puzzlement inflicted by surveillance on both sides of the lens. The heroine of Lynne Sharon Schwartz's *The Writing on the Wall* concludes the novel by saying "Nothing can ever be the way it was" in flawed Arabic (295). Adams goes past this symbolic invocation of the Other as language by mingling the Algerians' awkward English with covert Arabic cadences to create the sense of an imprecise translation, the rough draft of a report whose loose ends are yet to be tied together. And no aspect of the novel so collapses the distinction between thematic and structural surveillance tropes as its rendering of dialogue. Conversations often read like the transcript of a surveillance tape, where motivations are merely alluded to, possibly in code.

Memory fragments inserted into the story of Aziz and his friends further divert the narrative sequence. The function of this backstory is to frustrate readers tempted to categorize Aziz as knowable merely because he serves as the novel's "central intelligence" (to use Henry James's term in a context that enriches its original meaning). In ethical terms, the memories of the terrorist acts he committed, watched, or condoned in Algeria have gradually corroded Aziz's belief in moral choice. His disabused verdict that "there are no right sides, no wrong sides, no sides on any sides" (184) communicates a distinct post-9/11 sensibility, challenging at the same time the prejudices and moral radicalism used to justify the doctrine of preemption and blanket surveillance in the War on Terror. "What reality could any one person know?" Aziz asks, deciding that no image of the world he constructs is likely to be more objectively accurate than anybody else's. The tardy revelation that his betrothed was beheaded before his very eyes nevertheless instills in him the fear that the puzzle pieces of his life may at any moment come together to deal him another painful blow. This constant paranoia transforms "each strange rich creature into one person with only one quality" (i.e., potential danger) and his new surroundings into "a world where there was only one person beside himself: a person to run from" (230).

To some extent this insecurity is also a function of exile. Like Hemon's Vladimir Brik, Aziz is plagued by depression and melancholia, his role as a labeled box on the FBI's investigative charts closely echoing his own diminished sense of self: "His place in the order of things was not a place; maybe, as he came to think of it, it was an insert, a scooping out, into which he belonged, but if he were to die or to quit or not be there for some reason, another, not like him but adequate to his function, would be fitted in and, like the tab in his cereal box, would keep it neat and closed" (65). Aziz also shares with Brik a fascination with America as cavernous absence, marked by a lack of history and of violence. The serenity of his Boston life often interferes with his ability to remember Algeria's atrocities: "He willed the massacres into animation across the street, trying to see their Boston version. He imagined a sidewalk exploding, a handbag flying, a baby's hat plopped on a manhole cover. But these dioramas melted in the radiance before him: the metallic of cars, the kid of a caramel glove, the creamy red of brake lights. The pretty new nothing that was America—he wanted to watch that" (66). Those watching *him* imagine precisely such devastation to be his purported plan. The Algerians are in fact as concerned about being watched as the FBI task force is about watching them. Aziz's brother Mourad develops an obsession with surveillance that bespeaks his desire to become a bona fide American, even though he can acquire this "negative" citizenship only by first landing in the crosshairs of the authorities. The precision and stealth of the modern devices aimed at him are enough to give him an identity boost and free him from distasteful associations with his primitive homeland: "He looked everywhere when he came home from work and when he left for work, and he could see nothing, but he knew these were not baboons like back home that you could see plain. These were Americans, and they knew how to watch without bringing attention. They may have even bought the house across the street—he had heard from talk at work that the FBI did this, that they bought houses and waited and watched for *years*" (147).

And the FBI does watch for years, accumulating a massive amount of data. Despite their confidence in "patterns" and "repeats" (233), however, the FBI's perspective is no less simplifying than Aziz's amoral "no side" theory. As a more experienced agent admits, "The variants are essentially endless": databases such as phone company records are "riddled with errors," a problem compounded by Arabic to English transliteration. While the FBI's image of the Algerians becomes increasingly blurred (which, of course, doesn't prevent them from making arbitrary guesses and arrests), Aziz's worldview gradually regains a moral polarity sustained by the realization "that there were distinctions, that running from all—or loving all, he had to see that too—was little improvement over renouncing the subtlety of discernment because it led to excuses. Some explanations were footnotes. But some were a lens that focused" (248–49). Aziz ultimately seeks to reconcile his reductive views of Algeria ("permanent unfathomable confusion") and the United States ("prettiness walled off from his touch") within a "larger understanding" defined and refined by what he calls "fuller contradictions." Notably this is akin to the ethical challenge of surveillance as the artificial, morally overdetermined production of omniscience: Once the facts are on the table, what is the "larger understanding" that will admit them all, what lens focuses our inferences, and how do we reflect on the processes through which intelligence begets active involvement, whether as sanction or preemption?

Like the wall in the FBI's conference room, the novel is "covered with faces, names, dotted lines" (250) purveying no definitive plot or irrefutable causal links. Occasionally the hopelessly fumbling FBI takes center stage as the main culprit for the protracted failure of the War on Terror; then it's the Algerians themselves and their internecine terror campaigns perpetrating unspeakable horrors below the radar of global media, in ways that permanently cripple the Algerians' own psyche and their ability for social adjustment: "The sound of a man dying in Algeria is not even a whisper in the world. Arab man dies in Palestine, it is five orchestras, every instrument playing. Palestine boy huddled under his father, killed by a Jew, everywhere his picture goes. But where are the pictures of Muslim boys killed by Muslims in Blida? . . . Who makes this? It is not the Jew. It is not the CIA. It is us. *Us*" (278). The implications of this self-destructive war—its pidgin portrait a blunt correlative for its self-incriminating morality—do not escape the FBI investigators, who justify their suspicions of the Algerian "cell" by invoking the situation in Algeria, "as old as the Balkans. Intractable" (285), all while conflating evil and national belonging much the same way that the Chicago police and the Bush administration vilify outsiders of Jewish and Muslim faith in Hemon's *Lazarus Project*. Adams locates evil, as Hemon does, along the fault lines that separate peoples and nations in the form of a "blurriness" (286) into which the novel's characters fade and out of which they reemerge unexpectedly, challenging the investigators to clear up the fog in this war of suspicion and connect the dots. Piecing everything together, the FBI admits, is illusory, and any half-drawn picture inherently "flawed" (282). To demonstrate this predicament, at the end of the final chapter the novel simply stops, casually losing sight of its protagonists as if a surveillance camera had suddenly been switched off.

All in all, a complex development can be traced in the foregoing surveillance fictions from technologies that can track individual behavior, such as Orwell's telescreens or current CCTV cameras (from which data are collated by humans or observed in real time) to the eyeless sight and industrialized supervision of more discreet tracking devices. This evolution, in which 9/11 marks a nodal point, collocates with an ethical challenge that shifts the focus from the individual target of surveillance to screened populations or demographics. Not only is the private self besieged by invasive technologies, but a global self—designed according to the very architectures of communication that enabled mass surveillance—also threatens to lose its sense of cohesion and moral guidance. And thus these narratives' point about the ethics of surveillance is not the obvious one (that technologies increasingly fence in individuals and limit their agency, curtailing their fundamental right to freedom), but one more easily missed: that the technologies on which surveillance is based have entered plot, fictional subjectivity, and language in ways that provocatively turn the formal dynamic of global surveillance into a site for reflection.

My argument has been that the governing mode of interaction between the state and its citizens (as well as among citizens themselves) in these novels is a rigidly defined supervision and specularity that infiltrates the narrative itself. Barker anticipates the collusion of thematic and structural surveillance by scrutinizing, in an artwork series, the transition from surveillance as a strategy of self-control (with a psychoanalytic and vaguely religious subtext, embodied in the Christ figure) toward the diffuse paranoia propagated by the watchful cluster of hijackers. Kirn, Raban, and Gibson enfold the surveillance paradigm within the rhizomatic strategies of their novels, pieced together according to a dynamic of suspicion. Particularly in *The Unbinding*, a string of vignettes that blend seamlessly into one another, knowledge disappears into information, each bite equivalent and tied to all the others in an endless seriality through which the reader is left to sift. Flanagan and Adams underline, through the inconclusiveness of their narratives, the danger of demonizing suspicious citizens as likely terrorists, given that such assumptions hold great potential for mistakes and miscarriages of justice.[26] The task of not only the literary critic but of all readers, even those less traditionally conceived ("footageheads" and bureaucrats in charge of wading through surveillance data), is to draw connections, supply meanings, and extract significant intelligence from the morass of detail. Thus in the all-encompassing metaphor of "pattern recognition," the process of literary production and consumption converge.

We shouldn't forget that the worlds these novels inhabit are also partly hypothetical, demanding an ethical inspection of the boundary that separates the real from the virtual—a boundary that they partly occlude and one that post-9/11 surveillance policies have effectively abandoned in favor of trenchant moral dichotomies. What these fictions propose (and simultaneously enact) is an ethics of incompleteness able to interrupt and operate in excess of traditional moral distinctions that divide truth from illusion, reality from appearance, and good from evil. To that extent they usurp the central function of surveillance, which is to prove that the random and inchoate secretly cohere into a larger, intelligible design. In these novels the science of intelligence is inexact and its excavation largely unsuccessful, revealing an underlying concern about the broader moral narrative of the War on Terror as a misguided ethical principle laced with fabrication and innuendo. Overall these fictions' engagement with intelligence not only casts doubt on the starkly moralistic information-gathering enterprise that underlies the War on Terror but ardently espouses an open-circuit transnational ethics (as opposed to closed-circuit television) to counter the fantasy of completeness currently governing counterterrorist practices.

CONCLUSION

Postincendiary Circumstances

In November 2009 the whistleblower website Wikileaks released over half a million pager messages intercepted in the order officials and witnesses sent them on September 11, 2001. Media outlets seized the opportunity to discuss the ethical implications of these revelations on a global scale. Although comprehensive testimonial archives already exist, these messages resonate with greater force for being released by a truth-telling organization in a context of greater political and moral ambiguity than the solemn piousness that dominated the tenth anniversary of the attacks two years later. Within a few days the messages entered public discourse with the insistence of traumatic flashbacks, barely submerged beneath current political agendas aptly summarized by Wikileaks' concomitant revelations (especially of classified diplomatic documents exposing abuses and disinformation in the Afghanistan war). The 9/11 pager notes offer a brief, if harrowing, respite from these controversies. They range from factual reports—that Cantor Fitzgerald, for instance, suddenly went "offline" (they were, of course, hit by the first plane and lost over six hundred employees)—to the abstract and impassioned question "Why?" This question indeed belongs in the public realm not for any final answers we might provide, but for its ability to provoke more localized, manageable questions. Why, in particular, is it so difficult in the War on Terror to employ "the means, however imperfectly, that are the moral equivalent of the end we seek" (Booth and Dunne, "Worlds in Collision" 21)? Or, as Lynne Sharon Schwartz puts it in an exasperated comment on the moral logic of the Bush administration, "Who ever thought of separating means and ends? Every means becomes an end. There is no end to means" (146). In

CONCLUSION

tones that range as much as the pager messages do from the factual to the visceral, post-9/11 writing has vibrated with the same incomprehension and has strived to establish a sense of accountability, for political players and literature alike, in the aftermath of terror. To help articulate the aims of this writing, I want to recall here the voyage I promised in the opening pages, and recast it in terms that will allow me to establish why an ethical reading of post-9/11 fiction has a clear bearing on influential debates in literary and ethical studies reaching far beyond the specific questions asked of these texts. And since I am framing these remarks in a journalistic perspective, let me begin by establishing my coordinates in more generally narrative terms, before turning to recent literature that confirms several patterns I have outlined in this book.

Amitav Ghosh's essay collection *Incendiary Circumstances: A Chronicle of the Turmoil of Our Times* includes a piece written in 2001 and entitled "September 11," a concise autobiographical parable centered on the experiences of a couple whom Ghosh had befriended prior to the attacks. Frank and Nicole de Martini are two architects working for the engineering firm that built the World Trade Center (one as a construction manager, the other as a surveillance engineer) and occupying offices in the towers. Especially to Frank, the WTC epitomizes a pinnacle of worldly achievement, an assessment that he sees confirmed by the buildings' resistance to the 1993 bombing. "They represented an incredible human feat," Ghosh writes, channeling Nicole. "He was awed by their scale and magnitude, by their design, and by the efficiency of the use of materials. One of his most repeated sayings about the towers is that they were built to take the impact of a light airplane" (33). The attacks find the couple at their desks. Frank makes sure that Nicole exits the building, yet he stays behind to help evacuate other workers and never comes out. The remainder of the text lucidly describes the aftermath of this loss for the two families, lingering for a very brief moment on Nicole's suffering, which appears strangely subdued. In the story's last paragraph, Nicole is cited as noting, in a tone that betrays her admiration for her husband's martyrdom, that Frank "loved the towers and had complete faith in them" (35). Ghosh clearly intended this piece as homage to a friend who lost his life under horrific circumstances that he defied with bracing heroism. In an austere, hagiographic format, his essay glorifies the selflessness of an American hero and the unequivocal moral virtues of self-sacrifice.

Now compare Ghosh's piece with the *post*incendiary three-page account of a night spent at Ground Zero by the *New York Times* war correspondent Dexter Filkins in his book *The Forever War*, a sprawling documentary of the chaos in Afghanistan and Iraq since the beginning of the post-9/11 campaign against terror, real and imagined. Having witnessed similar and even worse catastrophes in other politically volatile regions, Filkins suggests that the disaster in New York by no means exceeds the destruction taking place every day in chronically war-torn countries. This view places Filkins in the company of Susan Sontag, who similarly cringed at the melodramatic and apocalyptic pronouncements by American mass media whipping up excessive patriotism and marshalling support for the War on Terror, rather than soberly assessing the reasons why the attacks may have been, at least symbolically, a self-inflicted wound (Sontag, Untitled). Filkins's memory of the hours he spent at Ground Zero serves to "ground" his narrative of the war he observed closely, not unlike Stephen Sharkey's obsessive recollection of the rape victim in Sarajevo punctuating his semipeaceful holiday from reality against the cozy backdrop of the English countryside in Pat Barker's *Double Vision*. *The Forever War*, however, reverses the coordinates: the remembered crime did not occur in a country like Bosnia, routinely plagued by ethnic conflict and street skirmishes, but in the heart of the United States, a place that up until September 11 had appeared heavily armored against assaults from the outside. Filkins's mind is flooded by analogies between the harrowing remains at Ground Zero and other horrors he has seen. "As I moved in closer," he begins,

> my eyes went to a gray-green thing spread across the puddles and rocks. Elongated, unrolled, sitting there, unnoticed. An intestine. It kind of jumped out at me, presented itself. It's amazing how the eyes do that, go right to the human flesh, spot it amid the heaviest camouflage of rubble and dirt and glass, as if it were glowing green in an infrared scope. I saw the same phenomenon later on, at a suicide bombing in Tel Aviv, the Orthodox volunteers with their spatulas

and bags, frantically running and scooping every bit of flesh, no matter how tiny, to save the various souls. Down here, in what had been an intersection south of the Twin Towers, I stood and looked at the gray-green mass, thought about whose it was, how it got there; whether, for instance, it had come from one of the airplane passengers, or from one of the people inside one of the buildings. Or even, against the odds, from one of the hijackers. (45)

Through the reference to the mechanized and disembodied vision of infrared cameras deployed in combat zones, the contrast between what Paul Virilio deplored as the mechanization of surveillance on the one hand and the unmediated encounter with human flesh on the other hand could not have been any starker or more disquieting. On video screens infrared images conceal the disturbing remains of human lives lost in phantom battles in which barely visible opponents wordlessly take each other out. The effect of this occlusion is a moral leveling that blurs the distinction between friend and foe. In similar ways the level of destruction in Lower Manhattan seems to preclude moralistic assumptions about the identity and allegiance of its victims. To Filkins, it matters little whose life was shattered. What counts is one's responsibility to "put cruelty first"— that is, bear witness to this loss and retell his experience, whose grittiness sets it miles apart from Ghosh's much more cosmetic and reader-friendly narrative in the tradition of the *New York Times* "Portraits of Grief." Over the seven-year interval between the publication of Ghosh's essay and Filkins's book, literature has assisted in bringing home to us the significance of the 9/11 moment and of the global responsibilities it incurs. To concisely restate my argument and its implications, I want to focus briefly on three short stories that I haven't as yet included in my analysis and that coherently summarize the ethical injunctions discussed in this book in ways that are symptomatic of the broader literary field I am delineating.

Chris Adrian's "The Vision of Peter Damien" is the first in a series of post-9/11 stories first published in 2007 and included in Adrian's collection, *A Better Angel*. "The Vision" is about how "we," both as individuals and as a nation, take 9/11 personally, albeit in a much more literal sense than any other narrative I have addressed here. Adrian himself stated in an interview that neither he nor the American people, particularly in New York, could avoid this personal involvement, because everyone's "imagination had been hijacked" (Nellins n.p.). "The Vision" provides a literal transcription of this trope: a group of children display mysterious symptoms that suggest they are possessed by the iconic specters of 9/11—the towers, the planes, and the jumpers. What haunts Peter Damien at first is the "empty blue sky" of September 11, with "a woman falling through it" (88). In ways that distinctly recall Helen Schulman's orchestrated duet between a young Tribeca mother and a WTC jumper, the falling woman tangles Peter up in her descent until they spin together down the side of the burning towers. "Arrested in her fall" (90), the woman re-creates the disheveled posture of Richard Drew's photograph, yet Adrian's vision pushes far beyond Drew's tasteful suspension of the fall in a perpetual present.

Adrian autopsies, as Filkins does, the aftereffects of that aestheticized moment, splattering the page with its bloody aftermath: "He heard a hard thump to his left. There was a lady there broken on the ground. Another fell on his right, a man this time—Peter collapsed, sure that he was felled by the rushing flight of something escaping from the man's body. He had never seen such a thing as a body twisted and ruptured like this, and he wondered if anyone ever had seen such a thing" (94). Most post-9/11 fiction takes a circuitous, oblique path toward representing bodily pain (Tristram is an obvious exception), partly because such physical amputations threaten to compromise the narrative's arterial flow. Suturing and partly reanimating Adrian's story is a form of ventriloquism not unlike Spiegelman's appropriation of the jumper's body. Before he can understand "the mystery beneath the affliction, and the reason that we are all suffering" (107), Peter himself becomes a flaming tower with people "leaping from out of his hair, dropping from his nose, squeezing like tears from the corners of his eyes" (106). Peter's depersonification is his apotheosis. For him, as for Michael Cunningham's Whitman-obsessed youths, dying is luckier—it is resurrection "dressed in a raiment of fire and destruction and grief" (109).

Although on the surface they perish so spectacularly, the victims of the terrorist attacks, all 2,998 of them, live on as undead specters in the mind of a little boy, Carl, on whom Adrian's pathological study "The Changeling" focuses with disturbing equanimity. (The story begins with waffles and ends with an ax.) To Carl, the toasted waffles "rise slow and stately," as if out of a grave (134), but even this veiled morbidity foreshadows little of what is to come. Carl is possessed by the souls of 9/11 victims demanding "blood sacrifice" (136). Taken at face value, this vision of bloodthirsty spirits acts out a scathing indictment of the equally vengeful War on Terror, yet Carl insists that only "sincerity and sacrifice" (144) will assuage the still-smoldering core of pain and penitence. Over and over the spirits speak through Carl of an "arithmetic of obligation" (147), defined in terms of self-flagellating remorse. And the only sacrifice capable of binding broken promises whole again is blood. "Have you made the change I asked you for?" Carl presses his father in much the same way that Schulman and Barker push their narratives toward rehabilitation and change. "You were supposed to become your better self" (153), the child insists, until his father saws off his own hand to appease him. The stump marks both an amputation and a growth—toward a fuller selfhood and, above all, toward the promise to the wandering spirits that we should "never step out of the shadow of the day they died, if that's what it means now to be good" (154).

In "Why Antichrist?" this idea of goodness after 9/11 is broached with derisiveness that turns insidiously into a deeply rewarding surprise. Yet another possession is at work here. The unnamed first-person narrator shares a bond with Cindy, whose father died in the WTC. Both adolescents go to parties and engage in petting, drinking, and games with an Ouija board, which claims that the narrator is the son of the Devil. This is particularly fascinating to Cindy, for whom nothing after 9/11 "was ever going to be the same" (213), and she is keen to ensnare her boyfriend into her apocalyptic vision. After projecting 9/11 footage on each other's naked bodies in a corporeal inscription of the ethical gaze and its libidinal subtext—"When you do it this way," Cindy proffers, "then you can almost feel what they were feeling" (226)—the boy cryptically accepts his

Luciferian identity, "grateful and happy" (227) for the catastrophe and ruin he has wrought. Both he and Carl's self-mutilating father react to the evil of terrorism by mimicking its practices and turning them, physically, against themselves.

I began this book by talking about self-binding and the withdrawal of judgment as primary ethical modes of constructing Otherness. The production of Otherness, Dorothy Hale observes, is what hurts—here very literally through the amputation of limbs or collapse by proxy, as memories of the crumbling towers inflict corporeal damage. Through narratives of barefaced cruelty, McGrath, Tristram, Halaby, Adams, and Flanagan are also adept at sowing guilt and discomfort, but Adrian sets particularly high ethical stakes. If we are to trust the plot of "Why Antichrist?," Cindy's posttraumatic condition seems to sharpen her self-destructive instincts, which conforms, of course, to the classic pathology of trauma, yet in hurting herself Cindy simultaneously wishes everything else to disappear. "I want you to put your fist through the whole world like you did to those two towers" (218), she begs the "Antichrist" with whom she is about to have sex. We feel that something is "wrong" (227)—morally and psychologically—not only with the children, but also with these preposterous narratives themselves. As is not often the case in post-9/11 fiction, Adrian himself, as a writer, assumes a risk that is aesthetically self-flagellating. Parallel to the self-mutilation carried out by Carl's father to exorcise his son's demons, Adrian "chops off" his stories, drawing the reader into their inexplicable and cathartic violence, asking us not only to remember those who perished on September 11, but also to honor their memory through sacrifice—be it only by exposing ourselves to the perversity of these stories. We close Adrian's book with a lingering question: What have *we* done for the dead today? And how does literature help us position ourselves to better intercept their voices?

An essential attribute of post-9/11 fiction resides in its concrete suggestions about how the experience of terror can be sublimated into an empathetic code of conduct. What we often encounter in these novels are people who went on to implement changes in their lives, ranging from enhanced attention to the small-scale visibility of everyday life (DeLillo), through an updated ecology of personal relationships and family responsibilities (Schulman), to a desire to atone for past moral failures and allow the potential of inchoate emotional ties to materialize (Barker). Yet some of the energy generated by the attacks produces abhorrent and often perplexing responses. In McGrath's "Ground Zero," the New York analyst treating a patient traumatized by the attacks and wooing a Chinese prostitute cannot detach her resentment of the Other (as potential terrorist) from her jealousy of this woman, who lures her client away from a relationship that appears to have emotionally sustained the analyst for years. Tristram's unnamed protagonist in *After* lashes out against an innocent Persian to avenge her husband's death at the hands of Islamic fundamentalists. In Australia Flanagan focuses on a TV investigator who rides the wave of global antiterror media with utter disregard for the catastrophic human toll of his inaccurate reports.

Despite some patently condemnable behavior, the cumulative effect of reading these fictions is not merely (and never directly) the promulgation of specific moral principles or the prescriptive delineation of how to interpret or respond to Otherness, be it in the form of a person or a discursive mode. Rather the novels I have discussed seek to train what may be called the reader's moral intuition. The process of empathetic connection they effect does not single out the producer or the recipient of compassion, but aims to prepare and decongest the channels of compassion itself. Finally, at the end of these stories' traffic of responsibilities is the implied reader. In reading these fictions, we witness textual authority changing hands and, ultimately, falling into our own. I am, of course, aware of the dangers of collapsing the difference between textual worlds and everyday experience; the limits bounding narrative ethics in fiction cannot be facilely breached in order to derive lessons for everyday life. However, this literature does foster awareness of the vicissitudes and trappings of ethical response, as well as embarrassment and shame about the immorality or injustice of one's own actions and of larger political idioms that have followed ethically illiterate precepts by triggering the cycle of violence following upon the attacks.

Circling back to the critical evaluation of new ethical theory offered in the introduction, and bearing in mind what can be derived from the intervening chapters, I want to suggest that far from enacting a turn away from politics, ethical engagement with and within literature can redirect the political away from the moralism of counterterrorist policies, expose its textured "fictional" narratives, and assert the legitimacy of moral ambivalence, deliberation, and ambiguity in a culture whose postnational contours are rigidly molded around moral crusades and what George W. Bush would call decision points. Prior to the 9/11 attacks John Guillory proposed that "the turn to ethics is a turn away from the political" and thus "risks abandoning politics itself to the forces of reaction" (29). Guillory's assessment of the unfortunate pairing of politics and morality seems uncannily prescient. Confirming my earlier contention that punctual events can indeed reverberate through the deeper layers of political life and public discourse, he singles out the Clinton impeachment scandal as a turning point in the marriage of politics and morality in the United States. "The reduction of politics to morality, to the spectacle of a morality play," he writes, "is just what has occurred in the political public sphere, culminating in the impeachment proceedings of 1999. Discourse in the public sphere often seems driven by the political right, which sees all political questions in terms of an absolutist morality. In the light of this development, any 'turn to ethics' must be regarded, at least initially, with suspicion" (29–30).

Guillory seems to conflate ethics with the public apportioning of moral guilt rather than regarding morality as a case-oriented manifestation of ethics, one that is easily mobilized in the service of ideology and needs to be permanently questioned through ethical critique. The more evident and trenchant part of his argument pertains to the role of reading as a bridge between the academic discipline of literary studies and the realities of political life. Guillory does not regard such mediation as entirely feasible, dismissing it as a "political fantasy" (31). This, I believe, is exactly where the benefits of studying contemporary narrative through an ethical lens becomes glaringly manifest. What post-9/11 fiction wrestles to do is replace the spectacle of politics as morality play with a shrewdly politicized narrative order free of constitutive presuppositions. In Fredric Jameson's terms, the goal of these texts is "escaping from the purely individualizing categories of ethics, of transcending the categories into which our existence as individual subjects necessarily locks us and opening up the radically distinct transindividual perspectives of collective life or historical process" (*The Political Unconscious* 103). Transplanted in a concrete historical context, whose particulars (towers, planes, jumpers, torture cells, and ubiquitous cameras) are ritualistically inventoried in post-9/11 fiction, the "conceptual *antinomy*" of fossilized ethical codes is newly grasped as a "*contradiction*" (104).

To be more specific: in attending to the moral discourses that proliferated after the September 11 attacks, fiction has sought to strike a balance between an ethics of witnessing and mourning on the one hand, and the need to challenge the abuse of moralism in the implementation of expedient political agendas on the other hand. Each of the texts to which I have attended suggests how individuals can intervene in the ethical flows of a culture—which often dictate affective responses—as well as in the political plots that such flows energize. DeLillo shows that the problems and conflicts between "us" and "them"—inasmuch as such oppositions are tenable—begin in our dissimilar understandings of images and the patterns that shape our reactions to them. *In the Shadow of No Towers* proposes that we should respond to the media intoxication following upon the attacks by identifying with the victims of discrimination and political violence in ways that engage our personal history. Without hinting at the wars that the attacks precipitated, Schulman's *A Day at the Beach* argues in favor of a meticulous, consummate kind of "resistant" mourning (that works through trauma but does not entirely forget its root causes) pitted against the premature and ill-considered solutions that parlayed national victimization into an ill-thought pretext for a Middle East crusade. McGrath's novella "Ground Zero" takes this one step further in exposing how easy it was to accept (in subtle and self-denying ways) the crackdown on terror suspects and enemy combatants in the weeks and months following the attacks. As a scapegoat who is burdened with moral responsibility for the events, the Chinese woman whom McGrath's analyst viciously maligns acts as a stand-in and lightning rod for the resentment churning underneath post-9/11 political moralism and for readers' conflicting expectations as to how fiction should encode and allay their fears, exculpating them from the need for further introspection. Hemon seconds this critique by unmasking the provisionality of moral pronouncements in the longer history of American racial relations and more recently in the Bosnian War. For Barker, the post-9/11 world is permanently marked by the sudden irruption of random violence, which forces its victims down two distinct paths: one of immediate response (as a result of a cataleptic epiphany inducing temporary sympathy with the Other) and one of patient assimilation of events, less like the painful severance of illusions and more in the manner of a slow growth toward compassion and the acknowledgment of one's own vulnerability. By incorporating surveillance practices, post-9/11 fiction also approaches media as, according to W. J. T. Mitchell, "something that can be addressed, that can be hailed, greeted, and challenged" (*What Do Pictures Want?* 208). Mitchell does not invoke the ethical implications of this practice, although they are impossible to ignore. By cladding in vulnerable human forms the political and media discourses that mark the post-9/11 era, such fiction underscores the spectacular ductility of ethics as a transnational narrative with the potential to explode the literary conventions that shore up national interests as well as the entrenched moralism of contemporary politics, which could profit from the historicizing perspective and ethical self-doubt that permeate post-9/11 literary culture.

To weave together the various threads of this book, let me reiterate what must have seemed obvious to everyone: that September 11 marked a change. The way I see this change does not, however, presuppose a dichotomy between before and after, but the conscious effort to understand exactly when and how causes became effects, when history and geography converged to deal the blow that amazes us to this day. September 11 marked, above all, a moment of introspection, a moment that inspired the tremendously salutary condition called disorientation. This is the bafflement that Butler and Spivak associate with ethics—and with the novel in particular—as a medium that carries an endless potential to befuddle and exasperate. The outcomes of this awakening in fiction range from torture to healing and resignation. For Suzannah Falktopf, after September 11 things fall into place; for Gina Davies they fall apart. Lorraine Adams begins a career, while Don DeLillo softly announces his retirement. Jonathan Franzen writes a post-9/11 novel almost sarcastically entitled *Freedom*, wherein disoriented, footloose Americans are "straining futilely to extract dark sustenance from an atmosphere of approval and plenitude" (193), an atmosphere of patriotic revivalism emanating like a poisonous cloud from "the World Trade Center's floodlit cicatrix" (198). Against the "self-dramatizing and self-pitying and self-deceiving and other noxious self-things" (507–08) that Franzen diagnoses in his protagonists and in the moral disorder of their lives, the fictions I addressed in this book collectively formulate a self-binding imperative, not as an idea external to literature, but as the very premise and promise of its infinitely desirable, if unrealizable, fulfillment.

And although such pronouncements generally seem glib and hasty, a generation of writers appears to have been replaced by another, for which ethics is not an approach to literature, but rather its condition of being—a sense of hesitant accountability that enables and inflects narrative itself. I discovered along the way that these novels had things to say that were more provocatively ambiguous and meaningful than what I may have tried to impose on them by applying clear-cut moralistic readings. The value of post-9/11 literature thus lies less in its precise historical realism than in the unsure suggestiveness of its language, less in its statements than in its understatements, in its confused narrative silences and their interactions with the gaps and inconsistencies of a larger post-9/11 justice plot relentlessly seeking judgment and resolution in Wars on Terror and ever wider and more disruptive global interventions, from Iraq and Afghanistan to Libya and Pakistan. The imperative motivating this book has been not so much to clarify or answer the questions raised by these texts, as to understand the workings of textual ambiguity and its ethical function while estimating the ways the censorious discourse of this literature regarding the current state of the ethical subject in the War on Terror might be "transferred" into the political and social realms to displace some of their most egregious moral certainties.

NOTES

Introduction

1. This is one of the greatest honors conferred on a 9/11 novel to date. Also in 2009 Joseph O'Neill's novel *Netherland* was awarded the PEN/Faulkner Award for Fiction.

2. An interesting, transnational special issue on literature after 9/11 appeared in the *Journal of Postcolonial Writing* in 2010. *Modern Fiction Studies* published a special issue ten years after the attacks.

3. My approach does not modify the conventional difference between the narrow understanding of values and social norms (morality) and the philosophy that negotiates these values (ethics). For a clear application of this distinction to fiction, see Wayne Booth: "The word 'ethical' may mistakenly suggest a project concentrating on quite limited moral standards: of honesty, perhaps, or of decency or tolerance. I am interested in a much broader topic, the entire range of effects on the 'character' or 'person' or 'self.' Moral judgments are only a small part of it. . . . For us here the word must cover all qualities in the character, or ethos, of authors and readers, whether these are judged as good or bad" (*The Company We Keep* 8).

4. On the political relevance and strategic power of translation as a humanistic and diplomatic tool, see Emily Apter's *The Translation Zone: A New Comparative Literature*, which argues in a post-9/11 context that "war is the continuation of extreme mistranslation or disagreement by other means . . . a condition of nontranslatability or translation failure at its most violent peak" (16). On mistranslation and intelligence in post-9/11 fiction, see chapter 5.

5. The texts I have chosen to discuss in this book have less to say about Iraq than might be expected, not because 9/11 literature has avoided the issue altogether (it hasn't), but simply because fictional treatments of the Iraq War remain marginal to broader discussions of the post-9/11 condition. This may partly stem from the impulse to regard Iraq ethically as unrelated to the terrorist attacks. Where 9/11 and Iraq are intertwined, the narrative tilts toward an interpretation

of the war as a superfluous sequel to Vietnam or more vaguely as a traumatic case of misrecognition. See McEwan, *Saturday*; O'Hagan, *Be Near Me*.

6. Jonathan Crary, among others, has argued compellingly that the technological mechanisms and optical devices of a historical period as "sites of both knowledge and power" (7) influence the visual regime of contemporaneous arts.

7. See Banita, "Raymond Williams and Online Video."

8. For an illustration of how superficially visual studies have incorporated ethical discourse, see Mitchell's cursory remark on Levinas in his essay "Showing Seeing": "Visual culture would find its primal scene, then, in what Emmanuel Levinas calls the face of the Other (beginning, I suppose, with the face of the Mother): the face-to-face encounter, the evidently hard-wired disposition to recognize the eyes of another organism (what Lacan and Sartre call the gaze)" (175).

9. Applying another of Levinas's oppositions, vision corresponds to what he terms "the Saying," defined as "the performative stating, proposing, or expressive position of myself facing the Other. It is a verbal or non-verbal ethical performance, whose essence cannot be caught in constative propositions." By contrast, "the Said" (which I equate here to the image) "is a statement, assertion, or proposition" whose "truth or falsity can be ascertained" (Critchley, *The Ethics of Deconstruction* 7).

10. See Attridge 21. His definition of the Other is worth citing here: "Whatever its precise complexion, the other in these accounts is primarily an impingement from outside that challenges assumptions, habits, and values and that demands a response" (23).

11. For a definition of this concept, see Derrida.

12. Amy Kaplan defines historical exceptionalism as "the often heard claim that the world was radically altered by 9/11, that the world will never be the same, that Americans have lost their former innocence about their safety and invulnerability at home" (83).

13. Rancière defines politics as a system that dynamically includes the elements it has excluded: "Politics exists when the natural order of domination is interrupted by the institution of a part of those who have no part" (11).

14. As recently as 2011 Elizabeth Anker writes that "for the most part nonwhite characters are virtually absent from the 9/11 novel, an obstruction that mirrors American myopia as well as signals a damaging denial of that event's global repercussions" (468). A critical myopia might also be at work here, since so many post-9/11 fictions engage nonwhite characters in a vibrantly transnational context.

15. For an explicit example of this focalization, see Martin Amis's short story "The Last Days of Muhammad Atta," which follows the iconic 9/11 hijacker from a hotel in Portland, Maine, through his flight to Boston's Logan Airport, and finally onto the doomed American Airlines flight 11 that crashed into the North Tower (in *The Second Plane*).

16. The word *cataleptic* originates in the Greek *kataleptikē*, an adjective derived from the verb *katalambanein*, meaning "to apprehend," "grasp," or "grasp firmly."

1. Falling Man Fiction

1. Evidence of these deaths was uniformly repressed until they entered the realm of the Internet. Readers of newspapers that did run such images reprehended their intolerable realism. See Frost, "Still Life"; Brottman; Junod, "The Falling Man."

2. As a synecdochic stand-in for a larger massacre, the image draws on a robust tradition of iconic photographs in which death was actual or presumed, such as the picture of the naked girl running down the road after a napalm attack in the Vietnam War, or the little boy with his hands up in the Warsaw ghetto. Zelizer refers to this visual pedigree of a memorable image as its "voice": "Seen here as the dimensions of an image that propel it to link with other events at other times and places, voice helps explain how the image takes on an already provided meaning upon its initial appearance" ("The Voice of the Visual" 162). See also Zelizer's study *About to Die: How News Images Move the Public*. For a lengthy analysis of how visual representations of 9/11 bore the imprint of previous iconic pictures of America at war, see Engle.

3. The only exception of which I am aware is the photograph of a severed hand that appeared in the *New York Daily News* (September 13, 2001, evening edition).

4. From among a plethora of texts relating in some way to Drew's memorable image, I have selected these three for their ability to assimilate the visuality of the picture in ethically relevant ways and to intervene in the cultural reception of the image. In 2009 the mythology of the falling man received an oblique, historically sophisticated treatment in Colum McCann's *Let the Great World Spin*, where Philippe Petit's audacious skywalk between the Twin Towers in 1974 operates as the still point around which a cluster of moral failures of the late Nixonian era come into focus. The novels by DeLillo, Spiegelman, and Schulman interest me here as the first to explore the cultural embeddedness of the falling man image and the ethical narratives it has spawned.

5. Several reviewers have remarked on the characters' failure to provoke the reader's sympathy. See, for instance, Heller McAlpin: "More than towers fall in DeLillo's novel. But the social harnesses that keep his characters from hitting the pavement—marriage, family, church, poker—don't arrest their descents altogether. One wishes DeLillo had written a book that made us want to reach out and catch them ourselves" (15).

6. As Lauren Berlant has argued, this focus on emotional intimacy has usurped the public sphere as a space for social antagonism, reframing nationality as a question of feelings and traumas (3–10). For a compelling analysis of highly affective patterns of melodrama in shaping politically correct responses to the attacks and drumming up support for retaliatory action, see Elisabeth Anker.

7. The performances take place where crowds are likely to form and disappear again rapidly, so as to ensure maximum impact of exposure. As DeLillo remarks in a brief essay on the collective properties of image making and image reception, "Images have something to do with crowds. An image is a crowd in a way, a smear of impressions. Images tend to draw people together, create mass identity" ("The Image and the Crowd" 72–73). See also DeLillo, *Conversations with Don DeLillo* (interview with Maria Nadotti): "The photographic image is a kind of crowd in itself, a jumble of impressions very different in kind from a book in which the printed lines follow one another in a linear order. There's something in the image that seems to collide with the very idea of individual identity" (110).

8. In his discussion of collective practices in dealing with trauma, Edward S. Casey notes the salutary effects of paying homage to the dead in the context of a community experience rather than individually. His example is a vigil in Union Square Park on September 17, 2001: "There was a distinct sense of relief to find oneself in the presence of others—albeit strangers—with whom to share grief. But more than relief was at stake in this extraordinary circumstance: something constructive was in the air. What was this?" (28). Although Casey does not spell it out, the constructive mood emerges precisely from the lack of familiarity among the spectators and their collective effort to overcome their individual anxieties.

9. The performance act might even be said to replicate, ironically, the terrorist attacks themselves, which may be seen to contain an element of performance art pushed to the limits of authenticity. Lentricchia and McAuliffe make a very similar point, namely that "the suicide terrorists who struck New York may be said to have made—with the cooperation of American television—performance art with political designs on its American audience" (13).

10. Marianne Hirsch writes, "I use the term postmemory to describe the relationship of children of survivors of cultural or collective trauma to the experiences of their parents, experiences that they 'remember' only as the stories and images with which they grew up, but that are so powerful, so monumental, as to constitute memories in their own right" ("Projected Memory" 8). Early critics of the book have noted the perils of a comparison between 9/11 and the Holocaust, yet they also absolved Spiegelman of any unseemly or unethical transgressions. See, for instance, Hajdu: "Spiegelman clearly sees Sept. 11 as his Holocaust (or the nearest thing his generation will have to personal experience with anything remotely correlative), and in *In the Shadow of No Towers* [he] makes explicit parallels between the events without diminishing the incomparable evil of the death camps" (13).

11. In the following I refer to the narrator in *Maus* as Artie when he is engaged in dialogue with his father and as Art when he reflects on the transmission of Vladek's story and the problems of vicarious experience. See also Bosmajian: "Artie is . . . a lesser Art Spiegelman, an orphaned voice and self that seems more lost than his author" (27). For *In the Shadow of No Towers* I accept the critical consensus that the book projects Spiegelman's own voice. The narrator in this case is simply Spiegelman.

12. For an alternative reading of suicide as a literary trope in 9/11 literature, see Elizabeth Anker's "Allegories of Falling and the 9/11 Novel," which correlates suicide with the allied plot of male midlife crisis and the weight of imperial impotence.

13. As Katalin Orbán aptly remarks, "The destruction of Anja's papers responds to the violent disorder of her self-destruction and to the memories of what destroyed both Anja and her diaries in the first place" (*Ethical Diversions* 72).

14. See also Hungerford: "Art calls his father a 'murderer' for burning the diaries of his dead wife, as if the destruction of Anja's record of her experiences at Auschwitz were somehow equivalent to the kinds of destruction that took place at Auschwitz" (*The Holocaust of Texts* 73).

15. As Marianne Hirsch notes, "Not seeing becomes visible and even audible, as graphic as the absent towers. Words, images, and word-images work together to enact the impossibility of seeing and the impossibility of not looking" ("Editor's Column" 1213).

16. See Young; McGlothlin. Spiegelman himself lays out the blueprint for this narrative mapping in his interview with Lawrence Weschler. What concerns him

in *Maus* is "not so much whether my father was telling the truth, but rather, just what had he actually lived through—what did he understand of what he experienced, what did he tell of what he understood, what did I understand of what he told, and what do I tell?" (Weschler 56).

17. See also Chute: "In *Maus*, Spiegelman drew the character Artie's smoke as the smoke of human flesh drifting upwards from Auschwitz, a move that implied Artie's guilt at commercializing the Holocaust and also the impossibility of escape from the traumas of the past" ("Temporality and Seriality" 233). "The figure of the smoke screen," Michael Levine writes, is "key to the principle of displacement operative in the text" (326).

18. As Andreas Huyssen describes the martyred victims disguised as mice, "We see persecuted little animals drawn with a human body and wearing human clothes and with a highly abstracted, non-expressive mouse physiognomy. 'Maus' here means vulnerability, unalloyed suffering, victimization" ("Of Mice and Mimesis" 75).

19. About unrepresentable and indescribable smells both in *Maus* and *In the Shadow of No Towers*, Katalin Orbán writes, "This connection between the two events and stories marks both crises as cases of traumatic memory in a multigenerational chain of remembering, transmission, and reenactment anchored in the body." The link thus epitomizes Spiegelman's "effort to reorient the reader from the 'awesome' sublime to a more contingent history that does not transcend material bodies and traces" ("Trauma and Visuality" 58).

20. See Barbara Kirshenblatt-Gimblett: "For some, it was the smell of smoke that broke the cinematic spell" (18).

21. See also Richard Klein, who provides a sophisticated reading of smoking in the tradition of the Kantian sublime.

22. See Dawn Marlan for an interpretation of smoking as "a pleasure that involves an experience of emptiness" (256).

23. Cathy Caruth defines posttraumatic stress disorder as "a response . . . to an overwhelming event or events, which takes the form of repeated, intrusive hallucinations, dreams, thoughts or behaviors stemming from the event" (*Trauma* 4).

24. Klein's description of smoking, in which "every single cigarette numerically implies all the other cigarettes, exactly alike, that the smoker consumes in a series; each cigarette immediately calls forth its inevitable successor" (26), best epitomizes the anaphoric, almost mathematical structure of this habit.

25. In *Windows on the World*, Frédéric Beigbeder includes smoking in his fictional, tongue-in-cheek U.S. Immigration Service questionnaire, next to other

socially reviled or even criminal activities, such as pedophilia and the tendency to "regularly masturbate in front of photographs of dismembered corpses" (163).

26. To resort to a useful distinction by the painter Jasper Johns—to whom the novel refers repeatedly—in directing her gaze toward the TV set, Suzannah's posture corresponds to the position of the "watchman" who falls into the trap of looking, while in gazing out the window she is a "spy," her senses alert and set to memorize and remember perceptions. See Perloff 218.

27. See Raymond Williams, "From Medium to Social Practice" 158–64; Mitchell, *What Do Pictures Want?* 203–04.

28. On the critical role of creating narratives about what has happened in order to absorb and work through trauma, see Caruth, *Unclaimed Experience*; Brison; Wigren; as well as LaCapra's "Consciousness and Working-Through" in *Representing the Holocaust*.

29. Opulent objecthood and surface complexity are the main features of Johns's works that the novel invokes. For Johns, "composition must be decentered, non-hierarchical, each part of the canvas as important as every other part" (Perloff 199). Just as the endless loop of the WTC collapse engenders a sense of visual saturation and/or displacement, so too does Johns strip ordinary domestic objects of their common associations and recontextualizes them in new juxtapositions that challenge viewers' notions of how a visual field should be organized.

30. See Abraham and Torok 125–38.

31. http://www.guardian.co.uk/politics/2001/oct/02/labourconference.labour7.

2. Sex and Sense

1. For a discussion of the intertextual linkages among the three stories, see Duggan, who makes the compelling suggestion that such intertextual networks echo "the repetitive structure and temporal leaps characteristic of trauma itself" (390).

2. On the differences between the terms *client* and *patient*, see Kahn. In my analysis I use these terms interchangeably. Kahn distinguishes between the two, associating with *patient* a sense of pathology that he seeks to avoid (6). In the context of my discussion, I consider it important to retain both the idea of pathology (since the text deals with the issue of PTSD and the acknowledgment of this condition as pathological constituted a major breakthrough in psychiatry) and that of a social contract between the two parties involved in the analytic alliance. Moreover, as I will show, the text features both an analyst (who deals with

a patient) and a prostitute (who serves a client), but analogies are posited between the two that justify my use of the two terms as largely overlapping.

3. For a selection of materials from this collection, see Marshall Clark et al. The 9/11 Response and Recovery Project (financed by the *New York Times* 9/11 Neediest Fund), which has supplied background information for this chapter, contains sixty-five interviews with responders in the fields of philanthropy, trauma services, unemployment relief, law, and education. The interview genre strikes me as an appropriate point of comparison in establishing the main features of trauma therapy after 9/11, especially when the respondents are themselves therapists and provide evidence, personal or generic, of vicarious traumatization. Moreover the motto of the Oral History Research Office, "Telling Lives," fits the aims and means of psychotherapy, where patients live to tell (recounting their survival) and at the same time tell to live (using the narrative as a means of regaining control over their lives).

4. See Girard, "Mimesis and Violence" 9–19.

5. On this triangulation, see Girard, *Deceit, Desire*.

6. See also T. Douglas. The purpose of the scapegoating ritual, Douglas notes, "was to cleanse the community of its sins by the process of transferring the sins to an animal and allowing it to escape into the wilderness" (9).

7. See Ferguson 234. Most of McGrath's narrators are blatantly biased or diseased, their perception of reality severely tainted by trauma and/or psychological confusion.

8. This corresponds to Wayne C. Booth's understanding of narratorial unreliability (*The Rhetoric of Fiction* 174–75).

9. *After* was published in 2004, but according to the author's website, the American publisher Farrar, Straus and Giroux acquired the book as early as July 2003. It is therefore safe to assume that for Claire Tristram and early readers of her novel, the revelation of the images of torture inflicted upon Iraqi detainees by U.S. soldiers at Abu Ghraib came as a surprise on April 28, 2004.

10. Only the man is given a name in the novel, and this occurs toward the end of the narrative. The widow (like McGrath's analyst) remains unnamed.

11. On the ways American freedom and citizenship are defined in terms of freedom in the private sphere, see Haag; Dillon.

12. Despite its overlaps with that most controversial of Abu Ghraib revelations—torture inflicted by female guards—the novel ventures beyond gendered moral issues in the War on Terror. In the words of the writer and activist Barbara Ehrenreich, "the strategy and vision" of feminism, which suffered a massive

blow from the release of the torture images, "rested on the assumption, implicit or stated outright, that women were morally superior to men" (3). That women are held to a more rigorous ethical standard than men is a notion that Tristram's novel initially espouses but then sets out to dispute, applying moral standards gender-neutrally to all kinds of victims and perpetrators, male and female. Tristram thus suggests that only by acknowledging that moral rules can be breached by anyone, that cruelty is a common transgression, can we effectively limit its destructive potential.

13. Her wish recalls another abusive white woman turning against a Muslim male in Jeff Stanzler's 2005 film *Sorry, Haters*. In this story a young accountant rattled by the 9/11 attacks deceives and manipulates a New York cab driver to the point of carrying out a subway suicide bombing in which the man is not only killed but also framed as the suicide bomber. Stanzler's heroine justifies her own behavior in a monologue that discloses an obsession with the 9/11 attacks as the kind of horror scenario that can eradicate the boundaries between her own sense of failure and other people's apparent self-sufficiency. That day, she suggests, everyone was the same, that is, like herself: "That day I wasn't a failure. I wasn't powerless because everybody was powerless. Everybody was. I just wanted that day back."

14. On this point, see Feinman: "Utilizing the assumptions of distinctly gendered cultures, the white female U.S. soldier proceeds to violate the physical and religious (or cultural) integrity of the Arab male prisoner. From smearing (fake) menstrual blood on the Arab prisoner to enacting sexually explicit behaviors and sexually harassing him, the white female soldier creates a stunning environment of humiliation and distress" (68–69).

15. As Cathy Caruth explains, "The event is not assimilated or experienced fully at the time, but only belatedly, in its repeated possession of the one who experiences it" (*Trauma* 4).

16. "Trauma," Lynne Layton writes, "splits the experience of power and powerlessness, domination and submission in extremely marked ways" (114).

17. A broad swath of scholarship on sexuality in trauma literature too readily assumes that "sex threatens to undercut trauma literature's ethical impulse . . . by subsuming moral, ideological, and political concerns under a text's aesthetic and affective effects and, ultimately, its saleability" (Kohlke 229; see also Yaeger). Contrary to this view, Kohlke argues that by "strategically asserting individuals' desiring humanity" (232) against politically repressive formations, sexuality in trauma literature does indeed help to configure acts of resistance. But to accept

this emollient premise unquestioningly would be to simplify sexuality itself as well as the sum of connotations around issues such as sexual violence, performance, and victimization. In Tristram's novel, sexuality has less to do with the reconstitution of identity and self-worth than with their productive destruction, a destruction that is symptomatic of what Shklar calls the practice of putting cruelty first: above the self, the individual, and consolation.

3. Moral Crusades

1. Among literary texts by ethnic American writers that uniformly condemn racial profiling, Sherman Alexie's *Flight* is a puzzling exception. In one segment of this episodic novel, an Arab American pilot in training approaches a flight instructor who unquestioningly takes him on. The would-be pilot is extremely grateful for this: "When I came to your door, when I said, I want to be a pilot, you immediately thought of September eleventh. You immediately thought I was another crazy terrorist who wanted to learn how to fly planes into skyscrapers. . . . I was turned away from seven flight instructors before I came to you. One flight instructor pulled a gun on me. . . . He called me a sand nigger and said he was going to blow off my head if I didn't get the fuck out of his place of business" (111). So far so fair, but it turns out that the pilot was secretly planning a terrorist attack, which he eventually manages to carry out by crashing his small plane into downtown Chicago. This, of course, is not sufficient reason to claim that the novel, or even Alexie himself, may be condoning racial profiling—which may or may not have prevented the massacre. Yet the novel is certainly more ambiguous and leaves more ethical questions unresolved than the other texts I am discussing here.

2. A similar argument is proposed by John Updike's *Terrorist*, which sees the "dozing giant of American racism, lulled by decades of official liberal singsong" (43), stir anew as "people want to go back to simple—black and white, right and wrong, when things aren't simple" (202).

3. For an impassioned discussion of race and the genealogy of hate violence against Arab and Muslim communities after 9/11, see Ahmad.

4. According to the sociologist Stanley Cohen, moral panic occurs when "a condition, episode, person or group of persons emerges to become defined as a threat to societal values and interest; its nature is presented in a stylized and stereotypical fashion by the mass media and politicians" (9).

5. See Sontag, "Regarding the Torture of Others."

6. This sexualized xenophobia is also in line with the discursive practices of

European colonialism, wherein, according to Anne McClintock, "the rhetoric of *gender* was used to make increasingly refined distinctions among the different races" (55).

7. My argument here assumes an opposition between racialization as a morality-based phenomenon (explained in the first part of this chapter) and risk assessment as an alternative to moral thinking. This is not to say, however, that morality and risk may not become conjoined in other contexts. Amoore and de Goede, for example, make the interesting observation that "risk avoidance has become a moral enterprise relating to issues of self-control, self-knowledge and self-improvement" (12).

8. Halaby may be said to carry the coincidence plot to the extreme by having the victim of the car accident purchase drugs from Salwa's lover prior to his deadly encounter with Jassim. While certainly useful in establishing narrative interconnectedness, such coincidences lack an important aspect that narratologists associate with an effective coincidence plot, namely the moment of recognition (see Dannenberg 89–108). Neither Jassim nor Salwa nor Jack can ultimately connect the dots, which is perhaps meant to reflect the inability of risk assessors to accurately anticipate terrorist events and other hazards.

9. In a landmark essay on Don DeLillo and Richard Powers, Ursula Heise compellingly argues that "a consideration of risk and the kind of narrative articulation it requires has potentially important implications for the analysis of narrative form" (747).

10. Husband and wife are subjected to different forms of repression, he to institutional detention, she to public opprobrium based on her appearance. This chimes with Nadine Naber's observation that "federal government policies disproportionately targeted men while hate crimes and incidents of harassment in the public sphere disproportionately targeted women" ("Look, Mohammed" 293).

11. On the broader level of political rhetoric and media discourse, Joan Kirkby has exposed the neoconservative appropriation of Whitman to legitimize the "democratic vistas" of the War on Terror. But while neoconservatives use Whitman to tap into subconscious national mythology, Cunningham cites the poet in ways that appear nondoctrinal, questioning (or dismissing) the poet's oft-invoked allegiance to an exceptionalist American ideal. See Kirkby.

12. Ironically the woman calling herself Walt Whitman and the children she has hoarded and trained as terrorists purportedly employ the apparatus of fear and risk only to protect their vision, loosely inspired by Whitman, of a world as

yet uncolonized by technology, industrialization, and precisely the kinds of hazards to which she herself contributes. "Whitman," she claims, "was the last great man who really and truly loved the world. The machinery was just starting up when he lived. If we can return to a time like Whitman's, maybe we can love the world again" (Cunningham 188).

13. On the "personality defect" model of terrorism, which holds that terrorists suffer from pathological personalities emerging from a damaged sense of self, see Post; Ruby. A similar idea is proposed by Reynolds Price in his novel *The Good Priest's Son*. In this case the terrorists are considered to be emotionally and morally impoverished due to inadequate fathering: "What did the hugely successful attack on New York buildings and lives . . . represent but the momentarily triumphant assertion by nineteen young men that people should *cease* (millions of people, maybe all Americans, surely all infidels) since those young men had simply lacked fathers? Or adequate fathers" (258).

4. The Internationalization of Conscience

1. North American fiction set against a Balkan backdrop has become increasingly popular and critically acclaimed over the past few years. See also Banita, "Escaping Binarism." For a recent example of American fiction drawing on the history and legacy of the Balkan wars, see Téa Obrecht's novel *The Tiger's Wife*, winner of the 2011 Orange Prize for Fiction.

2. As a cipher for the human cost of ethnic conflict and the responsibilities it places on global civil society, the Bosnian War features briefly in Richard Flanagan's post-9/11 novel *The Unknown Terrorist* (see chapter 5).

3. All paragraphs cited from or inspired by historical sources are italicized in the novel.

4. The specter of radicalism in Chicago also mirrors post-9/11 discourse in terms of the technological dynamics allowing formerly powerless individuals to bring about damage on a massive scale. Writing on the invention of dynamite prior to the Haymarket riots, James Green observes that "the weakest, most wretched elements of society had a weapon that could inflict incalculable damage" (10). Similar discussions emerged about the use of commercial airliners on September 11 and the increasing vulnerability of the West to chemical and bioweapons.

5. Along the same lines, see also Žižek's Lacanian statement that "the most dangerous form of betrayal is not a direct yielding to our pathological impulses

but, rather, a reference to some kind of Good" (*The Metastases of Enjoyment* 68). I discuss the psychoethical implications of "betraying one's desire" in chapter 2.

6. To some extent the designer chic of violence testifies to a growing obsession with evil in contemporary culture. "Evil," Jennifer Geddes notes, "has become an object of aesthetic fascination, rather than moral concern," taking on "a glamorous sheen ... beyond rational consideration" (7). Sontag makes a similar argument in her essay "Regarding the Torture of Others": "Violent crime is down, yet the easy delight taken in violence seems to have grown. From the harsh torments inflicted on incoming students in many American suburban high schools—depicted in Richard Linklater's 1993 film, *Dazed and Confused*—to the hazing rituals of physical brutality and sexual humiliation in college fraternities and on sports teams, America has become a country in which the fantasies and the practice of violence are seen as good entertainment, fun" (28).

7. According to Hannah Arendt, the banality of evil consists in its thoughtlessness and emotional remoteness, but today this thoughtlessness can be more readily found in what Sherene Razack calls "the repetition of simple truths meant to convince us that we are locked into a moment in history when 'the axis of evil' must be defeated at all costs" (*Dark Threats* 162). "As ordinary people," Razack continues, "we succumb to 'thoughtlessness' when we believe that we are mysteriously imbued with values of democracy and peace, more so than anyone else" (163).

8. This is a common interpretation of how the notion of evil can be used to trump logic and rupture arguments. See also Dews ("The label 'evil' often functions as an intellectual and ethical shrug of the shoulders. We do not need to question or ponder any longer: we just know that this human being, or that social or religious group, has an irrational commitment to chaos and moral mayhem" [1]) and Žižek ("The overpowering horror of violent acts and empathy with the victims inexorably function as a lure which prevents us from thinking" [*Violence* 3]).

9. Hemon has made some interesting comments on the ways the label "ethnic" does or does not apply to his work: "My work is most definitely not ethnic literature, because my ethnicity is unclear. . . . But the most important characteristic of immigrant literature in my opinion is that writers of this literature enter the country under certain political conditions and not with a certain ethnicity. I suppose ethnic literature does exist out there as such, but for me this is a very dangerous term. Writers who are considered to be ethnic may be great writers, but to have that as a border around your work is dangerous and difficult. . . .

I don't write books with Bosnia in mind. I write books with books in mind.... Things happen according to what is inside the book. I don't use the book as any sort of propaganda. At some point I want to write a book that is going to be completely un-Bosnian. No Bosnian characters. Nothing" (Blazan 257, 260).

10. On the related concepts of disaggregated, lean, and flexible citizenship, see Benhabib; Thaa; Ong.

11. As Anthony Appiah has written, linking ethics to readily available communication channels, "The worldwide web of information—radio, television, telephones, the Internet—means not only that we can affect lives everywhere but that we can learn about life anywhere, too. Each person you know about and can affect is someone to whom you have responsibilities: to say this is just to affirm the very idea of morality" (xiii).

12. Photography at Ground Zero has produced several volumes of collected images (among them *Endure* and *Eleven*) as well as memorable individual works by James Nachtwey and Annie Leibovitz. The following remark by David Campbell provides further proof of how iconic the site became in the aftermath of the WTC collapse: "On the Friday after the September 11, 2001, attacks, two news programs in England concluded their broadcasts with a series of still images, each static on the screen for much longer than usual, to the accompaniment of somber music" (100). Barker makes a similar comment: "The fact that 9/11 is known to us as a visual image . . . is a reason why it hasn't gone away. It doesn't become something that people can assimilate and control at all. It is simply there, and the horror is just a fact. It isn't something that we progress through and beyond" (Brannigan, "An Interview" 384).

13. Particularly in his *Disasters of War* (which Barker revisits from the perspective of a world confronted, again, with pain and mutilation), Goya initiated what Sontag calls "a new standard for responsiveness to suffering" in art (*Regarding the Pain of Others* 45). *Los Desastres de la Guerra* are a numbered sequence of eighty-three etchings completed between 1810 and 1820, all of which were published in 1863, thirty-five years after Goya's death. *Double Vision* illustrates the ethics of representation by referencing Goya as a prototype for the artist concerned with the importance of representing war as faithfully and penetratingly as possible, in other words, with representation for its own sake in a way that precludes the necessity of spectatorship. "This is another thing that fascinates me about representation," Barker remarks. "It's writing something for its own sake. It's telling the truth for the sake of the truth, not for the sake of telling it.

It's Goya grinding away at those etchings of the disasters of war, showing them to nobody throughout his life, not even planning to or trying to" (Brannigan, "An Interview" 372).

14. Barker seems to regard the events of September 11 and the subsequent invasion of Afghanistan and Iraq as mere blips on a temporal map where previous conflagrations such as World War I appear to register more evidently. After having devoted thousands of pages to the First World War, Barker confesses that more recent historical events do not constitute "a fruitful way forward" for her fiction: "For one thing, the topical reference is instantly outdated. In ten years' time, people will be thinking of dates and trying to figure out, was that the first war in Iraq or the second war in Iraq? Even 9/11 one day will have faded into history" (Brannigan, "An Interview" 387). *Double Vision* is, however, more insightful about the long-term effects of 9/11 than these remarks might suggest.

15. Sharon Monteith, for instance, cursorily dismisses the 9/11 subtext of *Double Vision* as "the weakest moment in the novel" (287).

16. In *Another World* the veteran's state of mind is meticulously recorded by a scholar who is interested in "the interaction between the individual veteran's memories of his combat experience, and the changing public perception of the war" (81).

17. On the concept of compassion fatigue, especially as it relates to the transmission of atrocity rather than to the direct experience of it, see Moeller.

18. Goya's biographer Julia Blackburn paraphrases this injunction as the paradox of a double vision mobilizing both obligation and guilt: "You have to look at what he shows you and yet you cannot look without looking away, ashamed of what you have seen" (116).

19. As the columnist Ellen Goodman noted in December 2001, "When terrorists struck on September 11, there was only one side. No editor demanded a quote from someone saying why it was fine to fly airplanes into buildings. No one expected reporters to take an 'objective' view of the terrorists" (B12). In the words of Michael Schudson, "Much reporting after September 11 turned toward a prose of solidarity rather than a prose of information" (41).

20. Korte usefully applies Pierre Bourdieu's notion of habitus to illuminate the performativity that guides the behavior of war correspondents, a form of theatricality that becomes especially visible in an era of mediatic overexposure, and which enhances the distancing effects I am articulating here—between the reporter and the conflict he is witnessing, as well as between life in combat and life at home.

5. Reading for the Pattern

1. The "Cornell box" referenced in the text points to the work of the American assemblage artist Joseph Cornell (1903–72), whose signature artworks were simple, glass-fronted boxed assemblages containing found objects in poetic configurations. Gibson is no stranger to Cornell's work: in his novel *Count Zero*, a gallery owner is recruited to track down the creator of Cornell-style boxes of intricate, futuristic design.

2. While the essence of surveillance lies in witnessing a transgression, crime, or potential deviance, strategies of control increasingly rely on forms of observation that move away from the visible. "The sharply visualized panoptic space of contemporary culture," Timothy Druckrey avers, "is rapidly shifting towards a post-optic one in which observation is quickly giving way to information gathering systems, databases, and the monitoring of biological and chemical agents" (151). Yet the primary engine of surveillance, especially as pictured in literature, remains the injunction to vision, and modes of visibility and spectatorship indeed define electronic data mining as well, despite or perhaps even due to its focus on invisibility, transparency, and the psychological simulation of surveillance. This also implies a rehabilitation of sight as a mode of perception, acting against the resistance to the supremacy of vision that dominated the discourse of the twentieth century (see Jay).

3. Data mining is the automated review of large quantities of data to discern patterns and predict or influence behavior. This occurs in both commercial and political contexts.

4. For further studies on surveillance in literature, see Breight. For a cross-media analysis, see S. P. Miller.

5. See, for instance, Seltzer; Boone.

6. See Deleuze and Guattari 208–31.

7. This reading corresponds to the use of surveillance in humanitarian situations rather than preventive social control, where potential criminals are being observed.

8. On the dramatic intensification of surveillance in the aftermath of 9/11, see Ball and Webster.

9. Elizabeth Swanson Goldberg astutely observes that the novel features countless such moments of separation (or conflation) of two distinct realms—one signifying safety, the other trauma—which are often organized around the trope of the transitional point or threshold: "Pat Barker's *Double Vision* sets up

border economies in suggestive spatial terms that figure safety and vulnerability within the broader frame of the potential for human connection in relation to the traumatic event. In *Double Vision*, that border is figured by the hearth or the threshold, and the transitional grammar employed in the text can be discerned in the leave-takings that accumulate at the end of nearly every one of the novel's twenty-seven chapters" (166).

10. The plot of this novel bears some resemblance to that of the film *Red Road* (dir. Andrea Arnold, 2006), a British production centered on a CCTV operator working in Glasgow. The operator obsessively observes residents in the shady parts of town, tracking the movements of one man in particular with whom she has some shared experience about which the viewer is kept guessing until the very end of the film. The plot unfolds very slowly, with few (though sensitively sprinkled) hints at the connection between the surveillance agent and her subject. The often frustrating process of watching the film thus mirrors the CCTV operator's task of sorting through random data, looking for meaning (for although she happens to know this particular man, generally her subjects are as puzzling to her as this man is to the audience).

11. In the words of John E. McGrath, "At root, all of our experiences of surveillance are structured by the expectation of death" (vii).

12. The boldface words mark a hyperlink in the digital version of the text. The websites are listed on a webpage, where the reader of the printed book can follow the original links.

13. The agency of the self is also endangered, as this increased visual perception from the outside suggests a subjecting panopticon rather than a subjective self-perception. Paradoxically, then, a stricter organization of the body through obsessive monitorization of its surfaces leads merely to its dis-organ-ization. Such watchful dismemberment also recalls Deleuze and Guattari's paradigm of the "body without organs," the fluid, transitory particles and singularities of the body's virtual rather than actual dimensions (165), and undercuts the narrative concept of a coherent and unitary organism, revealing instead the fragmented nature of consciousness.

14. This emplotment of surveillance confirms Thomas Y. Levin's diagnosis that "the locus of surveillance has thus shifted, imperceptibly but decidedly, away from the space of the story, to the very condition of possibility of that story" (583).

15. For a discussion of the precautionary principle, see Ewald, "Insurance and Risk" and "The Return of Descartes's Malicious Demon." While the "principle

of precaution" defined by Hans Jonas in the 1970s is derived from an ethics of responsibility and prudence, its contemporary incarnation erases much of its original ethical urgency. Instead it underlies a watchful politics based on permanent fear—a feeling that Jonas himself prescribes as the preliminary imperative of his ethics, though primarily as a punctual emotion that invites immediate action rather than as a pervasive affective environment. See Jonas.

16. Paul Giles has stressed the paradox at the heart of "homeland security" by defining the alignment of the two terms as oxymoronic: "To turn a home into a 'homeland' is, by definition, to move from a zone in which domestic comforts and protection could be taken for granted to one in which they had to be guarded anxiously and self-consciously; in that sense, the very phrase 'homeland security' could be seen as a contradiction in terms, since it rhetorically evokes the very insecurity it is designed to assuage" (17).

17. As part of a global surveillance system that is now over fifty years old and is operated by stations run in the United States, Britain, Canada, Australia, and New Zealand, Echelon intercepts and processes international communications traversing communication satellites. See Duncan Campbell.

18. The Council on Foreign Relations is a policy-developing organization that aims to have a hand in shaping U.S. foreign policy, either by putting forward suggestions through its various events and its journal *Foreign Affairs* or through the impact of its members, many of whom hold influential government positions.

19. "I was about 100 pages into the book on Sept 10th.... But that was completely swept aside by my recognition at that point that my world no longer existed and that the meaning of everything—I felt that just as strongly as I've ever felt anything in my life—the meaning of everything, *ever* that had gone before had to be reconsidered in the light of something that had happened" (Leonard n.p.).

20. See Hardt and Negri 108–15.

21. The anonymity of the maker and the digital dissemination of the footage call to mind the unedited and unnarrated witness videos of the 9/11 attacks, which provide a prime example of what Thomas Mathiesen calls "the viewer society" or the "synopticon" (where the many watch the few). These videos verify the massive dispersal of information systems, which may help redefine visuality in a world that is constantly visible, although the question of who is doing the seeing can never be definitively answered. As David Brin pointed out with reference to the terrorist attacks and the burgeoning of amateur surveillance, "Despite repeated efforts by our own hierarchs to justify one-way information flows,

the true record of the last generation has been an indisputable and overwhelming dispersal of knowledge and the power to see. People are becoming addicted to knowing. Take the events that surrounded the tragedies of September 11, 2001. Most of the video we saw was taken by private citizens, a potentially crucial element in future emergencies. Private cell phones spread word more rapidly than official media. So did email and instant messaging when the telephone system got swamped.... Is this a true and unstoppable trend? Only time will tell" (227–28). Gibson's surveillance thriller demonstrates that individual vigilance might indeed move the parameters of surveillance toward more private, grassroots forms.

22. N. Katherine Hayles notes the lack of plot over a large portion of the narrative and subsumes it to the search patterns of the novel as a whole, in which the characters are expected to detect hidden data rather than undergo significant transformations: "The effect of delaying all the decisive action until the end is to envelop the reader in an atmosphere of murky apprehension, searching for the pattern amidst a welter of precisely drawn details that do not quite cohere into plot" (146).

23. This perhaps shouldn't seem surprising if one considers that before writing her debut novel, Adams was known as a Pulitzer Prize–winning investigative journalist reporting on the millennium terrorist plot in which explosives would have been driven across the Canadian border and detonated at Los Angeles International Airport.

24. Tangible links between armed groups in Algeria (including Islamist militants abroad) and bin Laden certainly predate September 11, 2001. After the attacks, the Bush administration strongly endorsed the Algerian regime's counterterrorist strategies (Evans and Phillips 278–79).

25. See Kumamoto 85. Evans and Phillips have argued that Algeria became "a nodal point in the growing 'war' against international Islamic terrorism" in the 1990s, which eventually led to the CIA's closely monitoring the situation by the end of that decade (253). See also Connelly: "There *is* a transnational system emerging from events like the Algerian War and the underlying trends they represent" (286).

26. In collecting information rather than following a coherent narrative pattern, the post-9/11 surveillance novel may be said to illustrate the tendency diagnosed by Lev Manovich toward the replacement of narrative by the database as a fundamental cultural form and artistic paradigm of the digital age (227).

BIBLIOGRAPHY

Abel, Marco. "Don DeLillo's 'In the Ruins of the Future': Literature, Images, and the Rhetoric of Seeing 9/11." *PMLA* 118.5 (2003): 1236–50.

Abraham, Nicolas, and Maria Torok. *The Shell and the Kernel: Renewals of Psychoanalysis*. Vol. 1. Ed. and trans. Nicholas Rand. Chicago: University of Chicago Press, 1994.

Abramowicz, Janet. *Giorgio Morandi: The Art of Silence*. New Haven CT: Yale University Press, 2004.

Adams, Lorraine. *Harbor*. New York: Knopf, 2004.

———. *The Room and the Chair*. New York: Knopf, 2010.

Adrian, Chris. *A Better Angel: Stories*. New York: Farrar, Straus and Giroux, 2008.

Agamben, Giorgio. "Security and Terror." *Theory and Event* 5.4 (2002), http://muse.jhu.edu/.

Ahmad, Muneer. "Homeland Insecurities: Racial Violence the Day after September 11." *Social Text* 20.3 (2002): 101–15.

Alcorn, Marshall W. *Narcissism and the Literary Libido: Rhetoric, Text, and Subjectivity*. New York: NYU Press, 1997.

Alexie, Sherman. *Flight*. New York: Black Cat, 2007.

Ali, Kazim. *The Disappearance of Seth*. Wilkes Barre PA: Etruscan Press, 2009.

Amis, Martin. *The Second Plane*. London: Jonathan Cape, 2008.

Amoore, Louise. "Vigilant Visualities: The Watchful Politics of the War on Terror." *Security Dialogue* 38.2 (2007): 215–32.

Amoore, Louise, and Marieke de Goede. "Introduction: Governing by Risk in the War on Terror." *Risk and the War on Terror*. Ed. Louise Amoore and Marieke de Goede. London: Routledge, 2008. 5–19.

Anker, Elisabeth. "The Only Thing We Have to Fear . . ." *Theory & Event* 8.3 (2005), http://muse.jhu.edu/.

———. "Villains, Victims and Heroes: Melodrama, Media, and September 11." *Journal of Communication* 55.1 (2005): 22–37.

Anker, Elizabeth S. "Allegories of Falling and the 9/11 Novel." *American Literary History* 23.3 (2011): 463–82.

Antor, Heinz. "Unreliable Narration and (Dis-)Orientation in the Postmodern Neo-Gothic Novel: Reflections on Patrick McGrath's *The Grotesque* (1989)." *Miscelánea: A Journal of English and American Studies* 24 (2001): 11–37.

Appiah, Kwame Anthony. *Cosmopolitanism: Ethics in a World of Strangers*. New York: Norton, 2006.

Apter, Emily S. "On Oneworldedness: Or Paranoia as a World System." *American Literary History* 18.2 (2006): 365–89.

———. *The Translation Zone: A New Comparative Literature*. Princeton NJ: Princeton University Press, 2006.

Arondekar, Anjali. "Border/Line Sex: Queer Postcolonialities, or How Race Matters Outside the United States." *Interventions* 7.2 (2005): 236–50.

Attridge, Derek. "Innovation, Literature, Ethics: Relating to the Other." *PMLA* 114 (1999): 20–31.

Auster, Paul. *Sunset Park*. New York: Faber and Faber, 2010.

Avrich, Paul. *The Haymarket Tragedy*. Princeton NJ: Princeton University Press, 1984.

Bachelard, Gaston. *Le Rationnalisme appliqué*. Paris: Presses Universitaires de France, 1949.

Badiou, Alain. *Ethics: An Essay on the Understanding of Evil*. Trans. and introduction by Peter Hallward. London: Verso, 2001.

———. *Handbook of Inaesthetics*. Trans. Alberto Toscano. Stanford: Stanford University Press, 2005.

Bal, Mieke. "The Commitment to Look." *Journal of Visual Culture* 4.2 (2005): 145–62.

Ball, Kristie, and Frank Webster, eds. *The Intensification of Surveillance: Crime, Terrorism and Warfare in the Information Age*. London: Pluto Press, 2003.

Ballard, J. G. *Millennium People*. London: Flamingo 2003.

Banerjee, Mita. "'Whiteness of a Different Color'? Racial Profiling in John Updike's *Terrorist*." *Neohelicon* 35.2 (2008): 13–28.

Banita, Georgiana. "Escaping Binarism: The Bosnian War in the Canadian Imagination." *Zeitschrift für Kanada-Studien* 30.2 (2010): 1–18.

———. "Raymond Williams and Online Video: The Tragedy of Technology." *About Raymond Williams*. Ed. Monika Seidl, Roman Horak, and Lawrence Grossberg. London: Routledge, 2010. 94–105.

Barker, Pat. *Another World*. London: Penguin, 1999.

———. *Double Vision*. London: Hamish Hamilton, 2003.

Barthes, Roland. "Shock-Photos." *The Eiffel Tower and Other Mythologies*. Trans. Richard Howard. New York: Hill and Wang, 1979. 71–74.

Baudrillard, Jean. "The Ecstasy of Communication." Trans. John Johnston. *The Anti-Aesthetic: Essays on Postmodern Culture*. Ed. Hal Foster. Seattle: Bay Press, 1983. 126–33.

———. "L'Esprit du Terrorisme." In Hauerwas and Lentricchia 149–61.

———. *The Spirit of Terrorism and Other Essays*. Trans. Chris Turner. New York: Verso, 2003.

Bauman, Zygmunt. *Postmodern Ethics*. Oxford: Blackwell, 1993.

Beck, Ulrich. *Risk Society: Towards a New Modernity*. London: Sage, 1992.

Beigbeder, Frédéric. *Windows on the World*. London: Harper Perennial, 2005.

Bell, Martin. "The Truth Is Our Currency." *Press/Politics* 3.1 (1998): 102–09.

Bengley, Adam. "Image of Twin Towers Ablaze Haunts Narcissistic Cartoonist." Review of *In the Shadow of No Towers*, by Art Spiegelman. *New York Observer*, September 13, 2004.

Benhabib, Seyla. *The Rights of Others: Aliens, Residents and Citizens*. Cambridge, England: Cambridge University Press, 2004.

Bennett, Jill. "The Limits of Empathy and the Global Politics of Belonging." In Greenberg 132–38.

Bergoffen, Debra B. "9/11: America and the Politics of Innocence." In Sullivan and Schmidt 72–87.

Berlant, Lauren. *The Queen of America Goes to Washington City: Essays on Sex and Citizenship*. Durham NC: Duke University Press, 1997.

Bersani, Leo, and Adam Phillips. *Intimacies*. Chicago: University of Chicago Press, 2008.

Blackburn, Julia. *Old Man Goya*. New York: Pantheon Books, 2002.

Blazan, Sladja. *American Fictionary: Postsozialistische Migration in der amerikanischen Literatur*. Heidelberg: Winter, 2006.

Bohan, Ruth L. "'I Sing the Body Electric': Isadora Duncan, Whitman, and the Dance." *The Cambridge Companion to Walt Whitman*. Ed. Ezra Greenspan. Cambridge, England: Cambridge University Press, 1995. 166–93.

Boltanski, Luc. *Distant Suffering: Morality, Media and Politics*. Cambridge, England: Cambridge University Press, 1999.

Boone, Joseph A. "Depolicing *Villette*: Surveillance, Invisibility, and the Female Erotics of 'Heretic Narrative.'" *NOVEL: A Forum on Fiction* 26.1 (1992): 20–42.

Booth, Ken, and Tim Dunne. "Worlds in Collision." In Booth and Dunne 1–23.

———. *Worlds in Collision: Terror and the Future of Global Order.* New York: Palgrave Macmillan, 2002.

Booth, Wayne. *The Company We Keep: An Ethics of Fiction.* Berkeley: University of California Press, 1988.

Booth, Wayne C. *The Rhetoric of Fiction.* 2nd ed. Chicago: University of Chicago Press, 1983.

Borradori, Giovanna. *Philosophy in a Time of Terror: Dialogues with Jürgen Habermas and Jacques Derrida.* Chicago: University of Chicago Press, 2003.

Bosmajian, Hamida. "The Orphaned Voice in Art Spiegelman's *Maus* I & II." *Considering "Maus": Approaches to Art Spiegelman's "Survivor's Tale" of the Holocaust.* Tuscaloosa: University of Alabama Press, 2003. 26–43.

Boulanger, Ghislaine. Interview with Mary Marshall Clark. 9/11 Response and Recovery Project. Columbia University Oral History Research Department. June 24, 2005.

Braidotti, Rosi. *Transpositions: On Nomadic Ethics.* Cambridge, England: Polity Press, 2006.

Brandeis, Gayle. *Self Storage.* New York: Ballantine Books, 2008.

Brannigan, John. "An Interview with Pat Barker." *Contemporary Literature* 46.3 (2005): 366–92.

———. *Pat Barker.* Manchester, England: Manchester University Press, 2005.

Breight, Curtis C. *Surveillance, Militarism, and Drama in the Elizabethan Era.* New York: St. Martin's Press, 1996.

Brin, David. "The Self-Preventing Prophecy; or, How a Dose of Nightmare Can Help Tame Tomorrow's Perils." *On "Nineteen Eighty-Four": Orwell and Our Future.* Ed. Abbot Gleason, Jack Goldsmith, and Martha C. Nussbaum. Princeton NJ: Princeton University Press, 2005. 222–30.

Brison, S. "The Uses of Narrative in the Aftermath of Violence." *On Feminist Ethics and Politics.* Ed. Claudia Card. Lawrence: University of Kansas Press, 1999. 200–225.

Brooks, David. "What Whitman Knew." *Atlantic Monthly* 291.4 (2003): 32–33.

Brooks, Peter. "Narrative Transaction and Transference (Unburying 'Le Colonel Chabert')." *NOVEL: A Forum on Fiction* 15.2 (1982): 101–10.

Brottman, Mikita. "The Fascination of the Abomination: The Censored Images of 9/11." *Film and Television after 9/11.* Ed. Wheeler Winston Dixon. Carbondale: Southern Illinois University Press, 2004. 163–77.

Brown, Joshua. "Of Mice and Memory." *Oral History Review* 16.1 (1988): 91–109.

Burke, Anthony. *Beyond Security, Ethics and Violence: War against the Other.* New York: Routledge, 2007.

Butler, Judith. *Precarious Life: The Powers of Mourning and Violence*. New York: Verso, 2004.

———. "Values of Difficulty." *Just Being Difficult? Academic Writing in the Public Arena*. Ed. Jonathan Culler and Kevin Lamb. Stanford: Stanford University Press, 2003. 199–215.

Buzan, Barry. "Who May We Bomb?" In Booth and Dunne 85–94.

Campbell, David. "Representing Contemporary War." *Ethics & International Affairs* 17.2 (2003): 99–108.

Campbell, Duncan. "Inside Echelon: The History, Structure, and Function of the Global Surveillance System Known as Echelon." *Ctrl (Space): Rhetorics of Surveillance from Bentham to Big Brother*. Ed. Thomas Y. Levin, Ursula Frohne, and Peter Weibel. Cambridge MA: MIT Press, 2002. 158–69.

Carey, J. W. "American Journalism On, Before, and After September 11." *Journalism after September 11*. Ed. Barbie Zelizer and Stuart Allan. London: Routledge, 2002. 71–90.

Caruth, Cathy, ed. *Trauma: Explorations in Memory*. Baltimore: Johns Hopkins University Press, 1995.

———. *Unclaimed Experience: Trauma, Narrative, and History*. Baltimore: Johns Hopkins University Press, 1996.

Casey, Edward S. "Public Memory in Place and Time." *Framing Public Memory*. Ed. Kendall Phillips. Tuscaloosa: University of Alabama Press, 2004. 17–44.

Chemtob, Claude M. "Delayed Debriefing: After a Disaster." *Psychological Debriefing: Theory, Practice and Evidence*. Ed. Beverley Raphael and John P. Wilson. Cambridge, England: Cambridge University Press, 2000. 227–40.

———. Interview with Sharon Kofman. 9/11 Response and Recovery Project. Columbia University Oral History Research Department. February 8, 2005.

Chow, Rey. *Ethics after Idealism: Theory—Culture—Ethnicity—Reading*. Bloomington: Indiana University Press, 1998.

———. "Toward an Ethics of Postvisuality: Some Thoughts on the Recent Work of Zhang Yimou." *Poetics Today* 25.4 (2004): 673–88.

Chute, Hillary. "'The Shadow of a Past Time': History and Graphic Representation in *Maus*." *Twentieth Century Literature* 52.2 (2006): 199–230.

———. "Temporality and Seriality in Spiegelman's *In the Shadow of No Towers*." *American Periodicals* 17.2 (2007): 228–44.

Cilano, Cara, ed. *From Solidarity to Schisms: 9/11 and After in Fiction and Film from Outside the U.S.* Amsterdam: Rodopi, 2009.

Cohen, Samuel S. *After the End of History: American Fiction in the 1990s*. Iowa City: University of Iowa Press, 2009.

Cohen, Stanley. *Folk Devils and Moral Panics: The Creation of Mods and Rockers.* 3rd ed. London: Routledge, 2002.

Connelly, Matthew. *A Diplomatic Revolution: Algeria's Fight for Independence and the Origins of the Post–Cold War Era.* Oxford: Oxford University Press, 2002.

Crary, Jonathan. *Techniques of the Observer: On Vision and Modernity in the Nineteenth Century.* Cambridge MA: MIT Press, 1991.

Critchley, Simon. *The Ethics of Deconstruction: Derrida and Levinas.* Oxford: Blackwell, 1992.

———. *Infinitely Demanding: Ethics of Commitment, Politics of Resistance.* London: Verso, 2007.

Cunningham, Michael. *Specimen Days.* London: Harper Perennial, 2006.

Dannenberg, Hilary. *Coincidence and Counterfactuality: Plotting Time and Space in Narrative Fiction.* Lincoln: University of Nebraska Press, 2008.

Dean, Tim. "Art as Symptom: Žižek and the Ethics of Psychoanalytic Criticism." *Diacritics* 32.2 (2002): 21–41.

Deleuze, Gilles. "Postscript on Societies of Control." *October* 59 (1993): 3–7.

Deleuze, Gilles, and Félix Guattari. *A Thousand Plateaus.* Trans. Brian Massumi. Minneapolis: University of Minnesota Press, 1987.

DeLillo, Don. *Conversations with Don DeLillo.* Ed. Thomas DePietro. Jackson: University Press of Mississippi, 2005.

———. *Falling Man.* New York: Scribner, 2007.

———. "The Image and the Crowd." *Creative Camera*, April/May 1993, 72–73.

———. *Mao II.* New York: Viking, 1991.

de Man, Paul. *Allegories of Reading: Figural Language in Rousseau, Nietzsche, Rilke, and Proust.* New Haven CT: Yale University Press, 1979.

Der Derian, James. *Virtuous War: Mapping the Military-Industrial Media Entertainment Network.* Boulder CO: Westview, 2001.

———. "The War of Networks." *Theory and Event* 5.4 (2002), http://muse.jhu.edu/journals/theory_and_event/v005/5.4derderian.html.

Derrida, Jacques. "That Dangerous Supplement." *Acts of Literature.* Ed. Derek Attridge. London: Routledge, 1992. 76–109.

Dews, Peter. *The Idea of Evil.* Malden MA: Blackwell, 2008.

Dillon, Elizabeth Maddock. *The Gender of Freedom: Fictions of Liberalism and the Literary Public Sphere.* Stanford: Stanford University Press, 2004.

Dimock, Wai Chee. "Literature for the Planet." *PMLA* 116.1 (2001): 173–88.

———. "Whitman, Syntax, and Political Theory." *Breaking Bounds: Whitman and American Cultural Studies*. Ed. Betsy Erkkila and Jay Grossman. Oxford: Oxford University Press, 1996. 62–79.

Divakaruni, Chitra. *Queen of Dreams*. London: Abacus, 2005.

Doherty, Thomas. "Art Spiegelman's *Maus*: Graphic Art and the Holocaust." *American Literature* 68 (1996): 69–84.

Douglas, Mary, and Aaron Wildavsky. *Risk and Culture: An Essay on the Selection of Technological and Environmental Dangers*. Berkeley: University of California Press, 1983.

Douglas, Tom. *Scapegoats: Transferring Blame*. London: Routledge, 1995.

Druckrey, Timothy. "Secreted Agents, Security Leaks, Immune Systems, Spore Wars..." *Ctrl (Space): Rhetorics of Surveillance from Bentham to Big Brother*. Ed. Thomas Y. Levin, Ursula Frohne, and Peter Weibel. Cambridge MA: MIT Press, 2002. 150–57.

Duggan, Robert. "Ghosts of Gotham: 9/11 Mourning in Patrick McGrath's *Ghost Town* and Michael Cunningham's *Specimen Days*." *Journal of Postcolonial Writing* 46.3 (2010): 381–93.

Eaglestone, Robert. *Ethical Criticism: Reading after Levinas*. Edinburgh: Edinburgh University Press, 1997.

———. "Flaws: James, Nussbaum, Miller, Levinas." *Critical Ethics: Text, Theory and Responsibility*. Ed. Dominic Rainsford and Tim Woods. Basingstoke, England: Macmillan, 1999. 77–87.

Eagleton, Terry. *Holy Terror*. Oxford: Oxford University Press, 2005.

———. *On Evil*. New Haven CT: Yale University Press, 2010.

———. *Trouble with Strangers: A Study of Ethics*. Malden MA: Blackwell, 2009.

Ehrenreich, Barbara. "Foreword: Feminism's Assumptions Upended." *One of the Guys: Women as Aggressors and Torturers*. Ed. Tara McKelvey. Emeryville CA: Seal Press, 2007. 1–5.

Ellis, J. *Seeing Things: Television in the Age of Uncertainty*. London: I. B. Tauris, 2000.

———. *Visible Fictions: Cinema: Television: Video*. London: Routledge, 2000.

Elshtain, Jean Bethke. "How to Fight a Just War." In Booth and Dunne 263–69.

Endure: Renewal from Ground Zero. New York: Rockefeller Foundation, 2001.

Engle, Karen. *Seeing Ghosts: 9/11 and the Visual Imagination*. Montreal: McGill-Queen's University Press, 2009.

Ensler, Eve. *The Treatment*. New York: Dramatists Play Service, 2007.

Ericson, Richard V., and Aaron Doyle, eds. *Risk and Morality*. Toronto: University of Toronto Press, 2003.

Evans, Martin, and John Phillips. *Algeria: Anger of the Dispossessed*. New Haven CT: Yale University Press, 2007.

Ewald, François. "Insurance and Risk." *The Foucault Effect: Studies in Governmentality*. Ed. Graham Burchell, Colin Gordon, and Peter Miller. Chicago: University of Chicago Press, 1991. 197–210.

———. "The Return of Descartes's Malicious Demon: An Outline of a Philosophy of Precaution." *Embracing Risk: The Changing Culture of Insurance and Responsibility*. Ed. Tom Baker and Jonathan Simon. Chicago: University of Chicago Press, 2002. 273–302.

Feinman, Ilene. "Shock and Awe: Abu Ghraib, Women Soldiers, and Racially Gendered Torture." *One of the Guys: Women as Aggressors and Torturers*. Ed. Tara McKelvey. Emeryville CA: Seal Press, 2007. 57–80.

Felman, Shoshana. "The Return of the Voice: Claude Lanzmann's *Shoah*." *Testimony: Crises of Witnessing in Literature, Psychoanalysis and History*. Ed. Shoshana Felman and Dori Laub. New York: Routledge, 1992. 204–83.

———. "Turning the Screw of Interpretation." "Literature and Psychoanalysis. The Question of Reading: Otherwise." Special issue of *Yale French Studies* 55/56 (1977): 94–207.

Ferguson, Christine. "Dr. McGrath's Disease: Radical Pathology in Patrick McGrath's Neo-Gothicism." *Spectral Readings: Toward a Gothic Geography*. Ed. Glennis Byron and David Punter. London: Macmillan, 1999. 233–43.

Filkins, Dexter. *The Forever War*. New York: Knopf, 2008.

Fischl, Eric. "The Trauma of 9/11 and Its Impact on Artists." *Ethics and the Visual Arts*. Ed. Elaine A. King and Gail Levin. New York: Allworth Press, 2006.

Fisher, Jennifer. "Interperformance: The Live Tableaux Vivants of Suzanne Lacy, Janine Antoni, and Martina Abramovic." *Art Journal* 56 (1997): 28–33.

Flanagan, Richard. *The Unknown Terrorist*. Sydney: Picador, 2006.

Foer, Jonathan Safran. *Extremely Loud and Incredibly Close*. New York: Houghton Mifflin, 2005.

Forter, Greg. "Freud, Faulkner, Caruth: Trauma and the Politics of Literary Form." *Narrative* 15.3 (2007): 259–85.

Foster Wallace, D. "E Unibus Pluram: Television and U.S. Fiction." *A Supposedly Fun Thing I'll Never Do Again: Essays and Arguments*. London: Abacus, 2006. 21–82.

Foucault, Michel. *The History of Sexuality*. Trans. Robert Hurley. New York: Pantheon, 1977.

Fox, Paula. *Desperate Characters*. New York: Norton, 1999.
Franzen, Jonathan. *Freedom*. London: Fourth Estate, 2010.
Freud, Sigmund. "An Autobiographical Study." *Standard Edition* 20 (1925). London: Hogarth Press, 1959.
———. *The Ego and the Id. Standard Edition*. Trans. Joan Riviere. Ed. James Strachey. New York: Norton, 1990.
Friend, David. *Watching the World Change: The Stories behind the Images of 9/11*. New York: Picador, 2006.
Frosh Paul, and Amit Pinchevski, eds. *Media Witnessing: Testimony in the Age of Mass Communication*. Basingstoke, England: Palgrave Macmillan, 2009.
Frost, Laura. "Falling Man's Precarious Balance." *American Prospect*, May 11, 2007.
———. "Photography/Pornography/Torture: The Politics of Seeing Abu Ghraib." *One of the Guys: Women as Aggressors and Torturers*. Ed. Tara McKelvey. Emeryville CA: Seal Press, 2007. 135–44.
———. "Still Life: 9/11's Falling Bodies." *Literature after 9/11*. Ed. Ann Keniston and Jeanne Follansbee Quinn. New York: Routledge, 2008. 180–205.
Furedi, Frank. *Culture of Fear: Risk-Taking and the Morality of Low Expectation*. London: Cassell, 1997.
Garland, David. *The Culture of Control: Crime and Social Order in Contemporary Society*. Chicago: University of Chicago Press, 2001.
Geddes, Jennifer L. Introduction. *Evil after Postmodernism: Histories, Narratives, and Ethics*. Ed. Jennifer L. Geddes. London: Routledge, 2001. 1–8.
Ghosh, Amitav. *Incendiary Circumstances: A Chronicle of the Turmoil of Our Times*. New York: Houghton Mifflin, 2005.
———. *Pattern Recognition*. New York: Berkeley Books, 2003.
Giles, Paul. *The Global Remapping of American Literature*. Princeton NJ: Princeton University Press, 2011.
Girard, René. *Deceit, Desire and the Novel: Self and Other in Literary Structure*. Baltimore: Johns Hopkins University Press, 1965.
———. "Mimesis and Violence: Perspectives in Cultural Criticism." *Berkshire Review* 14 (1979): 9–19.
———. *The Scapegoat*. Baltimore: Johns Hopkins University Press, 1986.
Glejzer, Richard. "Witnessing 9/11: Art Spiegelman and the Persistence of Trauma." *Literature after 9/11*. Ed. Ann Keniston and Jeanne Follansbee Quinn. New York: Routledge, 2008. 99–119.
Goldberg, Elizabeth Swanson. *Beyond Terror: Gender, Narrative, Human Rights*. New Brunswick NJ: Rutgers University Press, 2007.

Goodman, Ellen. "Post-September 11 Dilemmas for Journalists." *San Diego Tribune*, December 7, 2001.

Gray, Louise. "The Power of Perspective." *Art Review* 40 (2004): 51–52.

Gray, Richard. *After the Fall: American Literature since 9/11*. Malden MA: Wiley-Blackwell, 2011.

———."Open Doors, Closed Minds: American Prose Writing at a Time of Crisis." *American Literary History* 21.1 (2009): 128–48.

Green, James. *Death in the Haymarket: A Story of Chicago, the First Labor Movement and the Bombing That Divided Gilded Age America*. New York: Pantheon Books, 2006.

Greenberg, Judith, ed. *Trauma at Home: After 9/11*. Lincoln: University of Nebraska Press, 2003.

Greenberg, Karen J. "Split Screens." *One of the Guys: Women as Aggressors and Torturers*. Ed. Tara McKelvey. Emeryville CA: Seal Press, 2007. 37–44.

Greenwald Smith, Rachel. "Organic Shrapnel: Affect and Aesthetics in September 11 Fiction." *American Literature* 83.1 (2011): 153–74.

Gronnvoll, Marita. "Gender (In)Visibility at Abu Ghraib." *Rhetoric & Public Affairs* 10.3 (2007): 371–98.

Guillory, John. "The Ethical Practice of Modernity: The Example of Reading." *The Turn to Ethics*. Ed. Marjorie Garber, Beatrice Hanssen, and Rebecca L. Walkowitz. New York: Routledge, 2000. 29–46.

Haag, Pamela. *Consent: Sexual Rights and the Transformation of American Liberalism*. Ithaca NY: Cornell University Press, 1999.

Hajdu, David. "In the Shadow of No Towers: Homeland Insecurity." *New York Times*, September 12, 2004, http://www.nytimes.com/2004/09/12/books/review/12HAJDU.html?pagewanted=all.

Halaby, Laila. *Once in a Promised Land*. Boston: Beacon Press, 2007.

Hale, Dorothy J. "Aesthetics and the New Ethics: Theorizing the Novel in the Twenty-First Century." *PMLA* 124.1 (2009): 896–905.

———. "Fiction as Restriction: Self-Binding in New Ethical Theories of the Novel." *Narrative* 15.2 (2007): 187–206.

Halliwell, Martin, and Catherine Morley, eds. *American Thought and Culture in the 21st Century*. Edinburgh: Edinburgh University Press, 2008.

Hamid, Mohsin. *The Reluctant Fundamentalist*. London: Penguin, 2007.

Hammad, Suheir. "first writing since." In Greenberg 139–43.

Hardt, Michael, and Antonio Negri. *Multitude: War and Democracy in the Age of Empire*. New York: Penguin, 2004.

Harpham, Geoffrey. "Ethics." *Critical Terms for Literary Studies*. Ed. Frank Lentricchia and Thomas McLaughlin. Chicago: University of Chicago Press, 1995. 387–405.

———. *Getting It Right: Language, Literature, and Ethics*. Chicago: University of Chicago Press, 1992.

Hartman, Geoffrey. *Scars of the Spirit: The Struggle against Inauthenticity*. Basingstoke, England: Palgrave Macmillan, 2002.

Hauerwas, Stanley, and Frank Lentricchia, eds. *Dissent from the Homeland: Essays after September 11*. Durham NC: Duke University Press, 2003.

Hayles, N. Katherine. "Traumas of Code." *Critical Inquiry* 33.1 (2006): 136–57.

Heise, Ursula K. "Toxins, Drugs, and Global Systems: Risk and Narrative in the Contemporary Novel." *American Literature* 74.4 (2002): 747–78.

Hemon, Aleksandar. *The Lazarus Project*. New York: Riverhead Books, 2008.

———. *Love and Obstacles: Stories*. New York: Riverhead Books, 2009.

———. *Nowhere Man: The Pronek Fantasies*. New York: Nan A. Talese, 2002.

Herman, J. *Trauma and Recovery: The Aftermath of Violence—From Domestic Abuse to Political Terror*. New York: Basic, 1992.

Hersh, Seymour M. *Chain of Command: The Road from 9/11 to Abu Ghraib*. New York: HarperCollins, 2004.

Hirsch, Joshua. *Afterimage: Film, Trauma, and the Holocaust*. Philadelphia: Temple University Press, 2004.

Hirsch, Marianne. "Editor's Column: Collateral Damage." PMLA 119.5 (2004): 1209–15.

———. "I Took Pictures: September 2001 and Beyond." In Greenberg 69–86.

———. "Projected Memory: Holocaust Photographs in Personal and Public Fantasy." *Acts of Memory: Cultural Recall in the Present*. Ed. Mieke Bal, Jonathan Crewe, and Leo Spitzer. Hanover NH: University Press of New England, 1999. 3–23.

Hong, Terry. "Responding with Hope to 9/11: A Talk with Chitra Banerjee Divakaruni about Her Latest Novel, *Queen of Dreams*." *Bloomsbury Review* 24.6 (2004), http://www.bloomsburyreview.com/Archives/2004/Chitra%20 Divakaruni.pdf.

Howe, Peter. *Shooting Under Fire: The World of the War Photographer*. New York: Artisan, 2002.

Huehls, Mitchum. "Foer, Spiegelman, and 9/11's Timely Traumas." *Literature after 9/11*. Ed. Ann Keniston and Jeanne Follansbee Quinn. New York: Routledge, 2008. 42–59.

Huffer, Lynne. "'There Is No Gomorrah': Narrative Ethics in Feminist and Queer Theory." *Differences* 12.3 (2001): 1–32.

Human Rights Watch. *We Are Not the Enemy: Hate Crimes against Arabs, Muslims, and Those Perceived to Be Arab or Muslim after September 11*. New York: Human Rights Watch, 2002.

Hungerford, Amy. *The Holocaust of Texts: Genocide, Literature, and Personification*. Chicago: University of Chicago Press, 2003.

———. "On the Period Formerly Known as Contemporary." *American Literary History* 20.1–2 (2008): 410–19.

Hunt, Krista. "'Embedded Feminism' and the War on Terror." In Hunt and Rygiel 51–71.

Hunt, Krista, and Kim Rygiel, eds. *(En)Gendering the War on Terror: War Stories and Camouflaged Politics*. Aldershot, England: Ashgate, 2007.

Huyssen, Andreas. "Of Mice and Mimesis: Reading Spiegelman with Adorno." *New German Critique* 81 (2000): 65–82.

———. "Von Mauschwitz in die Catskills und zurück: Art Spiegelman's Holocaust Comic *Maus*." *Bilder des Holocaust: Literatur—Film—bildende Kunst*. Ed. Manuel Köppen and Klaus Scherpe. Cologne: Böhlau, 1997. 171–89.

Ignatieff, Michael. *The Warrior's Honor: Ethnic War and the Modern Conscience*. London: Chatto and Windus, 1998.

Jameson, Fredric. *Archeologies of the Future: The Desire Called Utopia and Other Science Fictions*. London: Verso, 2005.

———. *The Political Unconscious: Narrative as a Socially Symbolic Act*. Ithaca NY: Cornell University Press, 1981.

Jay, Martin. *Downcast Eyes: The Denigration of Vision in Twentieth-Century French Thought*. Berkeley: University of California Press, 1993.

Jonas, Hans. *The Imperative of Responsibility: In Search of Ethics for the Technological Age*. Chicago: University of Chicago Press, 1979.

Junod, Tom. "The Falling Man." *Esquire* 140 (2003): 176–99.

———. "The Man Who Invented 9/11." *Esquire* 147.6 (2007): 38.

Just, Ward. *Forgetfulness*. Boston: Houghton Mifflin, 2006.

Kacandes, I. "9/11/01=1/27/01: The Changed Posttraumatic Self." In Greenberg 169–83.

Kahn, Michael. *Between Therapist and Client: The New Relationship*. New York: W. H. Freeman, 1991.

Kalfus, Ken. *A Disorder Peculiar to the Country*. New York: HarperCollins, 2006.

Kaplan, Amy. "Homeland Insecurities: Reflections on Language and Space." *Radical History Review* 85 (2003): 82–93.

Kaplan, E. Ann. *Trauma Culture: The Politics of Terror and Loss in Media and Literature*. New Brunswick NJ: Rutgers University Press, 2005.

Kauffman, Linda S. "The Wake of Terror: Don DeLillo's 'In the Ruins of the Future,' 'Baader-Meinhof,' and *Falling Man*." *Modern Fiction Studies* 54.2 (2008): 353–77.

Kaufman-Osborn, Timothy. "Gender Trouble at Abu Ghraib?" *Politics and Gender* 1 (2005): 597–619.

Keniston, Ann, and Jeanne Follansbee Quinn, eds. *Literature after 9/11*. New York: Routledge, 2009.

Kennedy-Pipe, Caroline, and Penny Stanley. "Rape in War: Lessons of the Balkan Conflicts in the 1990s." *The Kosovo Tragedy: The Human Rights Dimensions*. Ed. Ken Booth. London: Cass, 2001. 67–84.

Kernberg, Otto F. "Countertransference, Transference Regression, and the Incapacity to Depend." In Meyers 49–61.

Kirkby, Joan. "Reading Neocon Rhetoric: Walt Whitman and the War on Terror." *Interrogating the War on Terror*. Ed. Deborah Staines. Newcastle, England: Cambridge Scholars Publishing, 2007. 30–48.

Kirn, Walter. *The Unbinding*. New York: Anchor Books, 2006.

Kirshenblatt-Gimblett, Barbara. "Kodak Moments, Flashbulb Memories: Reflections on 9/11." *Drama Review* 47.1 (2003): 11–48.

Klein, Richard. *Cigarettes Are Sublime*. Durham NC: Duke University Press, 1993.

Knightley, Phillip. *The First Casualty: The War Correspondent as Hero and Myth-Maker from the Crimea to Iraq*. Baltimore: Johns Hopkins University Press, 2002.

Kohlke, Marie-Luise. "Sexuality in Extremity: Trauma Literature, Violence and Counter-Erotics." *Sexual Politics of Desire and Belonging*. Ed. Nick Rumens and Alejandro Cervantes-Carson. Amsterdam: Rodopi, 2007. 229–47.

Korte, Barbara. *Represented Reporters: Images of War Correspondents in Memoirs and Fiction*. Bielefeld, Germany: Transcript, 2009.

Kumamoto, Robert. *International Terrorism and American Foreign Relations 1945–1976*. Boston: Northeastern University Press, 1999.

Lacan, Jacques. *The Seminar of Jacques Lacan. Book 7: The Ethics of Psychoanalysis 1959–1960*. Ed. Jacques-Alain Miller. Trans. Dennis Porter. New York: Norton, 1992.

LaCapra, Dominick. *Representing the Holocaust: History, Theory, Trauma.* Ithaca NY: Cornell University Press, 1996.

Lane, Anthony. "This Is Not a Movie." *New Yorker*, September 24, 2001, 79.

Laub, Dori. "Bearing Witness, or the Vicissitudes of Listening." *Testimony: Crises of Witnessing in Literature, Psychoanalysis, and History.* By Shoshana Felman and Dori Laub. New York: Routledge, 1992. 57–74.

Layton, Lynne. "Trauma, Gender Identity and Sexuality: Discourses of Fragmentation." *American Imago* 52.1 (1995): 107–25.

Lentricchia, Frank, and Jody McAuliffe. *Crimes of Art and Terror.* Chicago: University of Chicago Press, 2003.

Leonard, Andrew. "Nodal Point." Interview with William Gibson. *Salon*, February 14, 2003, http://www.salon.com/2003/02/14/gibson_5/.

Levin, Thomas Y. "Rhetoric of the Temporal Index: Surveillant Nation and the Cinema of 'Real Time.'" *Ctrl (Space): Rhetorics of Surveillance from Bentham to Big Brother.* Ed. Thomas Y. Levin, Ursula Frohne, and Peter Weibel. Cambridge MA: MIT Press, 2002. 578–93.

Levinas, Emmanuel. *Basic Philosophical Writings.* Ed. Adriaan T. Peperzak, Simon Critchley, and Robert Bernasconi. Bloomington: Indiana University Press, 1996.

———. *Ethics and Infinity: Conversations with Philippe Nemo.* Trans. Richard A. Cohen. Pittsburgh PA: Duquesne University Press, 1985.

———. "Ethics of the Infinite." *States of Mind: Dialogues with Contemporary Thinkers on the European Mind.* Ed. Richard Kearney. Manchester, England: Manchester University Press, 1995. 177–99.

———. *Totality and Infinity.* Pittsburgh PA: Duquesne University Press, 1969.

Levine, Michael G. "Necessary Stains: Spiegelman's *Maus* and the Bleeding of History." *American Imago* 59.3 (2002): 317–41.

Lifton, Robert Jay. *Death in Life: Survivors of Hiroshima.* New York: Random House, 1967.

———. "An Interview with Robert Jay Lifton." In Caruth 128–47.

Lisle, Debbie. *The Global Politics of Contemporary Travel Writing.* Cambridge, England: Cambridge University Press, 2006.

Lurie, Susan. "Falling Persons and National Embodiment: The Reconstruction of Safe Spectatorship in the Photographic Record of 9/11." *Terror, Culture, Politics.* Ed. Daniel J. Sherman and Terry Nardin. Bloomington: Indiana University Press, 2006. 44–68.

Lyon, David. "The Search for Surveillance Theories." *Theorizing Surveillance: The Panopticon and Beyond*. Ed. David Lyon. Devon, England: Willan, 2006. 3–20.

———. *Surveillance after September 11*. Malden MA: Polity Press, 2003.

———. *Surveillance Studies: An Overview*. Cambridge, England: Polity, 2007.

MacLeod, Lewis. "Matters of Care and Control: Surveillance, Omniscience, and Narrative Power in *The Abbess of Crewe* and *Loitering with Intent*." *Modern Fiction Studies* 54.3 (2008): 574–94.

Majaj, Lisa Suhair. "Arab-Americans and the Meanings of Race." *Postcolonial Theory and the United States: Race, Ethnicity, and Literature*. Ed. Amritjit Singh and Peter Schmidt. Jackson: University Press of Mississippi, 2000. 320–37.

Manovich, Lev. *The Language of New Media*. Cambridge MA: MIT Press, 2001.

Margolis, Joseph. *Moral Philosophy after 9/11*. University Park: Pennsylvania State University Press, 2004.

Marlan, Dawn. "Emblems of Emptiness: Smoking as a Way of Life in Jean Eustache's *La Maman et la Putain*." *Smoke: A Global History of Smoking*. Ed. Sander L. Gilman and Zhou Xun. London: Reaktion, 2004. 256–64.

Marshall, Randall D. Interview with Sharon Kofman. 9/11 Response and Recovery Project. Columbia University Oral History Research Department. March 8, 2005.

Marshall Clark, Mary, et al., eds. *After the Fall: New Yorkers Remember September 2001 and the Years That Followed*. New York: New Press, 2011.

Mathiesen, Thomas. "The Viewer Society." *Theoretical Criminology* 1.2 (1997): 215–34.

McAlpin, Heller. "Falling Man: The Day It All Came Down." *Christian Science Monitor*, May 29, 2007, 13–15.

McCann, Colum. *Let the Great World Spin*. New York: Random House, 2009.

McClintock, Anne. *Imperial Leather: Race, Gender and Sexuality in the Colonial Contest*. New York: Routledge, 1995.

McClure, John A. "Postmodern/Post-Secular: Contemporary Fiction and Spirituality." *Modern Fiction Studies* 41 (1995): 141–63.

McEwan, Ian. *Saturday*. London: Jonathan Cape, 2005.

McGlothlin, Erin. "No Time Like the Present: Narrative and Time in Art Spiegelman's *Maus*." *Narrative* 11.2 (2003): 177–98.

McGrath, John E. *Loving Big Brother: Performance, Privacy and Surveillance Space*. London: Routledge, 2004.

McGrath, Patrick. "A Childhood in Broadmoor Hospital." *Granta* 29 (1989): 157–62.

———. *Ghost Town: Tales of Manhattan Then and Now*. London: Bloomsbury, 2006.

———. *Trauma*. London: Bloomsbury, 2008.

McLaughlin, Greg. *The War Correspondent*. London: Pluto Press, 2002.

Melley, Timothy. "'Stalked by Love': Female Paranoia and the Stalker Novel." *Differences: A Journal of Feminist Cultural Studies* 8.2 (1996): 68–100.

Melnick, Jeffrey Paul. *9/11 Culture: America under Construction*. New York: Wiley, 2009.

Mendelsohn, Eric R. Interviews with Fride Vedde and Ann Cvetkovich. 9/11 Response and Recovery Project. Columbia University Oral History Research Department. November 1, 2001; June 20, 2003.

Mendieta, Eduardo. "The Intimacy of Strangers: The Difficulty of Closeness and the Ethics of Distance." In Sullivan and Schmidt 112–27.

Merleau-Ponty, Maurice. *The Visible and the Invisible*. Ed. Claude Lefort. Trans. Alphonso Lingis. Evanston IL: Northwestern University Press, 1968.

Meštrović, Stjepan G. *The Balkanization of the West: The Confluence of Postmodernism and Postcommunism*. London: Routledge, 1994.

Metres, Philip. "Remaking/Unmaking: Abu Ghraib and Poetry." *PMLA* 123.5 (2008): 1596–610.

Meyers, Helen C., ed. *Between Analyst and Patient: New Dimensions in Countertransference and Transference*. Hillsdale NJ: Analytic Press, 1986.

Miller, J. Hillis. *The Ethics of Reading: Kant, de Man, Eliot, Trollope, James, and Benjamin*. New York: Columbia University Press, 1987.

Miller, Stephen Paul. "'Self-Portrait in a Convex Mirror,' the Watergate Affair, and Johns's Crosshatch Paintings: Surveillance and Reality-Testing in the Mid-Seventies." *Boundary 2* 20.2 (1993): 84–115.

Mitchell, W. J. T. "Response to Griselda Pollock: Ethics, Aesthetics, and Trauma Photographs." *The Life and Death of Images: Ethics and Aesthetics*. Ed. Diarmuid Costello and Dominic Willson. Ithaca NY: Cornell University Press, 2008. 236–40.

———. "Showing Seeing: A Critique of Visual Culture." *Journal of Visual Culture* 1.2 (2002): 165–81.

———. *What Do Pictures Want? The Lives and Loves of Images*. Chicago: University of Chicago Press, 2005.

Moeller, Susan D. *Compassion Fatigue: How the Media Sell Disease, Famine, War and Death*. New York: Routledge, 1999.

Monteith, Sharon, et al. *Critical Perspectives on Pat Barker*. Columbia: University of South Carolina Press, 2005.

Moore, Lorrie. *A Gate at the Stairs*. New York: Knopf, 2009.

Morley, Catherine. "Writing in the Wake of 9/11." In Halliwell and Morley 245–58.

Morris, Peter. *Guardians*. London: Oberon Books, 2005.

Mulvey, Laura. "Some Thoughts on Theories of Fetishism in the Context of Contemporary Culture." *October* 65 (1993): 3–20.

Mutimer, David. "Sovereign Contradictions: Maher Arar and the Indefinite Future." *The Logics of Biopower and the War on Terror: Living, Dying, Surviving*. Ed. Elizabeth Dauphinee and Cristina Masters. Basingstoke, England: Palgrave Macmillan, 2007. 159–79.

Naber, Nadine. "Ambiguous Insiders: An Investigation of Arab American Invisibility." *Ethnic and Racial Studies* 23.1 (2000): 37–61.

———. "'Look, Mohammed the Terrorist Is Coming!' Cultural Racism, Nation-Based Racism, and the Intersectionality of Oppressions after 9/11." *Race and Arab Americans before and after 9/11: From Invisible Citizens to Visible Subjects*. Ed. Amaney Jamal and Nadine Naber. Syracuse NY: Syracuse University Press, 2008. 276–304.

Naqvi, H. M. *Home Boy*. New York: Shaye Areheart Books, 2009.

Nellins, Drew. "An Interview with Chris Adrian." *Bookslut*, August 2008, http://www.bookslut.com/features/2008_08_013241.php.

Nelson, Deborah. "The Virtues of Heartlessness: Mary McCarthy, Hannah Arendt, and the Anesthetics of Empathy." *American Literary History* 18.1 (2006): 86–101.

Newton, Adam Zachary. *Narrative Ethics*. Cambridge MA: Harvard University Press, 1995.

Nicholson, C. Bríd. *Emma Goldman: Still Dangerous*. Montreal: Black Rose Books, 2010.

Nissenson, Hugh. *The Days of Awe*. Naperville IL: Sourcebooks, 2005.

Nussbaum, Martha. *Cultivating Humanity: A Classical Defense of Reform in Liberal Education*. Cambridge MA: Harvard University Press, 1997.

———. "Exactly and Responsibly: A Defense of Ethical Criticism." *Philosophy and Literature* 22.2 (1998): 343–65.

———. *The Fragility of Goodness: Luck and Ethics in Greek Tragedy and Philosophy*. Cambridge, England: Cambridge University Press, 1986.

———. *Love's Knowledge: Essays on Philosophy and Literature*. New York: Oxford University Press, 1990.

Oates, Joyce Carol. "Dimming the Lights." *New York Review of Books*, April 6, 2006, http://www.nybooks.com/articles/18836.

———. *I Am No One You Know*. New York: HarperCollins, 2005.

Obreht, Téa. *The Tiger's Wife*. New York: Random House, 2011.

O'Donnell, Patrick. *The American Novel Now: Reading Contemporary American Fiction since 1980*. Malden MA: Wiley-Blackwell, 2010.

O'Hagan, Andrew. *Be Near Me*. London: Faber and Faber, 2006.

Oliver, Kelly. *Witnessing: Beyond Recognition*. Minneapolis: University of Minnesota Press, 2001.

O'Neill, Joseph. *Netherland*. New York: Pantheon Books, 2008.

Ong, Aihwa. *Flexible Citizenship: The Cultural Logic of Transnationality*. Durham NC: Duke University Press, 1999.

Orbán, Katalin. *Ethical Diversions: The Post-Holocaust Narratives of Pynchon, Abish, DeLillo, and Spiegelman*. New York: Routledge, 2005.

———. "Trauma and Visuality: Art Spiegelman's *Maus* and *In the Shadow of No Towers*." *Representations* 97 (2007): 57–89.

O'Reilly, Nathanael. "Government, Media, and Power: Terrorism in the Australian Novel since 9/11." In Cilano 295–315.

Orwell, George. *Nineteen Eighty-Four: A Novel*. Harmondsworth, England: Penguin, 1974.

Patai, Raphael. *The Arab Mind*. New York: Scribner, 1976.

Pease, Donald. "From Virgin Land to Ground Zero: Interrogating the Mythological Foundations of the Master Fiction of the Homeland Security State." *A Companion to American Literature and Culture*. Ed. Paul Lauter. Malden MA: Wiley-Blackwell, 2010. 637–54.

Perloff, Marjorie. "Watchman, Spy, and Dead Man: Jasper Johns, Frank O'Hara, John Cage and the 'Aesthetic of Indifference.'" *Modernism/Modernity* 8.2 (2001): 197–223.

Peters, Cynthia. "What Does Feminism Have to Say?" *September 11, 2001: Feminist Perspectives*. Ed. Susan Hawthorne and Bronwyn Winter. Melbourne: Spinifex Press, 2002. 120–26.

Plato. *Timaeus*. Trans. Desmond Lee. Harmondsworth, England: Penguin, 1965.

Pledge, Robert, ed. *Eleven: Witnessing the World Trade Center 1974–2001*. New York: Contact Press Images, 2002.

Pollock, Griselda. "Dying, Seeing, Feeling: Transforming the Ethical Space of Feminist Aesthetics." *The Life and Death of Images: Ethics and Aesthetics*. Ed. Diarmuid Costello and Dominic Willson. Ithaca NY: Cornell University Press, 2008. 213–35.

Post, Jerrold. "Notes on a Psychodynamic Theory of Terrorist Behavior." *Terrorism: An International Journal* 7 (1984): 241–56.

Price, Reynolds. *The Good Priest's Son*. New York: Scribner, 2005.

Puar, Jasbir K. *Terrorist Assemblages: Homonationalism in Queer Times*. Durham NC: Duke University Press, 2007.

Puar, Jasbir K., and Amit S. Rai. "Monster, Terrorist, Fag: The War on Terrorism and the Production of Docile Patriots." *Social Text* 20.3 (2002): 117–48.

———. "The Remaking of a Model Minority: Perverse Projectiles under the Specter of (Counter)Terrorism." *Social Text* 22.3 (2004): 75–104.

Raban, Jonathan. *Surveillance*. London: Picador, 2006.

———. "We Have Mutated into a Surveillance Society—and Must Share the Blame." *Guardian*, May 20, 2006.

Rancière, Jacques. *Dis-agreement: Politics and Philosophy*. Minneapolis: University of Minnesota Press, 1999.

Razack, Sherene H. *Casting Out: The Eviction of Muslims from Western Law and Politics*. Toronto: University of Toronto Press, 2008.

———. *Dark Threats and White Knights: The Somalia Affair, Peacekeeping, and the New Imperialism*. Toronto: University of Toronto Press, 2004.

Reich, Annie. "On Counter-Transference." *International Journal of Psycho-Analysis* 32 (1951): 25–31.

Reyn, Irina. "Exile on Any Street: Irinia Reyn and Aleksandar Hemon in Conversation." *Guernica: A Magazine of Art and Politics*, February 2010, http://www.guernicamag.com/interviews/1532/not_melted_into_the_pot.

Reynolds, David S. "Politics and Poetry: *Leaves of Grass* and the Social Crisis of the 1850s." *The Cambridge Companion to Walt Whitman*. Ed. Ezra Greenspan. Cambridge, England: Cambridge University Press, 1995. 66–91.

Rorty, Richard. Introduction to *Pale Fire*, by Vladimir Nabokov. New York: Knopf, 1992. v–xvii.

Rose, Jacqueline. "Entryism." Review of *Specimen Days*, by Michael Cunningham. *London Review of Books* 27.18 (2005): 25–26.

Ross, Sarah C. E. "Regeneration, Redemption, Resurrection: Pat Barker and the Problem of Evil." *The Contemporary British Novel since 1980*. Ed. James Acheson and Sarah C. E. Ross. New York: Palgrave Macmillan, 2005. 131–41.

Rothberg, Michael. "A Failure of the Imagination: Diagnosing the post-9/11 Novel: A Response to Richard Gray." *American Literary History* 21.1 (2009): 152–58.

———. "'There Is No Poetry in This': Writing, Trauma, and Home." In Greenberg 147–57.

———. *Traumatic Realism: The Demands of Holocaust Representation*. Minneapolis: University of Minnesota Press, 2000.

Royle, Nicholas. "Hotel Psychoanalysis: Some Remarks on Mark Twain and Sigmund Freud." *Angelaki* 9.1 (2004): 3–14.

Ruby, Charles L. "Are Terrorists Mentally Deranged?" *Analyses of Social Issues and Public Policy* 2.1 (2002): 15–26.

Salaita, Steven. *Anti-Arab Racism in the USA: Where It Comes from and What It Means for Politics Today*. London: Pluto Press, 2006.

Satner, Eric L. "History beyond the Pleasure Principle: Some Thoughts on the Representation of Trauma." *Probing the Limits of Representation: Nazism and the "Final Solution."* Ed. Saul Friedlander. Cambridge MA: Harvard University Press, 1992. 143–54.

Schudson, Michael. "What's Unusual about Covering Politics as Usual?" *Journalism after September 11*. Ed. Barbie Zelizer and Stuart Allan. New York: Routledge, 2002. 36–47.

Schulman, Helen. *A Day at the Beach*. New York: Houghton Mifflin, 2007.

Schwartz, Lynne Sharon. *The Writing on the Wall*. New York: Counterpoint, 2005.

Seltzer, Mark. "*The Princess Casamassima*: Realism and the Fantasy of Surveillance." *Nineteenth-Century Fiction* 35.4 (1981): 506–34.

Shapiro, Michael J. "Every Move You Make: Bodies, Surveillance, and Media." *Social Text* 23.2 (2005): 21–34.

Shklar, Judith N. *The Faces of Injustice*. New Haven CT: Yale University Press, 1990.

———. "The Liberalism of Fear." *Liberalism and the Moral Life*. Ed. Nancy L. Rosenblum. Cambridge MA: Harvard University Press, 1989. 21–38.

———. *Ordinary Vices*. Cambridge MA: Harvard University Press, 1984.

Silverman, Kaja. *The Threshold of the Visible World*. New York: Routledge, 1996.

Simpson, David. *9/11: The Culture of Commemoration*. Chicago: University of Chicago Press, 2006.

Smith, Wendy. "Of Death and Deadlines." *Publishers Weekly*, December 15, 2003, 48.

Sontag, Susan. *Regarding the Pain of Others*. New York: Farrar, Straus and Giroux, 2003.

———. "Regarding the Torture of Others." *New York Times Magazine*, May 23, 2004, 24–29, 42.

———. [Untitled]. *New Yorker*, September 24, 2001.

Spiegelman, Art. *In the Shadow of No Towers*. New York: Pantheon, 2004.

———. *Maus: A Survivor's Tale.* New York: Pantheon Books, 1986.

———. *Maus II.* New York: Pantheon Books 1991.

Spivak, Gayatri Chakravorty. *Death of a Discipline.* New York: Columbia University Press, 2003.

———. "Ethics and Politics in Tagore, Coetzee, and Certain Scenes of Teaching." *Diacritics* 32.3–4 (2002): 17–31.

Sreberny, Annabelle. "Trauma Talk: Reconfiguring the Inside and Outside." *Journalism after September 11.* Ed. Barbie Zelizer and Stuart Allan. London: Routledge, 2002. 220–34.

Stark, Jared. "Suicide after Auschwitz." *Yale Journal of Criticism* 14.1 (2001): 93–114.

Stow, Simon. "Reading Our Way to Democracy? Literature and Public Ethics." *Philosophy and Literature* 30 (2006): 410–23.

Sturken, Marita. "Memorializing Absence." *Understanding September 11.* Ed. Craig Calhoun, Paul Price, and Ashley Timmer. New York: New Press, 2002. 374–84.

Sullivan, Shannon, and Dennis J. Schmidt, eds. *Difficulties of Ethical Life.* New York: Fordham University Press, 2008.

———. Introduction. In Sullivan and Schmidt 1–8.

Tabachnick, Stephen E. "The Religious Meaning of Art Spiegelman's *Maus.*" *Shofar: An Interdisciplinary Journal of Jewish Studies* 22.4 (2004): 1–13.

Tester, K. *Compassion, Morality and the Media.* Buckingham, England: Open University Press, 2001.

Thaa, Winfried. "'Lean Citizenship': The Fading Away of the Political in Transnational Democracy." *European Journal of International Relations* 7.4 (2001): 503–25.

Thomas, Glen. "History, Biography, and Narrative in Don DeLillo's *Libra.*" *Twentieth Century Literature* 43.1 (1997): 106–24.

Trilling, Lionel. "Manners, Morals, and the Novel." *Kenyon Review* 10 (1948): 11–27.

Tristram, Claire. *After.* New York: Farrar, Straus and Giroux, 2004.

Updike, John. *Terrorist.* New York: Knopf, 2006.

van Alphen, Ernst. "Caught by Images: Visual Imprints in Holocaust Testimonies." *Image and Remembrance: Representation and the Holocaust.* Ed. Shelley Hornstein and Florence Jacobowitz. Bloomington: Indiana University Press, 2003. 97–113.

Versluys, Kristiaan. "Art Spiegelman's *In the Shadow of No Towers*: 9/11 and the Representation of Trauma." *Modern Fiction Studies* 52.4 (2006): 980–1003.

———. *Out of the Blue: September 11 and the Novel*. New York: Columbia University Press, 2009.

Virilio, Paul. *Open Sky*. Trans. Julie Rose. London: Verso, 2008.

———. "The Overexposed City." *Zone* 1/2 (1986): 14–39.

———. *Strategy of Deception*. Trans. Chris Turner. London: Verso, 2000.

———. *The Vision Machine*. Bloomington: Indiana University Press, 1994.

———. "The Visual Crash." *Ctrl (Space): Rhetorics of Surveillance from Bentham to Big Brother*. Ed. Thomas Y. Levin, Ursula Frohne, and Peter Weibel. Cambridge MA: MIT Press, 2002. 108–13.

Walter, Jess. *The Zero*. New York: ReganBooks, 2006.

Walzer, Michael. *Arguing about War*. New Haven CT: Yale University Press, 2004.

Weber, Cynthia. "Fahrenheit 9/11: The Temperature Where Morality Burns." *Journal of American Studies* 40.1 (2006): 113–31.

———. *Imagining America at War: Morality, Politics and Film*. New York: Routledge, 2006.

Wegner, Phillip E. *Life between Two Deaths, 1989–2001: U.S. Culture in the Long Nineties*. Durham NC: Duke University Press, 2009.

———. "Recognizing the Patterns." *New Literary History* 38 (2007): 183–200.

Welch, Michael. *Scapegoats of September 11: Hate Crimes and State Crimes in the War on Terror*. New Brunswick NJ: Rutgers University Press, 2006.

Weschler, Lawrence. *Shapinski's Karma, Bogg's Bills, and Other True-Life Tales*. San Francisco: Northpoint Press, 1988.

Whitman, Walt. *Prose Works 1892*. Ed. Floyd Stovall. New York: New York University Press, 1961.

———. "Starting from Paumanok." *The Complete Poems*. Ed. Francis Murphy. London: Penguin, 1986. 50–62.

Wigren, Jodie. "Narrative Completion in the Treatment of Trauma." *Psychotherapy* 31.3 (1994): 415–23.

Wihl, Gary S. "Liberalism and the Articulation of Cruelty: An Essay on Judith Shklar and D. M. Thomas." *Texas Studies in Literature and Language* 43.4 (2001): 465–88.

Williams, Bernard. *Ethics and the Limits of Philosophy*. London: Fontana, 1985.

Williams, Raymond. "From Medium to Social Practice." *Marxism and Literature*. New York: Oxford University Press, 1977. 158–64.

Wood, James. "Black Noise." *New Republic*, July 2, 2007, 47–50.

Yack, Bernard. "Liberalism without Illusions: An Introduction to Judith Shklar's

Political Thought." *Liberalism without Illusions: Essays on Liberal Theory and the Political Vision of Judith Shklar*. Ed. Bernard Yack. Chicago: University of Chicago Press, 1996. 1–13.

Yaeger, Patricia. "Consuming Trauma; or, The Pleasures of Merely Circulating." *Extremities: Trauma, Testimony, and Community*. Ed. Nancy K. Miller and Jason Tougaw. Urbana: University of Illinois Press, 2002. 25–51.

Young, James. "The Holocaust as Vicarious Past: Art Spiegelman's *Maus* and the Afterimages of History." *Critical Inquiry* 24 (1998): 666–99.

Zelizer, Barbie. *About to Die: How News Images Move the Public*. Oxford: Oxford University Press, 2010.

———. "Photography, Journalism, and Trauma." *Journalism after September 11*. Ed. Barbie Zelizer and Stuart Allan. New York: Routledge, 2002. 48–68.

———. "The Voice of the Visual in Memory." *Framing Public Memory*. Ed. Kendall Phillips. Tuscaloosa: University of Alabama Press, 2004. 157–86.

Zine, Jasmin. "Between Orientalism and Fundamentalism: Muslim Women and Feminist Engagement." In Hunt and Rygiel 27–49.

Žižek, Slavoj. *The Metastases of Enjoyment: Six Essays on Women and Causality*. London: Verso, 2005.

———. *The Sublime Object of Ideology*. London: Verso, 1989.

———. *Violence: Six Sideways Reflections*. London: Profile Books, 2008.

———. "Welcome to the Desert of the Real!" In Hauerwas and Lentricchia 131–35.

INDEX

Abel, Marco, 64
Abraham, Nicolas, 105
Abu Ghraib scandal, 15, 16, 30, 52, 133, 134–35, 145–46, 270, 308n12; *After* compared to, 151–52, 158, 159; compared to Balkan War atrocities, 216, 218–19; compared to lynchings, 171
abuse, 137–41
Adams, Lorraine, 25, 31, 257, 288, 295, 299–300; *Harbor*, 15, 55, 252, 270, 281–88; *The Room and the Chair*, 15
Adrian, Chris, 55; *A Better Angel*, 292; "The Changeling," 294; "The Vision of Peter Damien," 292–95; "Why Antichrist?" 294–95
"Aesthetics" (Hale), 25, 26, 45
Afghanistan, 24, 30, 31, 56, 282
African Americans, lynchings of, 171
After (Tristram), 15, 52, 62, 110, 132–35, 139, 141–64, 187, 296; compared to Abu Ghraib scandal, 151–52, 158, 159; and Otherness, 163–64; plot of, 141–50; power politics and, 158–64; sexuality in, 152–53, 156–58; themes of, 155
After the End of History (Cohen), 3
After the Fall (Gray), 2
Agamben, Giorgio, 271

Alcorn, Marshall: *Narcissism and the Literary Libido*, 161–62
Alexie, Sherman: *Flight*, 310n1
Ali, Kazim: *The Disappearance of Seth*, 206
"Allegories of Falling" (Anker), 111
allegory, 110–32
Al Qaeda, 90, 282
ambiguity, 204, 226, 259, 289, 297, 300; in Bosnian War, 237; ending of *After* and, 146; and evil, 220; and the falling man, 72; imbalance of power and, 152–52; of insignificant happenings, 66; in literature, 2; moral vision of, 19; as organizing principle, 50; and politics, 28; as seduction and solace, 67; and sexual explicitness, 154
Ambuhl, Megan, 137
The American Novel Now (O'Donnell), 48
Amoore, Louise, 183
anarchists, 209–15
Anker, Elisabeth, 92
Anker, Elizabeth: "Allegories of Falling," 111
Another World (Barker), 231
Antor, Heinz, 129
Applied Rationalism (Bachelard), 267

INDEX

Apter, Emily: "On Oneworldedness," 46
Arab Americans, backlash against, 169–83
Arab culture, 138
The Arab Mind (Patai), 138
Archeologies of the Future (Jameson), 272, 275, 276
Arondekar, Anjali, 150
Ashcroft, John, 119–20
Atta, Mohammed, 50
Auster, Paul: *Sunset Park*, 11
An Autobiographical Study (Freud), 116
Avrich, Paul, 213
Axis of Evil, 213

Bachelard, Gaston: *Applied Rationalism*, 267
Badiou, Alain, 210; *Ethics*, 215, 216–17, 224–25; *Handbook of Inaesthetics*, 225
Bal, Mieke, 38–39
Balkan civil war, 19, 47, 207–10, 218–19
Ballard, J. G.: *Millennium People*, 6
Banerjee, Mita, 184
Barker, Pat, 25, 44, 294, 299, 314n13, 315n14; *Another World*, 231; *Double Vision*, 24, 27, 54, 161, 207, 229–49, 252, 258–61, 290; *Life Class*, 231, 232
Barthes, Roland: "Shock-Photos," 59
Baudrillard, Jean, 15, 44–45, 278; "L'Esprit du Terrorisme," 45
Bauman, Zygmunt, 51
Beck, Ulrich, 167, 198
Beigbeder, Frédéric, 49
Bell, Martin, 236–37
Bengley, Adam, 84
Bennett, Jill, 45
Bentham, Jeremy, 255
Bergoffen, Debra, 33–34

Bergstrom, Lucy, 270
Bersani, Leo, 52, 140, 159–60, 162–63
A Better Angel (Adrian), 292
Bin Laden, Osama, 16, 84, 174, 278
Blair, Tony, 107
Blazan, Sladja, 208, 222
Booth, Ken: "Worlds in Collision," 289
Booth, Wayne, 34
Borradori, Giovanna, 50
Bosnian War, 13, 44, 53–54, 206–07, 229, 238–40, 299
Boulanger, Ghislaine, 113, 114
Boy 381 (Vanags), 270
Braidotti, Rosi, 29
Brandeis, Gayle, 24, 31; *Self Storage*, 53, 166, 167, 185–97, 199–200; and Walt Whitman, 186, 190–95
Brannigan, John: "An Interview," 232, 243; *Pat Barker*, 232
Brin, David, 252
Brontë, Charlotte, 252
Brooks, David, 197
Brooks, Peter, 52
Burke, Anthony, 31
Bush, George W., 7, 16, 172, 177, 192, 208, 211, 218, 286; Axis of Evil and, 213; critique of, 30, 289; on decision points, 297; on overcoming evil, 216; social decay and, 87
Bush Doctrine, 32
Butler, Judith, 21, 25, 27, 73, 138, 146, 299; *Precarious Life*, 248; "Values of Difficulty," 26

Cantor Fitzgerald, 289
Carey, James W., 98
Caruth, Cathy, 110; *Unclaimed Experience*, 4, 81

Casting Out (Razack), 216
Cavani, Liliana: *The Night Porter*, 27, 148–49
"The Changeling" (Adrian), 294
Chemtob, Claude, 118–19
"A Childhood" (McGrath), 112
"The Children's Crusade" (Cunningham), 196–201
Chow, Rey, 56; "Toward an Ethics of Postvisuality," 38–39
Chute, Hillary, 77–78; "The Shadow," 77
Cilano, Cara, 2
civil liberties, 120
Clinton, Bill, 297
closure, 130
Cohen, Samuel S.: *After the End of History*, 3
cold war era, 3, 16, 47, 210, 217
Columbia University, 117–18
"The Conductor" (Hemon), 207–08
confinement, 8
conscience, internationalization of, 241
Cooksey, John, 180
countertransference, 116, 130
cruelty, 1, 25, 47, 53, 133–40, 145–64, 218, 238–39, 240, 242, 248, 292, 295, 309n12, 310n17
Cultivating Humanity (Nussbaum), 20
Cunningham, Michael, 12, 31, 293; "The Children's Crusade," 196–201; *Specimen Days*, 53, 166–67, 185, 186, 195–203; Walt Whitman and, 196–97, 201

data mining, 28–29
A Day at the Beach (Schulman), 51, 61, 92–108, 251
The Days of Awe (Nissenson), 7, 92–93
Dean, Tim, 163
death, 225–26, 278–81
Death of a Discipline (Spivak), 26, 43
De Goede, Marieke, 183
Deleuze, Gilles, 255
DeLillo, Don, 3, 12, 24, 99, 107–08, 112, 231, 251, 300; *Falling Man*, 5, 14, 49, 51, 61–74, 93, 109, 152, 251; "In the Ruins of the Future," 64; *Mao II*, 69; *Point Omega*, 14; *White Noise*, 268
De Man, Paul, 111
Derian, James Der, 31
Derrida, Jacques, 50
Dickens, Charles, 23
Dimock, Wai Chee, 50; "Literature for the Planet," 43; "Whitman, Syntax," 194, 201, 202, 203
The Disappearance of Seth (Ali), 206
disciplinary aesthetics, 252
A Disorder Peculiar to the Country (Kalfus), 53, 92–93, 109, 166, 171–73
Dissent from the Homeland (Hauerwas and Lentricchia), 44
Divakaruni, Chitra, 171, 182, 185; *Queen of Dreams*, 53, 166, 173–76, 203–04
Double Vision (Barker), 24, 27, 54, 161, 207, 229–36, 252, 290; catalepsis after 9/11 and, 241–49; ethics of representation in, 231–36; pain of others in, 236–41; plot of, 229–31; surveillance in, 258–61
Douglas, Mary, 183, 203
dreams, 113–14
Drew, Richard, 26, 59–61, 293, 303n4; Art Spiegelman and, 83–85; Don DeLillo and, 71, 73
Dunne, Tim: "Worlds in Collision," 289

Eaglestone, Robert: "Flaws," 226
Eagleton, Terry: *Holy Terror*, 219; *On Evil*, 219–20, 222, 226; *Trouble with Strangers*, 218
The Ego and the Id (Freud), 156
Eisenhower, Dwight D., 282
Eliot, George, 23
Ellis, John, 52; *Seeing Things*, 94, 97, 100; *Visible Fictions*, 99
Elshtain, Jean Bethke, 31
empathy, 191–92, 195
England, Lynndie, 137, 138, 140, 151, 159, 172
Ensler, Eve: *The Treatment*, 140–41
Ethical Diversions (Orbán), 78
ethics: abuse of goodness and, 216–17; and causality and immanence, 17–21; evil and, 224–25; and justice and security, 29–34; literary, 4, 5–12; narrative, 18–19, 201–03; new theory of, 21–23, 296–99; Otherness provocation and, 21–29; of representation, 231–36; of risk, 183–85; scapegoating and, 132; spectatorship and, 34–42, 64–66; surveillance and, 254–58, 271–77; transnational, 43–50, 221–27, 299
Ethics (Badiou), 215, 216–17, 224–25
Ethics and Infinity (Levinas), 39
"Ethics and Politics" (Spivak), 28
The Ethics of Psychoanalysis (Lacan), 121
The Ethics of Reading (Miller), 20, 28
"Ethics of the Infinite" (Levinas), 257
Ettinger, Bracha, 71
evil, 24–25, 31, 132; and abuse of goodness, 215–21; obsession with, 313n6; recognition of, 115–24; and War on Terror, 217–21, 227; and world-changing events, 217
Ewald, François: "Insurance and Risk," 183; "The Return of Descartes's Malicious Demon," 263
Extremely Loud and Incredibly Close (Foer), 41, 62–63

The Faces of Injustice (Shklar), 156
Fahrenheit 9/11 (Moore), 30
"A Failure of the Imagination" (Rothberg), 167–68
Falling Man (DeLillo), 5, 14, 49, 51, 61–74, 93, 109, 152, 251; conclusion of, 63; and the eternal in art, 66–70; performance art and, 70–74; spectatorship and, 64–66; visual attention in, 61–64
Federal Bureau of Investigation (FBI), 282–87
Felman, Shoshana, 52, 154–55, 230; "Turning the Screw," 154
feminism, 188–89
"Fiction as Restriction" (Hale), 21–26
Filkins, Dexter: *The Forever War*, 290–91
Flanagan, Richard, 6, 25, 257, 283, 288, 295; *The Unknown Terrorist*, 55, 252, 275, 278–81
"Flaws" (Eaglestone), 226
Flight (Alexie), 310n1
Foer, Jonathan Safran, 49, 73, 79; *Extremely Loud and Incredibly Close*, 41, 62–63
The Forever War (Filkins), 290–91
Forgetfulness (Just), 8–10
Forter, Greg, 131
Foucault, Michel, 255, 271
Fox, Robert, 244
The Fragility of Goodness (Nussbaum), 202–03

INDEX

Franzen, Jonathan: *Freedom*, 10–11, 300
Freedom (Franzen), 10–11, 300
Freud, Sigmund, 78–79, 115, 121, 154, 161; *An Autobiographical Study*, 116; *The Ego and the Id*, 156
Friend, David, 59, 83
"From Medium to Social Practice" (Williams), 96
Frosh, Paul, 52, 95, 104
Frost, Laura, 62–63, 138–39; "Photography/Pornography/Torture," 139, 152; "Still Life," 63, 73
Furedi, Frank, 184–85

A Gate at the Stairs (Moore), 168
Geneva Conventions, 137
Ghosh, Amitav: *Incendiary Circumstances*, 289–90
Ghost Town (McGrath), 52, 111, 118
Gibson, William, 14, 25, 257, 283, 287; *Pattern Recognition*, 55, 251, 252, 272–77
Giles, Paul, 47, 48, 50
Girard, René, 52; *The Scapegoat*, 125, 128
globalization, 45, 48; of conscience, 248–49; journalism of attachment and, 236–37; surveillance and, 47–48, 257–58, 271–77; war and, 206–07
Goldberg, Elizabeth Swanson, 232, 258
The Golden Bowl (James), 226
Goldman, Emma, 209
The Good Life (McInerney), 92–93, 108, 109, 152
The Good Priest's Son (Price), 7–8
Google, 268
Goya, Francisco de, 229, 234–35, 237, 249, 314n13
Gray, Louise, 138

Gray, Richard, 110, 112, 131, 165–66, 167, 187; *After the Fall*, 2; "Open Doors, Closed Minds," 109
Green, James, 213
Greenberg, Karen, 137, 141
Greenwald Smith, Rachel, 109–10
Gronnvoll, Marita, 151
The Grotesque (McGrath), 129
"Ground Zero" (McGrath), 110, 141, 220, 296, 298; cruelty in, 159–61; evil in, 115–24; narrative unreliability in, 127–32; scapegoating in, 111–32
Guardians (Morris), 140
Guillory, John, 55, 297

Halaby, Laila, 24, 31, 33, 171, 182, 185, 295; *Once in a Promised Land*, 53, 166, 176–81, 204, 205
Hale, Dorothy J., 4, 50, 73, 104, 146, 162, 295; "Aesthetics," 25, 26, 45; "Fiction as Restriction," 21–26
Halliwell, Martin, 44
Hamid, Mohsin, 53; *The Reluctant Fundamentalist*, 53, 167, 182–83, 199, 205
Hammad, Suheir, 46
Handbook of Inaesthetics (Badiou), 225
Harbor (Adams), 15, 55, 252, 270, 281–88
Harman, Sabrina, 137, 151
Harpham, Geoffrey, 17, 37–38
Hartman, Geoffrey, 76
hate crimes, 174–75
Hauerwas, Stanley: *Dissent from the Homeland*, 44
Hemon, Aleksandar, 6, 25, 44, 209–15, 221–27, 231, 299; "The Conductor," 207–08; *The Lazarus Project*, 22, 53–54, 207–27; *Love and Obstacles*, 207–08; *Nowhere Man*, 221, 223

349

Hersh, Seymour, 137–38
Hirsch, Joshua, 94
Hirsch, Marianne, 75; "I Took Pictures," 71
Holocaust, 19, 47, 81, 92, 101, 133, 270; Art Spiegelman and, 75–76, 79, 81–83; narrative fetishism and, 79–80
Holy Terror (Eagleton), 219
Home Boy (Naqvi), 205
Homeland Security policies, 30
Hong, Terry, 173
Howe, Peter, 228, 242
Huehls, Mitchum, 84
Huffer, Lynne, 24
Hungerford, Amy, 15, 16; "On the Period Formerly Known as Contemporary," 12–13
Hunt, Krista, 188
Huntington, Samuel, 29
Hussein, Saddam, 213

I Am No One You Know (Oates), 114
Ignatieff, Michael, 230, 241
Imagining America at War (Weber), 30
The Immensity of the Here and Now (West), 79
imperativity, factor of, 17
Incendiary Circumstances (Ghosh), 289–90
innocence, 33
"Insurance and Risk" (Ewald), 183
Internet, 268–69
"An Interview" (Brannigan), 232, 243
"An Interview" (Lifton), 105
"In the Ruins of the Future" (DeLillo), 64
In the Shadow of No Towers (Spiegelman), 51, 61, 75–92, 251

Iraq, 8, 24, 28, 30, 56, 86, 301n5
"I Took Pictures" (Hirsch), 71

James, Henry, 37, 62; *The Golden Bowl*, 226; *The Turn of the Screw*, 154; *Washington Square*, 27
Jameson, Fredric: *Archeologies of the Future*, 272, 275, 276; *The Political Unconscious*, 29, 297–98
jihad, 205
journalism of attachment, 236–38
Junod, Tom: "The Man Who Invented 9/11," 73
Just, Ward: *Forgetfulness*, 8–10

Kacandes, Irene, 101–02
Kalfus, Ken: *A Disorder Peculiar to the Country*, 53, 92–93, 109, 166, 171–73
Kaplan, Amy, 44, 57
Kaplan, E. Ann, 94
Kauffman, Linda S., 62
Kaufman-Osborn, Timothy, 151
Keniston, Ann, 2
Kennedy, John F., 282
Kennedy-Pipe, Caroline, 239
Kernberg, Otto F., 116
Kirn, Walter, 25, 257, 267, 274, 283, 287; *The Unbinding*, 55, 252, 262–66, 288
Korte, Barbara, 241

Lacan, Jacques, 19, 52, 132, 161; *The Ethics of Psychoanalysis*, 121
Lane, Anthony, 60
Laub, Dori, 117–18
The Lazarus Project (Hemon), 22, 53–54, 207–27
Lentricchia, Frank: *Dissent from the Homeland*, 44

INDEX

"L'Esprit du Terrorisme" (Baudrillard), 45
Let the Great World Spin (McCann), 14
Levinas, Emmanuel, 35, 38–40; *Ethics and Infinity*, 39; "Ethics of the Infinite," 257; *Totality and Infinity*, 39
Levine, Michael, 88–89
"The Liberalism of Fear" (Shklar), 136
Life between Two Deaths, 1989–2001 (Wegner), 3
Life Class (Barker), 231, 232
Lifton, Robert: "An Interview," 105
Lisle, Debbie, 223–24
"Literature for the Planet" (Dimock), 43
Locke, John, 136
"Look, Mohammed" (Naber), 182
love, 24, 245–48
Love and Obstacles (Hemon), 207–08
Love's Knowledge (Nussbaum), 18, 19, 23, 43, 54, 231, 243, 244–48
Lurie, Susan, 61
Lyon, David, 257; "The Search for Surveillance Theories," 280; *Surveillance after September 11*, 255; *Surveillance Studies*, 256

MacLeod, Lewis, 254
Majaj, Lisa Suhair, 169
"The Man Who Invented 9/11" (Junod), 73
Mao II (DeLillo), 69
Margolis, Joseph: *Moral Philosophy after 9/11*, 29
Marshall, Randall D., 116–17
Maus (Spiegelman), 51, 75–76, 77, 78, 80, 82, 85, 87–88, 92
McCann, Colum: *Let the Great World Spin*, 14

McClure, John, 62
McEwan, Ian: *Saturday*, 94
McGlothlin, Erin, 82
McGrath, Patrick, 6, 12, 24, 33, 207, 295; "A Childhood," 112; *Ghost Town*, 52, 111, 118; *The Grotesque*, 129; "Ground Zero," 110, 111–32, 141, 159–61, 220, 296, 298
McInerney, Jay: *The Good Life*, 92–93, 108, 109, 152
McLaughlin, Greg, 228, 233, 238, 244
Melley, Timothy, 259
Melnick, Jeffrey Paul, 43
Mendelsohn, Eric R., 117
Mendieta, Eduardo, 37
Merleau-Ponty, Maurice, 35
The Metastases of Enjoyment (Žižek), 139
Metres, Philip, 137
Millennium People (Ballard), 6
Miller, D. A.: *The Novel and the Police*, 253
Miller, J. Hillis, 18, 20–21, 25, 34; *The Ethics of Reading*, 20, 28
Mitchell, W. J. T.: *What Do Pictures Want?* 299
modernism, long, 15–16
"Monster, Terrorist, Fag" (Puar and Rai), 171, 180, 187, 188
Moore, Lorrie, 169; *A Gate at the Stairs*, 168
Moore, Michael: *Fahrenheit 9/11*, 30
morality, 6–7, 19–20, 31, 140–41
moral liberalism, 135–36
moral panic, 183–86
Moral Philosophy after 9/11 (Margolis), 29
moral racialization, 169–83
Morandi, Giorgio, 67–70, 99

Morley, Catherine, 44, 48–49
Morris, Christopher, 228, 242
Morris, Peter: *Guardians*, 140
multiculturalism, 13
Mulvey, Laura, 79
"The Mutants" (Oates), 114
Mutimer, David, 169

Naber, Nadine, 169; "Look, Mohammed," 182
Nachtwey, James, 228–29
Naqvi, H. M., 205–06; *Home Boy*, 205
Narcissism and the Literary Libido (Alcorn), 161–62
narrative fetishism, 79
narrative unreliability, 127–32, 263–65
Nellins, Drew, 293
Nelson, Deborah, 72
Netherland (O'Neill), 167–68
Newton, Adam Zachary, 17
New Yorker, 137
New York Times, 38, 59
Nicholson, C. Bríd, 214
The Night Porter (Cavani), 27, 148–49
Nineteen Eighty-Four (Orwell), 252–53, 262
Nissenson, Hugh: *The Days of Awe*, 7, 92–93
The Novel and the Police (Miller), 253
Nowhere Man (Hemon), 221, 223
Nussbaum, Martha, 17–20, 21, 23–24, 27, 28, 37, 244–48; *Cultivating Humanity*, 20; *The Fragility of Goodness*, 202–03; *Love's Knowledge*, 18, 19, 23, 43, 54, 231, 243, 244–48

Oates, Joyce Carol, 108; *I Am No One You Know*, 114; "The Mutants," 114

O'Donnell, Patrick: *The American Novel Now*, 48
Once in a Promised Land (Halaby), 53, 166, 176–81, 204, 205
O'Neill, Joseph: *Netherland*, 167–68
On Evil (Eagleton), 219–20, 222, 226
"On Oneworldedness" (Apter), 46
"On the Period Formerly Known as Contemporary" (Hungerford), 12–13
"Open Doors, Closed Minds" (Gray), 109
Open Sky (Virilio), 256
Operation Enduring Freedom, 16
Operation Iraqi Freedom, 16
Operation Phantom Fury, 16
oral history, 117–18
Orbán, Katalin: *Ethical Diversions*, 78
Ordinary Vices (Shklar), 135–36, 157
O'Reilly, Nathanael, 278
Orwell, George, 287; *Nineteen Eighty-Four*, 252–53, 262
Otherness, 12, 21–26, 30, 56; Bosnian Americans and, 208; cruelty and, 160, 161; empathy and, 195, 296; incomprehensibility of, 226–27; minority groups and, 48–49; mutilation and, 295; performance art and, 72; as property of discourse, 163–64; risk society and, 185–86; sameness and, 224; scapegoating and, 124; surveillance and, 257; vision and, 35, 37–38, 42
Out of the Blue (Versluys), 2, 49
"The Overexposed City" (Virilio), 268

pain, 8, 236–41
paranoia, 191
Patai, Raphael: *The Arab Mind*, 138

Pat Barker (Brannigan), 232
Patriot Act, 30, 87, 119–20, 257
patriotism, 86–87, 166, 290
Pattern Recognition (Gibson), 55, 251, 252, 272–77
Pearl, Daniel, 142, 145
Pease, Donald, 16, 44
performance art, 70–74, 304n7, 304n9
Persian Gulf War (1990–91), 206
personality defect theory, 312n13
Peters, Cynthia, 188
Petit, Philippe, 14
Phillips, Adam, 159, 162
photography, 303n2, 314n12; journalism of attachment and, 236–38; pain of others and, 236–41; of people falling from WTC, 26, 59–61, 71, 73, 83–85, 293, 303n4; war, 228–29
"Photography/Pornography/Torture" (Frost), 139, 152
The Pianist (Szpilman), 270
Piercy, Marge, 187
Pinchevski, Amit, 95
Plato: *Timaeus*, 35
Point Omega (DeLillo), 14
political reading process, 27–28, 297–98
The Political Unconscious (Jameson), 29, 297–98
Posner, Richard, 19
post-9/11 fiction, 1; American myopia in, 302n14; backdrop of, 30; contemporary culture and, 12–17; data mining and, 28–29; death by media in, 278–81; empathetic code of conduct and, 295–96; encounters with strangeness and, 165–66; ethical spectatorship and, 34–42; heterogeneity of, 1–2; historical context of, 3; justice and security in, 29–34; literary ethics and, 4, 5–12; moral topology of, 5–12; Otherness in, 12, 21–26; scholarship on, 14–17; sectarianism and, 13–14; surveillance and, 252–55; transnational ethics and, 43–50
posttraumatic stress disorder (PTSD), 112, 307n2
power politics, 158–64
Pratt, Mary Louise, 223
Precarious Life (Butler), 248
Price, Reynolds: *The Good Priest's Son*, 7–8
"Prisoner on the Hell Planet" (Spiegelman), 80
privacy, personal, 267–71
Prose Works (Whitman), 192, 193
psychoanalysis, 97, 127–32
psychotherapy, 112–24, 307n2
Puar, Jasbir, 151; "Monster, Terrorist, Fag," 171, 180, 187, 188; "The Remaking," 173–74; *Terrorist Assemblages*, 150

Queen of Dreams (Divakaruni), 53, 166, 173–76, 203–04
Quinn, Jeanne Follansbee, 2

Raban, Jonathan, 25, 257, 283, 287; *Surveillance*, 55, 252, 267–71; "We Have Mutated," 269
racial formation, 156–58, 166–69
racial profiling, 173–74, 176–81, 195, 198–99, 203–04, 310n1
Rai, Amit S.: "Monster, Terrorist, Fag," 171, 180, 187, 188; "The Remaking," 173–74
Rancière, Jacques, 46

rape, 238–40

Razack, Sherene: *Casting Out*, 216

Reagan, Ronald, 47

"Recognizing the Patterns" (Wegner), 273

Regarding the Pain of Others (Sontag), 60, 71

"Regarding the Torture of Others" (Sontag), 138

Reich, Annie, 116

The Reluctant Fundamentalist (Hamid), 53, 167, 182–83, 199, 205

"The Remaking" (Puar and Rai), 173–74

"The Return of Descartes's Malicious Demon" (Ewald), 263

Reynolds, David S., 193

risk, 166–67, 183–86

The Room and the Chair (Adams), 15

Rorty, Richard, 27, 28

Rose, Jacqueline, 197

Ross, Sarah, 248

Rothberg, Michael: "A Failure of the Imagination," 167–68; "There Is No Poetry in This," 46

Rousseau, Jean-Jacques, 136

Royle, Nicolas, 149

Rumsfeld, Donald, 138

Salaita, Steven, 169–70, 178–79, 186

sameness, 224

Satner, Eric, 52, 79

Saturday (McEwan), 94

The Scapegoat (Girard), 125, 128

scapegoating, 111–15, 124–64, 183–86, 298

Schmidt, Dennis J., 43

Schulman, Helen, 12, 24, 77, 95–109, 112, 148, 231, 293, 294, 296; *A Day at the Beach*, 51, 61, 92–108, 251

Schulz, Bruno, 221

Schwartz, Lynne Sharon, 289; *The Writing on the Wall*, 7, 94, 283–84

"The Search for Surveillance Theories" (Lyon), 280

sectarianism, 13–14

Seeing Things (Ellis), 94, 97, 100

self-awareness, 25–27

self-harm, 75, 78, 80–82, 85–86

Self Storage (Brandeis), 53, 166, 167, 185–97, 199–200

Seltzer, Mark, 253

September 11, 2001, 16, 299–300; American invincibility and, 33–34; American response to, 3, 8–9, 10, 165; backlash against Arab Americans after, 169–83; Balkanization of, 207–10; catalepsis after, 241–49; categorization of, 16–17; and cold war, 4; as continuation of conflicts, 47–48; and falling man photograph, 59–61; FBI after, 282–87; foreign relations after, 267–71; globalization and, 45; hate crimes after, 174–75; as national trauma, 45; pager messages sent on, 289; paranoia after, 191; Patriot Act and, 30, 87, 119–20, 257; personal privacy after, 267–71; racial formation after, 166–68; racial profiling after, 173–74, 176–81; surveillance after, 256; television and, 93–99; visualizations of Twin Towers and, 66–70

September 11 Response and Recovery Project, 113–14

sex/sexuality, 27; ambiguity of, 154–55; in Arab culture, 138; cruel, 152–54;

death and, 152–53; journalism of attachment and, 238–39; moral racialization and, 172; power politics and, 158–64; racial formation and, 156–58; torture and, 138–39, 141–58
"The Shadow" (Chute), 77
Shapiro, Michael, 258
Shklar, Judith, 52, 134, 155, 238; *The Faces of Injustice*, 156; "The Liberalism of Fear," 136; *Ordinary Vices*, 135–36, 157
"Shock-Photos" (Barthes), 59
Silverman, Kaja: *The Threshold of the Visible World*, 35–36
Simpson, David, 107
Singh, Sher, 174
Smith, Wendy, 232
smoke and smoking, 87–92
social decay, 86–87
"Song of Myself" (Whitman), 190, 192, 194
Sontag, Susan, 44, 52, 94, 139; *Regarding the Pain of Others*, 60, 71; "Regarding the Torture of Others," 138
Southeast Asian Americans, 173–74
Spark, Muriel, 252
Specimen Days (Cunningham), 53, 166–67, 185, 186, 195–203
spectatorship, 34–42, 64–66, 251–55
Spiegelman, Anja, 75, 80–83, 85–86
Spiegelman, Art, 12, 14, 24, 49, 61, 107–08, 109, 112, 251, 293; *In the Shadow of No Towers*, 51, 61, 75–92, 251; *Maus*, 51, 75–76, 77, 78, 80, 82, 85, 87–88, 92; "Prisoner on the Hell Planet," 80
Spiegelman, Vladek, 75, 81–83, 86
Spivak, Gayatri Chakravorty, 21, 26, 187, 299; *Death of a Discipline*, 26, 43; "Ethics and Politics," 28

Sreberny, Annabelle, 102
Stanley, Penny, 239
Stein, Gertrude, 168
Sterne, Laurence: *Tristram Shandy*, 225
"Still Life" (Frost), 63, 73
Strategy of Deception (Virilio), 256
The Sublime Object (Žižek), 163
suicide, 75, 78, 80–82, 85–86
Sullivan, Shannon, 43
Sunset Park (Auster), 11
surveillance, 287–88, 316n2; death by media and, 278–81; ethics and, 255–58; globalization and, 47–48, 257–58, 271–77; intelligence agencies and, 281–87; novels and, 252–55; peer-to-peer, 268–69, 318n21; plotting of, 262–66; trauma and, 258–61
Surveillance (Raban), 55, 252, 267–71
Surveillance after September 11 (Lyon), 255
Surveillance Studies (Lyon), 256
Szpilman, Wladyslaw: *The Pianist*, 270

Tabachnick, Stephen E., 80
television, 93–99, 106
Terrorist (Updike), 49
Terrorist Assemblages (Puar), 150
therapy, 112–24, 127–32, 143, 307n2
"There Is No Poetry in This" (Rothberg), 46
Thomas, D. M.: *The White Hotel*, 133, 149
Thomson, Alex, 228
The Threshold of the Visible World (Silverman), 35–36
Timaeus (Plato), 35
tolerance, 27
Torok, Maria, 105

torture, 137–58, 308n12
Totality and Infinity (Levinas), 39
"Toward an Ethics of Postvisuality" (Chow), 38–39
transference, 115–24
trauma: allegory of, 130–31; and evil, 115–24; and identity change, 100–108, 304n8; narrative unreliability and, 127–32; national, 45; neon effect of, 119; surveillance and, 258–61; survivors of, 305n10
The Treatment (Ensler), 140–41
Trilling, Lionel, 23, 24, 26
Tristram, Claire, 24, 27, 33, 207, 230, 293, 295; *After*, 15, 52, 62, 110, 132–35, 139, 141–64, 187, 296
Tristram Shandy (Sterne), 225
Trouble with Strangers (Eagleton), 218
"Turning the Screw" (Felman), 154
The Turn of the Screw (James), 154

The Unbinding (Kirn), 55, 252, 262–66, 288
Unclaimed Experience (Caruth), 4, 81
The Unknown Terrorist (Flanagan), 55, 252, 275, 278–81
Updike, John: *Terrorist*, 49

"Values of Difficulty" (Butler), 26
Vanags, August, 271; *Boy 381*, 270
Versluys, Kristiaan, 84; *Out of the Blue*, 2, 49
victimization, 135–36, 188–89, 217, 238–40
video, 36–38
Violence (Žižek), 216, 221
Virilio, Paul, 292; *Open Sky*, 256; "The Overexposed City," 268; *Strategy of Deception*, 256; *The Vision Machine*, 263; "The Visual Crash," 273
Visible Fictions (Ellis), 99
The Vision Machine (Virilio), 263
"The Vision of Peter Damien" (Adrian), 292–95
"The Visual Crash" (Virilio), 273
visual fetishism, 77–80
visual interventionism, 235–36
"The Voice of the Visual" (Zelizer), 61

Wallace, David Foster, 95
Walter, Jess, 5–6; *The Zero*, 5
Walzer, Michael, 31
war correspondents, 236–44, 290–91
War on Terror, 3, 8–9, 10, 24, 56, 165, 282, 288, 300; compared to Bosnian War, 208–09; compared to jihad, 205; and evil, 217–21, 227; foreign relations in, 267–71; justification of, 29; morality of, 30–31; moral racialization and, 169–83; personal privacy in, 267–71; and post-9/11 discourse, 167–68, 180; racial formation and, 166–69; risk management and, 183, 204; September 11, 2001, and, 17; sexuality and, 139–40; as transnational identification, 45
Washington Square (James), 27
Weber, Cynthia: *Imagining America at War*, 30
Wegner, Phillip E.: *Life between Two Deaths, 1989–2001*, 3; "Recognizing the Patterns," 273
"We Have Mutated" (Raban), 269
Welch, Michael, 180, 183, 185
"Welcome to the Desert of the Real!" (Žižek), 44

West, Paul: *The Immensity of the Here and Now*, 79
What Do Pictures Want? (Mitchell), 299
The White Hotel (Thomas), 133, 149
White Noise (DeLillo), 268
"Whitman, Syntax" (Dimock), 194, 201, 202, 203
Whitman, Walt, 53, 167, 190–97, 201, 293; *Prose Works*, 192, 193; "Song of Myself," 190, 192, 194
"Why Antichrist?" (Adrian), 294–95
Wiesel, Elie, 81
Wihl, Gary, 133–34, 135, 139, 152
Wikileaks, 289
Wildavsky, Aaron, 183, 203
Williams, Bernard, 166
Williams, Raymond, 52; "From Medium to Social Practice," 96
Wolfowitz, Paul, 28
Wood, James, 68
"Worlds in Collision" (Booth and Dunne), 289
The Writing on the Wall (Schwartz), 7, 94, 283–84

Young, James, 82

Zelizer, Barbie, 52, 60–61, 71; "The Voice of the Visual," 61
The Zero (Walter), 5
Žižek, Slavoj, 15; *The Metastases of Enjoyment*, 139; *The Sublime Object*, 163; *Violence*, 216, 221; "Welcome to the Desert of the Real!" 44